REGGAE, RASTA, REVOLUTION

Also edited by Chris Potash
THE JIMI HENDRIX COMPANION: THREE DECADES OF COMMENTARY

RASTA,
REVOLUTION

JAMAICAN MUSIC
FROM SKA TO DUB

EDITED BY

CHRIS POTASH

SCHIRMER BOOKS
An Imprint of SIMON & SCHUSTER MACMILLAN
NEW YORK

PRENTICE HALL INTERNATIONAL
LONDON · MEXICO CITY · NEW DELHI · SINGAPORE · SYDNEY · TORONTO

Copyright © 1997 Schirmer Books

Schirmer Books
An Imprint of Simon & Schuster Macmillan
1633 Broadway
New York, NY 10019

Book design by Charles B. Hames

Library of Congress Catalog Card Number: 97–19893

Printed in the United States of America

Printing number
1 2 3 4 5 6 7 8 9 10

Library of Congress Cataloging-in-Publication Data

Reggae, Rasta, revolution : Jamaican music from ska to dub / edited by
   Chris Potash.
       p.   cm.
   Includes bibliographical references (p. *****) and index.
   ISBN 0–02–864728–9 (alk. paper)
   1. Popular music—Jamaica—History and criticism.   I. Potash,
   Chris, 1964–   .
   ML3486.J3R44   1997
   781.464'097292—dc21   97–19893
                                                    CIP
                                                    MN

This paper meets the requirements of ANSI/MOSP 739.48–1992 {Permanence of Paper}.

To *those who feel it*—for *those who don't*

The songs from Jamaica, *sung and played by the Broadway cast and orchestra on a Victor recording, are, like their interpreters, uniformly genial. . . . I have only two trifling complaints to register, one being that, despite Mr. [Harold] Arlen's subtly shifting tempos, so much of the score is basically calypso. I understand that calypso is closely identified with the speech habits of some of the Caribbean islanders, but I am a crabby Northerner, and I lose patience with the innocent rhyming and the jerky rhythms rather quickly.*

"ISLAND HOPPING," THE NEW YORKER, 8 MARCH 1958

The songs of our early African inhabitants have been classified as sad, set in a minor key. But is it any wonder that they were sad when it is remembered that the native African and other slave-raiders never considered family ties—that the people were torn from all they loved and brought so far away from home and country that they realized that there was never an opportunity of returning? As slaves in their own native Africa an opportunity was often found of going home again, but with oceans separating them they realized that return was impossible, and like the Jewish captives as they sat, harp in hand by the waters of Babylon, their songs were the looking-glasses of their saddened spirits.

· · ·

But their songs, the songs which they had heard their fathers and mothers, sisters, brothers and countrymen sing from the days of their infancy, these no man could take away from them; these were planted deep down in their hearts and memories—these were hushed at the time of capture, but, humanlike, found voice again in their hour of misery as they lay huddled in the scant space of the slave-ship. And those of them who survived, not alone the perils of the sea, but the far greater inhumanity of Man, and arrived on our shores, remembered their native songs and would sing them after their hour of toil, only adding to them the bitterness of the soul in Captivity. Is it any wonder then that the songs of our early African settlers are characterized as sad and mournful? They had every inducement to make them so.

ASTLEY CLERK, THE MUSIC AND MUSICAL INSTRUMENTS OF JAMAICA, 1916

CONTENTS

x

ACKNOWLEDGMENTS

Respect to Denise Malek for her research and editorial assistance.

Thanks to Brian, lead singer of the Ska Blazers, for his insight, support, and the loan of the tapes, books, videos, etc.

For the music as well as the irie vibe, *peace!* to Armand's Records and Okey Ubah at 2nd Dimension, both in Philadelphia; Juicy "V" at Reggae Land Muzik in Miramar, Florida; and Delroy Bailey at High Times record store in the Kingston Mall.

Brendan McGowan in San Francisco taped a live Dub Mission session; Bryan Oettel forwarded *Catch a Fire* from New York; Ray Yaros and his cohorts Trevor and Mikey in the FLL holding yard supplied copies of *Dancehall Vibes* and *Now*; Jo Jo made the Cameo scene; and Carlos Suarez passed along the Johnny Dread CD as well as loaned me, years ago, his car for a fateful Key West road trip.

Thanks to the staff at the National Library of Jamaica in Kingston who helped in spite of not knowing exactly what to make of us; the Research Institute for the Study of Man on Manhattan's Upper East Side for their unique publications collection; and Jamaica Roots Ltd. of Spanish Town for the ginger wine I'm about to finish.

Thanks also to Dan Mausner and Desirée Bermani at Schirmer Books.

And here's to the authors I dealt with directly, and the conscientious permissions people who made life that much easier. I'd especially like to thank Evelyn Bernal, Max Block, Jamie Bogner, Louise Boundas, Pat Browne, Jennifer Canham, Louis Chude-Sokei, Peggi Clapham, Mary Flower, Allan Jones, Susan Kaplan, Tracey King, Lory Reyes, Pamela Sims, Carol Sullivan, Trainer, Virginia Turner, and Sarah Wells.

Cheers.

INTRODUCTION

"Reggae music!" yelled the guy on the bicycle as he cruised by us down the dusty side street. His exclamation was part question, but mostly command—after all, we were in Kingston, Jamaica.

Sure enough, the vinyl we carried under our arms in dog-eared sleeves was the real Jamaican deal.

We took the guy for Rasta. He took us for tourists. By the time I thought to look over my shoulder to acknowledge that I'd heard him and maybe nod in agreement, he was gone. Perhaps he'd turned a corner, or maybe he had said enough . . . just enough to begin this book with.

Reggae music: the unique sound of a special Caribbean nation, yes, but so much more to Jamaicans and fans abroad. Festivals like Sunsplash bring home the money; dancehall and neodub control foreign dance floors; the search for the next Marley drives local producers and brings the hope of stardom—however unlikely—to the youth. For the past twenty-five years or so the world's ears have more or less remained trained on the island, waiting for a new riddim to come and carry us away. And, often enough to keep those who listen interested, it has.

Bluebeat, rock steady, roots, version, lovers' rock, ragga—such labels are helpful to the extent that they illustrate the rich variety of styles leading up to the current sound of Jamaican music. The articles and essays collected in this book under the broader headings Roots, Marley, Reggae, Ska, Dub, Dancehall, and World introduce the performers most commonly associated with each "movement," if you will, and give the approximate dates and circumstances under which each held sway. In this way the development of the nation's popular music and its significance is plotted, from African slave songs and dances, through folk forms and the influence of American R&B, to even more extreme cross-cultural hybrids—and back. The seven parts are arranged not chronologically—most movements are still vital and mutually nonexclusive—but loosely for good measure.

Note that the writings in this anthology appear as they originally did in magazines, newspapers, books, journals, fanzines, and websites, save some stylistic changes such as spelling out numbers, equalizing punctuation, and, where approved and indicated, light copyediting intended to clarify. (One practical point: Three ellipsis points centered on a line indicate elided text.) The authors are critics, journalists, novelists, poets, producers, collectors, professors, and/or confirmed reggae fanatics. As the bibliography merely suggests, the literature on this topic is staggeringly multitudinous. There no doubt exist experts in all aspects of this topic, some of whom may not be cited. To those a simple "sorry" must suffice. May this unintentional slight nonetheless inspire you to publish elsewhere on this still underexposed subject.

In addition to the music itself (heard in concert as well as on cassettes, CDs, 45s, LPs, and radio), input that helped inform the selection and arrangement of the pieces came from movies, videos, photographs, television, and the Net. A goal was to expose myself to as many media as possible so as to ultimately strike an honorably modernist balance in my representation of the past and the present of reggae music.

Finally, please keep in mind that the whole of Jamaican music, as with anything worth not only studying but experiencing, is greater than the sum of its parts. Is Lee Perry a reggae or a dub artist? *Who feels it knows.* This is music we are discovering, after all.

The introductory notes that follow—presented in an order that echoes the organization of the book—act as prelude to our main selections. All of the articles mentioned herein, including those not reproduced in their entirety in the volume, are listed in the bibliography.

DREAD

Kingston buzzes like any city of size. There's a constant humming, a distant grumbling of commerce, of raucous, windowless public buses competing with careening automobiles for the road (maintained VW Transporters looking much sharper than the less-than-tuned English-make sports-car taxis). As a supporting chorus in suburban areas, dogs bark all night long. A hazy curtain of smoke from trash fires rises in front of the towering Blue Mountains, which apparently stop the sprawl from heading north. Beyond are the ganja fields, Nanny Town, Cudjoe's proud Maroon descendants, and the eerie Cockpit Country.

Downtown in the crucible of economic poverty known as the ghetto, a cultural alchemy took place in the 1960s and 1970s whereby the Rastafarians brought their beliefs to bear on Jamaican music. The effects of that revolution can still be felt today, in the beat on the streets and in the attitude of the people.

One of the few who have studied the Rastafarians in this urban environment is Father Joseph Owens, a social worker who moved to West Kingston in 1970 with the specific goal of living and reasoning with the brethren. Owens's findings, published in his fascinating social study *Dread*, reveal the unexpected root of the Rasta temperament: the Bible. Owens says the true Rasta "knows the Bible like the back alleys of his shantytown.... He sleeps, eats and does everything by it and never stops reading it and meditating on it."

Rastas speak with what Owens calls "an intrepid boldness" because they are confident that they are the righteous disciples of Jah Rastafari, Haile Selassie I, the *black* King of kings and Lord of lords. As God's (Jah's) chosen people, their words are Truth itself. Not coincidentally, "the creole which most Jamaicans speak is considered by the Rastafarians to be an admixture of English and their old African tongue and thus represents an attempt to free themselves from the old colonial regime." Very little, if anything, about Rasta is happenstance.

KNOTTY DREAD!

This deliberateness is manifested in Rasta's signature hairstyle, dreadlocks. "They that don't like the hair, it's because they are afraid of nature themselves," said Teddy, one of the brethren with whom Owens reasoned. "Anyone who fight against the hair fight against the self!"

These ropelike protuberances, which *dreads* carry proudly as natural and blessed expressions of their African heritage, are anything but natty, and yet that's how they've become known, popularized by Bob Marley's album of that name. Marley also made famous the dread act of flashing locks, or tossing them this way and that for effect. In concert or on the street, it's a dynamically intimate sight to behold.

Of course, simply wearing dreadlocks does not make one Rasta. The style has caught on as fashion, so much so that it's foolish to assign any special meaning to someone outside of Jamaica wearing locks; the same goes for those wearing the red, green, and gold knit locks cap. There are even dreadlock wigs available, for concertgoers who want a quick and temporary Dread Experience. Novelist Mario Vargas Llosa wrote for *The New York Times Magazine* on how his son turned "dread" while attending an exclusive English boarding school (the teen eventually grew out of it).

HERB

Another phenomenon rooted in Rasta theology but subsequently picked up by the world's pop culture is the smoking of the herb, or marijuana. The taking of *ganja*, as it is also known, is sacred; it is commonly burned in a hand-rolled cigarette called a *spliff*, or in a communal pipe or *chalice* as praises are offered to Jah. It is said to invoke inner clarity and to facilitate reasoning.

A widely held belief outside of Jamaica is that smoking ganja is necessary to really "get" reggae; that lighting up tunes one in. By extension, it is commonly assumed that all reggae musicians—and certainly all Rastas—smoke the herb. But this is not true. While many dreads partake more often than not, others are prevented by access, health, or constitution. Some even decry the herb, for reasons all their own.

Peter Tosh ("Legalize it/don't criticize it"), who formed the famed Wailers with Bob Marley and Bunny Livingston, was one of the most prominent ganja rights activists when he was alive and touring, especially as a solo artist. Marley, in one of his countless interviews with the foreign press, once said that it's better to start smoking ganja when young, "'cause it gives you a conscience." He suggested that if you come to it for the first time later in life it mash up your head. In 1982 Bob's wife, Rita, explained why women smoke less ganja than men do: "We can't afford to, 'cause you don't smoke and just get up and start working. . . . The woman has so many responsibilities she doesn't have much time to relax." Most recently, *High Times* magazine sent two of their own tokers to Kingston to elicit local color (mostly brown and green) while documenting the legalization movement thirty years after Haile Selassie's visit to the island. What Chris Simunek and photographer Brian Jahn experienced, however, was a dangerous clash of cultures. While attending a Rasta religious ceremony one night, the two white foreigners were menaced by youths apparently offended by their presence. The next day, according to Simunek, Kingston's *Sunday Gleaner* newspaper reported that their main tormentor had immolated himself after they'd left the gathering. Obviously, not every Jamaican welcomes Babylon's business.

Rock critic Lester Bangs had aesthetic reservations concerning indiscriminate use of the herb. As he disclosed in a 1978 drubbing of Marley's album *Kaya*, "It has long been a theory of mine that marijuana should only be legalized for Third World peoples, since ofays in general just can't handle it, becoming either paranoid, totally withdrawn or excruciatingly cosmic. When was the last time you saw an Arab or a Thai giggling all over him- or herself about the pattern in your carpet, or heard one of them say, 'If I say anything weird, let me know, 'cause I'm stoned'?"

Some consider herb to be God's own medicine, and in California a contentious debate has recently lead to the legalization of marijuana for medicinal use. As a result, the doors are legally open to the Cannabis Club in San Francisco, if you have the referral of a doctor. For sufferers of everything from AIDS to glaucoma, this is a good thing.

But, too much of a good thing . . .

Reggae producer Jah Life, who's worked with Sister Carol, Barrington Levi, and Mikey Jarrett, warned in a 1993 *Village Voice* article on city kids' copious consumption of "the Chronic" (street slang for marijuana cigars): "All smoking, including ganja, the holy herb, can be bad for the body. It is better to boil it and drink it as tea. Don't keep a blunt on you all the time, draw it and draw it until you lose the feeling, the enjoyment of it. Whatever you do, don't abuse it."

TUFF GONG

Bob Marley is still the single most prominent figure in reggae. In the 1970s he was one of the hottest performers on the international pop music scene. He's been identified, from various vantage points, as the Mick Jagger of reggae, the James Brown of the Caribbean, a black prince, a prophet, and God. As a spokesperson for his people he was fierce and tireless, and though he died in 1981 at the age of thirty-six, the music label he founded for his own freedom, Tuff Gong, lives on, doing the "works" he believed in so strongly, providing an outlet—and an in—for Jamaican musical talent.

Writer Alice Walker called Marley "a free spirit if ever there was one." She marveled at the vast energy and determination he must have had to come from a village in rural Jamaica and project himself into the world the way he did, winning acclaim, spreading love, toeing no line. Indeed, it is not enough to think of Marley's success in terms of records sold or concert receipts counted, or for his inclusion as reggae's token entry in rock reference books. Rather, his influence was and is worldwide, profound. His personal triumphs helped change attitudes immediately and forever.

Marley meant so much to his countrymen that a politically motivated attempt was made on his life in 1976; further indication of his popularity (and thus power) in Jamaica is the fact that then–Prime Minister Michael Manley interrupted his campaigning and flew immediately to Kingston to pay his respects to the wounded singer. Two years later Marley returned from a self-imposed exile to literally unite Manley and bitter political rival Edward Seaga, by joining their hands above his head onstage during the infamous One Love Peace Concert. His subsequent invitation to perform at the historic ceremonies celebrating sovereignty for Zimbabwe in 1980 was a coup for Third World peoples. Marley, an African-Jamaican and a Rasta, was there in his spiritual homeland to usher in freedom with his songs. Of all the words spoken that night, those chanted in unison by the black masses in attendance—singing along with Marley or merely enthusing—are the most freely repeated.

"Me have to laugh sometimes when dem scribes seh me like Mick Jagger or some superstar thing like that," Marley told *Rolling Stone* in 1976. "Dem have to listen close to the music, 'cause the message not the same. *Nooo,* mon, the reggae not the twist, mon!"

CULTIVATION

One function of reggae in the larger world, pioneered by Marley, has been to introduce into public discourse the "revolutionary" words of Garvey and Selassi (I enclose "revolutionary" in quotes because these leaders believed their Afrocentric ideals to be simple common sense), as well the works of such others as Frantz Fanon and Rex Nettleford. Scores of self-styled social philosophers (journalists) extended this dialogue via their reggae-centered interviews and reviews. Articles written in the mid-seventies—when reggae first began to attract mainstream press coverage—commonly start out talking about the music and then veer, with varying degrees of subtlety, into issues concerning the black diaspora.

The ideals of black pride and race consciousness came to the world's table partially on reggae's plate, and lyrics by the likes of Winston Rodney (aka Burning Spear) and lately Buju Banton continue that tradition. Marley himself sought the ear of the world's black populations to encourage the struggle toward racial unity and self-determination. At heart he hoped most to cultivate Rasta consciousness and black brotherhood, but, as befits someone with the nickname Tuff Gong, he dealt directly with the fact that the majority of his fans outside of Jamaica were white and mainly middle class. "Yeah, man. It's a black people's music," he told *Billboard*'s Leroy Robinson in 1973. "But I prefer *all* people to like our music."

GARDEN

Another way in which Bob Marley contributed was by tending his own garden—his family—and leaving behind the legacy of the Melody Makers.

"We're a family, not a group," eldest Marley son Ziggy (born David) told *Newsweek* back in 1988 when he was nineteen. Since then Ziggy Marley and the Melody Makers—which includes Ziggy's brother Stephen and sisters Sharon and Cedella, as well as various sit-ins—have played stages all over, reprising Dad's classics and jamming their own riddim.

While visiting the Bob Marley Museum at 56 Hope Road in Kingston, the site of the former Island House (where Bob lived after signing with Chris Blackwell and moving uptown), I happened upon Stephen hanging out with brothers Ziggy, Julian, and Damian, kicking a soccer ball near a wall covered with murals depicting high points in their father's life. Sitting on the front steps to take a rest before heading back into the first-floor studio to work on the new Melody Maker's disc, Stephen seemed open to approach.

After stuttering an introduction, I abruptly blurted out: "So, what was Bob's message?" I wanted to get right to the point, and to hear the answer from as near the source as possible. Eyeing me suspiciously, even heavy-liddedly, Stephen made reference to the unexpected: the Bible. The Bible again! Rasta consciousness was hammered home just that easy.

The young Marleys have learned their lessons well. And they see the big picture. For instance, Stephen suggests that the things they sing about are somewhat prescribed by their socioeconomic situation: in other words, because of who their dad is, they're set financially and can't in good conscience make like dancehall DJs and rap hard about freaky sex, cocaine, violence—nor would they want to. Instead, they deal with life's larger issues.

On my way out of the museum compound, walking around the squat but colorful statue of the elder Marley cradling his guitar while standing astride a cement soccer ball, I thought about how these Marley kids had one foot in each world: tied to the old ways by family, by roots planted wisely with a strong hand; and taking a step toward—aha—self-determination.

CAR/CULTURE

In 1976 "the air reverberated with the thundering beat and wailing voices of reggae...." So say the landmark liner notes for Culture's powerful debut album, *Two Sevens Clash*. The title refers to a premonition Joseph Hill, the group's music director, had while riding on a bus in Kingston. He envisioned that 1977 would be the year of judgment, an apocalyptic reckoning of Jamaica's political and economic troubles.

No outstanding event occurred that July 7 (7/7/77), though government forces were on alert; rather, the musical revolution begun by Bob Marley and Toots and the

Maytals and many others received welcome reinforcement. *Two Sevens Clash* was hailed as one of the best reggae albums ever and went on to encourage international interest in Rasta and Jamaican music.

Nearly twenty years later I recalled this as I was doing 77 mph down I-95 South, headed to Miami to catch a plane to Kingston. I maintained this speed throughout the drive as a tribute. After all, the Caribbean is a superstitious place, and it's wise to be aware of and even humor Fate. As Native Americans seek visions for clues to their callings, thus I allowed myself to be guided by the significance of the two sevens.

NATURAL MYSTIC

As pop music writer for the *Miami News* in the late 1980s, I had the enviable job of talking to acts who were touring at that time. My first reggae interview was with the aforementioned band Culture; then the group Inner Circle, whose song "Bad Boys" was resurrected as the opening song for the lamely realistic TV show *Cops,* worried to me about the damage Hurricane Gilbert had inflicted on the island. Speaking to Jimmy Cliff during a recording-session break was most memorable. CBS had just released *Hanging Fire,* a "pretty wild title" referring to the threat of nuclear annihilation that was very real in 1988. Twenty years earlier Cliff's first big hit had been lighter in tone and more general in interest. His cover of "Wonderful World, Beautiful People" had cast him as a potential international pop star—another Belafonte perhaps. But his lead role in *The Harder They Come* refocused the singer on spiritual fulfillment, and in 1973 Cliff converted from Rastafarianism to Islam. A year later his first trip to Africa had a profound effect on his life and music.

"Africa gave me a clearer understanding of the lifestyle and the behavior and beliefs of my ancestors," Cliff told me by phone from his Kingston studio. "Of course, modern Africa today still wants the American dream—though when I say 'America' it's also Britain, France, Holland—but at the same time there are the values of ancient Africa that remain, like the hospitality they extend to strangers and the belief in the source, the one spiritual source that feeds the universe. These things give me a more solid foundation to stand on."

A similar spiritual openness tempered with worldly concern marked the words of South African World Beat artist Alpha Blondy, who passed through Miami not long before Cliff's *Hanging Fire* tour. Blondy told me he also entertained religions other than Rasta (see World section). These first-person encounters are evidence enough for me that reggae runs on the energies of people of different beliefs; what makes the music essential are the spiritual vibes that move it. If smoking ganja is not necessary to appreciate reggae, then why shouldn't people in tune with man's mystic nature, regardless of their race, creed, or color, enjoy the music?

The double-edged beauty of reggae music: food for thought, a beat that moves bodies. As Cliff said in closing, "I just want to interject that life is physical as well as spiritual, and the spiritual side of us is the side that is more everlasting. We put food and water in our body to sustain our body, we should also nourish the spirit."

US VS. THEM

So, issues besides aesthetics enter the reggae mix. The nationality and race of artists sometimes come into play. Radio DJ David Rodigan made the observation in the on-line magazine *Yush* that in the 1970s and 1990s the reggae groups that regularly broke/break into the national charts were/are based in Jamaica, while in the 1980s mainly British acts ruled reggae. Producers such as Castro Brown; artists such as Aswad, Maxi Priest, Steel Pulse, Tipper Irie, Lloyd Brown, Smiley Culture, Pato Banton, and Macka B; and labels such as Ariwa (run by dub master Mad Professor), Greensleeves, Fashion, and Jet Star all made considerable contributions to the British reggae industry and thus made the form safe for High Street.

The case of British band UB40 illustrates how non-Jamaican performers have been disrespected by "purist" fans. As a mixed-race group prone to pop rather than that rude boy sound, UB40 got called on the critical carpet for everything from not relating to Jamaica to being white (a charged back-and-forth on the merits [or no] of the band is recorded in *Reggae on the Internet, Volume One,* a printout of Internet chat compiled in magazine form and distributed at Tower Records/Books, NYC, 1996).

There are those who genuinely enjoy UB40's music; those who dislike the group because they lack cultural credibility—they're not all Jamaican, or black, or sufferers; those who respect the band for forwarding the reggae vibe and promoting reggae around the world; and those who just don't listen because they're listening to something else. There is no consensus regarding whether world-based reggae (Them) can rival the home brew (Us).

Nonetheless, in an essay titled "The Dialectics of Reggae Music" which appeared in *Everybody's* magazine, Basil Wilson eloquently allows that "Under the rubric of Rastafari, the music nurtures the consciousness of black people without denying the humanity of any people. The beauty here, then, and certainly a paradox, is that despite the anti-colonial, anti-imperialistic leanings, the music is so all-encompassing that even those of European extraction obtain a special delight in singing along and have their consciousness raised."

SPLASH OR STING?

Reggae Sunsplash, the Jamaican music festival, was originally intended to increase tourism in June, the hottest time of the year on the island and thus officially the off-season. It is usually held in tourist-rich Montego Bay or Chukka Cove in Ocho Rios. Begun by Synergy Productions in 1978, Sunsplash has grown to become the premier international reggae event.

Reggae Sting (aka Bee Sting) is the more local and these days more vibrant reggae festival. Buju Banton, Beenie Man, Ninjaman, Lady Saw, Sister Carol, and others, mostly dancehall artists, have filled recent bills. Sting draws boisterous crowds who take this once-a-year opportunity to big-up or put down the current crop of DJs.

The tape-delayed feeds of 1996's Sunsplash and Sting concerts, available to First World fans via pay-per-view technology, illustrated where their respective market interests lie.

The Sunsplash program opened with a video montage that was surely supervised by the National Tourist Board. Toned Anglo couples frolic in the surf, step gingerly amid the rocks of Dunn's River Falls, dance a lighthearted step to some unseen rhythm—you get the picture. When the camera finally focuses on the festival, crowd shots show VIP guests sealed off from the rest of the audience by an intimidating metal wall, and European vacationers lounging on beach towels in the grass. Sting, on the other hand, opens with the action onstage and doesn't let up for two hours. The rambunctious crowd is involved to the max in hard-core support of reggae music and the strong personalities who paint it particularly Jamaican.

One spectacular Sting moment occurred when DJ Pinchers called out in a strong, lone voice above a fired up, chafing mass, potent in its blackness, poised for the response. It sounds trite, but the mystery of the music worked its magic at that moment. The call struck a nerve, caused a chill: the sight of such unity transcended what had begun as entertainment.

REGGAE GRAB BAG

- The 1973 movie *The Harder They Come* is set for a sequel starring the Fugees, the hip-hop group who moved "No Woman, No Cry's" government yard from Trench Town to Jersey. Wyclef and Pras—outspoken rap "refugees" proud of their Haitian backgrounds—and singer Lauryn Hill, who has a Puma Jones thing going on, *do* echo Black Uhuru's black-power trio setup. Nonetheless, set to be shot during the summer of 1997 in Jamaica and the Bronx, *The Harder They Fall* is encountering resistance from Perry Henzell, director of the original. Apparently Henzell objects to some aspect of Jimmy Cliff's involvement. How that turns out we'll have to wait and see.

- Marley backup singer Judy Mowatt, who formed the I-Threes along with Marcia Griffiths and Rita Marley, began her career as a creative dancer with a troupe performing fire and limbo dances for tourists at the island's resorts. Other reggae artists, such as Tony Bell of Bell and Kutchie, played on Caribbean cruise ships.

- Musical Youth, the teen group who served as Britain's answer to the Jackson Five, was assembled by reggae singer Freddie Waite and consisted of his two sons, Patrick and Junior, the Grant brothers, Michael and Kelvin, and Dennis Seaton. Their debut single, "Pass the Dutchie," reached No. 1 in 1982 and eventually sold four million copies. They were local heroes in Birmingham, role models for reggae wannabes the world over; they even won a Grammy for Best New Group before falling from grace into inactivity.

- The singer Ivanay was on Jamaican TV every few hours in late November '96 in a music video for the title song to her debut album, *Empower Me*. She comes across as a thoroughly modern woman—if a bit overhyped.

- Skateland, a roller-skating rink in Half Way Tree, Kingston, is a historic spot for the recording of such seminal DJs as Eek-a-Mouse, Brigadier Jerry, and Prince Jazzbo. Skankland—now closed—in Columbus, Ohio, set itself up as a parallel universe.

- A course called "The Rhetoric of Reggae Music" was a hit with students at the University of Vermont in Burlington during the spring 1996 semester.
- Byron Lee is credited by some sources with bringing the first electric bass guitar and bass amp to the island, thus establishing the bassline at the forefront of Jamaican music. (Says producer Lee Perry: "The drum is the beat of the heart, right? The bass is the brain.")
- In the magazine article "Jump Up!" music writer Timothy White related that Bunny Wailer warned producer Leslie Kong not to release a record called *The Best of the Wailers,* which Bunny considered premature. White quotes Bunny: "He went ahead anyways and that album came out. A month afterward Kong fell ill in the studio and went home—*and he died.* He was tryin' to kill us and it bounced back on *'im!*"

SKALARSHIP

One thing you may notice as you read through this volume is that there are nearly as many theories concerning the etymology of the words *reggae* and *ska* as there are writers who write about them.

In Jamaica, though, there is no talk of first, second, or third waves. Ska is simply oldies music, a bouncy, horny sound lumped under the aural umbrella of early reggae—kind of like how the Shirelles are rock and roll. Dancing is to ska as cooking is to a pot. Jay Cocks, writing in *Time* during the brief golden age of British second-wave (2 Tone) ska, called ska "flat-out party music played faster than reggae and meant to be, if not frivolous, then feckless" (see Ska section).

This same "sense of fun as strong as all that ganja Bob Marley goes on about" pervades the so-called first wave of Jamaican ska, too—tunes like "Carry Go Bring Come" by Justin Hinds and the Dominoes, "Strong Man Sampson," and "Hog in a Cocoa," all of which appear on a cassette compilation called *The Birth of Ska* (Sonic Sounds, no date) that I picked up at one of the Kingston airport duty-free shops. Interestingly enough, the cover design contains clip art of a decidedly white couple stiffly skanking. Weird.

The funnest ska show I've been to was maybe not a ska show at all. Today, *ska* is a tag used to describe such a range of pop music sounds that it's about as exact as *reggae,* which in some instances refers to 1970s-era songs suffused with the Rastafarian faith, and in other contexts can stand for all forms of Jamaican music at once. In ska's case, the term is applied to everything from the 1960s traditional sound of Don Drummond, through truly rude tunes from Bad Manners, to funky-fast Top 40 hits by the girl-fronted group No Doubt. One on-line ska discussion group (skagroup@list.pitt.edu) yielded the following rhetorical question from Brett (1/15/97), who has a point: "Why do 'we' insist on still calling so many third wave bands (or 2 Tone bands for that matter) 'ska' bands? Today's ska may have a lot in common with the original stuff but the sound is definitely different." (So—was the Skalars/Pietasters gig at the Hazleton [Pa.] Ska[te] Center "ska"?)

SKINS

Confusing the issue of what all this has to do with Jamaican music even more is the involvement of skinheads. The original skins came out of England in the 1960s, at about the same time as the mods; in fact, some have it that skins cut their hair shorter because they got in a lot of fights, and were called "hard mods." The early skins were not necessarily racist, like the worst of those who go by the name today. Rather, they steadfastly espoused working-class pride.

These sixties skins went to West Indian blues dances—the antecedents of punky reggae parties—in Notting Hill and Brixton to revel in the outlaw/outsider feeling . . . and to dance. Dime-store pocket paperbacks by British author Richard Allen chronicled the subculture in cartoon crudeness, with an occasional cursory mention of reggae for color. From *Skinhead Girls:* "Monday is a drag, I thought after Brian had left for his office. After Sunday's disco session it was an obscenity to thrust *reggae* and *soul* into the background and, instead, return to the mundane affairs of Mr Simms' sweat-shop." Pretty bald prose.

Some of the trappings of this brief affair between skins and Jamaican music have been adopted by subsequent ska fans. For example, black-and-white checkered band merchandise (to indicate black and white unity, though most third wavers are white), mod fashion (Fred Perry shirts, sharp-looking pants, etc.), hairstyles such as the Chelsea and the fringe, Vespa scooters—all can be seen at today's ska shows.

WHAT DUB?

At the High Times record store in downtown Kingston, the guy behind the turntable peered down and asked if I was German; or French perhaps, when I didn't answer immediately. "No, American," I said. He said he'd thought I was a European DJ because I'd asked for dub. He explained that he didn't have any dub, that dub was not a genre that was popular in Jamaica these days. Big in Belgium, though.

Dub is another style of music that's come out of Jamaica to find new life, or at least altered form, elsewhere. As *Melody Maker* columnist Richard Williams so successfully prophesied back in the seventies (see Dub section), this "aberrant form" has indeed insinuated itself into other musics.

Dub is the result of producers' playing their mixing boards like instruments. Back in the day, masters like King Tubby and Scientist dropped vocal tracks in and out of songs like so much karaoke haiku. "If reggae is Africa in the New World, then dub must be Africa on the moon; it's the psychedelic music I expected to hear in the sixties and didn't," wrote Luke Ehrlich in *Reggae International.* Ehrlich further characterizes the sound as "Musical coitus interruptus." Dick Hebdige, author of the acclaimed *Cut 'n' Mix,* on the occasion of Bob Marley's fiftieth birthday celebration (February 1995), delivered an address that just happened to open with a bit about dub: "Even as the bassline centred me and nailed me to the spot, dub taught me to question the security of every ground. It taught me not to get nervous when things aren't neatly framed." The liner notes from the CD anthology *Macro Dub Infection, Volume One* echo this outlook: "From out of the lab into the dance hall, dub proved there was an audience eager for insecurity" (K. Martin).

So, while it may be anachronistic, dub is still aurally antagonistic, in that it's so individualistic. The form's most infamous iconoclast, Lee Perry, is feted by a fanzine titled *The Upsetter* (edited by H. W. Targowski and David Katz). And acting out dub's desire to lean on the aural envelope are the singular DJs throughout the world who weave their shadowy or sleepy or sinuous dub webs: DJ Spooky in New York; Black Sifichi in Paris (Radio Nova); Bart Plantenga in Amsterdam (Radio Patapoe); Sep and Jah Bill in San Francisco (Dub Mission); many others.

Names for the new musics based in dub can be pretty opaque. Ben Neill is known as a pioneer of *illbient,* which is loosely described as dance music without the beats. Illbient DJs include Olive, Loop, and Kahn, who runs Temple Records. Tricky is said to do *trip-hop,* defined by Jon Pareles of the *New York Times* as "hip background music" with "added jagged noise to keep it ominous." If you're thinking this sound couldn't be further from the bob and weave of ska, you're right.

WALKING ON GRAVEL

Dub poets use the dark power of dub music to animate their lines. Critic Peter Kostakis points out that Linton Kwesi Johnson's "fluid brand of dread lacks innocence." That's the dub doing that.

Additionally, as performance artists, dub poets leverage their words against their bearing. This is dub-inspired, too. I'll never forget seeing Mutabaruka walking down a city sidewalk the afternoon before a spoken-word show in support of his album *The Mystery Unfolds.* Muta's gorgan dreads splayed out from his trademark white head-patch, his stride past onlookers was steady and strong—and he was barefoot! He was conspicuously *there.* This chance sighting of a man so literally out of step with his surroundings yet so sure of himself drove home the depth of his conviction.

Years later, a similar frisson occurred in a record store, where loosely attached to the wall was a rather battered copy of Oku Onuora's *Pressure Drop* LP, with a portrait of the artist staring back at me unflinching. (*Oku* means "fire." *Onuora* means "echo." Given name: Orlando Wong.) Onuora's countenance was that of a seer. I bought the album and was carrying it with me when the guy on the bike rode by and made his proclamation: Reggae music!

THE REVOLUTION WILL BE

To call something revolutionary can mean many different things. The invention of the microwave oven was revolutionary to some. In the case of reggae music, "revolutionary" refers to the political (best of Marley, etc.), the aural (dub pushes boundaries), and, most recently, the moral (dancehall pushes buttons).

The dancehall stylee jerked into being in 1985 with the release of an uncomplicated tune called "Under Me Sleng Teng." Recorded by Wayne Smith and produced by Prince Jammy, this recording-studio concoction caught on as the template for the dancehall sound: no bassline, cheap synth drum plink/plunk, raplike vocals. At best this basic formula—since exploited exponentially—can be seen as a simple musical structure to support ragga rhymes; at worst it seems to signal the end of reggae as we knew it.

Dancehall music appeals to young Jamaica. Its roguish reputation, while alienating roots-reggae lovers both at home and abroad since the late 1980s, has made the new style too big to ignore. "Some embraced the music while others were skeptical, but despite the struggle to integrate this natural part of us—the part that wants to humour, preach and rebel—into the Jamaican society, the dancehall has prevailed," wrote Alphea Saunders in a recent issue of *Reggae Times*.

Dancehall's takeover has been so complete in its land of origin that IRIE-FM, the Jamaican radio station so long synonymous with reggae and all it stands for, has become indistinguishable from other stations. *Give the people what they want* works as well in Jamaica as it does in the West. And why not? Although as an educational service, it might be interesting to hear a debate on the merits of dancehall in its own backyard.

Meanwhile, for better or worse, the tide of "slackness" DJs and "skin out" videos (focusing on the skimpiest, tightest, flashiest outfits worn by the wildest dancers in the hall) is upon us. First packaged and brought to America as the Ram Jam Dub Slam tour in 1991, dancehall reggae has made landfall.

THERE IS A REACTION TO ALL SATISFACTION

One Sunday morning I had the pleasure of "reasoning" with Trainer, the publisher of the reggae magazine *Dub Missive* who forwards the reggae vibe like a champion. The saying on the masthead of one issue of *DM* said, "If you are for the right thing, then you do it without thinking."

Trainer explained that the driving force behind dancehall—indeed behind Jamaican music from the time of Duke Reid on—is competition. From sound clashes to record wars to today's shocking lyrics, the harder, the badder, the better. He had no patience for the "reactionary" media who came down hard on dancehall after Buju Banton's apparently inflammatory single "Boom Bye Bye" was played on a New York radio station. Yet he granted that a radio DJ's ability to resist playing a song that could (most naturally would) cause a stink outside the dance hall is an expression of respect for his audience, and an indication of his/her talent. Trainer's article, reproduced in the Dancehall section of this book, sheds light on the inevitable clash of cultures that results when music crosses geographical as well as cultural borders.

Trainer also related that the audio anthology *Tougher Than Tough—The Story of Jamaican Music* was originally planned as a thirty-CD set, to cover thirty years of recording history, but was eventually downsized to four discs. Quite an editing job, that.

REGGAE WORLDWIDE

"I'll tell ya somet'ing, mon, me never t'ought reggae gon' become popular over da world, reachin' many ears, when it was beginnin'," Bob Marley once told Timothy White. "Was too much wickedness tryin' ta hold it down. De Devil was ev'rywheres."

Now that reggae—or what various retailers label as reggae—has broken the Jamaican sound on the pop scene, has the wickedness abated?

By most accounts, yes. The presence of reggae artists on the international scene has been a self-perpetuating Garveyist prophecy. The examples that Marley, Cliff, Hibbert, and others set encouraged artists like Brazil's Gilberto Gil, Zimbabwe's Thomas Mapfumo, and Gil Scott-Heron to explore their African roots.

Similarly, new artists traveling to foreign countries are perpetuating the trend established back in the 1970s. An article in the *Guyana Review* reports that Shabba Ranks, Maxi Priest, Chaka Demus and Pliers, Lovindeer, Louie Ranking, Papa San, and General Degree have become "household names" in that South American country, and that "Guyanese artists including Buster and Sister Sue, Roger B and Troy C who imitated the Jamaican dialect to good effect won applause for their efforts" in 1992.

Other reports of reggae's success are duly noted: In August 1996 the *Sunday Gleaner* reported that more than twenty thousand tickets had been sold to a Chaka Demus and Pliers show in Uganda. Also in '96, a dub poet, Yasus Afari, held the No. 1 reggae spot on Harare, Zimbabwe, radio. With revolutionary braggadocio, Nigerian reggae artist Majek Fashek, whose *Spirit of Love* album (Interscope, 1991) was produced by E Street Band alumnus Little Steven, remarks confidently in "Majek Fashek In A New York": "I've come to restore America." Female vocalist Sayoko cut a reggae reworking of the Japanese pop classic "Ue O Muite Aruko," better known abroad as "Sukiyaki," as an extended CD single that includes both the Japanese and English versions of the song, set to an infectious reggae beat laid down by Sly Dunbar and Robbie Shakespeare.

More: There have been reports of skanking at Jungle raves in London; the Welsh band Llwybr Llaethog cut a dub album, *Mewn Dyb (In Dub)* (ROIR, 1996); in Puerto Rico, ska carries on with groups like Skapulario, Los Pies Negros, and Los Discípulos de Chagua; the Nicaraguan reggae band Soul Vibrations wrote "Election Time" to protest the political victory of President Violeta Chamorro, who opposed the revolutionary Sandinistas; the reggae artist Johnny Dread, based in South Florida, represents his Caribbean roots and his cultural heroes in "My Island Cuba" off his self-produced CD *Scarecrow*—in the grand tradition of reggae as political mouthpiece, Dread pays tribute to José Martí, a poet and patriot who founded the Cuban Revolutionary party.

And it's not just on CDs, radio, and cassettes that Jamaican-influenced music is being heard. Diana King's song "Shy Guy" was in the movie *Bad Boys;* Sister Carol sang in *Something Wild;* Shaggy's "The Train Is Coming" was used in *The Money Train,* his "Summer Time" was in *Flipper,* and his "Boombastic" sold jeans for Levi Strauss; Bob Marley's "Jamming" sells beer for Budweiser (alas, not a well-done TV commercial); and Earl Chin's *Rockers TV,* the cable show, celebrated its fifteen-year anniversary in 1996.

"OUT OF MANY, ONE PEOPLE"

This Jamaican motto expresses the philosophy of unity that guides the commercial reggae scene outside its country of origin. On the international stage the music for the most part seeks common ground, and except for the occasional less-than-pointed sociopolitical wail, the sentiment World Beat usually shoots for is inclusion. Check Lucky Dube's *Together as One,* as well as, of course, Bob's "One Love." Also note the efforts of the support group Reggae Ambassadors Worldwide (RAW), who seek across-the-board cooperation using reggae as a hook.

"African reggae, it's like some 360 thing, mon," said Neville Garrick, the artist who illustrated several of Bob's album covers and who, with Rita Marley, administers the Bob Marley Foundation. Mark Jacobson spoke to Garrick in 1995 on assignment from *Natural History* magazine: "He [Garrick] notes the transcontinental cross-pollination of Latin rumba, mambo, and so on, which had their beginnings in African rhythms and then returned to the Mother Continent, becoming elemental to the development of soukous and Ghanaian 'high-life,' among others. 'The music come from there, Jamaicans mix it up, it go back,' Garrick says."

Whether reggae music, in the broadest sense, finds its way more often or less to the world's airways is mainly a commercial concern. More important is access—to the music and to its ideals of equality and unity. True equality is a tall order and not yet achieved; unity is a real feeling, not just some politically correct concept, and reaching for that feeling is a why behind this book. May the following words, by some people who feel it, stir the feeling in you.

Chris Potash
February 1997

PART ONE

ROOTS

Reggae, Rastafarianism and Cultural Identity

VERENA RECKORD

Jamaica Journal
August 1982

Reggae is Jamaica's greatest cultural export, the main force which identifies this country internationally. Ever since the advent of the ska in the late 1950s and with the coming of Independence in 1962, Jamaican popular music has experienced a phenomenal growth and evolution that has taken it from being a response to purely parochial needs to more sophisticated commercial international acceptance. Among the musical ambassadors responsible for transmitting the music abroad are: Byron Lee and the Dragonaires, Toots and the Maytals, the Sonny Bradshaw Seven, Count Ossie and the Mystic Revelation of Rastafari, Bob Marley and the Wailers, Third World, Peter Tosh, Dennis Brown, Jimmy Cliff, Desmond Dekker, the Mighty Diamonds, Zap Pow, Burning Spear, Ras Michael and the Sons of Negus, Culture, Alton Ellis, Papa Michigan and General Smiley, Leroy Sibles, Black Uhuru, the Revolutionaries, Lloyd Parkes and We the People Band, to name just a few (not in chronological order).

As music becomes more commercial, more accepted and performed by people of varying tastes and cultures, the tendency is to ignore the roots of its origin and its deeper meaning and function. This article attempts, however informally, to trace the development of Jamaican popular and Rasta music in an effort to show what functions these play in a people's search for identity.

Jamaican music is music of the majority, who are predominantly of African descent. The history of the music goes back over four hundred years to the earliest days of slavery. Very little is known (chronicled) of African music brought to Jamaica. What can be appreciated, by the evidence in African retentions, is that the slaves under severely repressive conditions preserved what they could of African culture, including music and dance, capsulated in extracts from larger ritual forms of their homelands. These were rituals rich in the spiritual vitality and emotionalism that characterized the expressions of the intensely religious Africans.

Today, existing African-influenced traditional and folk forms include Kumina, burru, Etu, Goombay, Pocomania, Revival, Jonkonnu, Maroon and Rasta music. All these musical forms have dance movements. In these the drum is the primary instrument, which provides a rich "polyridimic"[1] base for voice instruments. The importance of the polyridimic structure is reflected in all idioms of Jamaican popular music, which has gone through several clearly defined stages of development: mento; bluebeat; ska; rudie; rock steady; reggae. It is a music created by the majority, who cling steadfastly to their basic African roots because therein lies their identity.

In Jamaica's folk and traditional music the drum plays an important role. In Kumina, for instance, special care is taken of the drums (kbandu and playing cast), which function in rituals as the media for messages from the spirit world and vice versa. The drum in African culture is recognized as an instrument of communication. For Africans, the drum talks. For Jamaicans, the "ridim" talks. In Rastafarian ceremonies, in which music is an integral part, there can be no spiritual peaking,[2] as it were, unless the ridim is right. Sometimes virtuosos or group leaders, as in the Kumina situation, may be heard chiding drummers for not getting the right ridim to suit the needs of the moment.

In reggae the quality of the polyridimic structure of the music is extremely important to the meaning of the number to artistes and aficionados alike. You will hear people saying that such and such a ridim "macca" or "gummy" or "crabbit," meaning that the percussive intent of the music has touched the vulnerable emotional centre of the listener, causing him to respond favourably to the music.

The European slave master's instinctive efforts to civilize (deculturize) the slaves, and to preserve his own links with "home," introduced to the slaves Euro-Western religious and secular music, among other things. These were assimilated by the blacks, who in their subculture activities fused what appealed to them of white cultural practice with those retained from Africa. This fusion is evident in Jamaican religions like Revival, Pocomania, and even Kumina. "Borrowed" elements of music can also be seen, for instance, in the behaviour of things like harmony and melody in Jamaican music today.

African traditional music is usually based on a five-note scale which gives a certain minor tonality to their melodies. Many traditional Jamaican songs are in minor-sounding keys. And a lot of reggae artists seem to have a natural feel for the minor in their compositions, which can be quite off-putting to the ear conditioned to the "sweetness" of Euro-Western harmonic and melodic design. It is true that, as is frequently claimed, many popular Jamaican artistes are untrained musicians whose crude musical offerings are an insult to the sophisticated ear. Many critics are quick to make the blanket statement about most reggae artistes. What should be taken into consideration when the criticisms are being made is the fact that many listeners and practitioners of Jamaican pop music, especially in the area of "dub"[3] music, do not refer to works as music or song but as "sound." People will say that this or that artiste has released "a great sound"; not a *song* but a *sound,* which does not necessarily have anything to do with pleasing melodic flow and so on.

Some of the late Bob Marley's critics contended that Marley could not sing, that his songs were not melodious and that he spoke rather than sang. This is not totally true, as an examination of Marley's works will show. His expressions depended on the message of the particular song. What is true is that many of Marley's songs were written in minor keys, which may not be the first thing expected from a star on the international stage.

Another basic link with Africa, which is evident in Jamaican folk songs and which emerged in the popular music, is the call and response singing style which has its parallels in the wider musical expressions of the black diaspora.

With improved communications in the twentieth century, musical influences of the Americas and the Caribbean territories came to colour Jamaican music, mainly in terms of instrumentation and stylings.

FROM MENTO TO SKA

Mento is officially considered the first stage in the development of Jamaican popular music even though, according to our social historians,[4] it emerged in the nineteenth century as a figure in the popular quadrille dance of the time. Outside of the quadrille set of dances, mento is a song and dance form which was the métier of troubadours of the early days, who carried news, gossip and social commentary in lively songs and dances, playing on their mostly homemade drums, bamboo fifes and fiddles. It was then a music of the majority and expressed the people's views and their philosophy of life, not unlike the social role that reggae plays today. (The religious content so heavy in reggae was missing in mento, probably because there were so many risqué songs in mento, with its pelvic-centred dance movement.)

Early exponents of mento (from the 1930s onward) included people like Slim and Sam, Lord Flea, Lord Fly, Sugar Belly and Count Lasher, doing in their time songs like "The Naughty Flea," "Rukumbine," "Wheel and Tun Me," "Solja Man," "Linstead Market," "Solas Market," "Run Mongoose" and "Yuh No Yerri." As far as the mento expression was concerned, the response to African roots was total. There was the simple phraseology; the verses based on two main statements repeated; the call and response styling; the emphasis on polyridimic patterns; the pelvic-centred movement with complementary head, shoulder and arm movements coming out of other traditional forms like Kumina.

Mento suffered rises and falls in popularity during the history of Jamaican popular music. One dormant period was the first two decades of the century, when there was mass emigration of Jamaicans to Latin America, Cuba and the United States. The return of large numbers of émigrés in the post–World War I period contributed to external influences on indigenous music. The returning emigrants themselves brought back the songs and musical influences of the era; at the same time, modern developments—such as the availability of phonograph records—were also diffusing new forms of expression.

This period coincided with the development of black American music, particularly ragtime and swing. Jamaican musicians, by listening to records and imported sheet music, took their cues from the popular black musicians of America, especially the sounds of Basie, Ellington and others—the Dorsey Brothers, Glen Miller, etc. They adapted the arrangements to suit the available instrumentation in Jamaica. The Big Band was the rage. Popular bandleaders included Eric Deans, Redver Cook, Ivy Graydon, Roy Coburne, Roy White, Milton McPherson and Carlisle Demetrius and his Alpha Boys Band. These bands were usually Kingston based and played mainly for the rich and middle class. At the grassroots level it was still a mento scene but, as has always been the case, several individuals from the Big Band aggregations would do occasional "gigs" with the mento players in the less affluent areas of Kingston.

In the late 1940s to early 1950s the music scene in Kingston began to change. The Big Bands were breaking up, with individuals seeking "greener bread" abroad or in the developing tourist mecca on Jamaica's North Coast. This meant the absence of most of the musicians who jammed at ghetto sessions.

Grassroots impresarios like "Duke" Reid and Clement "Coxsone" Dodd were at the same time emerging with their "sound system" music (now called disco) to fill the musical needs of the majority. It was black American music that the people responded to most. Black soul, an Afro-American mix, threw up stars like Fats Domino, La Verne Baker, Louis Jordan, Nat Cole, Lloyd Price, the Drifters, the Coasters and the Platters. Friendly society halls like Forrester Hall on North Street and amusement park sites were the venues of these usually jam-packed events where the underprivileged danced their troubles away to the heavy thumping rhythm and blues sounds of America.

As musical rivalry between the leading sound system operators heightened, and as the public demand for novel sounds became more pressing, the North American source began to dry up. Reid and Coxsone went into producing their own sounds using local talent. Out of this early effort song stylists like Keith and Enid, Laurel Aitken and Jackie Edwards, to name a few, became popular. Many of the songs they did were borrowed North American material.

But the people's demand for their own artistes doing their own music soon saw the emergence of the "bluebeat," which the late great trombonist Don Drummond has been credited with creating. The bluebeat was the Jamaican musician's interpretation of American rhythm and blues tunes with a mento flavour. The combination worked, but the taste of success quickly erased the bluebeat as Jamaicans began composing their very own music while retaining the shuffle in the rhythm and blues rhythms and basic mento patterns as the dominant beat. The music became known as the ska.

Like all popular Jamaican dance forms, the ska came with its own set of movements; a kind of charade to music in which the dancers brought into play things like domestic activity (washing clothes, bathing), recreation (horse racing, cricket), actually anything that appealed to the ska dancer at the moment. Some really fancy and furious "foot works" came out of the ska period. In those days lyrics came hard to composers, and artistes would even sing nursery rhymes—like Eric Morris singing "Humpty Dumpty."

By the early sixties the record producers were multiplying. Leading the contingent were Coxsone, Reid, Chris Blackwell, and Ken Khouri. One of the first ska records to come out on Coxsone's label was Laurel Aitken's "Little Sheila." Soon the audience began to demand lyrics which reflected their own lifestyles and way of life—and songs like Drummond's "Easy Snappin," "Wings of a Dove" and "Oh Carolina" resulted.

What gave ska its big boost was Edward Seaga's cultural revival arising out of the Independence experience of 1962. The then Minister of Development and Welfare in strong nationalist terms pushed for the development of "things Jamaican" in all areas of cultural expression, including international exposure of the ska as popular indigenous music.

Mr. Seaga, who is now Prime Minister of Jamaica, was also an early record producer and is an authority on Jamaican folk music. His setting up of the Jamaica Festival as a vehicle for the annual exhibition of Jamaican arts was a great boost to the development of Jamaican popular music, as the Festival song contest forced participants to pay better attention to melody, lyrics, arrangement and performance. Because the song has to be about Jamaica, the contest also helps that much more to foster nationalism in Jamaican music. Festival songs from "Bam Bam" to "Noh Weh Noh Betta Dan Yard" (1981) can be seen as highly nationalistic, as the lyrics and musical arrangements come directly from and reflect Jamaican culture. However, Festival songs have a short life span and do not reflect the general concerns of Jamaican popular music.

BIG BAND JAZZ

In the meantime, the absent big dance bands were being gradually replaced by Big Band jazz with those musicians who worked the recording studios and in small combos in the night spots around Kingston. The movement had at the forefront people like Sonny Bradshaw, the Gaynair saxophonists "Bra" and "Bogey," "Little G" McNair, Billy Cook, Thaddy Mowatt, Viv Hall, Jackie Willacy, Roland Alphonso, Rupie Anderson, Don Drummond, Bertie King and Ossie Seymour, to name a few. They identified with black jazz stars like Dizzy Gillespie, Charlie Parker, Satchmo, Miles Davis, Ellington, Basie and Lester Young.

Out of the jazz voices of the day came another conscious musician—Carlos Malcolm, a Panamanian of Jamaican parentage, a trombonist/composer/arranger. In the late fifties to early sixties Malcolm enjoyed great popularity with his Afro-Jamaican Rhythms Orchestra, which featured Latin, jazz and Caribbean music; this identified Malcolm and his music not only with Jamaica but the wider black diaspora. The feeling was strong that Jamaica could produce our own exportable jazz.

Malcolm along with Bradshaw, Bertie King, Lennie Hibbert and other leading musicians formed a short-lived school of jazz which arose out of the founders' strong nationalist feelings. The school went under for several reasons—including lack of instruments and too many students who were too poor to pay even the small fees asked.

During that period also, newly independent Jamaica was attracting back home many musicians who had emigrated. Among those returning was tenor saxist Tommy McCook, who was soon to lead Jamaica's all-time great ska band, the Skatalites. McCooks's band included Don Drummond, who was by then well into Rastafarian philosophy and was steering Jamaican music, via his trombone, in new directions. There were also Roland Alphonso, Cluet Johnson, Lloyd Brevett, Lloyd Knibbs, Drumbago and others. This band made invaluable contributions to the development of music in Jamaica by its prolific output of good music by trained and highly skilled artistes; by taking the music live to the people of rural Jamaica; and by bringing together the musical tastes of grassroots and upper-class Jamaica. Skatalite solos and musical phrases from works like "Man In The Street," "Steaming," "Schooling the Duke" and "Easy Snappin" were on the lips of music lovers across the strata. They were the nation's property.

Singers in the limelight at the time included Laurel Aitken, Toots and the Maytals, Bunny and Skitter, the Wailing Wailers, Justin Hinds, Prince Buster and Millie Small. Byron Lee and the Dragonaires had by then risen to fame and were among the forerunners who took the marketable ska to the Caribbean and metropolitan countries. Crowded Independence dances in the metropole were where "Jamaicans out there" learnt the new music and dance steps from home brought by the Dragonaires and others like the Sonny Bradshaw Seven.

Meanwhile, the exotic Rasta drumming was significantly being introduced to Jamaican pop music by the leading exponent and credited originator of the form as it is known today, the late Oswald "Count Ossie" Williams, a Rastaman. In order to understand the importance of Rasta music in the cultural history of popular music, we need to take a brief look at the development of Rastafarianism itself.

RASTAFARIAN INPUT

In 1954 the Rastafarian stronghold at Pinnacle, near Spanish Town, was routed. It had been the home and communal farm of men, women and children ruled by "Gangunguru"[5] or "Gong" as he was called by his many wives. Gong preached the divinity of Haile Selassie, Ras Tafari of Ethiopia, and the repatriation back to Africa. The Rastafarians, as did their forefathers, always look to Africa as "the homeland." They see the black man in the diaspora as one in exile.

The displaced members of the self-contained Pinnacle community (over a thousand men, women and children who enjoyed certain security on Gong's vast ganja cultivation and through the earnings of their cottage industries) now found themselves joining the teeming dispossessed in the sprawling Back o' Wall slum of West Kingston. Up to then Rastafarianism did not boast a music of its own, and the early disciples like Howell and Joseph Hibbert[6] used at their street meetings Euro-Western church music, especially from the Baptist hymnal and "Sankey." At Back o' Wall the Rastas—by then social outcasts because of their self-imposed exile, antiestablishment way of life and black nationalist beliefs—met with another group of outcasts: the burru people.

The burru people were a dwindling breed of mostly criminals who were known for their virtuoso African drumming on akete drums supported by sansa (marimba box) and other instruments dating back to the days of slavery. The Rastas seized on the burru music because it presented them with something of a pure African form untouched by Western influences. The burru people in turn empathized with their fellow outcasts—often hiding their "wrong-doings" behind the mask of the Rasta's dreadlocks and dress. In time the burru people were absorbed by the larger and ever growing Rasta group with its messianic zeal to overthrow the cultural despotism of Europe.

In the later fifties Back o' Wall and West Kingston in general were the melting pot of African retentions and indigenous Afro-European forms: Kumina, burru, myal, Revivalism, Pocomania and a host of church mutations. It was there that Count Ossie, during regular trips to "reason" with other Rasta brethren on Garveyism, Rastafarianism, black culture and blackman redemption, learnt to play the burru drums. As the late Count told it, he learnt first to play the funde.[7] Then he graduated to the repeater or solo instrument on which he became a virtuoso. Ossie's teacher was a burru man called Bro. Joe.

The brethren reasoned that just as Europe had gone to great lengths to develop and preserve its cultural identity, so too should the black man—whether in Africa or in exile—seek to preserve his African identity. Since a dominant feature of African culture is music, and the chief instrument of communication is the drum, Ossie decided he was on the right track to developing a significant black music that suited the Rastafarian expression. He ordered a set of akete drums made to his specifications and soon worked out drumming stylings based on the burru patterns. In time he gave Rasta a music. It is a music of protest, one which expresses Rastafarian hopes and aspirations, a music which indoctrinates those interested in the philosophy of Rastafarianism.

Soon after this, Rasta music became a primary feature, a grounding force, at the mushrooming campsites of West Kingston and in the hills around the city. The demolition of Back o' Wall a few years later meant even greater dispersal of the Rastafarian brethren with their pulsating music and their message of black awareness.

Chief among the campsites was Count Ossie's camps, first at Adastra Road and later at the present premises on Glasspole Avenue in East Kingston where the MRR Community Centre built by Ossie now stands. Besides lawyers, doctors and "Indian chiefs," Ossie's camps attracted the cream of Jamaican jazz and pop musicians, including the Gaynairs, Tommy McCook, Viv Hall, Don Drummond, Ernest Ranglin, and even musicians from abroad. It was during these sessions of reasoning and music coming together that the compatibility of Rasta drumming and voice instruments and the creative excitement in the interchange were realized. It is said that it was out of this experience that the trombone of the great Don D (Drummond) took wing.

The experience also saw Ossie and his drummers as popular features at ghetto sound system dances, Coney Island and amusement park scenes. The general pattern was that come midnight, the blaring recorded music would come to a halt as Ossie and his drummers took the stage. Then the patrons, working-class Jamaica, would "grounds"[8] with the group until the wee hours of the morning.

Even if they did not all believe in the Rastafarian philosophy, they identified with the Rastas' symbolic beating down of "Babylon" (social oppressors) with their militant chants, Nyabingi[9] dancing and drumming which were at once entertaining and assuring. (Although the function and focus of Nyabingi are greatly altered today, the dance movement was a significant part of reggae king Bob Marley's movement onstage, which was often seen by the uninformed as prancing about.)

Ossie's music in the ghettos became the people's choice. Even those who did not "see Rasta"[10] or wished to go back to Africa found that they could forget their troubles and dance.

In time, Ossie became a performer on regular stages and in the recording studios. His drummers backing the Ffolkes Brothers resulted in the ska classic "Oh Carolina." Rasta music had made its mark on the popular recording scene, and ever since the ridims have been used by local pop musicians to create on. The music also gave to its ever growing audience Rasta chants which became popular dance numbers, chants like "Wings of a Dove," "Holy Mount Zion" and "Rivers of Babylon."

A significant boost to the popularity of Rasta music in the early sixties was the phenomenal migration of the young from multifocal Jamaican middle class toward the simple peace-and-love and black consciousness philosophy of Rastafarianism. It was a social phenomenon that the National Dance Theatre Company's Rex Nettleford saw fit to chronicle in the company's repertoire as *Two Drums for Babylon* in 1964. While Rasta roots were taking hold of the popular music expression, other indigenous influences had also been showing up in the music of pop stars like Toots and the Maytals and the Wailing Wailers. Toots Hibbert's music on the whole, including his well-known "Bam Bam" Festival-winning song, has the strong ridimic value and performance quality of Revivalism and the call and response influence of African traditions. Jimmy Cliff's early hits show the gospel-Poco-blues mix, as do works of people like the Heptones, Desmond Dekker and Justin Hinds. When Eric Donaldson came to sing his 1969–70 Festival song winner "Cherry Oh Baby," he brought a raw rural sound to the urban majority who immediately embraced it (which is understandable since most of the city's working class, and then some, are migrants from the rural areas).

ROCK STEADY TO REGGAE

There are no exact dates for the beginnings and endings of social and cultural periods, and so it is with music. Even while Rasta music seemed to have been dormant during the rock steady period, which followed the ska era, Rasta influences were budding beneath the surface, waiting for the spring of the rudie period and the magnificent florescence in the reggae period. In the later sixties the ska sound, which featured many horns on top of a basic ridim, was hit by the dispersal, again for economic reasons, of many horn men as well as by the death of culture hero Don Drummond.

Record producer Clement Dodd and people like Jackie Mittoo, a leading popular musical composer of the time, began experimenting with the basic ridim and what was left of voice instruments. The piano and the guitar were given more importance. The simple repetitive two- or three-chord progression of ska was retained, along with the ridim patterns; the formerly walking bass became more flexible; and the whole thing was coloured by an overall slow, bluesy beat as Jamaicans did the new rock steady to the tunes of Hopeton Lewis ("Sound and Pressure," "Take it Easy"), Alton Ellis ("Get Ready Rock Steady") and others.

At first rock steady was strictly for enjoyment, as was the ska on a whole, but the easy ridim was found suitable for lyrics of social commentary. Soon the artistes were coming to grips with the stifling social conditions which pervaded life in the ghetto, from which most of them came. This was so especially in the short "rudie" period which was part of the transition from ska to rock steady. Rudie lyrics commented on the new criminal elements among the ghetto youths, with their nihilistic view of life where the only goal was to live dangerously and die young for lack of real positive social goals.

Rudie songs included "Rude Boy," "Rudie O Rudie," "Rudie in Court," "Rudie Get Offa Circuit Charge," "See Dem a Come," "Rude Boy Train," "007," "Trying to Conquer Me," to name a few. Bob Marley and the Wailers, Desmond Dekker, Roy Shirley, Derrick Morgan, Delroy Wilson, Hopeton Lewis, Alton Ellis, were among the stars of the period.

In the early seventies Rasta doctrine, culture and outspoken criticism of the establishment, as well as its concern for black unity, freedom of Africa and the black and oppressed peoples of the world, became more widely accepted by the youth of the country, and it all came out in the popular music. The polyridimic influences of Rasta music became the driving force of reggae. Count Ossie's "Rasta Reggae" was the first reggae to incorporate fully the Rasta drums in the music. In time, the patterns of the three Rasta drums (bass, funde, repeater) were distributed[11] to the bass, rhythm guitar, keyboards and added percussions. The reggae era is now in full flower.

Generally speaking, reggae has three basic components: ridim—the polyridimic overlays in the percussive weave—melody and voice. As in Rasta music, the ridim in a reggae piece remains constant once it is set. But reggae tempo can be fast or slow, and as the emphasis is on the ridim instruments, aficionados will argue endlessly about whether a reggae is "roots rock reggae," "rock steady," "steady rock," "rumbling roots," "roots reggae rockers" or a host of others. A reggae piece can also be expressed in several permutations commonly called "versions": ridim minus melody; new melody on old ridim; speaking voice over set ridim; instrumental fills of a piece with just touches of the original ridim in punctuation. It goes on.

This extremely flexible music lends itself to almost endless musical exploitation. It is sought after by music makers and lovers all over the world.

Reggae's lasting qualities parallel those of African-influenced traditional and folk forms in that like them, reggae includes a great deal of emotionalism, spiritual vitality and gnomic function. For instance, nowhere else in the world is the popular music a basically religious music. Nowhere else do the people in the popular sense dance and shake their bodies exulting in a deity of their own making. And nowhere else is the popular music an integral part of the people's way of life as is reggae in Jamaica.

Added to this is the reggae artistes' concern through their lyrics for black awareness and unity and the freedom of the oppressed peoples of the world. This is understood and accepted by the reggae audiences in Jamaica and abroad. Most of the leading artistes profess to be Rastafarians, and their empathy with blacks and sufferers internationally points to a certain universal identity[12] of the Jamaican majority. Indeed, although the religious element is strongest, the music has also become the vehicle for the transmittal of wider cultural manifestations and for commentary on internal and international political and social affairs.

Going by the form, function and performance of reggae, one gets the feeling that the Jamaican majority are a people spiritually in transit, and that the heaven they identify with has nothing at all to do with that created by Euro-Christianity.

Jamaican popular music has influenced other art forms. It has given birth to the popular "dub poetry" with leading exponents Oku Onuora and Michael Smith. The National Dance Theatre Company has also seen fit to make valid social commentary in dance, using the music of the popular culture heroes: *Street People* (music of Desmond Dekker and other pop artistes), *Tribute to Cliff* (music of Jimmy Cliff), *Backlash* (music of Toots and the Maytals), *Court of Jah* (music of Bob Marley and the Wailers), *Rockstone Debate* (Bob Marley and traditional music).

Among Jamaican musicians responsible for the creation of reggae music for recreational, critical and inspirational purposes are the late Hon. Bob Marley, O.M.,[13] Toots and the Maytals, Third World, Ras Michael and the Sons of Negus, Jimmy Cliff, Peter Tosh, Pablo Moses, U-Roy, Big Youth, Culture, the Revolutionaries, the late Jacob Miller, Judy Mowatt, Rita Marley.

All the above reggae stars and more profess the faith of Rastafari. Over the years, in their music and otherwise, they have spoken of an intensely religious, peace-loving people who are nevertheless defiant of social oppression and Euro-Western cultural despotism, and strongly conscious of their black roots.

Even though they voice their love for Jamaica, in a spiritually significant sense they sing more of oneness with the black people of the world, which gives the music a strong universal identity as well.

NOTES

1. In Jamaican music "ridim" refers to the drum and percussion patterns and tempo.
2. Referred to by some Rastas as the "rising of the irix."
3. "Dub" refers to the dubbing on of new lyrics, usually "deejay" stylings on already existing ridim.
4. According to the late actor, social historian and folk hero Ranny Williams, the blacks in Jamaica added the indigenous mento to the set of quadrille dances to "liven up" the dance as well as to insert their own identity.
5. Leonard P. Howell, 1898–1981, claimed to speak several African languages; founded the Ethiopian Salvation Society in 1934; set out first basic principles of Rastafarianism.

6. Joseph Hibbert (born 1894) founded the Ethiopian Mystic Masons and several Rastafarian groups after the coronation of Haile Selassie.

7. It is customary for a student to learn to "hold" (play) the funde (one of three akete drums) before any of the others.

8. "Get down": identify; dance, etc.

9. Nyabingi: A Rasta term meaning "death to white oppressors and their black supporters."

10. "See Rasta": accept Haile Selassie as God.

11. Ossie felt that something of the importance of Rastafarianism to Jamaican music was lost when the ridims of the Rasta drums are simulated in other instruments. Today, reggae groups include one or more of the Rasta drums in their ridim sections.

12. This speaks more of a spiritual identity, which is very important to the highly religious Jamaicans, than of national identity, which is embraced by most artistes who see Jamaica as God's gift to the black man.

13. Robert Nesta Marley, reggae superstar, was given the third-highest civil honour of Jamaica (the Order of Merit) for his contribution internationally to Jamaican music and culture, before his death on May 11, 1981.

From "Reggae, Rastafarians and Revolution: Rock Music in the Third World"

JAMES A. WINDERS

The Journal of Popular Culture
1983

In recent years, reggae has become Jamaica's major new export—rivaling bauxite. As a result of this exposure of the rest of the world to Jamaica through this recorded music with growing participation of British and American record companies, people outside Jamaica have learned something of the explosive nature of Jamaican society. In particular, it is through the music that we have become more acquainted with the beliefs and customs of one of the world's most unusual subcultures: the Rastafarians (Brotherhood of Rastafari).

The Rastafarians, concentrated in Jamaica but with many followers among large Jamaican immigrant population centers such as London and New York, are variously described as a religious cult, as a political movement within Jamaica, as a criminal element associated with drug dealing and violence, or as irresponsible dropouts. They are objects of considerable scorn among many segments of Jamaican society—black and white alike—and their extensive cultivation and use of ganja/marijuana brings them frequent clashes with the police.[1] Rastafarians are categorized by the police as violent and a threat to Jamaican society, yet many of the nation's leading artists, craftspeople, athletes and especially musicians are Rastas (*Rasta* or *Rastaman* are used more frequently than *Rastafarian*).[2] They are the leading critics of Jamaica's government—the forces of Babylon to them—and their ideas dominate the lyrics of reggae songs to such an extent that recent albums by groups like Bob Marley and the Wailers and Burning Spear and artists like Peter Tosh and Max Romeo appear to have been intended more as Rastafarian sermons than as popular record albums.

There is no "official" Rastafarian theology; no canon; no church structure. Rastas agree on two principles of faith only (with wide differences on everything from personal appearance to whether or not Haile Selassie was the incarnate Christ or a god in his own right): (1) that Haile Selassie I—the king of kings, the lord of lords, Conquering Lion of the Tribe of Judah—is the living God, and (2) that Africa is the real home of the black man; his paradise.[3] They see themselves as the lost children of Israel captive in Babylon, awaiting deliverance and repatriation: when "Jah" (Rastafari, Haile Selassie) leads them back to "Zion" (Ethiopia).

The story of the Rastafarians begins with the career of a self-styled black prophet from Jamaica who gained great prominence in Harlem in the 1920s: Marcus Mosiah Garvey, a man much maligned and misunderstood in this country, but much beloved and esteemed as a prophet by his fellow black Jamaicans.[4] Born in Jamaica in 1887, Garvey emigrated to the United States in 1916 and, the following year, founded the Universal Negro Improvement Association (UNIA). Under Garvey's leadership, this organization became the leading exponent (to the horror of many middle-class blacks and liberal whites and to the delight of the Ku Klux Klan) of "redemption through repatriation" for blacks: Garvey taught that the Negro would always suffer as long as he was divorced from his true homeland—Africa.

Garvey wasted little time in taking steps to put his beliefs into practice. He founded his own newspaper, *The Negro World*, in New York soon after founding the UNIA. Garvey's black nationalist slogan, "One Aim, One God, One Destiny," became the official motto of the newspaper. But the venture that proved his undoing was the establishment in 1919 of the Black Star Line to "link the colored peoples of the world in commercial and industrial discourse." Garvey sold shares in this company, which he promoted to potential backers as the means for returning New World blacks to Africa. He even held meetings with the Klan to secure their investment in repatriation. Garvey traveled widely throughout the United States speaking in support of his schemes, even appearing in Harlem and elsewhere in what could only be called Napoleon regalia.

Garvey was a short, powerfully built man of regal bearing. His critics of course called him ostentatious. A proud man, he preached black pride and black consciousness in a Jim Crow era. As a result, the federal authorities were gunning for him. In 1922, after the Black Star Line went bankrupt, Garvey and three associates were indicted on several counts of mail fraud stemming from the sales campaign for the company's shares. Garvey was indicted for mail fraud in 1923, but was free on bond until 1925, when the conviction was upheld and he began serving a sentence in the federal penitentiary in Atlanta. President Coolidge commuted his sentence in 1927 and Garvey was deported to Jamaica.

Garvey was nevertheless a prophet with honor in his own country; indeed he had become something of an international celebrity. For example, in Kenya no less a personality than the young Jomo Kenyatta listened with great interest to Garvey's message of black strength and solidarity. Jamaicans listened enthusiastically to Garvey's talks in the months after his return, and he made something of a splash in Jamaican politics. He eventually grew impatient with his native country and moved to England in 1935, where he oversaw his dwindling international movement. He died there in 1940.[5]

But before Marcus left Jamaica behind he made a speech in Kingston that became the launching pad for Rastafarianism. In a Kingston church on a Sunday in 1927, Garvey proclaimed (prophesied), "Look to Africa, where a black king shall be crowned." Garvey's followers were thus extremely interested in November of 1930 when the Kingston *Daily Gleaner* ran on its front page the story that a relatively unknown tribal chieftain named Ras Tafari Mekonnen had been crowned Haile Selassie I (the name means "Power of the Holy Trinity"). Was this the black king Marcus had prophesied, the Garveyites wondered?[6] The faithful, like all Jamaicans steeped in a tradition of Bible-thumping revivalism, pored over the scriptures to find some clue about this Haile Selassie. And in Revelation 5:5 they found this: "Then one of the elders said to me, 'Weep not; lo, the lion of the tribe of Judah, the Root of David, has conquered, so that he can open the scroll and its seven seals.'"[7] (R.S.V.)

When Ethiopia won the world's admiration for its historic resistance to Mussolini in 1935, the excitement in Jamaica over Haile Selassie increased. Some began to call him "Jah," a word whose origins are obscure. It may, however, be related to a word used in certain Masonic rituals. The Masons, in fact, had been active in Jamaica. His followers regarded him as the Living God, and Marcus Garvey was elevated to a kind of John the Baptist status. Thus was born the brotherhood of Rastafari.[8]

Only gradually did other Jamaicans learn of the existence within their country of a growing body of people who rejected Jamaican society and longed to be transported to Africa. Through periodic confrontations with the law, the Rastas began to intrude more and more into the Jamaican consciousness. In 1933 a Rastafarian named L. P. Howell was imprisoned as a result of his attempt to sell five thousand pictures of Haile Selassie purported to be exclusive passports to Ethiopia. When Howell got out of prison in 1940, he moved with his followers into the remote hills of Jamaica, the historic place of refuge for the runaway slaves who came to be called "Maroons," and founded a settlement called Pinnacle. The police raided this settlement in 1941 and arrested seventy people on charges of growing ganja and violence.[9]

From this point on the Rastas began to be associated in the popular mind with violence and crime.[10] In the 1950s Rastas were often arrested, and sometimes flogged and forcibly shaved. Rastas even charged that in Trench Town the police deliberately burned many children to death.[11] Nineteen fifty-five in particular was a violent year of demonstrations over the subject of repatriation.[12] In 1960 several Rastas, anxious to alter the violent prejudices most Jamaicans had against them, asked some scholars at the University of the West Indies in Kingston to prepare a report on the Rastafarian movement. The results of the report, which concluded that most Rastafarians were nonviolent, that they really were sincere about repatriation and ought to be supported by the government in moving to Africa, did not please the government, either in Kingston or London, and the report was largely ignored.[13]

On April 21, 1966, one of the most extraordinary spectacles in postcolonial Jamaican history unfolded at Palisadoes Airport, where thousands of Rasta were on hand to greet the arrival of Emperor Haile Selassie I, who was on a state visit. When pandemonium erupted upon his landing, Selassie at first refused to leave his plane.

He expressed dismay over the hysterical crowd who were worshipping his divinity (he later emphatically denied his own divinity, but the Rastas were not swayed by this; even Jah, they said, could not gainsay the prophecy), but he finally relented and basked in the outpouring of affection from this and other gatherings in Jamaica. He appeared to enjoy himself immensely during his stay, and while some Jamaicans expressed surprise that "Jah" was a mere 5'4", most were pleased with his kingly demeanor.[14]

Ethiopians occasionally expressed some interest in the desires of the Jamaican brethren to settle in Ethiopia. In 1955 the Ethiopian government had set aside some five hundred acres of land for "the black peoples of the West," but only a few ever came. This was at the same time that large numbers of Jamaicans began to emigrate to London.[15] While Haile Selassie was willing to accept a few settlers from Jamaica, the thought of thousands of ganja-smoking unemployed aliens living in his country made him reluctant to make overtures to the eager Rastafarians.

The Jamaican government of Prime Minister Michael Manley, while—like its predecessors—opposed to the idea of wholesale repatriation of large numbers, was willing to play up the "Ethiopian connection" to win the support of the Rastas. When Manley visited Ethiopia before Haile Selassie was overthrown in the coup of 1973, Selassie gave him a handsome walking stick that Manley, with his flair for adopting the Biblical style of the Rastas, called "the rod of correction."[16] But despite signs from Manley that he, like the present more moderate government of Edward Seaga, was interested in maintaining good relations with the brotherhood of Rastafari (though not willing as yet to legalize marijuana, one of their chief demands), most Rastas still say they await the "return to Zion."[17]

> If I dream, mon, every Rastamon's dream, to fly home to Ethiopia and leave a-Babylon, where de politicians doan let I an' I brethren be free an live we own righteous way.[18]
>
> BOB MARLEY, QUOTED IN ROLLING STONE INTERVIEW, AUGUST 12, 1976

Although there is not universal agreement among Rastas concerning specific religious practices, the movement as a whole is known in Jamaica and abroad for two things in particular: the extensive use of and devotion to ganja as a way of life, and the practice among male members of wearing the hair, which they refuse to cut, in "locks" or "dreadlocks." Not all Rastas adopt this style, while many "false Rastas" do, and differences can be found among Rastafarians on matters of diet, sex, children and work. Use of ganja, however, is universal—true of many non-Rasta Jamaicans as well.[19]

Ganja has long been a part of Jamaican folk culture, though a likely explanation is that immigrants from India introduced cannabis to Jamaica in the mid-nineteenth century. *Ganja* is the Hindu word for marijuana, and "Kali," the name for an Indian black goddess, is also the name of a particularly potent grade of dark-colored ganja. For generations in Jamaica, ganja has been not only smoked, but brewed as tea and eaten as seasoning in soups and stews. Most of its uses have been medicinal (note recent discussions of marijuana and glaucoma), including use of ganja tea to calm upset stomach in children. Ganja is cultivated on a grand scale in Jamaica, and despite the activities of Jamaican and American authorities, ganja is the island's true cash crop.[20]

For Rastas, ganja—"herb"—has sacramental importance. The marijuana high is valued as something more than pleasurable; it is cherished as a "righteous" state, prayerful and contemplative. Much of Rasta theology is composed of specific and curious verses of scripture, and interpretations thereof, from the Old and New Testaments. Nowhere is this more obvious than on the subject of "herb." The specific verses used to support the copious sacramental use of marijuana are Psalm 18:8 and Revelation 22:2.[21] Psalm 18 also finds David giving thanks for a victory in battle, and then the Lord appears to David in anger. In verse 8 we are told that "Smoke went up from his nostrils, and devouring fire from his mouth," and this is taken by Rastafarians as evidence that God himself smokes the herb and urges his children to do so. The passage in Revelation is the "river and the tree of life" passage where "the leaves of the tree were for the healing of the nation." Ganja again?

Numbers 6:5 is another source from which the Rastas extract the scriptural authority for one of their most curious practices. This verse begins, "All the days of his separation no razor shall come upon his head."[22] Since Rastafarians take themselves to be "Israelites" separated from "Zion," this has been used as the scriptural basis of the refusal of many male Rastas to cut their hair. Many are "locksmen," wearing their hair in plaits, which they themselves smear with lard, called "dread-locks," often for convenience stuffing the mass of hair into large woolen caps, frequently in the red, green and gold of Ethiopia.[23] Other Rastas are "beardsmen," keeping the hair short above but allowing "no razor upon the beard." Some Rastas have both locks and beards, and some are "baldheads."[24] But tonsorial considerations should not be allowed to override concern with what lies within, as the Rasta saying about "false Rastas" who adopt the style without the real commitment reflects: "Him have locks on head but not in heart."[25]

Native Jamaicans speak a thick patois that reveals certain African survivals in their dialect, and Rastas have a dialect all their own. These Rasta linguistic inventions frequently find their way into reggae songs, where they provide the uninitiated with no end of confusion. Words like *Jah* we have mentioned, but then there is the mystifying tendency of Rastas to use the nominative case exclusively: "I," "I and I," "I and I brethren."[26] This extends to the substitution of an *I* prefix for the first syllable of a word, e.g.: "I-dren" (children) or "I-tal" (natural).[27] Reggae songs are literally peppered with Rasta slogans such as "I-Ree-Ites" ("Higher Heights," or perhaps "Israelites").[28]

Many Rastafarians are vegetarians and insist on "I-tal" food, emphasizing vegetables, fruits and grains. Some refuse to drink alcohol, while many enjoy Jamaica's Red Stripe Beer or Dragon Stout. Some, like Orthodox Jews and Muslims, will eat no pork, often preferring goat as their choice of meat. Such prohibitions are of course biblical, and many Rastas go beyond the dietary laws to enforce certain taboos such as the Old Testament admonition against sleeping with a woman who is menstruating. This stricture carries over into Jamaican popular culture generally, for the most violent curses and epithets are menstrual (Blood clot! Ras clot! Bumba clot!—all eligible for use as either nouns or adjectives). Some Rastafarians are polygamists, and there is generally no marriage ceremony.[29] Rastas are very much opposed to birth control, which they suspect is part of a white program to limit the size of the black race.[30] In V. S. Naipaul's novel *Guerrillas,* set in Jamaica, this item is noted among the graffiti along a busy Kingston thoroughfare: BIRTH CONTROL IS A PLOT AGAINST THE NEGRO RACE.[31]

Of crucial importance to Jamaica is the debate within the Rastafarian movement over whether to cooperate at all with "Babylon" and, if so, to what extent. Most Rastas are unemployed, chronic unemployment being a basic feature of Jamaican life, but many reject the idea of working "for Babylon" anyway. "Don't vote" is another familiar slogan found in places like Trench Town, and yet reggae songs have been used by both major political parties in recent elections,[32] an acknowledgment that reggae music, Rastafarian influences and all, has become a major cultural force in Jamaican life. For example, Prime Minister Michael Manley's campaign song in the 1972 election was a reggae hit called "Better Must Come."[33] Most recent reggae songs trumpet the certain downfall of Babylon, the Armageddon that will surely come, in much the same way that punk rock groups in Britain gloat over the diminishing power of the U.K.

Reggae is the music—part journalism, part prophecy—that captures the cultural contradictions of the new Jamaica, pounding them into the consciousness with a hypnotic beat.

NOTES

1. Kitzinger, Sheila. "Rastafarian Brethren of Jamaica." *Comparative Studies in Society and History* 9: 1 (October 1966), pp. 33–39.
2. Davis, Stephen, and Peter Simon. *Reggae Bloodlines: In Search of the Music and Culture of Jamaica.* Garden City, NY: Anchor, 1977, p. 69.
3. Ibid., p. 72.
4. Literature on Garvey is fascinating and extensive; see especially Edmund David Cronon, *Black Moses: The Story of Marcus Garvey and the Universal Negro Improvement Association* (Madison: University of Wisconsin Press, 1955); *Marcus Garvey,* ed. E. D. Cronon (Englewood Cliffs, NJ: Prentice-Hall, 1973), "Great Lives Observed" series; Amy Jacques Garvey, *Garvey and Garveyism* (New York: Collier, 1970); Tony Martin, *Race First: The Ideological and Organizational Struggles of Marcus Garvey and the Universal Negro Improvement Association* (Westport, CT: Greenwood, 1976); and Elton C. Fox, *Garvey: The Story of a Pioneer Black Nationalist* (New York: Dodd, Mead, 1972).

For speeches of Garvey and his followers see: *Philosophy and Opinions of Marcus Garvey,* ed. Amy Jacques Garvey (New York: Atheneum, 1970); *More Philosophy and Opinions of Marcus Garvey,* ed. E. U. Essien-Udom and Amy Jacques Garvey (London: Frank Cass, 1977); and *Black Redemption: Churchmen Speak for the Garvey Movement,* ed. Randall K. Burkett (Philadelphia: Temple University Press, 1978).

Reggae recordings are peppered with references to Garvey, especially the recordings of the Burning Spear, including their albums *Marcus Garvey* (Island Records, 1975) and *Garvey's*

Ghost (Mango Records, 1975). Additional references may be heard in Peter Tosh's recording of "The Prophets" on *Bush Doctor* (Rolling Stones Records, 1978) and in Bob Marley and the Wailers' "Kinky Reggae" on *Catch a Fire* (Island, 1973).

5. This summary is based chiefly on E. D. Cronon, "Introduction" and "Chronology of the Life of Marcus Garvey," *Marcus Garvey*, ed. Cronon, pp. 1–16, 17–18; Davis, pp. 66–68; and "Would You Believe Rasta Theology?" *High Times* (September 1976), pp. 58–59.

6. Davis, p. 69.

7. "Would You Believe Rasta Theology?" p. 59. See also Leonard Barrett, *The Rastafarians: Sounds of Cultural Dissonance* (Boston: Beacon, 1977), p. 83. Although this book has its flaws, the author demonstrates the ways in which Rastafarianism is rooted in various Jamaican revivalist traditions.

8. "Would You Believe . . .?" p. 59.

9. Kitzinger, p. 33.

10. The growing tension between the Rastafarians and the Jamaican authorities is treated in Rex M. Nettleford, *Identity, Race and Protest in Jamaica* (New York: Morrow, 1972), pp. 39–111.

11. Kitzinger, p. 33.

12. Ibid., p. 34.

13. Ibid., p. 36.

14. Davis, pp. 76–77.

15. Kitzinger, p. 34.

16. Thomas, Michael. "The Rastas Are Coming! The Rastas Are Coming!" *Rolling Stone* (August 12, 1976), p. 34.

17. Ibid., p. 37.

18. Bob Marley, quoted in Ed McCormack, "Bob Marley With a Bullet," *Rolling Stone* (August 12, 1976), p. 34.

19. Davis, pp. 70–75. See also Kitzinger, pp. 37–38.

20. Ibid., pp. 179–81.

21. Ibid., p. 75.

22. Kitzinger, p. 35.

23. "The *High Times* Guide to Jamaica" *High Times* (September 1976), p. 51.

24. This term is used to express disdain for non-Rastas, as in Marley's song "Crazy Baldhead," *Rastaman Vibration* (Island Records, 1976).

25. Davis, p. 75.

26. Kitzinger, p. 35.

27. Ibid., p. 35.

28. This last phrase is sung, e.g. by the "I-Threes," the three female singers in Bob Marley and the Wailers, as a refrain in the song "Positive Vibration," *Rastaman Vibration* (Island, 1976). One of the most popular songs of the Jamaican band "Third World" is called "Irie Ites," and can be heard on the 1979 Island Records release *The Story's Been Told*.

29. Davis, p. 75.

30. Kitzinger, p. 37.

31. V. S. Naipaul, *Guerrillas* (New York: Knopf, 1975), p. 3.

32. "Singing Them a Message," *Time* (March 22, 1976), p. 84.

33. Davis, pp. 172–73.

"Up-full Sounds": Language, Identity, and the Worldview of Rastafari

JOHN W. PULIS

Ethnic Groups
1993[1]

About a decade ago I asked a Rastafarian, a backcountry "rootsman," what the world-view of Rastafari was all about: "Jus word-sound-paawa, bradda, dat what I-n-I [Rastafari] a-deal wit, jus word-sound-paawa," was his reply. As I learned, the world-view of Rastafari was not as simple as suggested, but was bound up with ideas concerning language, identity, and history.

The Rastafarian brethren resemble what anthropologists refer to as a millennial or revitalization movement. The Rastafarians first emerged during the interwar decades in Jamaica, but are now present wherever Jamaicans have migrated. Their proclamations concerning Haile Selassie, their mediation of contemporary and biblical events, and their unique way of speaking, known as "Dread Talk," "I-ance," or "I-yaric," have been dismissed as the irrational prophesies of a Third World millennial cult.

This paper discusses a philosophy of language known as "word-sound-power." Rather than irrational prophecy, the author contends that word-sound-power is a way of speaking in which a tension between Creole and Standard English words and meanings are used to contest traditional constructions of identity. This paper opens with a background survey of language in Jamaica, proceeds to the presentation of a "reasoning" in which the writer participated, and concludes with a discussion of how a reconstituted understanding of language contests traditional constructions of identity.

BACKGROUND

The island of Jamaica was the crown jewel of the eighteenth-century British Empire. Anglophile planters and African laborers created a unique West Indian culture expressed by annual festivities such as Jonkonnu, the belief-system of Afro-Christianity, and a spoken language, a form of Creole-English known as Jamaica Talk.

Creole languages were long considered to be baby talk, slang, or broken dialects of European languages, be they French, English, or Dutch. Recent analyses of grammar, speech, and vocabulary have demonstrated that West Indian Creoles are not baby talk or slangs, but bona fide languages that originated in Africa and were reconstituted in the New World.

Such is the case of Jamaica Talk. As Alleyne (1988) and Cassidy (1982 [1961]) contend, Jamaica Talk constituted the disclosure of day-to-day life. It was spoken by Africans and Europeans in the sugar plantations, the slave villages, and the local markets. The vocabulary of Jamaica Talk contained English and African words and incorporated various performative and rhetorical genres, from African proverbs and English folktales to the talking drums and abengs of the Maroons.[2]

While Jamaica Talk was the discourse of everyday life, it was not politically neutral. On the one hand, it was subordinated to English as the official spoken and printed language of the colony. Lady Nugent, the North American wife of Governor George Nugent of Jamaica (1801–1806), made the following observations: "The Creole language is not confined to the Negroes. Many of their [European] ladies, who have not been educated in England, speak a sort of broken English, with an indolent drawling out of their words, that is very tiresome if not disgusting. I stood next to a lady one night, near a window, and, by way of saying something, remarked that the air was much cooler than usual; to which she answered, 'Yes, ma-am, him rail-ly too fraish'" (Jekyll, 1966 [1907]).

On the other hand, the drums and horns sounded during the slave rebellions and Maroon wars were by no means a secondary genre, but were means of communication clearly understood by Africans and Europeans alike. As Jamaica Talk was reconstituted from English and African dialects spoken in the eighteenth century, the word-sound-power of Dread Talk emerged from the urban enclaves of the twentieth century.

BALM YARDS AND DUNGLES

The interwar decades were turbulent years in Jamaican history. Events set in motion in the nineteenth century transformed involuntary laborers into a disenfranchised working class by the 1930s. Landless peasants and unemployed workers migrated to Central America to dig canals and build railroads. The population of Montego Bay and Kingston trebled, and urban enclaves, balm yards, and dungles became focal points of social and political unrest.

Pan-Africanists, trade unionists, and street preachers alike were active in Kingston contesting British colonialism. Labor leaders such as Alexander Bustamante and nationalists such as Norman Manley organized unions and laid the foundation for what became the People's National and Jamaican Labor Parties. Similarly, Pan-Africanists such as Marcus Garvey, "native-Baptists"[3] such as Alexander Bedward, and advocates of Rastafari such as Leonard Howell were also active; but they drew upon an alternate tradition of prophetic oratory and biblical interpretation to contest British hegemony.

Both street preachers and trade unionists mounted formidable challenges. On the one hand, street preaching and biblical interpretation expressed a continuity with the political and linguistic praxis of Afro-Jamaican culture. Slave leaders and native-Baptists fused religion and politics into an Afro-Jamaican worldview expressed not in the grammar and rhetoric of Standard English, but in the sounds and signs of Jamaica Talk.

On the other hand, international events such as the coronation of Haile Selassie and the Pan-African movement provided the context for the transformation of Jamaica Talk into Dread Talk. Jamaica Talk was the "chosen tongue," the means of communication by which trade unionists and street preachers assaulted British hegemony. It was the tonal semantics of Creole and the worldview of Afro-Christianity that inspired the publications of West Indian poets, historians, and political activists. It was not the printed word that inspired Dread Talk, but the spoken. In addition to verifying local prophesy concerning an African Messiah, the events that unfolded in Ethiopia substantiated a linguistic praxis that subordinated spoken and printed English to the tonal or sound-based semantics of Creole. The acoustic structure of English words and the grammatical structure of printed texts were "penetrated"; that is, read aloud, broken apart, and reassembled into a discourse that renegotiated traditional constructions of identity. If the words and sounds of this prophecy were first spoken during the 1930s in Kingston, by the 1980s they were heard in Africa, Europe, and North America, as a cohort of Rastafarians matured, a number of formal organizations were established, and an international music industry proliferated.

FOREGROUND

The proper way to frame an analysis of Dread Talk is not to focus on the sentence or the word, but on the context of communication. As important as grammatical analyses are, they tend to neglect the speaker, the setting, and the scene. Neglecting the speaker-hearer dyad is understandable in analyses of historic texts, but not in studies of spoken language where meaning is embedded in the context of communication.

The writer was introduced to the word-sounds of Dread Talk while discussing religion and culture with a Rastafarian we shall call Bongo.[4] The name Bongo is a pseudonym for a Jamaican who "turned dread," became a Rastafarian during the 1960s. Like many Jamaicans, Bongo was unable to support himself in the community in which he was born. He migrated to Kingston and established a residence in a Kingston yard where he learned or became "grounded" in the word-sound-power of Rastafari. Bongo remained in Kingston until the late 1970s when the "tribalism" or politically sponsored violence of the time forced him to establish a rural residence. The following conversation took place at Bongo's countryside household. It was the first in a series of "reasonings" about a variety of topics that took place over the course of two years.

BUTTA AND WATTA

"So da man move among dread," Bongo asked as I arrived at his "gates" or household.[5]

"Well, I would like to learn about Rastafari," I replied, as he plucked an orange from one of his trees, sliced off the skin, and offered me half.

"How long da man been ina Jam-roc [Jamaica]?"

"Only a few months, but I was here last year."

"So de man know de runnings?"

"Well . . . , not really, I mean, I've heard reggae and Bob Marley tunes in New York, but I don't know the ropes."

"Claudi tell I da man cite-up [read from the Holy Bible] in Town [Kingston]?"

"Somewhat, but I really want to talk to country people, you know, grass roots, get a feel for Rasta in rural areas."

"Yes I, de movement rooted here," he replied, adding, "still Town de center, times hard now, de beast ina *kon*-trol, Michael gone."

"You mean Manley?"

"*Dat* what I seh, *Michael*. Rea-gan install Seaga said way Tatcher [Thatcher] install him, ana de Pope install her, da man no see!"

"Are they all connected?" I asked, as we moved over and sat on some rocks in the shade.

"I na seh de connected, dem part of de system, said way."

"You mean Babylon?"

"Yes I, da system."

"Interesting . . ."

"Na *interesting, reality*, da man no see it."

"Well, reality yes, but only one view . . ."

"Only *one* reality, I-aya, na *views*. Da man's vision no clear, or maybe da man see images dat not exist. Se-las-sie-I, dat reality."

"This is what I want to find out, about . . . Se . . . las . . . sie-I and Babylon and what the consciousness . . . [of Rastafari is all about]."

"I-n-I," he interjected, "no deal wit no *kon*-scious-ness, I deal wit trut, rights, *wizmon*, na *kon* no one. Jah seh, 'Him dat have ears, . . . *Hear!* Him dat have eyes, . . . *See!*' I-n-I no *kon* no one. If dem wan see, dem mus jus open dem selves an dem see."

"Well, I didn't mean *con*, but . . ."

"*Well*, ha! dat fa watta, *but-ta*, ha! dat fa bread, mon, dem na *up-full* sounds, I-n-I no deal wit dem," he interjected once again, as he smiled and shrugged his shoulders.

"So," I asked, responding to his criticism and his shift or change in the conversation to language, "you drop out certain words."

"I na seh I-n-I *drop* dem, cause if dem bust [are spoken], dem mus bust. I na bust sounds dat deal wit down-press-ion or kon-sciousness, cause how I lif-up if I reason down? I-n-I deal wit *up-press-I*, I-sciousness, dem sounds *up-full*, deal wit *livity* [life] not death. I-n-I na *kon* no one, jus word, sound, paawa, bradda, word, sound, paawa," he declared, adding, "Tell I, da man mus cite-up more time?"

"Well, not really. I mean, I've heard biblical expressions but never really read anything."

"I tell da man, *well* . . . is fa watta, *but-ta* . . . fa bread, dem na *up-full* sounds."

"Why are they not . . . *up-full*?"

"Dem not heartical. I-n-I no deal wit Babylon words dat kon-fuse I, make I look in-a-da wrong place [pointing up to the sky and down to the ground]. I deal wit

I-scious words dat over-stand, cause how can I reason wit da man an under-stand," he declared, explaining, "dat mean to seh da man over I. Dat wishy-washy slave ting, when I-n-I mus humble I-self before dem false gods, an dem preacher, an dem bukkie-massa, no I-aya, times faawod. Da man mus know dis if him move among dread?"

"Well . . . ," and before the sounds passed through my lips I pulled them back and said, "ah . . . , I mean, I've only been here a short time and have a lot to learn."

"Yes I, Se-lassie different. How da man come to do dis?"

"What do you mean?"

"I na *you*, hail I dread or da I or Bongo. Na *you*, or *him*, or *he*, da man no see?"

"'Cause they're not up-full?"

"Ah . . . , *yes* I! Still, da man no know da runnings, da movements."

"I'm afraid not."

"What da man fear? I-n-I deal wit knowledge and wiz-mon, de trut na hurt no one, I-aya, I-n-I da source, da man mus acknowledge dat. True, de Bee-ble [Holy Bible] culture, dem change it to *kon*-fuse I, I cite cause I know, Bee-ble support I knowledge. Yes I, it de word of Jah. De system change de word, I-aya, mix em up, *kon*-fuse I-n-I, so I look in de wrong place. More times I rest pon hilltop and di I reveal H.I.M. [His Imperial Majesty] self. Da man no see it."

"How does Se-las-sie reveal himself?"

"Jah work differently, H.I.M. mystical. Se-lassie-I gives tanks wit blessings—da rain, H.I.M. put pon de ert all creation. Come, I show da man. Look pon dat, what da man see?" he asked, pointing at what appeared to me as a barren patch of his garden.

"Dirt, ground, weeds . . ."

"Ground? Yes, cause I-n-I trod pon de firmament. Dem na weeds, dem herbs! Dat na dirt, da ert! Creation dat. Dem spring fort from de ert, I na do nothing, da man see? Herbs spring fort from de I. Yes I-aya, de ert de lord and de fullness der of. Dat how Jah reveal himself to I. Look pon de hillside, da man see dem trees, dem bushes, farms too?"

"Yes, I see them."

"Se-las-sie-I put dem pon de ert for I-n-I, for I livity, da man see?"

"I think . . ."

"Da man na *tink*. Jah seh dem dat have eyes, see, and dem dat have ears, hear, dis here no duppy business, I-aya, no little spirit from above *kon-fuse* I. Jus word-sound-paawa, bradda, jus word-sound-paawa, da man no see?"

UP-FULL SOUNDS

It is beyond the scope of this article to submit the preceding dialogue to an extended analysis. I have discussed a speech event as "reasoning" and a form of textual inter-pretation known as "citing [sighting]-up" elsewhere. The following discussion focuses on the formation of word-sounds and their relationship to identity.

For Bongo, and all Rastafarians, language is an arena, a site of political struggle and personal transformation. Since English was associated with the enslavement of

African people, its grammar, phonology, and semantics were not considered to be "heartical," that is, capable of expressing African culture and consciousness. The phonological structure of English words was "penetrated"—that is, sounded out loud and broken apart to expose contradictions between sound and meaning—and then reassembled into new words called up-full sounds. For example, the *de* sound prefix in the word *dedicate* (pronounced *dead*-di-cate) was deleted because of its sound-sense similarity to the *de* sound in the English words *death* and *destruction*. The *de* prefix was replaced by a sound that signified its opposite, not in Creole, but in English, i.e., *live*, creating the up-full *liv-i-cate*. The *un* sound in words such as *understand* was replaced by the *o* sound of *over* as in *overstand*, implying that all speakers are competent, i.e., no speaker of Creole, English, or Dread Talk is under, beneath, or below another. The *up* sound in the word *oppression* was replaced by *down*, as in *down-press-I*, because, as Bongo stated, few people are "pushed up" in social or economic mobility, but many are pushed down. The *con* sound in words such as *kon-scious* and *kon-trol* was associated with the *k* sound in the Creole word *kunni*, meaning clever. It was replaced by the first-person pronoun *I*, as in *I-trol* and *I-scious*. Similarly, the suffix *dom* was deleted from the word *wisdom* because of its similarity to the word *dumb*. According to Bongo, the formation of English words from oppositional or contradictory meanings was not a natural but a political practice intended to foment confusion, or "kon-fuse I." How, Bongo reasoned, can a man be both wise and dumb at the same time? The Creole *mon*, i.e., man, replaced the suffix *dumb* creating the word-sound *wiz-mon*.

Transforming what Bongo referred to as "Babylon" words into "heartical" sounds was not an idiosyncratic or stylistic convention, but a political and linguistic praxis. While the various changes are suggestive of phonological rules, unique to Atlantic Creoles, in which syllables are omitted from the beginning, the middle, and end in Creole word formation, Rastafarians bring the tonal semantics of Creole to bear on transforming both Jamaica Talk and Standard English into Dread Talk. Dread Talk departs from Jamaica Talk, but does not replicate English, in its use of personal pronouns. The pronouns *him, she, we, you,* and especially the use of *me* as a first-person pronoun in Jamaica Talk were replaced by the singular *I* and noun phrase "I-n-I." The first-person *I* replaced the *u* or you-sound, the second-person derivative, in words such as *unity* and *human* creating the words *I-nity* and *I-man*, similar to the word-sounds *I-trol* and *I-scious*. The noun phrase "I-n-I" is a homophone. When used to signify a plurality, the first person *I* replaced the *me* and *we* of Jamaica Talk with "I-n[and]-I." When used in reference to person, self or individual, the *I* signified the cornerstone of a renegotiated construction of identity known as "I-n[within]-I."

Breaking apart English words enabled Rastafarians to key the meaning attached to up-full sounds to historical events and cultural constructs. Bongo was careful to stress that the word-sound-power of Rastafari was not to be confused with "duppy business." The word *duppy* or *dupe* is African in origin. It refers to a social construction in which identity is composed of multiple souls. What was known as a dupe was considered to be a spiritual force, and what was referred to as a shadow was considered its external expression.[6] The multiple-soul concept constitutes the core of character (duppy-soul) and an accompanying personality (shadow-spirit) that communicated during ecstatic trances in glossalia or "tongues" with a pantheon of Afro-Christian spirits in folk religions such as Revival and Pocomania.

The ecstatic trance, ritual embodiment, and "tongues" associated with traditional construction of identity were superseded by the multiple speaking voices of I-n[and]-I the up-full sounds of Dread Talk, and knowledge, or wiz-mon. As we mentioned earlier, the word-sound *wiz-mon* was used by Bongo to signify a wise as opposed to a dumb man. The knowledge associated with wiz-mon was not ahistorical but was keyed to international events. According to Bongo, the coronation of the Ethiopian emperor Haile Selassie in 1930 broke the seventh seal as recounted in the Revelation of John (chapters 6–19), releasing a knowledge or literacy to African peoples. Rather than a literacy born of printed texts, the seven seals were associated with sight, sound-speech, smell, and wiz-mon; a knowledge located in what Bongo referred to as the "foundation" in a foundation-structure embodiment.

The foundation-structure embodiment renegotiated traditional constructions of identity and history. According to Bongo, the personas and caricatures associated with duppies and spirits controlled body and mind, thought and activity, the relationship between foundation and structure. Known in the anthropological literature as possession-trance and ritual dissociation, "getting in the spirit," the culturally learned and socially performed embodiment, epitomized by the trumps, groanings, and shouts of Revival, reproduced knowledge about the structure. Groundation in the rhythms and semantics of up-full sounds renegotiated the traditional call-and-response, sender-receiver dyad. Rather than a pantheon of Afro-Christian spirits who resided in the heavens, communicated in tongues, and controlled the structure, Selassie was a living Messiah associated with a knowledge or literacy that emerged from the foundation. Inverting the sender-receiver dyad, placing foundation over structure, challenged accepted convention concerning history, identity, and social behavior. The millennium associated with the second coming of Christ was superseded by an apocalypse associated with Haile Selassie, a discourse of up-full sounds, and renegotiated identity known as I-n-I.

CONCLUSION

It is critically important not to reduce up-full sounds to grammatical categories, to situate them along a Creole linguistic continuum, or to classify them as irrational prophecy. Whether transmitted over radio waves, performed by reggae musicians, or spoken in local reasonings, the sounds of Dread Talk have inspired a society attempting to create a national identity, a national culture, and a national consciousness from a legacy of colonialism. While the vocabulary of Dread Talk contains both Creole and English words, it is not the word that constitutes the focus of their agenda, but the decolonization of thoughts and ideas, actions and behavior. It is likely to be an ongoing process.

ACKNOWLEDGMENTS: The author wishes to thank the Inter-America Foundation for a field-research fellowship; the Right Honorable Rex Nettleford and Dr. Carl Stone of the University of the West Indies, Jamaica, for their assistance; Michael J. Harner, Richard Blot, Carole Yawney, and John Homiak for their comments; and the rootsmen of St. Elizabeth and Manchester.

SELECT NOTES

1. An abbreviated version of this paper was presented at the 89th Annual Meeting of the American Anthropological Association in November 1990.

2. The Maroons were escaped slaves who established semiautonomous communities in the seventeenth century. An abeng was a cow-horn and/or conch-shell horn sounded during the Maroon Wars. See Mavis Campbell, *The Maroons of Jamaica* (1989).

3. *Native-Baptist* was the term applied to itinerant or folk preachers, epitomized by the activities of the Afro-Americans Moses Baker and George Liele in the eighteenth century; by the Afro-Jamaican Sam Sharpe in the nineteenth century; and by Alexander Bedward in the twentieth century.

4. Bongo's household was located in what was once a nineteenth-century Moravian mission village. While he was neither an "elder" nor an "ancient," he was without question a "rootsman," a Rastafarian who rejected the way of life associated with contemporary Jamaican society.

5. This conversation occurred on January 14, 1982. I have italicized words and sounds that were overdifferentiated or stressed in speech and hyphenated word-sounds that were inverted, deleted, or substituted. All such guides are relative.

6. Each individual is born with a unique character (duppy-soul) and an accompanying personality (shadow-spirit) associated with socially defined understandings of good and bad. When a person dies, a duppy travels to an otherwordly realm while a shadow is believed to lurk behind. In a series of rituals, the shadow is dispatched below the earth, insuring it cannot be used malevolently by an obeahman.

ABBREVIATED BIBLIOGRAPHY

Alleyne, Mervyn. *Roots of Jamaican Culture.* London: Pluto Press, 1988.

Campbell, Mavis. *The Maroons of Jamaica, 1655–1796: A History of Resistance, Collaboration and Betrayal.* Granby, MA: Bergin & Garvey, 1988.

Cassidy, Frederic. *Jamaica Talk: Three Hundred Years of the English Language in Jamaica.* London: Macmillan, 1982 (1961).

Jekyll, Walter. *Jamaican Song and Story.* New York: Dover, 1969 (1907).

[Notes and bibliography have been condensed for space. Please see original article for complete citations.]

From "Jamaica"

KENNETH BILBY

Caribbean Currents
1995

Jamaican popular music has always been more varied than the one-sided Rasta image that the music industry promoted for many years in its attempts to capitalize on the popularity of outstanding Rasta reggae artists Bob Marley, Peter Tosh, Bunny Wailer, Burning Spear, and others working in the same vein. Indeed, every phase the music has gone through, from ska to reggae, is replete with examples of continued borrowing from folk or traditional sources, of which Rastafarian Nyabinghi music is but one. It is not an exaggeration to say that Jamaican music has been fundamentally shaped by this ongoing interchange between new and old. As dub poet Oku Onuora says, "Because of the richness of reggae, because of the heritage of reggae . . . like African-derived rhythms like mento, Poco, Kumina, which gave rise to Rastafarian chants, drummin', which gave rise to ska and then to rock steady . . . because of this rich cultural heritage of the music, it is able to shift—the colorin', we are able to vary the color."[1]

The influence of mento, in particular, has been underrated. Not only would some argue that the characteristic ska afterbeat actually stems in part from the strumming patterns of the banjo or guitar in mento, but ska versions of traditional mento tunes were common during the early 1960s. One thinks of popular recordings such as "Penny Reel" by Eric Morris; "Rukumbine" by Shenley Duffus; "Sauce and Tea (Helena)" by the Monarchs; "Old Fowl Ska" by Roland Alphonso; and "Wheel and Turn" by Frank Anderson and Tommy McCook. There were also quite a few original ska compositions done in a mento-inspired style, such as "Sugar Bag" and "Tackoo" by Lee Perry. To some extent, this early infusion of mento was a sign of pride in the times, as the independence celebrations of 1962 were still fresh in Kingstonians' minds.

If anything, the influence of mento increased during the reggae era. The subtle weave of rhythm guitar and keyboards that distinguishes the afterbeat of mature reggae (at first played on guitar alone) from its rock-steady equivalent has a definite mento feel. The slower tempo of rock steady and reggae also brought them closer to mento. In fact, the historic 1967 recording that many argue to be the very first reggae song—"Nanny Goat" by Larry Marshall and Alvin Leslie—was unmistakably mento-based, as were other songs by Marshall, such as "Throw Me Corn" and "Son Son." Both "Throw Me Corn" and "Nanny Goat" were tremendously popular in Jamaica as dance numbers, and what is today called the "Nanny Goat riddim"—the drum-and-bass tracks from this recording—continues to be recycled in an endless series of new permutations.

Few listeners outside of Jamaica know that there was a whole substyle or genre of mento-reggae (sometimes called "country music") that enjoyed tremendous popularity in the island during the 1970s. Its most prolific exponent was Stanley Beckford, lead singer of the Starlights (also known as Stanley and the Turbynes), who released hit after hit, beginning in 1973 and continuing through the decade. Some of his better-known songs, such as "Healing in the Balm Yard," were reggae versions of older mento songs, while others, such as the huge hits "Soldering" and "Leave Mi Kisiloo," were his own mento-reggae compositions. Other singers working in this style of "country music" also had big hits, such as the Prince Brothers with "Open the Door (A Fe Mi Something)" and Calypso Williams (King Bed Bug) with "Screw the Cock (Cork) Tight." In 1977 a Trinidadian calypsonian based in Jamaica, Lord Laro, scored another smash hit in this vein called "Reggae Mento Rockers" (also released under the title "Disco Mento Rockers"), showing that interaction between Trinidadian calypso and Jamaican mento could cut both ways. Yet other locally prominent reggae artists have made contributions to this genre, such as Eric Donaldson (author of the famous song "Cherry Oh Baby," covered by the Rolling Stones and UB40), Bobby Ellis, the Fabulous Five, Orlando Folks and the Ideal, Lloyd Lovindeer, the Moonlights, Roy Rayon, Sugar Belly, and the Tellers; nor should it be forgotten that some of the mento singers of the 1950s, such as Count Lasher and Lord Tanamo, continued to compose and record into the 1970s, now backed by the current mento-reggae style (while others, such as Count Zebra, continued to record and have minor hits in the old acoustic style of mento). Despite the popularity of mento-reggae in its homeland, most foreign reggae fans heard little or none of it and thus remained oblivious to one of the sweetest and most thoroughly Jamaican sounds of that era.

The Afro-Protestant musical contribution to reggae has been given somewhat more recognition than that of mento. The 1972 film *The Harder They Come*, which did so much to popularize reggae abroad, includes an extended scene of Jimmy Cliff's character, an aspiring reggae star named Ivan, working up a sweat in the Revival-influenced choir of a Pentecostal "clap-hand" church. In another scene Ivan persuades one of the church musicians to back him on electric guitar while trying out a new reggae composition. Despite the fact that Ivan's love of "temporal" reggae music leads to a confrontation with the preacher, the existence of a connection between church music and secular reggae in downtown Kingston is made apparent by their juxtaposition in the film. Another reggae film that was popular with foreign audiences, *Rockers*, includes a scene with traditional Revivalist dancing and drumming, hinting at the possibility of a connection between old-time religion and reggae. Such fleeting images aside, few non-Jamaicans have the opportunity or the inclination to learn anything about Jamaican Revivalism, and thus most foreign reggae listeners remain unaware of the extent to which the influence of this indigenous Afro-Jamaican religion permeates Jamaican popular culture, including music.

The Revivalist influence on popular music goes back to the early days of ska, when Revival-tinged recordings such as "Six and Seven Books of Moses" and "Hallelujah" by the Maytals, "River Jordan" and "Freedom" by Clancy Eccles, and "River to the Bank" by Baba Brooks were among the mix of styles then to be heard on downtown sound systems. Even the Wailers, before fully embracing the Rastafarian faith, recorded a number of Revival-influenced spiritual songs during the ska period. With the ascendance of Rasta-oriented reggae, those elements of traditional Rastafarian music derived from Revivalist sources were transferred to urban popular music along with the rest, lending much of the reggae of the 1970s a hymnlike quality that would be familiar to the ears of churchgoers all over rural Jamaica. The melodies and chord progressions of many Rasta reggae songs, as well as the biblical language and prophetic messages that typify the genre, owe much to Revivalism.

Not all the Afro-Protestant influences in reggae, however, came by way of the medium of Rastafarian songs; some occurred more directly. This is particularly clear in the case of the Maytals, whose gospel-tinged sound sometimes reminds North American listeners of the black gospel tradition in the United States. Whatever resemblance the Maytals' style may bear to black religious music in the United States, it cannot be considered derivative. Although lead singer Toots Hibbert, like many of his contemporaries, listened to and admired U.S. gospel music sung by the likes of the young Sam Cooke (with the Soul Stirrers), he and the other Maytals were also steeped in local Revivalism. When they were making their ska records, they were simultaneously singing in a church choir. Not only is there a strong Jamaican Revivalist feeling in the Maytals' many religious reggae songs after the ska era—for example, "Loving Spirit," "In the Dark," and "Got to Be There"—but some songs even directly quote traditional Revival melodies. The appropriately named "Revival Reggae," for instance, sets the meaningless syllables of an old Revival chorus—a type of chanting often associated, in the traditional context, with the onset of spiritual possession—to a driving reggae rhythm.

Few reggae fans in other countries are aware that there exists in Jamaica a type of local gospel music, usually called "Christian music," that has close ties to the reggae industry. Often associated with Pentecostal congregations, this genre of recorded music—represented by singers and preachers like Gloria Bailey, Claudelle Clarke, the Gospel Blenders, the Grace Thrillers, Evangelist Higgins, the Don Sam Group, and Otis Wright—has assimilated both black and rural white gospel styles from the United States and blended them with various other foreign and local influences. Stylistically speaking, much of this music is quite close to reggae, but with certain distinguishing features, such as differently accented drum patterns, a busy tambourine, and sometimes prominent clapping; some of it, in fact, is reggae in all but name. This is not surprising, since these gospel singers share studios and producers with reggae artists. Many top studio musicians whose names are normally associated with reggae can also be heard on these Revivalist-influenced Christian recordings, among them Radcliffe "Dougie" Bryan (guitar), Harold Butler (keyboard), Ansel Collins (keyboard), Grub Cooper (drums and keyboard), Carlton "Santa" Davis (drums), and the internationally acclaimed Lowell "Sly" Dunbar (drums). Even some well-known reggae vocalists, such as Larry Marshall (Bro. Marshall), the Tamlins, and Carlene Davis, have had parallel careers as "Christian singers."

Like blues and gospel music in the United States, secular reggae and local gospel music have never really been entirely separate, and influences have gone both ways. This is but one more way in which the Afro-Protestant Revivalist heritage has continued to feed into popular culture and music in this intensely spiritual country.

♦ ♦ ♦

Like earlier forms of reggae, ragga music is stylistically more diverse than is generally recognized, partly because it has also drawn on deeply rooted older forms. By the early 1990s, even as foreign reggae fans and critics were complaining about what they saw as a desertion of the music's local roots for an artificial and "soulless" sound shaped by an imported digital technology, local musicians were remarking on its increasing debt to older, rural Jamaican musical forms. Asked in what direction Jamaican popular music was currently moving, Wayne Armond of the Kingston-based reggae band Chalice had this to say: "What it's encompassin' is very old Jamaican music—mento, Poco, you know, all the ethnic music from early Jamaica, only this is now being played on a drum machine, but the influences are valued. . . . You hear them in dancehall music. Not the old Studio One beats, further back than that. Before reggae, before even the advent of ska or rock steady, I'm talking about the things they call burru, way, way back from my great-grandfather in slavery days, that's what we're talking about."[2] Clearly, something more has been going on in recent Jamaican music than the foreign press is equipped to tell us about.

We can get a glimpse of what most foreign observers have missed by going back to 1984—just before "Under Me Sleng Teng" ushered in the "digital revolution"—to take a look at a lesser-known series of developments that would eventually bring the new music of Jamaica closer than ever to its rural roots, even as it was entering the present digital era. In that year a dancehall deejay named Lord Sassa Frass had a local hit with a record called "Pocomania Jump." Musically speaking, it was in the typical dancehall style of that era and owed little to traditional Revival music. Yet its fanciful lyrics, which brought together dancehall "posses" and "the parson, the deacon, and son" in Sassa Frass's imaginary "Revival tent," were full of references to the paraphernalia and spiritual workings of traditional Poco churches. "Poco jump, Poco jump, mek we do de Poco jump," went the chorus, and the piece ended with the heavy rhythmic breathing, or "trumping," associated with dancing and spiritual possession in the Revival religion.[3] (Sassa Frass's later-released LP also included a cut called "Kumina to

Kumina," which, despite the title, bore little or no evidence of musical influence from Kumina.) Virtually unnoticed outside of Jamaica, this locally popular record—despite its offhand, somewhat whimsical treatment of the subject—brought Pocomania and Revival once again into the public spotlight, and helped set the stage for the creation of a new style of dancehall music actually based on traditional Revival rhythms, though this would take several years to surface in full force.

Not long after the "Sleng Teng" riddim took hold, two studio musicians who had been instrumental in the popularization of the digital sound, Steely (Wycliffe Johnson) and Clevie (Cleveland Browne), began looking for a new sound. Their search led them to traditional sources. Taking a chance, they made a conscious decision to incorporate the drum rhythms of the Revival religion into their digital dancehall mix. What they came up with was a stripped-down version of a Revival beat played on a simulated snare drum. With its faster tempo and relatively busy drum rhythms, the new sound represented a dramatic departure from previous styles of dancehall reggae. While Steely and Clevie were experimenting, others were also looking to Revivalist sources for inspiration.

In 1989 a very popular dancehall deejay named Lloyd Lovindeer—yet another local Jamaican star who remains largely unknown outside the Caribbean—released an influential album called *One Day Christian.* Though the title cut satirized the hypocrisy of corrupt preachers (and was aimed especially at wealthy North American televangelists), the rest of the album simply reveled in the infectious new Revivalist-dancehall beat that it showcased. Saturated with Revivalist themes and musical influences—including the prominent snare drum that Steely and Clevie had been experimenting with—it was nevertheless primarily a party record, and it included two big local hits, "Pocomania Day" and "Poco Party." Lovindeer followed this with another Poco dancehall album called *Find Your Way.*

The success of *One Day Christian,* on which Steely and Clevie had played drums, keyboards, and bass, led the duo to produce an album called *Poco in the East,* released in 1990. One whole side was devoted to deejays toasting over electronic Poco dancehall rhythms. They followed this up later in the year with an entire album in the new genre, called *More Poco.* Poco dancehall had now become a bona fide trend, and even young deejays known for their gun lyrics and "bad boy" posturing began to come up with their own contributions, such as Cobra (aka Mad Cobra), who recorded a cut called "Poco Jump."

Although this explicitly Revivalist-based style of Poco dancehall music seems to have faded recently, its influence has been inestimable, owing to the enormous popularity of Steely and Clevie as producers. A large portion of what is called ragga today developed from this sound. Other producers have jumped on the bandwagon and are now manufacturing their own up-tempo digital tracks with similarly driving imitation drum rhythms. Much experimentation is going on in studios, resulting in greater variety. One can hear an increasing emphasis on stimulated bass-drums patterns, some of which are uncannily reminiscent of the rhythmic feel of the bandu drum of Kumina, though rarely duplicating its rhythms precisely. Some variants of this new percussion-centered digital sound still feature the high snare of Poco dancehall, while others combine various timbres and rhythms into new syntheses whose origins cannot be located in a particular traditional source but which sound thoroughly Jamaican, with occasional suggestions of Kumina, Poco, Nyabinghi, and other Afro-Jamaican forms.

The result of all this experimentation is a new genre that must be considered the most original trend in dancehall: a substyle of ragga music that has changed so much that, if one is to go by strictly musical criteria, it can no longer be considered reggae at all, since its stylistic connections with the music known by that name during the 1960s and 1970s are no longer clear. Though created with computer technology, it is closer in sound to the surviving neo-African music of rural Jamaica than any popular music before it. (It should be noted that because rhythm tracks in this style have no equivalent to a lead drum, this music usually lacks the rhythmic complexity produced by the improvisations of that instrument in a traditional ensemble; however, it could be argued that the more rhythmically innovative deejays function much like the missing lead drum.) In the words of dub poet Linton Kwesi Johnson, "With the discovery of digital recording, an extreme minimalism has emerged.... On the one hand, this music is totally technological; on the other the rhythms are far more Jamaican: they're drawn from Etu, Pocomania, Kumina—African-based religious cults who provide the rhythms used by Shabba Ranks or Buju Banton. So despite the extent of the technology being used, the music is becoming even rootsier, with a resonance even for quite old listeners, because it evokes back to what they first heard in rural Jamaica."[4]

There is considerable irony in the situation. North American devotees of what is now called the "classic" reggae sound of the 1970s may praise the music played by an old-style U.S.-based Rastafarian band with no following in Jamaica as "roots reggae" while dismissing the new ragga sound as a homogenized, commercial form of techno-pop that has strayed from the "roots." But part of what makes this ragga style less palatable to such listeners is the decreasing prominence of those elements of reggae that actually owe more to European and North American sources (and thus sound more familiar to foreign ears)—vocal and instrumental melodies and harmonies that stem largely from the Western tradition, for instance—in favor of an aesthetic that leans more toward the African side of Jamaica's musical heritage. The fact is that much of the new ragga music is more firmly rooted in local soil than ever. With its heavily percussive Afro-Jamaican sound, its debt to Jamaica's rich oral culture, and its lyrics that are almost exclusively in "deep" Jamaican Creole (or patwa—a language intelligible only to Jamaicans or foreigners who make the effort to learn it), it is, as reggae once was, definitely an acquired taste for those brought up on "mainstream" Euro-American pop.

Those foreign listeners who have learned enough of the Jamaican language to have access to texts may be disturbed by the sexual content, violent imagery, or vehemently antihomosexual rhetoric of many contemporary ragga recordings. Like recent stylistic changes in the music, this choice of subject matter reveals a tenaciously local orientation and says much about the degree to which the music continues to be rooted in the lived experience of its performers. The sexual "slackness" of many lyrics, overblown and sexist as it may have become, is nonetheless part of a tradition of sexual banter and double entendre in Jamaican popular music that goes back to mento and before. The violence of "gun lyrics" mirrors the harsh reality of life in a desperately poor part of Kingston that continues to be ravaged by political warfare, drugs, and crime. And the strident vilification of homosexuality is rooted in local values that have been shaped by a fundamentalist reading of biblical scripture. As young, downtown deejays have reclaimed Jamaica's indigenous popular music from the pretensions of international marketers aiming to please cosmopolitan audiences, it has become harder for foreign consumers of that music to romanticize the experience from which it springs or to see in it an entirely "progressive" response to social injustice.

However, the variety of themes treated in ragga lyrics should not be underestimated. Alternative emphases, including Rastafarian perspectives, have actually been present in dancehall music since it took over in the 1980s, and current releases indicate that social-protest and Rasta-oriented lyrics may once again be on the rise. Nor should dominant trends, such as the new ragga style discussed above, be allowed to conceal the variation that keeps Jamaican popular music alive. In an interview a few years back, veteran Jamaican singer Bob Andy described how established marketing categories have a tendency to create a false sense of stylistic homogeneity. "In Jamaica what we have long been doing is capsuling everything and calling it reggae," he said. "Reggae is but one aspect of Jamaican music," he added, pointing out that "Peter Tosh, Bunny Wailer, and myself have done songs that emphasize all of the beats— ranging from ska, mento, and rock steady to reggae and dancehall."[5] The dancehall music of today—often called "dancehall reggae," thereby ensuring some continuity with a previously established international marketing category—also draws from all these older sources (including many perennial "riddims" sampled directly from old Studio One recordings).

But it would be wrong to give the impression that ragga has looked only to the past or to local sources for musical ideas. Despite the current popularity of resurgent Afro-Jamaican rhythms, one can detect strains of hip-hop, contemporary R&B, rock, and other foreign genres in much of the recent music coming out of Jamaica. Stylistic experimentation continues, and novelty is as valued as ever. A rapid succession of new dances with such names as "cool and deadly," buttafly, "Santa Barbara," and bogle and of new rhythms and riffs with equally original names—for example, bangara, cordiroy (corduroy), Indian beat, and talking drums—keeps the music in a constant state of flux. Internationally prominent studio musicians such as Sly Dunbar travel across the world, listening to all kinds of music, and return with new ideas that eventually make their way onto the local music scene. Jamaica is, after all, hardly isolated from musical trends in the United States and Europe.

Indeed, the most obvious foreign influence on Jamaican music in recent years has been from hip-hop. The latest series of exchanges between urban African-American and Jamaican musics arose spontaneously out of contacts between black American and Jamaican communities in New York and other U.S. cities during the 1980s. More recently, following the success of crossover artists such as Shabba Ranks, collaborations between U.S. singers and Jamaican deejays have been promoted by record companies in a calculated manner. As of this writing, more than two dozen Jamaican deejays—crossover stars such as Buju Banton, Patra, and Tiger—have been signed by major labels. So far, those on the Jamaican side of the equation have managed to maintain their distinctive musical identity, using their own Jamaican Creole language even when toasting over an entirely hip-hop rhythm. (Shabba Ranks has even had some success introducing U.S. audiences to Poco-derived dancehall rhythms, not to mention the Rasta Nyabinghi drumming featured on a video he did with comedian Eddie Murphy.) Not only this, but dancehall/ragga has had a remarkable impact on African-American hip-hop artists as well, and the Jamaican presence is firmly established—for the time being, at least—on black-oriented radio in cities like New York and Washington, D.C. Back in Jamaica, however, there is much talk of the potential threat that fusions such as ragga–hip-hop might pose to the integrity of Jamaica's local popular music should the process go too far.

The tension between local identity and globalizing trends is likely to remain a fundamental theme in the future of Jamaican popular music. Reggae and dancehall varieties are now played by musicians on every continent, and non-Jamaican recording artists working in these genres have had major successes in several African countries, Europe, the United States, and Japan. Fusions based primarily on Jamaican styles, such as Asian-influenced bhangramuffin, have also led to gigantic record sales. Even ska continues to be marketable outside of Jamaica, and in the United States the recent emergence of a new generation of "Third Wave" ska bands (as well as a new hardcore, punk-influenced fusion dubbed "ska-core") has attracted the attention of major labels.

Meanwhile, hundreds of hopeful young raggamuffins congregate day after day in front of Kingston's dozens of recording studios, patiently waiting for auditions. One need not be as big as Bob Marley or a Shabba Ranks to escape from poverty. Jamaica, after all, is reputed to have the highest per capita output of records of any country in the world. An estimated two hundred new singles are released in Kingston every week, most of which will never leave the island.[6] No wonder Jamaica continues dancing to its own beat, hoping that the world will follow. So far, the producers searching for new sounds have known where to look. Here, in the place that gave the world reggae, uptown with its international connections may call the shots, but the greatest hope still lies with downtown.

NOTES

1. Oku Onuora, quoted in Brian Jahn and Tom Weber, *Reggae Island: Jamaican Music in the Digital Age* (Kingston: Kingston Publishers Limited, 1992), p. 91.

2. Wayne Armond, quoted in Jahn and Weber, *Reggae Island*, p. 129.

3. "Pocomania Jump," a 1984 twelve-inch 45 rpm record (Ashantites 010).

4. Linton Kwesi Johnson, "Introduction," in *Tougher than Tough: Thirty-five Years of Jamaican Hits* (booklet accompanying four-CD boxed set [1993] *Tougher than Tough: The Story of Jamaican Music* [Mango CD 1–4, 518 400–3]).

5. Bob Andy, "Jamaican Music Is Not Reggae," in *Jamaica Beat* (Kingston), no. 3 (February–March 1989): 5.

6. Maureen Sheridan, "Jamaican Studios Jumping with Success of Dancehall," *Billboard* 101 (July 18, 1992): 1.

PART TWO

MARLEY

Uptown Ghetto Living:
Bob Marley in His Own Backyard

VIVIEN GOLDMAN

Melody Maker
11 August 1979

As you drive through the white-pillared gates into the grounds of 56 Hope Road, the first thing you notice is that the road doesn't have any holes. Even here, uptown in New Kingston, the road surfaces are pitted and scarred, as if someone had scratched their spots; great boulders are kicked casually into the gutter. All the damage, we're told, is because of the recent flood; but the fact remains that in Bob Marley's yard, the tarmac is new, shiny, and unblemished.

One side of the house is a big record shop, in an airy room. There are BABYLON BY BUS and RAT RACE and TUFF GONG tie-dye T-shirts hanging on the walls, the most Western-style merchandising techniques I've ever seen in Jamaica. There's even a fanzine section on the counter, selling the Wailers fan club booklet, including I-tal recipes, and *Rasta Voice* magazine.

The Tuff Gong outfit is ensconced in what used to be Bob Marley's house. Other Wailers also used to live in the white mansion. The pillars at the front of the drive still say ISLAND HOUSE—that's because before Marley took over, it was Island Record's HQ. They don't have a Jamaican base anymore; in its place, Marley's own record company.

The yard has become a car park. While the whole island is full of cannibalised cars, bits of cars grafted onto other cars, as car and spare-part import bans reduce the available transport still further, there's a remarkably high collection of new, functional cars—including the BMW, the Wailers' favourite motorised vehicle (just check the initials).

The "straight" world of Jamaica is still making life difficult for the dreads, but here at ex–Island House it's Rasta country. Men and women sit on the steps, lean up against trees; Tuff Gong Records is obviously where the action is in Kingston these days.

◆ ◆ ◆

Inside the house is the ultimate proof that Marley, the local boy made good, is bringing it back home: a twenty-four-track studio—there's only one other on the island, at Harry J's. Channel One has only just gone up from four to sixteen tracks.

And what a studio. Very small, but the style . . . someone says it looks like Miami's Criteria Sound, but my terms of reference tell me that the stripped pine walls are strictly West Coast style. More roots; reggae has gone well international.

In the control room, watching the vertical strips of light that indicate the recording levels on each track flickering up and down, are Bob Marley and his brothers and sisters. Alex Sadkin has flown in from Miami to work with Bob, and Tuff Gong has poached Treasure Isle's engineer, Errol Thompson. They're mixing a new song: "Step it natty, step it inna—Zimbabwe . . . soon we'll find out who is—the real revolutionary. . . ."

Marley takes time out to talk. We go round the house, through a big beautifully carved wooden door, into an office. And that means a regular, Western-style office with new office furniture, even IBM typewriters, and phones with intercom systems.

MM: It's astonishing how much more direct and militant your new tunes are than *Kaya* . . .

MARLEY: This is getting to the point. What they said about *Kaya* is true, but you can't show aggression all the while. To make music is a *life* that I have to live. Sometimes you have to fight with music. So it's not just someone who studies and chats, it's a whole development. Right now is a more militant time on earth, because it's Jah Jah time. But me always militant, you know. Me *too* militant. That's why me did things like *Kaya*, to cool off the pace.

MM: If you were interested in being heard by an international market, maybe they were frightened off by militant music . . .

MARLEY: Of course, especially the parents.

MM: Did you feel under pressure to record for the States market, for example?

MARLEY: To tell you the truth, I don't even think that way. I just think more of an inner creativeness. Inna my chest. I don't make a tune specially for this and this; if the feeling comes nice into my soul according to a certain vibration—me no really a prostitute. Me just respect people like Taj Mahal and Bob Dylan for how they do with themselves. They respect their own talent, that means where they are and who they are. It *that* that people have to want, you dig, 'cos the people don't want to be pleased, they want to please someone, you dig, it goes both ways. So it's no use getting in this mechanical bag, because creativeness leave if you do that. That's why plenty of artists come just for a time and then you hear no more of them, because them no really be themselves. Because when you are yourself, boy, that's it, I think . . .

MM: Were you ever annoyed at Rasta being used as a sales gimmick?

MARLEY: As far as I'm concerned the record company might try and show the people a gimmick—we don't think we play at a place and tomorrow everyone is *Rasta*. It's not like that. It grows. You never can tell which vision you're going to get, or if God is going to call you. So Rastafari is God's new name, Head Creator. Africa is the cornerstone to the realisation of people's unity.

MM: You just went to Africa for the first time, after tying to get a visa for ages. Was it like you'd imagined?

MARLEY: When I got there it was the same thing I felt about Africa here, the same as I'd always imagined it would be. But nicer.

MM: How nicer?

MARLEY: Just nicer in terms of *living*, development, opportunity. When you go to Africa you see how useful you can be to mankind.

MM: You mean they need a lot of help out there?

MARLEY: Not in respect of the material element. It's like—Africa awaits its creators. It needs a lot of people who know how to do things. This is just a little studio. Africa is capable of plenty studios, but it's up to who really wants to deal with it.

MM: Some people in England regard Rasta as another offshoot of the colonial mentality, something that holds people down.

MARLEY: What one man thinks is great. But only a fool leans upon his one understanding. The truth is there. King Solomon and King David are the roots of black people and the roots of creation—they are Jacob's people. So when a black man says that Rasta is colonialist, he's turning it the other way in a sense of diplomacy, he's putting down his own thing, because he's learnt how to do it. Who teaches him? You dig what I'm saying?

MM: Just like they say that it's more important to confront the reality in England, for example, than to think of going to Africa.

MARLEY: I could agree with that, but why fight to stay in a place that's dirty, where the rivers are polluted? Why stay in a place where if God shook two earthquakes, all these stones are gonna fall on you and kill you? Africa for Africans at home and abroad. Like England for English people, America for Americans, Asia for the Chinese . . . but we're not saying that people can't mix together. But this world is funny, because you claim you're white and I claim I'm black, and we have a fight, because if you're not sensible, it becomes a barrier. But the truth is the truth, your father's name is Noah and my father's name is Noah and Shem's father's named Noah, so we all three people come from Noah so we're the same people. But right now it's just a few who search out their roots.

MM: Do you feel you could exert a lot of power in Jamaican politics?

MARLEY: Me can do a lot of things, anywhere.

MM: But, for example, after Claudie Massop (one of the organizers of last year's Peace Treaty in Kingston) was shot by the police, how did you feel about the Peace Concert?

MARLEY: I and I is *Rasta,* and the struggle continues.

MM: But where do you struggle? Do you feel that a Rasta musician should never get directly politically involved?

MARLEY: I don't involve myself. We don't support either the JLP or the PNP. Rasta is *different.* Claudie was my brethren. And a lot more people. But we know that we are Rastafarians, that we have something to offer. We have the Twelve Tribes of Israel, the Ethiopian Orthodox Church, the Theocratic Government. If a youth wants to go out there and fight politics, he can go. We have something that demands rights if you stand where me stand. If you don't do that, you'll be dying in the streets with your dreadlocks on, because you're not defending the thing you must defend. You can't be strong, you must be a weakling. It's just the truth. We defend His Majesty's philosophy. It's not political—it's only words that make it political. It's life—people—action.

MM: When you sing about militancy what do you expect people to do?

MARLEY: I expect if you're living by the gun, if gun is the fight, then *fire* gun. If where you come from, you fight with sticks and stones, then fight with sticks and stones. If the fight is spiritual, then fight spiritual, because everywhere the fight goes on. We don't have any alternatives. If a man fights you with machine guns and you throw stones, then—machine gun for machine gun! So the struggle continues. A lot of people defend South Africa, some secretly, some openly. A lot of white people defend South Africa, and when you keep the black man down in South Africa you keep him down all over the earth. Because Africa is Solomon's gold mine. So—war! Either I and I lives, or no one lives. You know what the big fight is? It's that black people—and only black people—mustn't say the truth about Rasta.

MM: I disagree—you can get lots of information about Rasta.

MARLEY: Of course, but say you love Rasta, and see a chance whereby mankind can set up something new to live by so that we can all say: THIS is how we want to live—the system won't support that. If all the leaders were to get up tomorrow morning and say they defend Rasta, what do you think would happen? But all of them can get up tomorrow and die. (Rastas reject the concept of death, won't attend funerals.)

MM: In the mid-sixties you worked in a car factory in Wilmington, Delaware. What was that like?

MARLEY: As a youth I was always active, never lazy. I learnt a trade, welding, so dealing with those things is part of my thing. I enjoy dealing with parts, part-work, and I never really mind because I just did it as much as I wanted to do it. Any time I felt fed up, I didn't really look for a job. I come from country, and country is always good. You grow everything.

You don't really have to go out there and kill yourself to get a place or have money, you can eat and bathe and make clothes and build your own house, but in a strange land you can't find a place or settle down to find a way to leave. The best way out is to organise and leave.

MM: Do you regard Jamaica as a strange land?

MARLEY: Jamaica is a place we know, but the system change and it a gets strange. It just change, and get strange . . . because I'm tired of saying it, I and I are tired of saying this: *Rastafari!* I and I not trying to push myself, it's just the truth, God knows . . . that's why sometimes I don't even bother to talk because it's just a waste of time, but I still have the urge. But when I talk to people, it seems sometimes we're not on the same wavelength. From Pope Paul's time, we knew we'd be under pressure. White man doesn't have any sympathy with Rasta, but he has to hear that, and perish in his own fornication that he deals with, his own fuckery and his own atomic and his own S.A.L.T. . . . . (Marley's voice sneers—he's referring to the Strategic Arms Limitation Treaty, and punning it with salt, which Rastas are forbidden to eat according to their dietary laws.) We haven't really come to save the white nation. But they are some of the people on earth, and they have to hear the truth. The white man has nothing he can give us, you know—only death. That's why I and I is Rasta, because we know death has nothing against I and I.

MM: But you're working within those white man's systems. Would you have got to be an international star if Chris Blackwell (head of Island Records) was a black man?

MARLEY: Watch me. If I wasn't capable of being something . . . Chris Blackwell didn't help me. I had to work *hard* while Blackwell flew out and enjoyed himself. But he had the contacts at the time that we felt we needed, and perhaps we did. But Blackwell did a lot for himself. I remember a time when he had nineteen Jamaican acts signed, and before my days he wouldn't touch one. The pressure of the way we had to work was why the Wailers (Marley's referring to the trio of himself, Peter Tosh and Bunny Livingstone) didn't agree, because we didn't get any help, we were out on tour under some steep conditions that first time . . . because if it was my *raasclaat* I'd have blown up the whole earth already, with its corruption. It's just pressure from all sides, we're born to get pressure, we come upon the earth to get pressure. You get pressure from your family, pressure from strangers, pressure from *all over*. So you've got to be mindful.

MM: One of the biggest pressures on you is being *the* international reggae messenger. That's why I felt "Running Away," where you defended yourself against people accusing you of doing that when you left Jamaica for Miami after they tried to shoot you, was *Kaya*'s most penetrating, sincere track.

43

MARLEY: People don't understand that we live in this earth, too. We don't sing these songs and live in the sky. I don't have an army behind me. If I did, I wouldn't care, I'd just get *more militant.* Because I'd know, well, I have 50,000 armed youth, and when I talk, I talk from strength. But you have to know how you're dealing. Maybe if I'd tried to make a heavier tune than "Kaya" they would have tried to assassinate me because I would have come too hard. I have to know how to run my life, because that's what I have, and nobody can tell me to put it on the line, you dig? Because no one understands these things. These things are heavier than anyone can understand. People that aren't involved don't know it, it's *my* work, and I know it outside in. I know when I am in danger and what to do to get out. I know when everything is cool, and I know when I tremble, do you understand? Because music is something that everyone follows, so it's a force, a terrible force. Someone like me, now—if I want to be a loudmouth, I'm a loudmouth, and someone can come out one day and BOOGAAAA!—shoot me. So, I'm a loud-mouth—and then I'm cool. Then I'll come out again. So someone might say, Yes, we have to defend this youth, because he deals with the right things, or else I go—WAWAWAWAWAAAAAAA! And one day—know what I mean? But I am a man that can sing any song, because I can never change. I've even tested myself to see if I can change, and there is no change.

MM: I don't know what you mean—everyone changes, all the time.

MARLEY: When I sing a tune like "Kaya," do I change? No. I'm more . . . *wickeder!* That's how the earth gets tricked. There are a lot of people just come upon the train, and me just say, right, it's this direction I'm going in, let's see who follows me, and who does their own thing. So I just say *"Kaya!"* and everybody just goes so, and now I come back and say *"Black survival!"* and—pure idiots, all they do is follow. Not one of them is a leader, they're all followers. So I hear people say, Bob Marley's gone soft, all he is, is a traitor to Bob Marley's cause. But how could they know who Bob Marley is, and how could Bob get soft? Bob grow inna this thing, the things that Bob sings about are his life, it's how he lives. I couldn't get any education that could change my way of thinking, you dig? I live the way I live. My struggle can never ever change. If it could have changed, it already would have, because I've been everywhere. I live in Miami the same way I live in Jamaica. But people don't under-stand that we're in contact with our own people, everywhere we go, our people come. It's not the place, it's the people. In Miami, my brethren are there, same way. So it's not a feeling like children waiting for Christmas, we're just natural people, soldiers, we just live a war every day. Because just imagine being a Rasta in this world which doesn't like Rasta. We could be enjoying being something else, but no. We say—*"We are Rasta!"*

MM: How come you're aware of the danger of being assassinated when you say there's no such thing as death?

MARLEY: Hold on, now. You think you can go out there and lay down in front of the car and let it run over you? If I go outside and see the big bus coming and put my head underneath it, what do you think will happen?

MM: Your head will be crushed. And what will you be then?

MARLEY: *(yells): Dead!* This is where people make a mistake. They say that the flesh doesn't value anything, but that's the biggest lie. This flesh is what you've got, what God put inside you is your life. That's the way I think, that's the way I'm organised, because I don't stray from my roots, and my roots is God. But sister, I understand what you're saying. You're saying a man can be dead in his flesh and his spirit still lives, but I respect my flesh too, and I know my spirit and what it's like. . . .

MM: So when you say you don't believe in death . . .

MARLEY: *(firmly):* I don't believe in death neither in flesh nor in spirit.

MM: But I don't understand, because one minute you're saying you don't believe in death, and the next minute you say you'll be shot, and . . .

MARLEY: Yes, but you have to *avoid* it! Some people don't figure it's such a great thing, they don't know how long they can preserve it. Preservation is the gift of God, the gift of God is life, the wages of sin is death. When a man does wickedness he's gone out there and dead.

MM: Oh, I thought you felt death didn't exist at all.

MARLEY: Death does not exist for me. I truly know God. He gives me this (life) and my estimation is: If he gives me this, why should he take it back? Only the Devil says that everybody has to die.

MM: Someone from Inner Circle told me that the money from the Peace Show never got to all the right people. Did you know about that?

MARLEY: All I know is that it went to everyone that wanted it. Too much people involved, too much people have too much thing to say and they don't know anything. So many people go on about how they're roots, and when did you last see them in the ghetto? They hide from the ghetto, they're not in *contact.*

MM: But you must find it difficult to keep in touch with the ghetto . . .

MARLEY: *(incredulous):* Find it difficult? Watch now. You look into my yard. It's a ghetto. This is a ghetto you're looking at. Look out there. I've just brought the ghetto uptown. My thing is, why must I stay in one place every day of my life, and all the days of my life I have to run from the police? Look in any other yard along the road and see if you see any one of my brethren out there in any other yard. When I lived in the ghetto, every day I had to jump fences, police trying to hold me, you dig? So my job all the while was to try to find one place where the police wouldn't run me down too much. So I don't want to stay in contact with the ghetto, in contact with the ghetto means in contact with a prison, in contact with everything that's bad all the while, not the people. When the law comes out, they send them into the ghetto first, not uptown. So how long does it take you to realise—boy, well they don't send them uptown, y'know! So we'll make a ghetto uptown. *Every day* I jumped fences from the police, for *years,* not a week. For *years.* So me get afraid now, me have to make some type of move. You either stay there and let bad people shoot you down, or you make a move and show people some improvement. Or else I would take up a gun and start shoot them off and then a lot of youths would follow me, and they'd be dead the same way. I want some improvement. It doesn't have to be materially but it can be freedom of thinking.

MM: The material things have helped you to spread a little bit of freedom out to a few people, but it hasn't helped all the people in the ghetto. Don't you think that only more direct political action can do that?

MARLEY: Something more direct would be if Queen Elizabeth would take her *raas* away from Jamaica, take away her Constitution, call away those ways of life they have down here.

MM: I thought that was supposed to happen when Jamaica became independent.

MARLEY: But it never happened. We still have a Governor-General. No one gives Jamaica people a chance, that's why we say that the earth is corrupted and everyone has to die and leave we. It's a selfish way of thinking, but . . . *(mutters)* fuck it . . . how long will they pressure we? We are the people who realise the place where they thieved us from, so we say, *Ah,* you took us from there, *ah,* this is what we are. But they still tell us, No, no, this is what you are! This is what you must be. . . . This yard (house), they call it Freedom Ground. Hardly anything can happen here. The greatest thing that could happen would never happen, so you could say God has we for a purpose and a reason.

MM: "Ambush in the Night" contains the clearest references you've ever made to colonialism.

MARLEY: *(absently):* We always try. There's a lot of good music we have in there, a whole heap of good stuff. . . . I don't like to talk, because the way I talk, I don't know if I can be understood. Or maybe somebody might understand me the wrong way. There's only one thing we have to say, that is, we are Rastafarian people the same way some people are Catholic. Some people are this, some people are this. They always want to interview I and I, but they don't want to know what we really want to say. It (Rasta) becomes unreal, like something we try and make . . . *raas* . . . truth is like food, man—when you say "food" you know you mean food, and when you say "truth," same way. You know, Vivien, sometimes me no get over too straight, because you are a woman, and you see things . . . me understand how you see things, but I can't please you by talking to make you feel pleased. Me just have to show you say—you have to be strong.

MM: Since you're always covering old tunes, I thought you should cover the tune "Rude Boy Get Bail." It's still so relevant.

MARLEY: Well, Bunny did that in '66, when I was in America, but me did other rude boy songs—that rude bwoy business, bad, bad music. Only them shouldn't have said "rude boy," them should have said "Rasta." You dig me? But in them times, me didn't know Rasta. Something was going on, you felt it, and didn't know if you were bad bad or good good—then I understood it's good, you're good—it's Rasta!

MM: When, or what, made you realise it was Rasta, not rudeness?

MARLEY: What is there to benefit from badness? I wondered, I looked at it and thought, boy, *bloodclaat*, if I thump this man here I feel the contact too. And then I said, it's the same God that lives in my hand lives in me, and that means that it's not him I thump, it's God I'm really thumping. So I used to wonder about this human feeling business . . . the whole thing is Rasta. The way I tell you, it's a whole experience, but you break it down and it's just—Rasta.

MM: Did you used to play lots of gigs in the early days?

MARLEY: Not a lot, just like Christmas morning and Easter, we'd be there up in the Carib Theatre. But we was always the underground, always the rebels. We came from *Trench Town*. So you'd hear about Byron Lee and all that society business, but we came from down so named *Wailers* from *Trench Town*. So we stay, and we're glad of it. You've got to be someone.

MM: So now you get society knocking on your door . . .

MARLEY: Turn them off. Tell them to come another day.

MM: Which bit of your career has meant the most?

MARLEY: I love the development of our music, that's what I really dig about the whole thing. How we've tried to develop, really try to understand what we're trying to do, you know? It grows. That's why every day people come forward with new songs. Music goes on forever.

Before we leave, Marley asks why I haven't tried to interview Family Man (I have tried) or one of the other Wailers.

"It's always me who has to talk," he says, "and I don't dig it either, because it gets me into problems . . ."

Marley in Zimbabwe

HORACE CAMPBELL

From *Rasta and Resistance: From Marcus Garvey to Walter Rodney*
1987

This author shared the joy and enthusiasm in Zimbabwe in April 1980 when it was announced that Bob Marley would perform at the official celebrations. It was an important tribute to the Rastafari, for in the limited four-hour programme of that historic evening on April 17, 1980, the African leaders gave Marley a billing at the celebrations at Rufaro Stadium in Harare Township. At 10:14 P.M. Bob Marley arrived onstage, after the technicians had spent the previous two hours setting up the forty tons of speaker boxes, tweeters, mixers, lights and other technological components that had been harnessed for the circulation of reggae.

Shouting "Viva Zimbabwe!" as he came onstage, Marley lifted the spirits of the audience as he moved straight into "Rastaman Vibrations," followed by the appropriate reminder of the inequalities "Them Belly Full but We Hungry." Rastafari culture beamed out to the delegates and Presidents from 104 states who had gathered to witness the lowering of the last British flag in Africa.

As Marley moved into "I Shot the Sheriff" there was bedlam in the stadium; everything seemed out of control. The policemen were running on the field, followed by the press. The band had stopped. The white Rhodesian police had dispersed tear gas on the throngs of African workers outside the stadium who were pulled by the rhythms of "Family Man" Barrett, the bass guitarist. The whole stadium was covered with tear gas. Order was only restored when guerrillas of the Zimbabwe African National Liberation Army (ZANLA) marched through the stadium with raised clenched fists, reassuring the people that the Rhodesian police could not stop the celebrations.

Marley returned to the stage after this fifteen-minute disruption and shouted *"Freedom!"* A crisp English voice at the other end of the stadium said, "Bob Marley, you have exactly two minutes left." In defiance, Marley sang "War." *O povo* (the people) jumped and chanted with Marley that "there will be war until South Africa is free." This exhilaration was the response of a people who were lifted out of the fear that the celebrations would be sabotaged by the racists who had said that black people in Zimbabwe would not achieve independence before the year 2035.

The hard drumming bass reverberated across the African sky as the band put everything into the music and Marley wailed "We Don't Need No More Trouble." All the energy, force, history and power of reggae filled the air as Neville Garrick, the dreadlocks engineer, frantically mixed the music so that the sounds from the forty-foot-high boxes beamed out to all the poor people who could not get into the stadium.

After fifteen minutes of the supposed two minutes, the Wailers sang "Africans a liberate Zimbabwe." In one section of the stadium the whole gathering stood and joined in chanting this song of freedom, saying that they did not want to be fooled by mercenaries. It was an experience filled with emotion, and Bob Marley responded with the slogans of Pan-African unity which were an essential part of his outlook as a Rastafari.[1]

The whole energising experience was repeated the following night, for on that occasion Marley gave a free concert for the forty thousand workers and unemployed who were not able to get into the stadium the previous evening. That evening Marley told the audience that the next time they performed in Africa they hoped it would be in a free Azania. During the whole week they were in Zimbabwe, Marley and the Wailers operated as Rastafari ambassadors to Africa, whether in the form of organising friendly football matches, attending a formal reception with the President—Canaan Banana—or in discussion with the guerrillas in the camps.

Back in the Caribbean, Marley, who by then must have known that he had terminal cancer, worked at the pace of a lion and sought to build up the newspaper of Tuff Gong (his recording studio), *Survival*, in a conscious effort to stop the confusion of the *Coptic Times*. Despite the concept of mysticism and the talk about the "teachings of His Majesty," Marley's paper was an effort to reach the youths. The masthead of the paper queried:

> *Are the youths tomorrow's leaders*
> *Or are they tomorrow's shame,*
> *You must not be their impeders*
> *Less on you they'll put the blame.*
> *Train the youths while they are tender*
> *For what things you want them to be,*
> *When old they will remember*
> *Lessons taught to them by thee.*[2]

Such a dedication to the youths was augmented by Marley's lasting testament to Rastafari:

I and I made our contribution to the Freedom of Zimbabwe. When we say Natty going to dub it up in a Zimbabwe, that's exactly what we mean, "give the people what they want." Now they got what they want do we want more? "Yes," the Freedom of South Africa. So Africa unite, unite, unite. You're so right and let's do it.[3]

And Rita Marley added her voice, declaring:

I and I firmly believe that music going to teach the world a lesson. Black women stand firm and keep the faith, for your reward shall be great. Zimbabwe now, South Africa next. When all Africa free, all black people free.

Bob Marley and Rita Marley raised their voices and their pens to push for full liberation of the continent of Africa, for they had understood the teachings of Walter Rodney, that full dignity would never be achieved by blacks until there was an end to white rule in Africa, and social justice.

NOTES

1. For a full account of the situation in Zimbabwe at the time, see "The Night the British Flag Was Lowered in Rhodesia" by Horace Campbell, *Westindian Digest,* June 1980, pp. 64–66. See also *Caribbean Contact,* July 1980, for a previous tribute to Bob Marley by this author.
2. *Survival,* volume 2 (June 1980), p. 1. This poem was part of Marley's support to the Hunger Project. Page 3 of the paper said, "Bob Marley has given his support in both moral and material forms. He has donated two songs to the cause."
3. Ibid., p. 8.

"So Much Things to Say": The Journey of Bob Marley

ISAAC FERGUSSON

The Village Voice
18 May 1982

He sat with his friends smoking and rapping. Bob Marley. During his lifetime this man had become a mythical figure, yet nothing in his easygoing manner identified a superstar. He did not overshadow or separate himself from the dozen or so Rastamen milling about his Essex House suite. His laughter was uproarious, unpretentious, and free. He blended so snugly with his peers that I could never have picked him out had his face not decorated record jackets, T-shirts, and posters everywhere. A year after his death, his words still sustain and warn and fulfill.

I had read about the millions of records Marley sold worldwide, and that he was a multimillionaire. Still I found it hard to reconcile the slightly built, denim-clad man with the explosive entertainer who danced across the stages of huge arenas or penetrated me with his stare from the cover of *Rolling Stone*. Marley got up and politely took leave of the jolly group. He led me to the bedroom. Lying casually across the bed, he carefully thumbed through a Bible. Tonight he will talk with me about Rastafari; tomorrow he will go up to Harlem's Apollo Theater and make more history, more legend.

Marley recorded his first song, "Judge Not," in 1961; he was sixteen years old then. A helter-skelter music industry was just developing in Kingston, JA, where the unemployment rate was 35 percent and Marley scuffed out a living as a welder. "Me grow stubborn, you know," he recalled when we talked. "Me grow without mother and father. Me no have no parent fe have no big influence pon me. Me just grow in de ghetto with de youth. Stubborn, no obey no one; but we had qualities and we were good to one another." In 1964 Marley, Peter Tosh, and Bunny Wailer formed the Wailing Wailers. From the beginning, Marley strove to convey meaningful content in his lyrics: "Nothing I do is in vain. There is nothing I ever do that goes away in the wind. Whatever I do shall prosper. Because I and I no compromise I and I music, I'm one of dem tough ones," Marley said.

Soon the world discovered that Marley was no ordinary singer whose words were designed to be hummed for moments and forgotten; here was a messenger whose lyrics call attention to our condition, to the reasons for suffering. The music brings lightness to the feet and makes them dance, but the beat is a marching drum, a call to struggle: "Get up, stand up/Stand up for your rights/Get up, stand up/Don't give up the fight."

Marley came to be widely respected as a songwriter with a reach that was broad and deep. Eric Clapton had a big hit with Marley's "I Shot the Sheriff"; Johnny Nash scored with Marley's "Stir It Up" and "Guava Jelly." In 1972 Marley and the Wailers signed with Island Records, a small London-based company headed by Chris Blackwell, a white Jamaican. Marley, who wrote his songs and arranged his music, made ten albums with Island. They all went gold; 500,000 copies sold within the first year in England, Europe, and Canada. Two albums, *Rastaman Vibration* and *Uprising*, made gold in the United States. His only comment when asked about his success was, "The man who does his work well, he shall be rewarded."

During the late 1960s the Wailers became the first popular Jamaican group to make Rastafari philosophies and Rasta drumming the main thrusts of their music. Inspired by the back-to-Africa beliefs of Rastafari, Marley took a deep interest in Africa and the slave trade and wrote some of the most devastating statements of black rage ever recorded. His songs were designed both to tell history and to instill pride and hope in a people indoctrinated with the lie of inferiority. "In my music I and I want people to see themselves," he said. "I and I are of the house of David. Our home is Timbuktu, Ethiopia, Africa, where we enjoyed a rich civilization long before the coming of the European. Marcus Garvey said that a people without knowledge of their past is like a tree without roots."

Soon, more and more of Jamaica's top musicians became Rastas, and reggae, the dominant music of Jamaica, became the main vehicle of expression for the Rastafari movement. Its radical ideas were carried by radio into every home, and soon Rastafari permeated the society. Reggae singers like Marley became more than mere entertainers, they became "revolutionary workers" and representatives of Kingston's poor: "Them belly full but we hungry/A hungry mob is an angry mob/A rain a fall but the dirt it tough/A pot a cook but the food no 'nough." Sung with simplicity and the clarity of Marley's skeletal voice, those ideas were easily understood and quickly absorbed by even the most illiterate among the poor. Through music, Marley and other Rasta musicians attacked Jamaica's skinocratic system that placed whites at the top, mulattos in the middle, and blacks nowhere. Marley sang in "Crazy Baldhead": "Didn't my people before me/Slave for this country/Now you look me with a scorn/Then you eat up all my corn."

The singer became the high priest, prophet, and pied piper of Rasta and captivated the people of the Third World. Unlike most religious cults, Rastafari has no written rules or procedures; its members are united by certain common beliefs and uncommon rituals. The rituals and even the beliefs vary from one Rasta group to another. Bongo-U, a college-trained pharmacologist and now a Rasta medicine man in Montego Bay, says: "You will never know the Rastaman through books. You can tell the Rastaman through deeds, but to know the Rastaman you must live the experience—it's the only way." Some Rastas are devoutly religious and of exemplary moral character; others are thieves and criminals. Some Rastas are hardworking and industrious; others believe employment means surrender to "Babylon." The only two beliefs all Rastas hold in common are: Haile Selassie is God; repatriation to Africa is the only true salvation for black people.

"Rasta is the most dominant, most important thing in my life," Marley once told me. "You have one man defend capitalist and other man defend socialist. . . . Finally you have I and I who defend Rastafari." Marley believed that in the Rastafari way of life there was an urgent message for the rest of the world. He believed that it was his divine mission to spread the word of the living, almighty "Jah," and also to inform blacks in the West that they are a lost tribe of Israelites sold into slavery in a Western hell called "Babylon." Marley came to help an uprooted and displaced people establish an identity. Bob Marley, who worked to explode the myth of a white God in a black society, was the first person to tell me that Israel was a man and not a place. He said the people who live in the country of that name are impostors. To Marley and all orthodox Rastas, blacks are the true Hebrews.

Rastas refer to themselves as "I and I," speaking always in the plural because they believe that God lives inside them. To express this divine presence they change the numeral in the title of Selassie I of Ethiopia and pronounce it like the personal pronoun. Most Rastas adhere to a strict vegetarian diet.

In the strictest Rastafari sect, called Niyabingi, Rastas take an oath pledging "death to black and white oppressors." Yet they refuse to carry weapons: "Violence," Bongo-U explains, "is left to Jah. God alone has the right to destroy." Niyabingi Rastas cite Genesis, saying that God made the earth with words—"'Let there be light,' Jah said, and there was light." They believe that when all Jah's children are united in one cry—"death to black and white oppressors"—destruction will surely come to the exploiters. "Rastas believe in mind power and in the power of the elements—lightning, earthquake, and thunder," Bongo-U says.

From the Book of Numbers, Marley and other Rastas took the command never to cut their hair: "All the days of the vow of his separation there shall no razor come upon his head, he shall be holy, and shall let the locks of the hair of his head grow." This is the path of the Nazarites which Jesus took. According to biblical injunction, Rastas cannot eat while others starve. They live communally, sharing goods and services among their community.

In the mid-sixties, when there was an unprecedented rise in gang warfare and violent robberies in the West Kingston ghettos, police and politicians alike blamed the Rastas. The government ordered an offensive against Rasta communes, and police viciously routed them and burned their homes. The worst attack involved the July 1966 destruction of Back o' Wall, a part of the slums where numerous Rastas had settled in makeshift tin-and-board shacks. At dawn, heavily armed police ringed the settlement with bulldozers while the occupants slept. Without warning they leveled the settlement, injuring and arresting scores of Rasta men, women, and children. This attack failed to destroy the Rastafari movement; instead it scattered throughout

Kingston and the rest of the island and soon began to challenge the norms, beliefs, and habits of Jamaicans throughout the island.

Once entrenched all over Kingston, the Rastafari, who had a history of self-reliance based on fishing, farming, and handicrafts, now inspired the youths to seek alternative employment outside the "shitstem!" Their call to "come out of Babylon" spurred an explosion of creative art, and today Rasta painters and woodcarvers are transforming Kingston into a showplace of talent that generates considerable tourist business for Jamaica. But the most important product of the Rasta artistic renaissance is reggae music. Numerous drumming brotherhoods developed in the Kingston ghettos as unemployed youths and former rude boys turned to music as a profession and creative outlet.

Until 1966, Marley's music consisted mostly of glorifications of the rude boy desperado lifestyle. He had had hits with "Rude Boy," "Rule Them Rudy," "I'm the Toughest," and the rude boy anthem "Steppin' Razor." But Marley came under the influence of Mortimo Planno, a high priest and a force among the West Kingston Rastafari, and his transformation began. Marley said Planno guided him to a consciousness which was always in him and which he only had to recognize. He emphasized that no one can make a person a Rasta: "You have to look inside yourself to see Rasta," he said. "Every black is a Rasta, dem only have to look inside themselves. No one had to tell me. Jah told me himself. I and I looked inside I self and I saw Jah Rastafari."

After Planno, Vernon Carrington—Gad the Prophet to Rastas and the founder of the Twelve Tribes of Israel Rastafari sect, to which Marley belonged—took the singer even further into Rastafari: "Gad revealed back to I and I the secret of the lost Twelve Tribes," said Marley, who learned that each person is assigned to a tribe according to the month of their birth. "I was born in February so I'm from the tribe of Joseph," he explained. "Somebody born in April could say they are Aries and that's what they will be, because the word is power and you live it. But if you say you are Reuben, then you realize you find your roots because you become Jacob's children, which is Israel. Jacob said thou art Reuben, thou art my firstborn, the beginning of my strength, the excellency of my dignity."

In "Redemption Song," Marley identified himself as the present-day incarnation of Joseph, son of Jacob: "But my hand was strengthened by the hand of the almighty." Genesis 49:24 says of Joseph: "But his bow abode in strength, and his hand was made strong by the hand of the almighty." Ramdeen, an East Indian dread, pointed to this biblical verse and said, "Same man that Bob Marley. Jah gave him the gift to write that music and put those words together. His mission was to deliver Israel through songs of redemption."

In 1967 Marley quit recording, left Kingston, and returned to the St. Ann mountain village where he was born. There in those hills he made a covenant with a new God, Jah Rastafari. This was to prove a pivotal event in his life, in his musical direction and in the history of the Rastafari movement itself. For a year Marley roamed the hills and practiced the ways of Rasta, and soon Rastafari permeated his entire being. When Marley returned to Kingston in late 1968, he brought with him a new music and a mission to take the word of Jah Rastafari to the people. His religion became the content of his music, and the music therefore became the medium through which he set out to take Rastafari to the world. Jamaica's ex–prime minister Michael Manley said, "Marley took what was a subculture in Jamaica and elevated it to a dominant culture. He took a folk art," he continued, "and he elevated it into a universal language of communication."

Marley's first song of religious testimony, "Selassie I Is the Temple," came in late 1968. This was followed by "Duppy Conqueror," "Small Axe," "Trench Town Rock"— these songs zeroed in on poverty, injustice, and the evil of power politics. Marley had experienced a rebirth, and ready or not, Jamaica and the Rastafari had a new prophet. By constantly calling attention to the social inequities and by threatening and demanding redress, Marley and the Rastafari, mainly through music, moved not just the poor, but also middle-class intellectuals to question the ethics of Jamaican society and the conduct of government officials. Tremendous pressure was brought to bear on politicians as the music urged the people to view them with distrust. During the months preceding the 1972 elections, the ruling Jamaica Labor Party (led by Prime Minister Hugh Shearer) reacted by banning such songs from the radio. But a brisk black market developed in reggae, and the music still played a big role in the defeat that year of the JLP by Michael Manley's People's National Party.

Without ever getting involved in power politics, Bob Marley, who said "me no sing politics, me sing bout freedom," became a political force to be reckoned with. He was quoted and courted by both factions of Jamaica's political establishment. Jamaican Albert Reid, a 63-year-old tractor operator, swore that if "Bob alone was in power in Jamaica we would have a lovely, peaceful country."

In Jamaica and abroad, Bob Marley transcended barriers of race, color, and class. Marley said to me, "The different peoples of the earth are the different flowers of the earth. Jah made them all." Indeed, people all over the world perceived that despite his pro-black stand he was not a racist; they knew he stood for love and respect for all peoples. Wailer vocalist Judy Mowatt says that "even people of different languages and different cultures understood because his message was simple. He sang about the need for love and unity amongst all people." The universality of the Rastafari message is perhaps the most important factor in the worldwide acceptance of Marley's music. Reggae music is also infusing new radical content into British and American popular music—the Wailers, Steel Pulse, Burning Spear are topping the charts. At a Marley concert in Madison Square Garden, Oja, a black American Rastaman, spoke of reggae's connection to blacks here: "Reggae can make the music much more relevant to the real-life experiences of black people in America. We listen to our radios more than we read or watch television, and what does most of the music say to us? Party, party, dance, dance, get down, get down. But a reggae song might deal with the lack of food for the people, or about the war in Zimbabwe, or the need for blacks to unite. That's why it's so important for our people to hear reggae."

In strife-torn Africa, where various nations are struggling for political power and self-determination, songs like Marley's "War" inspired the revolutionaries to keep up the struggle: "Until the ignoble and unhappy regimes/That now hold our brothers/In Angola/In Mozambique/South Africa/In subhuman bondage/Have been toppled/Utterly destroyed/Everywhere is war." His "Zimbabwe" became a war cry for SWAPO and ZANU guerrillas on the battlefield in what was then Rhodesia. This song internationalized the struggle and helped win world support for Zimbabwe's liberators. In 1978 the Senegalese Delegation to the United Nations presented Marley with the Third World Peace Medal, in tribute to his influence as a revolutionary artist.

Marley went even further in contributing to Zimbabwe. He headlined a concert at Boston's Harvard Stadium and raised money for the new nation. For the first time in modern history, a popular singer had thereby demonstrated that he could use his music and his popularity to influence the outcome of a war. This action won Marley worldwide acclaim, but it also earned him enemies. As Marley developed he became increasingly secular and international in scope. Consider his 1979 release, "Babylon System," which deals with workers passing their lives toiling in the capitalist profit machinery: "We've been treading on the/Wine press much too long/Rebel, rebel/Babylon system is a vampire." Marley called on the sufferers to take action to change their own lives. Such lyrics can be interpreted as anticapitalist and progressive, merely liberal, or anarchist—depending on the perspective of the listener: Like the Rastafari ideology from which it comes, the reggae message is open-ended. And as Rastafari and reggae become more widespread, people of diverse political ideologies read their own meanings into the religion and the music.

Some Marxists read and interpret the songs as invocations to the international working class to unite and overthrow capitalism. "Marley's reggae is the world's most powerful battle cry," said leftist economist Teresa Turner. "The task at hand is collecting the survivors of centuries of exploitation, racism, and degeneration—people who, as explained by Marx, are necessarily left out of the mainstream of society. Those survivors are potential revolutionaries, and Marley's reggae invokes them to keep up the fight as the life's work of this generation. The mission of Rasta is to re-create society on a moral basis of equality.

But theocratic Rastas like Marley are both anticapitalist and anticommunist, saying that both systems are evil and designed to oppress and destroy. They give allegiance to no authority but Jah Rastafari. Says Bongo-U: "We shall set politics against religion, religion against commerce, capitalism against communism, and set them to war! And they shall destroy themselves." Since each Rasta is in constant contact with God—reading a chapter of the Bible every day—there is no need for intermediaries. Thus there are no conventional leaders in the movement.

For the five years that preceded the diagnosis of cancer, Rasta prophet Bob Marley had been working incessantly, ignoring the advice of doctors and close associates that he stop and obtain a thorough medical examination. No, he wouldn't stop, he would have to quit the stage and it would take years to recoup the momentum. This was his time and he seized upon it. Whenever he went into his studio to record, he did enough songs for two albums. Marley would drink his fish tea, eat his rice-and-peas stew, roll himself about six spliffs, and go to work. With incredible energy and determination he kept strumming his guitar, maybe 12 hours, sometimes till day-break; but he had to get just what he wanted, always the perfectionist.

When Marley and the Wailers arrived in New York in September 1980 for their concert at Madison Square Garden, straight away I sought them out. Minion Phillips, a close friend of Marley's who traveled with the Wailers, was even then extremely worried. She had had some terrifying dreams. In one she dreamt that Bob stood before her and she saw a big serpent curled up and moving round and round in his stomach, eating it out. "I'm afraid for Bob," she said. "I have a feeling something terrible will happen. I don't think this tour will be completed."

"Marley! Marley! Marley!" resounded under the huge Madison Square Garden dome; then, amid thunderous applause, the audience of 20,000 jumped to its feet. There he stood, about 5 feet 4 inches, a slim man in denim jacket, jeans, and construction boots with his guitar held fast before him like a machine gun. He threw his head of ropelike hair about and it became a whirlwind around his small black face. The crack of a drum exploded into bass, into organ. And high above the roar of the audience, the sinewy terror sliced through the inky space like the shrill call of a seagull: "There's a natural mystic flowing through the air/If you listen carefully now you will hear/This could be the first trumpet, might as well be the last. . . ."

He became rock-still and intent at the microphone, a presence at once shocking and magical, totally in control. His eyes were dark holes in cheeks of slate. A huge crown of matted locks haloed his face and fell onto his back and shoulders. I jumped the barriers between seats and moved to different ends of the Garden, searching hard for signs of any weakness. Marley seemed in excellent form and the audience screamed for more each time he completed a song. "He's okay," I told myself, "he's got to be okay to perform like this."

The band was silent. Marley picked out a low note on his acoustic guitar: "Emancipate yourself from mental slavery/None but ourselves can free our minds. . . . These songs of freedom is all I ever had. . . ." But why was he singing this one alone? And why the past tense—"all I ever had"? The next day, Sunday, Marley collapsed while jogging in Central Park. Tuesday the same thing happened in Pittsburgh during what became his last concert. The following Saturday I visited Rita Marley and Judy Mowatt. "How's Bob?" I asked. Rita took my hand. "We don't know for sure," she answered, "the doctors say he has a tumor in his brain." I looked up at Minion Phillips and she was staring straight into my eyes. We both knew. The horror choked me.

The knowledge that Bob Marley might soon die haunted me those months he spent fighting for his life in Dr. Josef Issels' cancer clinic in West Germany. Still I was shocked when I heard that he had died in Miami on Monday, May 11, en route to Jamaica. He knew the work was over. While in the hospital he told his mother, Cedella Booker, that he had had enough of the needles which for seven months had pricked his flesh. Less than seventy pounds, he was too weak to lift the guitar he had hardly left alone for twenty years. Says Mrs. Booker, "He wasn't afraid or bitter at the end. He said he was going into the hills to rest for a while."

Bob slept and Rita Marley flew back to Jamaica. She journeyed to the mountains of Nine Miles Village, St. Ann. Marley had lived in a small house built by his father on the side of a steep hill overlooking the village in the valley below. There on that hill, Bob sat on a huge stone and wrote his classic "Trench Town Rock." There Rita had spent some of the happiest days of her life. Bob's tomb would stand beside the house, right where the stone sat. She carefully chose the spot.

Rita decided then to build a temple with a roof and space enough for her to sit and talk with Bob. He would not be buried under the earth but rest in a vault five feet above ground. She would embalm his body in the same way Egyptians and tribal Africans preserved their kings. Generations to come will be able to break the seals, draw Bob out, and gaze upon him. She would take him to his resting place with the pomp and glory befitting a king.

When a king dies, everyone has a theory; the reggae king is no exception. Some, like Fatso who sat behind me on the flight to Kingston, say that Marley committed suicide. Did Marley work himself to death at age thirty-six, or did he work so furiously because he knew he would die young? Marley was always rubbing his forehead and grimacing while performing. Did he know something no one else knew? "Who feels it knows it, Lord," he sang in his "Running Away" in 1978. "Bob spent too much time up in the ozone layer, that messed up his health," said his photographer friend, Fikisha.

There is talk of foul play, despite what police say. One dread told me Bob was killed because he was an important revolutionary. He argued that laser beams were hooked up between the spotlights while Bob performed and they "burn out 'im brain." Jamaican police sergeant Vernal Savane was certain marijuana killed Marley. "Ganja has destroyed a lot of youths," he insisted. To Rastas that claim is ridiculous. Rasta George, a Niyabingi dread, said, "The holy herb can kill no one, it can only heal I and I."

But the most controversial belief of the strict Niyabingi Rastafari is their total rejection of death. "Don't expect a man like Bunny Wailer and Peter Tosh at Bob's funeral," said Niyabingi Rasta Ras Joe, "them men are livers—they do not deal with death." Psalms 6:5 says, "For in the grave there is no remembrance of thee." Thus Niyabingi Rastas like Peter Tosh and Bunny Wailer say, "Let the dead bury the dead." They do not attend funerals. No hard feelings exist between the three founding members of the Wailers; indeed, if Peter had died Bob would not have shown up at his burial.

Marley, like other Rastas, believed that a person manifests himself again and again in the flesh. Thus Selassie is the same man, David. Marley has given up one body, but he will manifest himself again in a new body in the days to come. To Rastas who believe Marley was the "fleshical manifestation of Joseph, son of Jacob," his passing merely marked the departure of a great prophet and there was no sadness. Dread I-One, a one-legged Rastaman taxi driver, pointed into the starry blue sky and said there was no need to be sad because "we are numerous as the stars. Every prophet that falls, twelve are born."

Wednesday, May 20, was a national day of mourning, and by noon 12,000 persons had beaten me to the National Arena, viewed the body, and left. Another 10,000 gathered outside the Arena, trying to get in before 5 P.M. Thousands rushed the gate and police resorted to tear gas to repel them. Sister Sissy, aged sixty, held fast to a young man she did not know and fought her way forward as if she could not feel the tear gas biting at her skin. "Me never get tear gas on me befo," she said, "but me tek it only for Bob Marley. I never knew him, but oh I loved him. God knows he was a true prophet. I had to see 'pon his face before they bury him."

I stood there staring at what looked like a doll with Marley's face. It was a very eerie experience, hearing his voice, watching him lie there. His handsome face looked scrubbed, plastic from embalming, but the trance only increased its mystic magnetism. His majestic locks, scorched by radiation aimed at his brain, were laid in twisted ropes almost down to his waist. He was still wearing his gold, red, and green undervest and knitted wool cap in the colors of Rastafari, and his usual jeans and denim jacket. The stream of faces of a thousand different colors flowed slowly along in step to his voice wailing from huge loudspeakers: "So old man river don't cry for me/Cause I've got a running stream of love you see. . . ."

At 6 P.M. on Thursday, May 21, over 200 police officers and thousands of Jamaicans lined the road outside Kingston Max Field Park Ethiopian Church. His Eminence Archbishop Abouna Yesehay, the Western church head, came to Kingston to officiate at a members-and-invited-guests-only ceremony which began at eight. Inside the gates the bishops gathered, arrayed in splendid gowns of gold, silver, and crimson. Like wise kings from the East they mumbled prayers in Amharic and Geez as the Archbishop lit frankincense which filled the church. Drums pounded amid the tinkling of bells and the humming of songs and prayers. Journalists and television crews hustled in to take all the space between the altar and the congregation, blocking the view of church members and guests.

A motorcade quickly assembled after the service and cruised across West Kingston, passing by Marley's Tuff Gong Studios and then turning into the National Arena, where a state ceremony commenced at 11 A.M. The huge arena was filled to capacity. State politicians, ambassadors, international media, music stars, and thousands of Rastas dressed in white with red, green, and gold caps mingled and talked, and then the politicians took turns making speeches: [Governor-General] Sir Florizel Glasspole, Michael Manley, and finally Prime Minister Edward Seaga. He announced that a statue of Marley standing with his guitar is to be the first erected in Jamaica Park, a shrine for distinguished Jamaican heroes. "May his soul find contentment in the achievements of his life and rejoice in the embrace of Jah Rastafari," said Seaga, and the audience jumped to its feet. Thunderous shouts of "Rastafari! Rastafari!" punctuated the applause—in death, official society finally recognized Marley and his God.

At the end, Wailer musicians, incensed at the way the establishment co-opted the funeral, pushed aside police pallbearers, and Marley's lifelong companions bore him outside. Horse-mounted police forced a path through the huge crowd and the motorcade moved. People piled into trucks and buses, some rode motorcycles, others set out on foot. Down through Spanish Town, down past a thousand shanties, up into the mountain passes and through villages where people gathered in solid walls along both sides of the road, deeper and deeper into the heart of Jamaica, they traveled back to the hills from which Bob Marley came.

I arrived at a steep hill atop which the mausoleum stood and fought my way up. I pushed a black-suited man aside and came face to face with a smiling Edward Seaga standing on the threshold of Marley's tomb. Black-jacketed men flanked him. Seaga arrived by helicopter, avoiding the slow and grueling 55-mile trip in a 90-degree sunsplash. Yes, he had seen Jamaica come out that day. No, he had never seen a funeral like this, yes, it was an incredible sight. He moved aside; I stepped around him and saw the open vault waiting.

I heard the crowd exclaiming, and there came the police pallbearers battling uphill like packhorses straining under their heavy load. They headed straight for the vault and pushed the coffin in. "Bob Marley, King of Reggae, has chosen to come here to rest," someone announced over a loudspeaker. And 10,000 voices all rose up. Did they shout "Hail him"? Or was it "Praise him"? Coherence was lost in a roar that reached up to the sky. Again and again they hailed him.

The photographers scrambled to treetops and clambered to the roof of Bob's father's house. A trumpet pealed. The sun burst between the silhouettes atop the mountain and illuminated Bob's ledge. His wife and mother sang: "Angels of mercy, angels of light, singing to welcome the pilgrim of the night." The sun dropped behind the mountain and immediately it was cooler. Only the Archbishop's voice broke the silence, reading the final sermon. A stout man placed a red metal plate with a gold star of David—this was the first seal. One by one he inserted the studs and fastened a plyboard sheet in place and poured buckets of wet cement between plyboard and metal—this formed the third seal.

Darkness falls swiftly once the sun leaves those hills. The television crews, the police, and the politicians hurriedly boarded vehicles, engines roared, trucks and cars negotiated tricky turnabouts and rumbled downhill at 7 P.M. African drummer Olatunji walked around Marley's tomb ringing an agogo, a ceremonial bell. The drummer struck out a range of different pitches and rhythms. He stopped at Marley's head and rang out a long penetrating peal that ricocheted off the mountainsides and lingered in the still darkness. The mountains became giant lumps of coal. Down in the riverbed, a fire burned before a small house. Shadows danced and moved in and about the yard. Powerful speakers drove Marley's voice out the door; it resounded against the hills and filled the night: "Won't you help to sing/These songs of freedom . . . Redemption songs."

One-legged Abraham Morish came hopping uphill to the tomb on his crutch to welcome Bob home. "Bob made us hold our heads up. He has to call my father uncle, all of us in the village is one family. He gave us a message of honesty. I believe he is a prophet because many things he talk fulfill."

Marley Parley

SPEECH

Interview
January 1995

SPEECH: How are you all doing?

ZIGGY
MARLEY: We're good, Speech.

CEDELLA
MARLEY: How are you?

S: Beautiful. I'm calling you from Japan. We're over here on tour. Where are you?

CM: At home in Jamaica.

S: It's good to talk to you again. And I want you all to know that I'm very honored to do this interview.

RITA
MARLEY: Yeah, we're happy to talk to you, Speech.

S: OK, I'll start with my first question, then. The political message in brother Bob Marley's songs has been interpreted in many ways. What do you think the political message is?

ZM: Well, Speech, I don't think my father really went out to say he was writing political songs. To him it was a natural voicing out of feelings, his feelings, without directly striving to be political. Some artists try to be political, and some artists naturally state something which can be termed as being political.

S: I get what you're saying, because a lot of people say that about my music, and I feel the same way—that I don't try to be political, I just speak what's on my mind. So what do you think was the serious message that brother Bob Marley was trying to get across to people?

ZM: Each song really has a message within itself. If you listen to different songs of our father, you get different vibes, because each song points to a different part of the struggle, and the message in his songs was to not give up the struggle for freedom, the struggle for the black people in Africa. Not giving up and loving each other, you know? That's what I would say was the overall message.

S: Do you feel that his message helped effect the kinds of changes we see today—for instance, in South Africa? Because Bob Marley was one of the first musicians to make the rest of the world aware of the situation there.

CM: Yeah, and in a way just like Malcolm X's message brought about change. He spoke about change by any means necessary, whether it means we're gonna go with love or we're gonna have to go with arms. In South Africa they tried everything. They tried a little peace, they tried a little war, then they tried a little peace again. It took a lot of love and hate to get to where they are now. And I think that was the same thing Daddy was about, too—unity by any means necessary, even if you have to stick a man in his eye for him to see.

S: I agree with you, because I feel that his music has surely inspired a lot of people and kept them going when it didn't look like there was any hope for change. Which sort of leads me to my next question. Rita, you wrote in the introduction of the new Bob Marley biography, *Bob Marley: Songs of Freedom*, that there was a sense of sadness in Bob even while he was giving so much joy to others. What do you feel were some of the things that saddened him?

RM: I think one of the main things that I can identify was how long it took black Americans to respond to the music of Bob Marley—the lyrics especially. You remember his song about "stiff-necked fools"?

S: Uh-huh.

RM: "You think you are cool/To deny me for simplicity." Those are Bob Marley's words. And I think in that song he saw the fate of the black Americans. It took so long for them just to hear the message, to turn on to the music. Even at our concerts we would have a majority of white people coming to see us, more so than blacks in those days—even toward the end of his life. But Bob had seen what was happening in the world and realized, These are my people and this is what I'm about. It's not even about the color but is that these are my people.

S: Over time, Bob's music has positively affected so many people, including myself, and has led a lot of people to perceive him as a prophet. Is that how you all see him?

RM: You know, I told Bob exactly those same words. I said, "You are a prophet." He said, "What?!" "I don't mind," I said, "I know that you are."

ZM: But some people would make you believe that a prophet is a man with wings, a man who could make water come from the hills—a magician.

A prophet is a person who is walking on earth amongst us, who teaches us things that come from the inspiration of the Almighty. Which our father did, you understand. So, to us, calling our father a prophet is no big deal because we know that prophets walk amongst us every day.

S: In your opinion, what was prophetic about him?

ZM: The music. You know, in his songs are lyrics like "You never miss the water until the well run dry," which is a prophetic saying if you understand it, because it is something that affects everyone's life at some time. Every lyric that he sings affects someone's life some time or another. So just touching people's life like that is prophetic in a way.

S: Rita, in what ways do you think Bob's spirit has stayed in the world today, and in what ways do you feel the world has been unable to hear his message?

RM: I don't think the world is unable to hear his message. Any part of the world you go, Bob Marley is listened to, his message is heard, even more so now than when he was alive. Even the babies that are born today— you know, mothers tell me, "I have Baby listening to Bob Marley."

S: I definitely can relate to that. I just had a child twenty days ago and my child listens to Bob Marley, too. So that's cool. *[laughter]* I realize this next question is rather personal, but in what ways do each of you miss Bob Marley the most? Why don't you answer first, Rita.

RM: I don't want to think about missing him. I want to think about keeping him alive and loving him and sharing him. We are family and we all carry his message and his work forward—his vibe. So we're not really missing him of such here. And having many children is another way that his spirit is still alive.

ZM: When you miss somebody you're supposed to be sad, but I'm not sad because he's still here to me. So much of him is in me and in us. We believe in such high spirituality that it is like life still exists for our father, on a different level. That is our belief.

S: Cedella?

CM: I guess the thing that I probably miss is the father figure. Daddy passed on when I was thirteen years old. I'm twenty-seven now, so I've had a lot of time to get to know him spiritually. Because even while he was here physically, he wasn't here—he was on the road, on tour. And because of that I've gotten a better understanding of him now than before.

S: Yeah, my brother passed on when I was child and I didn't really get to know him until after he was gone. Now, I only know Bob Marley from his music, because I never met him personally, but I've always viewed him as such an energetic person, a person who was so full of life. Bob would have been fifty years old in February. How do you see him as a fifty-year-old man?

CM: Well, he'd probably have gray hairs here and there, because he's now a grandfather of fifteen. So he's gone a long way. *[laughs]* Musically, you can't think of what would have come next because Bob Marley is still at the top of the *Billboard* charts. The music is still there. But I do wish I could see him again, although Mama's forty-nine, so I can just look at her and imagine what he'd look like. *[laughs]*

S: I heard that.

CM: Mommy, your turn. How would you see Daddy at fifty?

RM: I think that's private. *[laughs]* I'm just trying to imagine him with gray hair in his hairline and a smile on his face. Because physically Bob would still look like he did when he was twenty-one! Even though Stephen and Ziggy and the rest of the boys are more physically built and more muscled than Bob ever was—

CM: That's because in those days they didn't have a Soloflex! *[all laugh]*

RM: But he would still be smiling at us and giving us a lot of approval that we are doing a good job.

S: And I know that this year Bob will be alive in so many different ways. The first Bob Marley biography authorized by the family will be published in February. *Legend 2* will be released in the spring, and a special tribute concert honoring Bob Marley's music will be held in Miami later in the year. Can you all talk a little bit about the year that's coming and what's on the agenda?

CM: Well, we're going to be having concerts worldwide, but the big one will be held in Kingston [Jamaica] on February 6. We plan to invite people like yourself to play, if you're available. *[laughs]*

S: I'd love to.

CM: Yeah, man, anybody who would like to be a part of it and just jam with the family—just have an irie time. Later on down the year, the I-Three and the Wailers will be releasing *Legend 2.* And here in Jamaica we are trying to have a real intimate dinner at the Bob Marley Museum. Also, I'm supposed to have a baby in February or March.

S: Congratulations.

CM: Thank you. So the family's really hyped up. *[laughs]* Then Ziggy Marley and the Melody Makers hit the road. So it should really be a Bob Marley year, marking his fiftieth birthday.

S: Cedella, you run Tuff Gong Records, which is the record company started by your father. What has Bob's musical legacy meant to you as a record producer?

CM: Boy, it's mostly meant chasing after lot of people who are pirates and vandals. *[laughs]* You know, so many people are like, "We played with Bob and we want half of his estate." It's been a real learning experience, because it's not everybody who smiles at you which mean you good. Especially being a young woman. Certain people believe that they can take advantage of you. They don't realize that I am a young black woman *[CM and S laugh]* who grew up in Jamaica and Wilmington, Delaware—that I came out of two tough black neighborhoods.

But there is another side to it, too. Because in Jamaica the young talent is extraordinary. And because a lot of the kids who are singing nowadays are from poor areas, that's their only way out. So you have to do a lot of counseling. I find myself counseling these kids more than even producing, because I can't fit everyone into the studio. You have to tell them, "Just because I can't do it right now, don't give up and don't turn to this and don't turn to that." Because not everybody goes to school here. We don't have free education, really. And when kids can't find one way, they turn to the next. So it's been a learning experience, but I'm hanging in there. I'm tough. *[laughs]* Like Tuff Gong.

S: I'm glad that you're helping the brothers and sisters out the way you do. That's really needed. Rita, you were married to Bob for almost fifteen years. How has his legacy touched you?

RM: I couldn't have done what I'm doing now without Bob's influence. I met him when I was nineteen years old. I remember how I would scream to hear his songs on the radio. But Bob's influence is more than just as a husband. We had more than a husband-and-wife relationship. We knew we were meant to be for a purpose. And that's a purpose I'm living through now, to show the world that this man was more than just a man in a life.

S: Brother Ziggy?

ZM: Yes, brother Speech.

S: I'm a big fan of your music, and I feel that you've contributed a lot to the uplifting of African people and people in general. I also want you to know that we as a people are very proud of what you've done, and that I see you as having your own identity. But I know many times people want to put you in your father's footsteps. Does that concern you?

ZM: Never. Some people will say that for good, that I am in my father's footsteps, and some will say it for negative, but I don't let it trouble me. Because it's a natural thing. You know that because you have a kid now; we all have kids and see what we've given to them. So if your kid acts like you, it's only natural. Everything is natural.

S: How do each of you feel the world is a different place now because of Bob Marley?

CM: For one thing, I think nowadays we kind of have a wider acceptance of interracial relationships, which our father helped bring about. His father was white, and his mother was black. Even now, lots of black people have a hard time really believing that. Meanwhile, a lot of white people just revel in them kind of revelations. *[CM and S laugh]* "Yeah! He was one of us!" But Daddy has done so much for so many different kinds of people. So often, I will meet someone who says, "I never really knew your father, but I was gonna take my life one day and I heard this song and I changed my mind." You know, I read fan mail sometimes, and it really blows you away when you realize the kind of power he has. It is the way he reached people individually, one and one, man and man.

RM: Every day at the Bob Marley Museum we have at least—at the very least about eighty people visit us. The people are still coming from all over, seeking and searching to hear about this man and just trying to take something for themselves that is of him. "Can I touch this? Can I sit here where he sat?" This man was special and is still special to the world. People are living their lives with his songs. And his songs mean their lives to them.

S: It seems to me that reggae in Bob's time had a very political and progressive edge to it. How do you feel about the changes reggae music has been through since Bob Marley?

ZM: The original stuff is still being loved and still being played. Where the music is going now is just another branch, another leaf off the same tree, but it hasn't overshadowed the root.

RM: We are living in a time where there will be changes in every aspect of the earth. If you look at [the book of] Revelation in the Bible, you see that we are living in that time now. So we anticipate all kinds of changes. But, as Ziggy says, the root still predominates. There are branches and leaves. Leaves fall, and there is winter. Then we have spring and it gets green again. It's just a development and a change, but it doesn't bother the music. As the saying goes, "All things shall perish from under the sky. Music alone shall live—never it shall die." There will always be music. And there will always be the roots where it comes from. And your music, Speech, means a lot to this generation. You must know that. And I'm proud of the impact that you're making. Like Bob, you're creating a great vibe in the history of music now, with this generation. So keep up the good work, brother, and Jah be with you in everything that you do.

S: Thank you. Well, that's it, brothers and sisters.

ALL: Yes!

S: *[laughs]* This was a good chance to talk to you all again. Hopefully, when I get back to the States, we'll be able to hook up.

RM: Yes. And we want to get the number where we can contact you, because we feel like a family here. We feel that you have just ordained yourself into the family tree. And it feels good.

PART THREE

REGGAE

West Indian Population Sparks
New U.K. Music Trend

Billboard
13 November 1971

About the same size as Devon and Somerset (two counties in the U.K.) combined, Jamaica boasts a population of nearly two million. By far the biggest percentage of the inhabitants are of African descent, but European, Chinese and East Indian have added to the variety of the national origin. Music has always been a major part of their lives, stemming from the tribal dances in Africa—to the lament sung by the slave in captivity.

Several years ago West Indian music came to the U.K. via immigrants setting up home. The demand for their music was met, and soon the music became a part of the British record industry.

The current term for this music is *reggae*—believed to have derived from a Jamaican sweet made from sugarcane and crushed fruits; the sweetness of the food was likened to the music.

Reggae is nothing new, only the name has been changed, but the music still has the same hypnotic and relaxing beat as it did in the early 1960s, when the Jamaican teenager danced to the music in the steamy clubs of the east end of the Jamaican capital, Kingston.

The Jamaican recording industry is small and highly personal. Nearly every producer has his own record label and distributes his records direct to the stores. In nearly all cases the producer will issue a white-label copy of a record to the shops to judge its reaction. Selling records in Jamaica is cut and dried. If the demand is there it is made available, and it is this method of selling that to a certain extent has been employed in the U.K. Several record stores in a highly populated coloured area receive white-label copies direct from Kingston to gauge customer reaction, and these initial releases might sell at around $2.40.

Reggae music came to the U.K. shores as bluebeat, and later through names like ska and rock steady. One of the earliest successful bluebeat records issued here was "My Boy Lollipop" by Millie (on Fantana). At this time bluebeat had no commercial appeal to the major record manufacturer, so it was left to the small independent to meet the demand. The two earliest bluebeat records ever issued in the U.K. were "Oh Carolina" by the Ffolkes Brothers on Emil Shallit's Melodisc label, and "Independent Jamaica" by the Lord Creator. This disc marked the debut of Island, formed by Chris Blackwell and Graham Goodhall in 1962. Blackwell was one of the main persons responsible for bringing West Indian music to the U.K. He started in Jamaica in 1960 recording several local singers. Goodhall worked for Radio Jamaica in Kingston for seven years. These years in Kingston cemented the foundations for their future activities, although Goodhall broke away from Island in 1965 to introduce his own Doctor Bird label group, also specialising in West Indian music.

This early start gave Island the monopoly in the market. But with Blackwell's continued diversification into contemporary rock music, a new association was formed with Lee Gopthall. He had previously been an accountant and in the mail-order business and had ventured into the record business via his Musicland record-shop chain and his Trojan and Coxsone labels. Trojan became the main U.K. outlet for reggae.

At this time record dealers were apprehensive over stocking West Indian music, so selling was concentrated among a few select shops in areas with a high coloured population. To supplement its efforts in the field, Island spent a great deal of money getting airplay on the now-outlawed pirate radio stations and succeeded in breaking several records.

However, it was not until around 1969 that West Indian music, in the form of reggae, began to achieve national recognition. This sudden surge in the popularity of reggae can be attributed to many factors. It is interesting to note that a song, "The Liquidator," had been featured in the U.K. Top 50, published by *Record and Tape Retailer,* several weeks before the BBC featured the number on its *Top of the Pops* TV show. Perhaps two of the most important factors in reggae's development have been personal appearances by the acts concerned and the activities of mobile sound system operators.

There are several clubs in London and the provinces which are essentially for the coloured population. Two of the most famous clubs in London are the Cue Club in Praed Street and the Roaring Twenties in Carnaby Street. All these clubs receive the latest records issued, and many of the sound system operators come from the West Indies bringing with them the latest records and sounds.

It is these two main areas, clubs and mobiles, on which companies like Trojan concentrate. Trojan issues products on a variety of labels, and the cream of the releases are mailed direct to the clubs and specialist record stores. The company, apart from advertising in the trade musical press, also uses the *Daily Gleaner,* one of the main local papers in Kingston and widely read in the U.K. by the coloured population.

Other companies concentrating on the reggae market are Pama Records and Junior Lincoln's Bamboo label. Pama, run by Harry and Carl Palmer, scored a considerable hit a while back with Max Romeo's controversial "Wet Dream," which although banned by the BBC achieved strong sales. Bamboo operates from Junior Lincoln's record store, which is reported to be one of the major dealers in West Indian music.

Rob Bell, label manager at Trojan, estimates that 90 percent of the reggae records issued are original records acquired from Jamaica. Many are sent to London just as a backing track, and arrangements plus added string accompaniment are finished in London. Another interesting aspect of the reggae records is their price. It is virtually impossible to issue a record of this kind at full price. A reggae album is more likely to be in the $2.40 price bracket or below.

"It appears," says Bell, "that the customer prefers to buy a single to a full-priced album." Bell cites the case of an album, soon to be released, which features live recordings by Dandy, Greyhound and the Pioneers and will be issued at mid-price.

"There are two main markets for reggae material," adds Bell. "The black market, which automatically buys the record, plus the club circuit." Bell says that this area is very important in breaking a reggae record into the white market.

There is now a healthy acceptance of West Indian music, and the airplay allotted to this music has increased favourably. However, apart from the records which actually break into the national charts, there are many which become turntable hits around the clubs and chalk up impressive sales figures.

Bell says that the average sale of a record to the ethnic market could be between 4,000 and 5,000, but some records can reach 40,000, which for the kind of market companies like Trojan are involved in is very attractive. And these sales are often achieved with little if any radio exposure.

This type of music was a small part of the U.K. record industry but the main source of income for a then-small record company—Island. One man's belief in the music led others to follow suit, making West Indian music a good financial proposition.

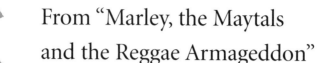

From "Marley, the Maytals and the Reggae Armageddon"

MICHAEL GOODWIN

Rolling Stone
11 September 1975

SAN FRANCISCO— . . . Less than forty-eight hours later [after Bob Marley and the Wailers had "taken the town"], Toots and the Maytals walked onto the stage at Winterland for the first of three performances. The crowd wasn't large—about one thousand people had shown up—but it was stone reggae freaks, some of them in Wailers or Maytals T-shirts. And it was familiar enough with the reggae scene to expect a very different sort of concert. It was.

If Bob Marley is finally breaking reggae for the American audience, "Toots" Hibbert, who may have invented it, isn't far behind. In fact, there is a sizable group of music-industry people that feels Hibbert even has the potential to surpass Marley, given the necessary exposure and promotion.

Toots, Raleigh Gordon and Jerry Mathias formed the Maytals in 1963 (Toots was seventeen at the time), and they've been going strong ever since, without a single personnel change. When ska was happening, they sang ska. When rock steady (an infectious, medium-tempo shuffle beat that sounds a bit like the Memphis Jug Band) began to break in 1965, they sang rock steady. And in 1968, when the rock steady rhythm began to speed up, when the electric bass turned into the lead instrument and no one knew what to call the new style, Toots wrote "Do the Reggay," the first time the word appeared in a song.

The roots of reggae can be heard in the earliest Maytals recordings—the African quarter tones, the insistent polyrhythms, the repeated phrases trembling on the edge of a wordless chant. These were not common elements at the time; the Wailers were moving in the same direction, but they were also cutting ska cover versions of "What's New Pussycat?" In any case, when the new style swept Jamaica in 1968, Toots was the one to give it a name.

Like most reggae groups (the Wailers being a notable exception), the Maytals are essentially vocalists and use handpicked studio musicians for recording sessions. Toots's tireless, high-energy vocals, easily the most exciting in reggae, are instantly recognizable by their astonishing range and the subtle bends and slurs that seem to come direct from Africa. His lead is matched by the rich contrapuntal harmonies of the Maytals—harmonies that have roots in African chant, New Orleans rock and roll and particularly black gospel music.

Like Marley, Toots is a brilliant (and prolific) songwriter—and, as a devout Rastaman, the main body of his work is religious. "I make most of my songs out of the Bible," he says. "It doesn't take a lot of time like it takes some people. I just concentrate, meditate. I pray and I give tongues to God."

For thirteen years the Maytals have remained consistent favorites with Jamaican audiences. They have eight best-selling LPs, countless singles ("whole lot, whole lot," says Toots, "over two hundred all going") and they've taken first place in the Jamaican Song Festival no fewer than three times ("Bam Bam" in 1966, "Sweet and Dandy" in 1969, "Pomps and Pride" in 1972). No other group, not even the Wailers, has equaled their phenomenal popularity in Jamaica. And yet, aside from two obscure singles on Shelter, the only Maytals sides available in the States are two tracks on *The Harder They Come*.

In the days preceding the San Francisco concert, reports began to circulate that the Maytals had signed with Island Records. This should change the picture so far as the Maytals' exposure goes, but at the time of this first major U.S. concert—with no Maytals records even in the stores—the group remained a legend. As a result, the crowd at Winterland was both exultant and a bit uneasy. In Jamaica, reggae is street music—rough, rude and funky. And while the Maytals showed they were professionals, they remained professionals on Jamaican terms.

The first Winterland performance seemed designed to reinforce the stories about reggae funk. Everything that could possibly go wrong went wrong: The Inner Circle, Toots's backup band for the date, was missing a keyboard player; the microphone kept cutting out; the Maytals, who had stepped off a plane less than four hours before show time, were obviously exhausted and there had been no chance for rehearsal.

But none of it mattered. When Toots, wearing a fire-red zoot suit, took the stage and Raleigh and Jerry stepped up to the microphones on either side, the audience exploded with cheers. Toots played it straight for a few songs, letting the music carry him, and then he started bringing the audience into the action. He insisted that people sing along, and as soon as he had them hooked he started changing the arrangements. He pulled people up onto the stage to teach them how to do the reggae. He danced across the front of the stage, touching people's hands. It was an ecstatic revival meeting, powered by a pounding, irresistible wave of bass-heavy reggae rhythm.

The music was rough but the energy pouring from the stage carried it. The audience was transfigured and stayed that way until Toots and his brethren staggered offstage after an hour that seemed like fifteen minutes.

Toots Hibbert is a small, soft-spoken man with short hair and a neatly trimmed beard. Sitting on the bed in his hotel room, a long spliff burning down between his fingers, it's hard to believe that he's the greatest reggae singer in the world.

"I always want to be a prophet when I was small," says Toots, speaking slowly—partly so I can understand him and partly because of the spliff, which is the latest in a series of spliffs. "And that's why on most of my records, people thought I must . . ." He trails off, his eyes drawn to the western movie unreeling on the color TV. "But I never used to go to church," he continues after a moment, "never join a church. I'm a Rastaman and my name is love. If you have love, all things are possible."

As the smoke gets heavier, so does Toots's accent. It's a typical reggae interview: one-third stoned, one-third unintelligible, one-third revelation. Toots is trying hard; being a prophet has its responsibilities.

What's the connection between reggae and the Rastafari brethren?

I's a Rastaman and the music is love. And God is love. I am love. So . . . if a thing is good it got to come through love. Because all song is Rasta music. It's the roots of Rasta, roots of black man music. Whether you Rasta or not, it is just black people music.

Was "54-46" real? Did you get busted?

Yeah, really. It was in '66. They frame me for herbs. I didn't really have it, but still the same thing. I was there for twelve months. I was happy, really, knowing that I was there innocently. I get my guitar and make a lot of music there. I have to show them the work of God, them have to know it's just God, I'm just God. Rasta, Jah.

In The Harder They Come, *the Jamaican music industry is portrayed as extremely exploitive. Is that accurate?*

The show is true, it's reality. It's true when you just coming in the business and you don't understand. You get tied down until a certain time when you realize everything. In those time, me and Jimmy Cliff comin' up, there's nothing you could do about it. 'Cause you're so excited about it until you don't know what they're doing to you. . . .

Are things different now?

We have money but the amount of money we get in Jamaica couldn't suffice, so we have to travel. We don't worry about the money as long as we have love. Love make we comfortable. If we would make a fight over money, we would get better treatment. But Rastaman make them jump on they one soul. They rob me but they rob themself. They thought it's me they rob. So since I know that and that's what God say, I don't worry be rich. I'm rich in salvation. If you're rich in salvation you don't need no money, 'cause you have all your testimony.

Does it bother you at all that your audience here is mainly white?

It feels lovely. It make me feel good, man. I can feel everyone now gathering a certain amount of love in righteousness and trying to know God. Everyone, black or white, now's the time when everyone should really try to *know*, and know their rights. I'm a musician and God himself teach me that. Those works are miracles. Not only me could do that. You could do that, because my God suppose to be your God.

How to Learn to Love Reggae

LESTER BANGS

Stereo Review
April 1977

> *Marcus Garvey words come to pass*
> *Can't get no food to eat*
> *Can't get no money to spend . . .*

These lines from the title song of the album *Marcus Garvey* by Winston Rodney, also known as the Burning Spear, have nothing to do with you. They have nothing to do with me either. They have to do with a bunch of pot smokers down in Jamaica who have invented the quasi-political religion called Rastafarianism, which posits the dogma that the late Haile Selassie, Emperor of Ethiopia, is (was) God, that Marcus Garvey was his prophet, and that pretty soon God is gonna do a Second Coming and take all black Jamaicans back to Africa on Black Star liners.

But you already know about all that, for by now you have already read, skimmed, or passed up most of those ten thousand articles celebrating Bob Marley as some kind of Mick Jagger with spiritual overtones and outlining in unscrupulous detail the religion that put him in the Top 40. It is therefore only fair to warn you that this article is not going to be about Bob Marley, Haile Selassie, or Marcus Garvey, but if it succeeds in its purpose it *will* take you to armchair Ethiopia. This article is being written first of all on the assumption that, whether you are white or black, you have lots of money to spend (which is only one of the reasons the Burning Spear lyrics quoted above have nothing to do with you), and on the further assumption that you bought *Rastaman Vibration* or at least have a certain amount of curiosity about all this *reggae* jive and are wondering where to go to satisfy it. Since, as with practically any other musical idiom, a great many reggae albums are terrible, I will tell you which ones are not and help you navigate through the floodgates of vinyl product that the commercial success of *Rastaman Vibration* has opened up.

I have already declared that Rastafarianism, Marcus Garvey, and all the rest are irrelevant, since if you are white you are automatically excluded, and if you are black I doubt that you are dying to hotfoot it to Africa, where you might, for your innocence, end up as a crocodile's lunch. But reggae, the musical form that came out of all this, is fascinating, hypnotic, multifaceted (contrary to the claims of its critics), and startlingly beautiful *once you get it*. It is not the laid-back, coconut-clonk, ricky-tick redundancy it might at first seem; it brims over with passion, love, rage, pain, anguish, and joy, just like the best of all music. And though most American listeners don't "get" it at first exposure, perceiving it and even becoming addicted to it are not at all the artificial, hip-liberal-motivated processes you might think. Hell, when I finally began to dig reggae myself I discovered that it had taken me so long only because I didn't particularly dig Bob Marley, whose music was all I had been exposed to.

That is one reason I'm not going to talk about any of Marley's work here. Another is that there is simply too much fine reggae coming out of the other artists who have received considerably less hype, and space is limited. Assuming that the average listener finds reggae moderately to totally inaccessible, I will try to take you through seven stages of acculturation, beginning with music very close to American soul and ending up in the primeval African mud and a haze of cannabis fumes. Wherever you choose to stop down the line depends simply on your level of tolerance for the (to normal American ears, anyway) musically *outré*.

One problem with presenting reggae to an LP-oriented American audience is that this music is almost totally singles-oriented in its homeland. On albums, reggae artists, like so many Bo Diddleys, tend to repeat a hit formula until it keels over and dies, resulting in whole disc sides that are deadly dull. But my job is to steer you clear of such quagmires; this is a directory of the *good* stuff. The jadedness of music critics is legendary, so if it turns *me* on it ought to have you hopping for joy.

1. ANTHOLOGIES

One answer to the problem of reconciling an LP market with a singles culture is, of course, the anthology, which ideally not only separates out the dross, but also exposes you to artists who may have had only one or two great songs in them. Jamaica has the largest per capita weekly release of singles of any country in the world, so theoretically there should be an unlimited supply of satisfying reggae oldies and greatest-hits collections. There *are* probably more than anybody but a fanatic has time to listen to, but unfortunately a great many of them are unavailable in the United States, and the albums that are obtainable here are not always of equal quality. More than many other forms of music, reggae frustrates objective qualification—a record that most listeners would find impossibly murky or so deep into monotony-as-mesmerism as to be terminally boring will strike other, perhaps more hard-core, fans as the "real" roots music—maybe just because it *is* so murky and monotonous. This results in anthologies, both English and American, that are often as erratic as albums by individual artists.

The reason for this, I suspect, is that many record companies just buy up the rights to whatever they can lay their hands on and put it out on the off chance it will sell—they have no real idea of how good (or how bad) any of it actually is. Even Island, which prides itself on being the white record company most sensitive to the nuances of black Jamaican consciousness and generally delivers the goods to prove it, still manages to give the feeling that they are not *quite* sure of the sales potential of much of what they are releasing. If they were, they'd probably promote it better. They don't seem to be able to decide whether to push the more commercial aspects of reggae or just settle for its being one of the strongest musical cults around. Their two samplers, volumes one and two of *This Is Reggae Music* (ILPS 9251 and 9327), mostly take the commercial approach, and while one could hardly call Third World's American soul–infused "Freedom Song" or Arthur Louis's cover of Bob Dylan's "Knockin' on Heaven's Door" (with Eric Clapton accompaniment) the last word in Trench Town roots music, both these albums are totally accessible, providing enjoyable listening for all but the most diehard aural reactionaries.

A better set, if you don't already own it, is the soundtrack from *The Harder They Come* (Mango 9202), the underground-classic reggae movie starring Jimmy Cliff, who leads off a collection of some of the very greatest examples of earlier reggae by several acknowledged masters. Some of the songs on this album—the Slickers' "Johnny Too Bad," Cliff's own "You Can Get It If You Really Want" and "Many Rivers to Cross," and the title tune—have already become standards. Certainly Cliff has never been as strong since this tour de force display of deceptively lilting Otis Redding vocal turns and street-tough lyrics, and every one of the other artists is equally compelling. *The Harder They Come* achieves total commercial accessibility without compromising its hard-won political principles or their religious base, nor does it teeter on the edge of the abyss of self-parody as so much subsequent topical reggae does. Convincing evidence in support of the argument that reggae is the soul music of the seventies (American soul having been all but decimated by disco), this album will stand as a masterpiece for years and should be the cornerstone of any reggae collection, serious or otherwise. Incidentally, it received an honorable mention in *Stereo Review*'s Record of the Year awards for 1973, and Cliff himself received another for his *Unlimited* album (Warner Bros. MS 2147) in 1974.

One of the best reggae anthologies I have ever heard is the three-record set called *Feelin' High*, assembled by Don Williams of Shelter Records and originally released on the Columbia Special Products label only to the press, disc jockeys, and record-club members. Part of it, also selected by Williams, will shortly be available as a single LP disc under the title *Roots* on the Shelter label, but neither its exact contents nor its number-to-be are known at this time. What makes the three-disc set truly important (as well as a sheer delight) is that, although Marley and Toots are both present, the larger part of the material is by performers even more obscure than most of those on any album already mentioned. There is simply no way to convey the somehow beatific sadness of Freddie McKay's "Sweet You, Sour You" in mere prose, or the way this one song impresses itself indelibly on the listener's sensibilities by transforming the condition of heartbreak into something very like a state of grace.

Feelin' High is also noteworthy for its inclusion of obscure early recordings by artists familiar to confirmed reggae fans. There is Marley's "Duppy Conqueror" in its original (superior) version, the first-day-of-summer motorcycle peel-out of Prince Jazzbo's "School," the ribald hilarity of I-Roy's "Flashing My Whip," the Motown-influenced dynamism of "I Come from Jamaica" by Black Eagles, and Desmond Dekker's 1969 U.S. hit "Israelites," just to put it all in a little perspective. These three records make up the most diversified reggae anthology I've heard; they are long on musicality and short on the ecclesiastical didacticism that is perhaps attractive to some listeners but probably puts many more off as boringly preachy. *Feelin' High* is the record that turned me into a reggae fan, so I probably have a soft spot for it; once you've heard it I think you will too.

An excellent anthology of more current reggae is *The Front Line,* a Virgin Records sampler (VC-503) available on import at a price so reasonable you may suspect the quality of the product. Besides two beautiful cuts by the Mighty Diamonds, it has the very best songs from recent albums by U-Roy, I-Roy (no relation), Johnny Clarke, the Gladiators, Delroy Washington, and Keith Hudson. Most of those albums weren't very well sustained, but listening to *The Front Line* again just now I was struck by how vital and complementary to each other these individual songs sounded removed from the oppressive redundance of their original contexts. These discs are especially recommended for listeners whose musical curiosity has a tendency to outstrip their cash supply.

2. TOOTS AND THE MAYTALS

With his deep, groaning, bluesy voice and the relentlessly churning arrangements that support it, Toots Hibbert and the Maytals should be instantly relevant to anybody who grew up on American soul music of the sixties. Like Jimmy Cliff, Toots has absorbed Otis Redding well, but his understanding of the message is grittier, more down-home, and, with an occasional James Brown edge to the rhythms, his music *rocks* more solidly than just about anyone else's in reggae. Some critics have labeled Toots negatively as an "old-fashioned" performer, but I can see that only as a compliment. Toots' music, far from the velvet insinuations of Cliff or the supercool apocalypses of Marley, *cooks* in the flat-out, no-apologies-to-MOR manner of the great Stax/Volt sides of a decade ago. Add to this the fact that Toots has a real feel for pop music (he even recorded an audaciously brilliant cover version of John Denver's hit "Take Me Home, Country Roads") and you can see there is ample reason why this man, perhaps the most dynamic reggae artist alive (on records, anyway) should be able to break through to the mass American audience.

Toots has lots of albums out in Jamaica, of course, though only two have been released so far here, both on Island. I find the second, *Reggae Got Soul* (ILPS 9374), a bit strained, although the title track is a classic. But *Funky Kingston* (ILPS 9330), his first American set (and a *Stereo Review* 1976 Record of the Year Award winner) is absolutely essential to any collection of *contemporary* music, let alone reggae. It contains the juiciest cuts from *two* albums released in Jamaica and Britain on the Dragon label—*Funky Kingston* and *In the Dark,* which you can get from your friendly local import service if you don't like abridged editions; both are well worth the money. But the American *Funky Kingston* is perfection, the most exciting and diversified set of reggae tunes by a single artist yet released. Besides the revelatory reworkings of "Country Roads" and "Louie Louie," it contains Toots' most unforgettable evocations of Jamaica—"Time Tough," "Pressure Drop," and the title song—all rolling along in the great, blustery, scalding-funk style that has become Toots' trademark. Toots' songs have a universality that many of his peers' odes to Jah Rastafari fall far short of, and the vocal backings of the Maytals as well as the instrumental work by the rest of the band are never less than vital. If you want more after that, there is some very early Maytals work available on import. Most listeners will probably find *Never Grow Old* a little too primitively raucous, but *From the Roots* (both discs on Trojan) strikes the perfect balance between barnyard squawk and uptown strut, and even includes a humorously gutsy version of "Give Peace a Chance."

3. PRINCE BUSTER

I am probably going to get in trouble with white true believers in the primacy of Rastafarian doctrine for this inclusion, but I figure if we're going to be in any way comprehensive in this thing, we should have at least one example of the music that immediately preceded the advent of reggae in Jamaica—the outgrowth of calypso known variously as ska, rock steady, and bluebeat. There is a lot of out-and-out calypso still available, but I imagine you got enough of that with Harry Belafonte. Anyway, from the Mighty Sparrow to Byron Lee (an old commercializer masquerading as a reggae artist) it's not very listenable stuff. The *real* bluebeat, though, was as woolly a permutation of black American music as reggae, blessed not only with the R&B charge but with a plenitude of wit. Enter Prince Buster.

You have probably heard Prince Buster before. "Ten Commandments," a hit in the United States and much of the rest of the world in 1967, was a prototype for most of his other work. It is characterized by a drivingly repetitive Latin riff over which Buster firmly (and with no little irony) declaims "The Ten Commandments of *man,* given to *wo*-man." A diatribe of sexism so fanatical it becomes a form of burlesque, it abounds in such gems as Commandment Seven—"Thou shalt not shout my name in the streets if I am walking with another woman, but wait intelligently until I come home, then we both can have it out decently"—and Commandment Ten—"Thou shalt not call my attention to anything that may be for sale in any stores, for I will not give thee anything but what you actually need for your purpose."

At his best, as in "Earthquake" and "Judge Dread," Buster combines his talent for aural cartoons with a wry, sly perception of the violence and oppression besetting Jamaican society, themes that would come to fruition with the flowering of reggae. All the songs mentioned here can be found on a wonderful Melodisc import called *Prince Buster: Fabulous Greatest Hits* (FAB MS 1).

4. THE MIGHTY DIAMONDS

In the work of the Mighty Diamonds we encounter not only solid, mainstream reggae, but the fulfillment in blood and tears of Buster's caricatures of bullet-riddled turmoil. The song titles alone testify: "Why Me Black Brother, Why?"; "Gnashing of Teeth"; "I Need a Roof"; "Go Seek Your Rights." Like the blues, this is music issuing directly from conditions of squalor and oppression so extreme that white listeners may not be able to resist disbelief in some of the lyrics, while black Americans may find them a bit embarrassing in their candor.

There is obvious danger of self-parody in this stuff, as there is in much Rastafarian reggae, but even if you couldn't care less about the subject matter, the musical setting is so rhythmically provocative and downright beautiful that you'll find yourself forgetting all about the sociopolitical baggage and just flowing with the mesmerizing sound. The Diamonds are built on a classic vocal-group sound: the alternately supple and urgent lead tenor of Donald Sharpe meshes perfectly with the almost whispered exhortations and lovely, fluid Smokey Robinson–like falsetto harmonies of Fitzroy Simpson and Lloyd Ferguson to create some of the most heartbreakingly lyrical sides in all of reggae. The gentle lyricism works in precise counterpoint both to the militancy of the lyrics and the tense, choppingly percussive piano and guitar. In their green army-surplus fatigues and red berets, their faces stoned, cold masks of hostile appraisal, the Diamonds look like they just got out of prison only to be immediately conscripted by the SLA. If the central subject of all the best Rasta reggae is the paradox of the velvet knife, as many of Bob Marley's followers assert, then the Diamonds may be deemed master assassins. Anybody who has ever swooned to Smokey Robinson will welcome the blade. Album: *Right Time* (Virgin PZ 34235).

5. BURNING SPEAR

Now, true to this piece's already stated spirit of gradually increasing obscurity, we enter the realm marked Not for Everybody. You're on your own from here on out— there'll be no more hand-holding and one-toe dipping in those currents of reggae more amenable to infidels, so if you don't like any of the records discussed henceforth, don't come crying to me.

Burning Spear is a group that even many professed reggae fans find boring, or too laid-back, or too something. I find them utterly hypnotic, a slow vortex of spiraling rhythms, tidal horns, and sedimentary piano over which Rupert Willington and Delroy Hines wave sad, brooding harmonies that sway like looming kelp behind Winston Rodney's sinuous, plaintive, hauntingly primitive chants which alternately telegraph or painfully cry out tribal philippics, painting stark images of slave ships and shackles around the legs.

See?

Burning Spear's music is so personal to me it's almost embarrassing, partly because I suppose they really *aren't* the most quietly powerful sound in years or more people would be into them, partly because I'm white, after all. I've never been one for indulging in liberal guilt, so it seems just a wee bit anomalous that I should become so lost in and entranced by these little slices of black history originally addressed to such a specific and ultimately foreign audience. It is partly Jack Ruby's production and partly the magnificent band employed that make *Marcus Garvey* (Island 9377),

Spear's first Island album, so intensely evocative that you can drift away from yourself and general external awareness in the magnetic currents of the music. But there's more than technical genius and picturesque filigree at work here. Winston Rodney is a kind of folk-historian/sociologist/poet, and it is his vision and his overriding sense of mission that finally make this music so powerful, so troubled and troubling for listeners of any cultural or ethnic persuasion. When he sings about Marcus Garvey, he's not just brandishing a name that by now has become a reggae cliché, but telling the story of *a man.*

Like all great artists, Rodney is continually interested in moving on, transcending the statements he's already made. The result is that, although the basically tribal melodies are almost identical, the subject matter in the *Marcus Garvey* follow-up, *Man in the Hills* (Island 9412), has changed. Where the earlier album dealt with black history and figures like Garvey and Jamaican Prime Ministers Bustamente and Norman Washington Manley, *Man* concentrates on present-day Jamaican family life in rural villages and Trench Town shacks. I find the earlier disc more moving by far, though whether that's because of subject matter or the limited nature of Rodney's melodic materials is open to question. Don't miss *Marcus Garvey* if these descriptions spark you at all, and if you find in the record the same wealth of feeling and musical artistry that I did, then pick up *Man* as well as *Garvey's Ghost* (Mango 9382), a mostly instrumental dub version of the first album that makes tremendous background music.

6. DUB

Dub is one of the most fascinating and, to many non-Jamaican Caucasian ears, most comprehension-frustrating forms of reggae. An audacious innovation comparable to putting the beat on *two* instead of on *one* (the basis of all reggae), dub may also be this music's one truly revolutionary contribution to the technology of recorded sound.

Certainly one cannot remember a previous instance in the history of the phonograph when artists routinely took records by other people, overdubbed their own interpretations of the basic track, and then released the product under their own names. Dub originated when Jamaican record companies began filling the flip sides of singles with "versions" of the A sides that usually consisted of the vocals almost entirely mixed out and the rhythm tracks mixed up through a lava-haze of reverb. The result, as might be imagined, is fairly strange—a snatch of a barely comprehensible vocal hissing in and out like a quick draft from a door opened for five seconds and then slammed shut, then a seemingly endless stretch of guitars and piano vamping submissively to a metronomically unvarying beat which itself becomes something very like the star of the proceedings. Nobody solos—the track just clacks along in this molten rigidity until it runs out, and, as with the A sides, the endings are often abrupt.

The innovation came when producers, technicians, and artists in Jamaican studios devised a sort of jive-spieler's vocal counterpoint to the remixed versions, overdubbed the result, and released it. It was perhaps natural that such recordings should become hits in Jamaica—after all, they sounded like recent hits because, at least instrumentally, they *were*—but they have remained something between an unlistenable curiosity and a druggies' cult in America.

One of the earliest and still-surviving dub artists was I-Roy, whose "Flashing My Whip" is a highlight of the *Feelin' High* anthology. The record he was dubbing opened with a Mills Brothers–type vocal group crooning with almost ludicrous sweetness, "Yoooo, and your smiling face," over which I-Roy suddenly barged, booming his insinuations: "Flashin' my whip, flashin' my whip! We gotta move, we gotta move!" It was a great comic moment. Since then, I-Roy has released five stunningly dull albums in Jamaica and Britain on which almost every cut sounds the same. I have them all, never ever play any of them, and have no idea why I keep them, except that an artist who holds on being this boring for this long must be respected for an eccentric persistence that borders on the avant-garde.

But I wouldn't be going on at this length if I didn't feel dub was worth your while. For one thing, rest assured that there is absolutely nothing like it anywhere else; also, dub records are just beginning to be released in America, so you might as well know what you're up against—one of these days a new purchase may make you think there is something wrong with your record player. Certainly it is the most violent-*sounding* form of reggae—the bass notes in some dub records are enough to blow out speakers, the mix can be hot enough to melt your stylus, and the whole sound is a kind of cacophonous clattering smog. This invests dub with more psychedelic properties than most other reggae, and in Jamaica there are large numbers of people so flipped out that they made best-sellers of certain dub records that didn't even have the grace to bother with the vocal overlays.

Assuming that you haven't reached that point yet, I can steer you in the direction of some "artists" so accomplished at their curious and arcane art that their space-outs may make better listening than the original records they've mutilated. Big Youth (aka Manley Buchanan) is a wildly dreadlocked hipster grinning insanely through jeweled front teeth. He usually wears a pair of reflector shades to go with these—and he is the best dub artist on the island. His records are truly entertaining because he brings not only broad wit and enormous verbal invention to everything he does, but a strong sense of pop music too. His best material can be found on *Dread Locks Dread* (Klik KLP 9001), where, as usual, he half sings, half talks the words in a voice midway between a choked cry and a hooting laugh, delivering as much a running commentary on the Kingston street scene as Rastafarian rant.

I recommend this album in the face of the fact that five of the eleven songs are the purest filler, dull instrumentals with a harmonica riffing over an indifferent rhythm section. The rest is magnificent, especially his apocalyptic dub of Burning Spear's title track from *Marcus Garvey* and "Train to Rhodesia," a brilliant performance that opens with Big Youth singing "Is there always gonna be/One more bridge to cross?" and then cuts abruptly back with an overdubbed holler of "Black people, do we really really really have to fight?" The whole leaps and swoops to the middle section, where the vocal from the original record sifts in and out, dancing in the counterpoint to Big

Youth's own loping verbal improvisations. The effect is nothing short of breath-taking, a dizzying play of rhythms not quite like anything else you've ever heard.

Natty Cultural Dread (Trojan TRLS 123) is a more consistent album, and although nothing on it is as instantaneously gripping as "Train to Rhodesia," it's probably a better buy, especially for such smoldering slag-slings as "Wolf in Sheep's Clothing" and "Hell Is for Heroes." He sings more here, and the results range from the joyously catchy "Every Nigger Is a Star" to, so help me God, "Touch Me in the Morning," which he does *straight* (I think). Big Youth's pop bent is even more pronounced on the recent and only intermittently successful *Hit the Road Jack,* on which, besides reworking the title track, he makes demolition sites out of Jackie DeShannon's version of "What the World Needs Now" and Marvin Gaye's "What's Going On."

All of Big Youth's records are imports; it doesn't look like any American company will risk him, although they have begun to pick up other dub albums with far less commercial appeal. The best is U-Roy's *Dread in a Babylon* (Virgin PZ 34234), a dense, dazing record that is nevertheless thoroughly enjoyable and as good a place to begin steeping yourself in dub as any. Beware, though, of the follow-up, *Natty Rebel* (also Virgin), which is uninspired.

Similarly, Island/Mango has just put out two dub albums by Lee Perry, the most gifted producer in Jamaica. *Colombia Colly* (Mango 9386, listed as being by a myth-ical artist called Jah Lion) blazes for most of the first side and is fascinating for Perry's studio mastery, which includes particularly effective use of sound effects. Side two, in the grand reggae tradition, is all filler. The accompanying album, *Super Ape* (Island 9414, listed under the Upsetters), is almost totally unlistenable.

7. RAS MICHAEL

There is an element of drag (as in real slow plod) indigenous to all reggae. It's predictable when the rhythm is staggered this way. The best reggae uses drag propen-sities to suck the listener into the total drone and keep him hypnotized, but in less fortuitous circumstances it makes for astoundingly dull listening. One way or another it's got to be dealt with, and one way of dealing with any challenge is to fling yourself headlong into it and *wallow,* which is probably why I love Ras Michael and the Sons of Negus so.

Ras Michael is one of the most interesting reggae artists in Jamaica by dint of the fact that in his music the element of drag has permeated so far as to be absolutely central. Though hand-drums aplenty go bip-bap all around a Ras Michael song, the music itself seems to have almost no momentum whatsoever, but to be at a near standstill in a primeval African bog. Meanwhile, Ras Michael himself groans about Jah and Zion in a voice so flat and leaden it makes a mere Nico seem fleet and airy by comparison. I mean, if you think reggae is just a big thud-plod in the first place, you're not going to *believe* this stuff.

The most peculiar aspect of Ras Michael's music is its tromping, chantlike struc-ture. Yet glaringly modern sounds keep cropping up on his albums. Each of his three discs embodies this contradiction, and each is quite different. *Freedom Sounds*

(Dynamic DYLP 3004) is the most primitive—the songs are long, groaning chants and seem to have no motion at all. But out of this sonic morass, which you might call garage reggae, rise two electric guitars riffing in a manner unmistakably reminiscent of white American rock solo styles of the sixties. The effect is like a prehistoric Grateful Dead, and though the lead guitarist, Earl "Chinna" Smith, is one of the most ubiquitous session guitarists in Jamaica, he plays like this only with Ras Michael—which must indicate something exceedingly odd about the musical personality of Michael himself.

Tribute to the Emperor (Trojan TRLS 132), by Ras Michael and the Sons of Negus with Jazzboe Abubaka (whoever the latter may be), embodies similar yet distinct contradictions. Again the songs are ceremonially pedestrian hymns of praise to Jah, their non-Western character underlined by the fact that in this case many of the lyrics seem to be in some African tongue (Amharic?). Yet the musicians are allowed to take relatively extended solos, something that happens on all three Ras Michael sets but not many other reggae albums, lending a jazz quality to such instrumentals as "Jazzboe Abubaka at Large" and "Tribute to Rastofori" [sic], showcases for guitar and trombone which sound like something out of a *Peter Gunn* soundtrack. Also, in line with the "tribute" theme of the album, there is a stately, even ornamental quality to much of the music that is in direct contrast to the almost grim dogma of *Freedom Sounds*.

The third Ras Michael album, *Rastafari* (Vulcan VULP 005), is more commercial than the other two. Though still chantlike and relatively sluggish, the songs are upbeat by comparison. Some songs, like "None a Jah Jah Children No Cry" (a direct steal from Marley's "No Woman, No Cry"), even have enough melody to be called catchy, and effective use is made of female backup vocalists. I hear what sounds like a xylophone soloing in "Birds in the Treetop," and "In Zion" is a fairly straight copy of the Drifters' "On Broadway."

Ras Michael's records, all imports, are some of the most unusual, even bewildering items I have heard in some time. I am not at all sure most people will find them particularly listenable, although in their reconciliation of musical polarities I find an experimentalism that makes them not only valuable documents but also highly appealing. This very quality, in fact—of having one foot in villages antedating recorded history and the other in jazz and electric rock—makes these discs ultimate statements of what reggae, behind the religious cultism and sociological interest, is all about. Today you can hear the entire history of black music coming out of that little island below Cuba, different genres and even eras thriving side by side. Given the political climate of the place and the fickle temperament of the larger pop audience outside its borders, there's no telling how long this boom will last or how big it will get (I suspect it will never catch on here in a big way). What *is* certain is that there has never been anything quite like this before, that it's far more diversified than it seems on first hearing, and that if you care at all about a living, healthy contemporary music you owe it to yourself to check it out.

Jimmy Cliff: Paving the Way for Reggae

Rolling Stone
6 August 1981

By his own estimate, Jimmy Cliff has been making records since he was fourteen. Now the reggae vocalist and songwriter, best known for his role in *The Harder They Come*, is set to star in a new film, *Bongo Man*, and hopes at last to reach American audiences with his latest LP, *I Am the Living*. We caught up with Cliff one morning during his recent U.S. tour and chatted about his career, aspirations and remembrances.

RS: Your publicity suggests that you might be the new reggae leader now that Bob Marley is dead. Is that how you view yourself?

CLIFF: No! I'm not into that. I think it was Shakespeare who said the world is a stage, and everyone has a part to play. I've always been playing my part, and Bob's been playing his part. None of us can play another's part. I've been doing what I had to do, which is like a shepherd's work within the reggae idiom. The shepherd is the one who opens the gate. That has always been my part, you know, to make the way. And that is still what I'm doing: the live and living African ambassador.

RS: In a personal sense, what meaning did Marley's death have for you?

CLIFF: What I know now is that Bob finished all he had to do on this earth, and he's gone to a higher plane to do some higher work. Emotionally, I may feel it, because I know that we shared artistic feelings and human feelings. And when you think, "I'm not going to see this man physically again," you feel it. But when you come to the reality of what life is really about, I don't know.

RS: After the success of *The Harder They Come*, it seemed as if your career would take off. What happened?

CLIFF: I changed. I went into a heavy spiritual and cultural thing, which I felt was more important. I still made records, but my interest wasn't a hundred percent into the music. But by about 1977, after I satisfied myself spiritually and culturally, I started seriously getting back into music.

RS: At one point there was some confusion about your image. On one album cover you wore a suit and tie.

CLIFF: That was *Unlimited;* those were my Moslem days. From the late sixties and into the seventies there was a strong racial consciousness in England, and I started listening to Malcolm X and penetrated the religion of Islam. Hence, the suit and tie.

RS: Are you still a practicing Moslem?

CLIFF: Well, no, I don't belong to any religion. All religions belong to I. It's clear that there's only really one creator, and religion, as it is now, is like a device to rob people. So I believe in the Koran, I believe in the Bible, I believe in all the prophets.

RS: But you're not a Rasta . . .

CLIFF: I am Rasta. Rasta belongs to me, you know, because I knew Rasta before I knew Islam, and when you check it out as an organized religion, Rasta is really orthodox Christianity.

RS: Do you see your new album as a change in direction?

CLIFF: *I Am the Living* was really made with the idea of penetrating black America. I went out to Los Angeles and wrote two songs—"I Am the Living" and "It's the Beginning of the End"—with Deniece Williams and Alee Willis. We put them down in demo and it turned out great, so I recorded all but three of the songs in California with Luther Dixon and Chuck Tranel as producers.

RS: Why do you think reggae hasn't penetrated black America?

CLIFF: Black America's got a music of their own, and it's part of their lifestyle, like reggae's a part of the lifestyle of black kids in England. To give them another form of music you have to take it to them and say, "Look, reggae music is black music." We played to about twenty thousand black people in Houston the other night and they loved it.

RS: How do American audiences respond to you, as opposed to European audiences?

CLIFF: European audiences are, I think, more enthusiastic and more excited, but it is growing rapidly in America. The media were hyping reggae as if it was going to be the next thing. I never expected that, but it's going the way I expected it to—timely.

RS: Why didn't you think it would catch on quickly?

CLIFF: Because reggae is not a fad music—something that's big this year and next year it's gone. It's a music of the people, and it's a music that goes with the times. So as people change, it moves with the people, is timely with the people.

Remember Reggae?

GEORGE DE STEFANO

The Nation
26 January 1985

Back in the mid-1970s, rock critics proclaimed that the sound of Jamaica would be the next big thing in pop music. With hindsight, the naïveté of that claim becomes obvious. During that time, the music market fragmented; no longer did any one form dominate popular tastes, as rock had in the 1960s. Reggae, a foreign music with a funny beat, performed by singers whose accents confounded American ears, hardly stood a chance of conquering the mass market. Several reggae artists, most notably Jimmy "The Harder They Come" Cliff and Peter Tosh, tried to overcome the resistance by diluting their music. The gamble succeeded only in alienating the small but loyal audience of serious fans.

Today few reggae records crack the pop charts, and without hits, groups or solo artists don't get much chance to tour. While undiluted reggae hangs onto the periphery of the pop market, reggae-derived hits by such non-Jamaican superstars as Boy George, Tina Turner and Sting get all the glory.

Why such a comedown for an idiom that was touted both as great dance music and as a force for spiritual renewal and political revolt? Music journalist Nelson George blames a fickle white audience for reggae's commercial collapse. George, who is black, says hip young whites have tired of reggae and are looking to other styles—urban funk, the African pop of such artists as Nigeria's King Sunny Adé—for their fix of black exotica.

There's some truth to George's observation, but he fails to account for the disenchantment of the many nontrendy fans. The fact is, reggae has lost its cutting edge: it seems unable to challenge and surprise its listeners. Rather than expand its formal vocabulary, much of the new reggae absorbs, often awkwardly, elements of rock and funk. Although celebrated for its acute social consciousness, 1980s reggae has little on its mind except the familiar Rastafarian moral precepts, not to mention the moon/June clichés of romantic balladry. Rebellion, restless energy and a commitment to truth-telling drew many to reggae, but those qualities are getting harder to find. An unmistakable sign of the music's decline is the success of Yellowman. Currently the hottest thing in reggae, Yellowman is less a singer than a rapper, Jamaican-style, who specializes in smutty, sexist doggerel.

Shortly before his death, in 1981, Bob Marley, the singer-songwriter who was reggae's most gifted and charismatic exponent, was expanding the music's stylistic range and capturing a mass following in America. But it wasn't only the loss of Marley that contributed to reggae's slump. Two other factors must be figured in: the change in Jamaica's political climate signaled by the 1980 election of right-wing Prime Minister Edward Seaga, and the exhaustion of Rastafarianism.

Although Marley and most reggae musicians kept their distance from Jamaican politics, it's undeniable that reggae's greatest creative period coincided with the eight years when Prime Minister Michael Manley and his People's National Party held power. Socialism, anti-imperialism and solidarity with other developing nations dominated Jamaican political discourse in the Manley era, and that climate nurtured the radical ruminations in the best of reggae. Not all Jamaican music was so sober-minded; for every militant reggae broadside there was a sentimental love song or bawdy novelty tune. But in the mid to late 1970s reggae so forcefully articulated the restless mood of the island's poor that certain records were banned from the airwaves.

Rastafari, the millennial religious-cultural movement whose followers deify the late Ethiopian emperor Haile Selassie and reject "Babylon" (capitalism and its institutions), claimed the allegiance of nearly all reggae artists and much of Jamaica's youth and urban poor. At its peak, Rasta seemed to be pitting its black nationalist, anticapitalist ethos against that of bourgeois Creole society. But Rasta's atavisms—its disdain for politics and collective action, its religious obscurantism and its sometimes virulent sexism—prevented it from becoming the force for radical reform many hoped it would be.

Recent records by two bands steeped in Rastafari reflect reggae's current lassitude and loss of direction. Steel Pulse, a sextet composed of expatriate West Indians living in England, and Black Uhuru, a Kingston-based aggregation, write and play reggae that, like Bob Marley's, celebrates the economic and racial struggles of ordinary folk. But it's a long way down from *Tribute to the Martyrs,* Steel Pulse's second and best album, to their fifth and latest effort, *Earth Crisis* (Elektra). What sounded fresh and vibrant on earlier records has turned mechanical. The band plods on, displaying little of the flair for dynamics and exciting rhythm contrasts that once distinguished their playing. The banal lyrics by lead singer David Hinds tell us that children are the hope of the future, that the bodyguards of dictators are nasty fellows and that humanity is in the midst of an "earth crisis." Hinds brings no special details, no sharp observations to these themes; he simply milks the ready-mades of Rastafarian lore. Worse, the reactionary side of Rasta gets aired in "Wild Goose Chase," with lyrics that condemn contraception and call abortion "legal murder."

The core of Black Uhuru is a vocal trio which is backed by a band comprising some of Jamaica's best studio musicians. The group's songs are more often minor-key chants framed by catchy refrains than conventional pop tunes. Their eerie, sometimes mournful quality suits lead singer Michael Rose's lyrics, which tend to dwell on adversity and struggle. Black Uhuru's approach succeeded brilliantly on their 1981 album, *Red*. Alas, the follow-up was the desultory *Chill Out*, and now, after a lengthy silence, the group has released *Anthem* (Island), a mixed bag indeed.

The album's sound, harder and more angular than the "spongy reggae" (Rose's term) of previous records, relies heavily on synthesizers and electronically distorted vocals, and on straightforward rock backbeats in addition to the familiar reggae syncopations. The results are occasionally exhilarating, but more often these touches prove gimmicky rather than innovative. For the first time Michael Rose hasn't written all the songs; backup vocalist Duckie Simpson has contributed several of his unremarkable compositions. (Puma Jones, the third singer and one of the few women prominent in reggae, has yet to write for the group.) Although there's no shortage of good riffs and insinuating, melodic hooks here, the lyrics are vague, insubstantial and sometimes embarrassingly trite. (The best number, "Solidarity," was written by Steve Van Zandt, Bruce Springteen's former E Street Band compère.) *Anthem* finds Black Uhuru coasting on tired formulas.

Linton Kwesi Johnson, an expatriate Jamaican poet who doesn't even consider himself a reggae artist, spends much of his time doing political work in London's black communities. Every few years, in defiance of the recording industry's constant demand for new "product," he makes an album of his poetry set to reggae music. *Making History* (Mango) is his first release in four years, but it was worth the wait. Johnson's record was easily the best reggae album of 1984, maybe the best since Black Uhuru's *Red*.

Not a singer, Johnson declaims his verse in cadences that ride the surging reggae rhythms. Since he uses the patois of working-class West Indians, one must listen closely to grasp the words. (The notes on the album jacket provide some assistance.) Johnson comes across as a sophisticated black Marxist who hasn't lost touch with the streets. He has no use for Rasta religiosity; on an earlier album he gently trashed the sect's penchant for foggy mysticism and its obsession with a mythical African paradise that supposedly existed before the white man arrived.

Making History is antiracist, proletarian reggae that you can dance to. "Wat About di Workin' Claas," Johnson's critique of Soviet-style socialism and Western capitalism ("di two a' dem di workers do contest") is set to a swinging, jazz-reggae arrangement spiced by blustery trombone and fluent guitar. "Di Great Insohreckshan," a salute to the 1981 uprising of blacks and some white youth in Brixton, a poor section of London, has a compulsive rhythm of the sort Jamaican musicians like to call "sticky." The stunning title track expresses Johnson's unsentimental faith in the ability of working-class people to transform their lives. The superb band, led by veteran reggae musicians and producer Dennis Bovell, churns out a pumping rhythm punctuated by martial-sounding horns. The inexorable momentum of the performance evokes insurrection more powerfully than anything else in reggae or, for that matter, in rock or folkie protest music. When Johnson defiantly declares, "Now tell me something, mister right-wing mon!" he's chilling. When on other tracks he eulogizes his father, who died poor in Jamaica, or mourns the assassinated West Indian radical Walter Rodney, he's terribly moving.

Drawing upon the political and social struggles of his community—an extended one, to be sure—and portraying them with critical intelligence and passion, Linton Kwesi Johnson shows one way out of the reggae cul-de-sac. He says, enough of moralizing, enough of nostalgia for dead emperors, enough of abstract, unfocused protest. Let's talk about our lives now, what we need and how we're going to get it. No need to make self-deluding myths when we could be making history.

The Stone that the Builder Refused . . .

RANDALL GRASS

The Reggae and African Beat
December 1987

Peter Tosh is no longer with us—at least not like before. Never again will we see him stalk an audience, whirl into his personalized, karatelike ballet, peer over his ever-present dark glasses with surprisingly mild eyes even as he utters words pulsating with bitter anger or preaches interminably. He was the only artist left on the reggae scene who could magnetize a stadium full of people, make them feel they were in the presence of someone who could explode into some transcendent realm or perhaps shatter the mundane mediocrity of everyday reality. He was the one whose very presence was a challenge, a shock, to the system he reviled. He did not go quietly.

The news came as a shock—an early morning phone call blasting into my sleep-cocoon. I felt a sort of numb fatalism. But as days passed and reflections multiplied, emotions came rushing forward. And with the emotions came a comprehension of what we have lost.

What can we learn from Peter Tosh's passing? Let us reflect on the absence of great personalities in the generation coming after the founding fathers—Bob Marley, Peter Tosh, Bunny Wailer, Burning Spear, Joe Higgs (the godfather), Jimmy Cliff and the Ethiopians, to name a few. Theirs was a generation of great personalities shaped by the hard knocks of the old school, an abject apprenticeship, hardened by the relentless forces of oppression. There was no quick route to success. One had to be worthy, to prove worthiness, to even be given an opportunity—like the old jazz players who would not allow an upstart talent onstage unless he could demonstrate a certain level of competence that was earned by paying a certain set of dues. They had learned the tradition. I think of Joe Higgs onstage at S.O.B.'s in New York, conducting and scolding his backup musicians, the excellent band assembled by Ras Tesfa; every false note was heard and rejected by Higgs because his standards would not tolerate anything less than perfection.

Of the next generation, only a handful have shown flashes of the stature of their predecessors—people like Mutabaruka, Joseph Hill of Culture, Big Youth and precious few others. They grew as last witnesses to the tradition, the old ways, learning first-hand from the masters. But the newest reggae generation offers almost no one; maybe Michael Rose or David Hinds have the potential to achieve greatness. The new generation has come of age in a time of shattered families, of impatience borne of inflated expectations, of discredited values, of disconnection. There is no time for apprenticeship—anyone can make a record, anyone can grab for the gold. And, too often, gold is what it's all about

Lust for gold killed Peter. Right now in Jamaica, musicians are targets. Word has it that musicians have been put on notice by certain thieves that musicians must have money when the thieves come or they'll be killed. A recent Jamaican *Daily Gleaner* news story reported that Yellowman, stopped and searched for drugs at a police road-block (they found none), protested, only to be asked by a policeman: "You waan go like Tosh?" The sad thing is, even the most successful musicians in Jamaica are not rich; it's only an illusion that they are wealthy, believed by the youth because the musicians have a little more, just enough to fuel a Hollywood fantasy. The really rich people in Jamaica are not accessible to thieves; the musicians, of, by and from the people, make easy targets.

Increasingly, life means nothing to many of the youth. And this is just as true in the United States as in Jamaica—perhaps more true. The same forces are operating worldwide (the film *River's Edge* shows similar dynamics at work among a bunch of affluent suburban teens in Northern California). Life means nothing because connections between human beings are being systematically blocked . . . by the system, yes, but also by greed for money, material pleasures and power (and its flip-side, security). If there is no family, if you have no one to depend on for emotional or physical substance, if acquiring material things becomes more important than maintaining human relationships, then what could a human life mean to an isolated, self-sufficient, greed-intoxicated person? Instant gratification fuels violence and makes bad music.

Peter Tosh was not perfect. And maybe some of his faults helped lead to his murder. But no one can say he didn't aspire to greatness. No one can say he ever took the easy way out. No one can say he was selfish in his approach to life. He cared, maybe too much. He left us some great music that will be ever inspiring, as well as a standard of fearlessness and dedication to the betterment of humanity that was, and is, unsurpassed. Yes, he is a great spirit. In a better world he wouldn't have had to be so courageous, so hard, so often. But in a better world he would still be physically with us.

Third World Vision

MAUREEN SHERIDAN

Down Beat
January 1986

From the beginning, they knew what they wanted. Third World—the progressive reggae group started in Kingston, Jamaica, in 1973 by keyboarder Michael "Ibo" Cooper and guitarist Stephen "Cat" Coore, and completed shortly thereafter with the addition of rhythm guitarist William "Rugs" Clarke, bassist Ritchie Daley, drummer Willie Stewart, and now-departed percussionist Irving "Carrot" Jarrett—wanted a sound of its own, a sound that would support its vision of one universal musical and social harmony without betraying the group's Jamaican roots. And from its 1975 debut album onward, Third World has delivered that sound.

The uniqueness of the Third World sound, says Ibo, as he sits on the radiator ("It's cold up here") in a bare dressing room on the Toronto stop of the band's recent Reggae Sunsplash tour, "comes from its members . . . from the way we've united different people. Everyone in the group stems from the same root, but each one of us has absorbed different musical influences." He explains that he and Cat both have classical and jazz backgrounds and a fondness for rock; rhythm man Rugs and bassist Ritchie are basically "roots," the word used to describe an indefinable Jamaican essence, but roots that have mingled with a little R&B or funky topsoil; and Willie, the only member born outside of Jamaica, has a penchant for African drum rhythms.

Put it all together over a reggae base, add lyrics that reach further than the Rasta-ese of many reggae groups, and you have Third World. "Roots reggae is a good foundation," Ibo tells me, "but we get impatient with the static form. What we do is add to it and stretch it further."

And stretch reggae music further is precisely what they've done over the past ten years, using the complementary rhythms of funk, rock, jazz, and Africa. In their most recent CBS album, *Sense of Purpose,* the album they consider their best, they've stretched even further with a little Sugar Hill–style rap and U.K. electro-pop. Aren't they afraid that by delving into all of these diverse styles they will dilute or lose their sense of direction? "No," says Ibo, "once you're rooted, you're free to take off anywhere."

Ibo Cooper studied at Kingston's Royal School of Music (the "Royal" a holdover from colonial times and since deleted), beginning on piano, an instrument that "combines the harp of biblical times with the rhythm of drums," and later taking up clarinet, organ, synthesizer, and percussion. Cat Coore's main teacher was his mother, Rita, recognized by critics as "one of the best [teachers] in the Caribbean," from whom he learned to play the guitar, cello, bass, and harmonica. Such formal musical training is unusual among reggae musicians, most of whom are self-taught. It is this added dimension of theory and discipline—balanced by the less-structured self-expression and considerable practical experience contributed by Rugs, Ritchie, and Willie—that propelled Third World into musical areas not previously explored by reggae groups.

The development of the Third World sound came naturally from the group's frequent need to cover soul and reggae tunes during its early gigs as a resident and backing band for Bob Marley and others. Third World was the first band to funk up the reggae beat, according to Ibo, having done "seven years ago what others are just beginning to do now. Our music has influenced many international groups, including the Police. As a matter of fact, Sting told me when we opened for them in New York that he was a bit afraid to come on after us because of this."

There is little doubt that Third World is at the cutting edge of reggae (not to mention video and performance art, since way back in 1980 the group made the long-form *Prisoner in the Streets,* and before that it had performed the experimental musical plays *Explanitations* and *Transmigration*). Third World was, for example, the first reggae group to add synthesizer, and it originated the poetry-read-to-reggae art form known as dub poetry.

First signed by Island Records, the band left the label after its 1978 hit *Now That We've Found Love* and a half-dozen successful albums because of the label's heavy promotional concentration on its best-seller, Bob Marley. The move to CBS came at approximately the same time as the band's beginning of a now-strong link with Stevie Wonder, who was one of the first black Americans to pick up on the potential of reggae and bring its rhythms into his own music ("Master Blaster [Jammin']," "Ebony and Ivory," and others). "We met when Stevie came down to perform at Reggae Sunsplash '81 in honor of Bob Marley, and it was meant that we work with him." Anyone who was present at Stevie's Third World–backed performance would have to agree: nothing that magical could have been otherwise—Stevie singing "jammin' till the break of dawn" as the sultry tropical sun rose on the horizon and the multinational multiracial audience jammed as one.

Next came the collaboration with Stevie on the Wonder-written single "Try Jah Love," a crossover pioneer and worldwide hit. "Stevie has done a lot for reggae," says

Cat. "He really helped to break it in North America." He also helped, by his endorsement, to integrate Third World's mostly white Stateside audiences.

In the last two years reggae's strength in North America in terms of record sales and concert attendance has surged dramatically. In addition to the earlier acceptance of the music by white audiences, cemented by Wonder and groups like the Police, Men at Work, and Culture Club, people like Jimmy Cliff, Musical Youth, Donna Summer, and Tina Turner have at last opened black America's ears to the power of Jamaican funk. Like rock, reggae is beginning to diversify, a sure sign of growth and burgeoning demand. "You have Jamaican reggae, British reggae, the American version—Tina Turner—and now there's a new reggae sound starting in Florida," Ritchie Daley tells me.

Does Third World resent the much greater exposure accorded U.S. or English groups who play reggae? "No," answers Cat, "these people are playing our music, they believe in it. How could we resent them?" But Rugs Clarke, disappearing through a door, remarked, "Police dem tieves." A few minutes later, Rugs returns with another thought: "Reggae is a spiritual force you see, a positive force for black people." I smile and ask, "Do you want to keep it just for yourselves?" "No, no," he smiles back, "we'll share it."

Third World's Kingston headquarters-cum-theatre-cum–rehearsal hall is housed in a low, white building in the uptown area of the city known as New Kingston, which is so different from its "old" or downtown counterpart that many Kingstonians never cross the invisible border between the two. To the downtowner, Third World plays uptown reggae, a variant that has traveled too far from the ghetto to be "roots."

"No one ever says we can't play roots; they just say we don't," Ibo explains. "If roots is basic rhythm, then you must be able to move on from that to communicate to a wider audience. Music is energy and comes from the ultimate source, and how can you limit that? That would limit the ultimate possibilities of the music."

"Music," interjects Willie, "communicates through natural energy with a power so great that it makes mechanical means of communication unnecessary. You can't block or limit anything that powerful." Willie's words echo those of Marshall McLuhan, who saw the music of the eighties as "blowing the horse blinders off the old restrictive technology by asserting a tribal or more human way to communicate." Halfway through the decade there are signs that this may be happening.

"We don't believe in categories or classifications," Ibo says. "We believe in being cosmopolitan. The narrow-minded man meets no one and gets nowhere." Third World's deep spiritual commitment to the Rastafarian ideal of the unity of mankind is the source of its members' open minds, and it's apparent in everything they do. Even the musical influences they cite are far more eclectic than one would expect, given the semiclosed airwaves (now slowly opening) and natural insularity of the island. In fact, so many names pour forth from their lips that the following is a distilled list of three pages of notes. Collectively they cite Stevie Wonder, James Brown, Bob Marley, Sly and the Family Stone, Earth, Wind and Fire, Mighty Sparrow, and Ashanti (from the Ivory Coast). Individually, Willie cites Alton Ellis, Eric Donaldson, Desi Jones, Lenny White, Buddy Rich, Buddy Miles, and Carl Darkin; Rugs names Nat King Cole, Sam Cooke, Aretha Franklin, Nancy Wilson, and most crucially, his father, who "always sang at weddings" and who overruled his mother's objections when Rugs got his first gig at the age of sixteen; Ritchie lists Carlos Malcolm, Desmond Dekker, and the Beatles; Cat adds Ernie Ranglin, Jimi Hendrix, Santana, Toots Maytal, Pat Metheny, Leslie and Harold Butler, and ("I wouldn't say he's an influence, but I do listen to") Van Halen; while Ibo cites Herbie Hancock, Jackie Mittoo, Keith Jarrett, and Mtume.

What do they listen to now? To everything that's current in rap, rock, U.K. pop, and jazz, but mostly to reggae—all forms of reggae, including the ubiquitous (in Jamaica) dancehall or DJ style personified by Yellowman. Third World prefers Brigadier Jerry: "Him swing, man." They also listen to Eddy Grant, Papa Levi (U.K. toast rapide king), and a couple of them listen to juju.

I turn the conversation to *Sense of Purpose*, an album that reinforces the group's reputation as innovators. ("There's a new generation listening to our music," notes Ibo, "and we must communicate to them—a father cannot stay away from his children.") Recorded in both Jamaica and New Jersey—the band prefers laying down the basic tracks in Jamaica before mixing in final touches in the States—ten of the eleven cuts on the album are self-produced, and nine of them are original Third World songs. The major songwriters in the group are Ibo, Cat, and Rugs, but Ritchie explains that by the time a song is recorded each man's contributions are such that in many cases they feel they all wrote it, and credit is given accordingly. The actual songwriting process, according to Cat, is usually a lone endeavor, a tape of which is brought in for the others to hear. "Sometimes, not often, a song is created spontaneously in rehearsal," he says.

With *Sense of Purpose* appearing on pop, black, and dance charts and the Brit-hit Island remix of *Now That We've Found Love* offering yet more proof of the band's position in the vanguard of sound, where does Third World go next? (Apart, that is, from solo projects—like Ibo and Cat's production of Canadian twin act Syren and Willie's production of such artists as Jamaica's Carlene Davis.) "We don't know. We won't know until we get there," answers Ibo, glancing at Ritchie. "Stevie [Wonder] asked us the same question, and Ritchie told him we'd be doing a further extension of the same thing."

Bob's Son Ziggy
Proves to Be a Reggae Biggie

CHRIS POTASH

The Miami News
28 April 1988

Dreadlocked and serious, the fallen prophet's eldest son returned the music to the people Sunday.

Like vindicated followers, the 2,300-plus reggae fans who packed Club 1235 roared their allegiance to Ziggy Marley and the Melody Makers on a night filled with high expectations and good cheer.

Marijuana smoke filtered through the air, and the Rasta-love spirit of Bob Marley was everywhere. The side aisles of the old art deco theater were so clogged with people that pumped-up security hulks could hardly file through, even sideways. The massive dance floor was a tangled mass of hopping, thumping, squirming human sardines as the house disc jockey spun song after reggae song.

By 11:30 P.M. the place was poised for action. Miami-scene types—well-dressed Anglo and Hispanic trendies—swarmed the ground floor, while hardcore reggaers and Rastafari roosted in the balcony. When the tour's road manager finally took the stage to recite the Ethiopian introduction to the song "Dreams of Home" off the band's latest album, *Conscious Party*, the over-capacity crowd lurched forward and broke into an all-encompassing, unrestrained boogie.

Ziggy walked onstage, greeted like he was the reincarnation of his father. A chunky, muscular man in a red T-shirt and jeans dropped his head back and let out a whoop, like he had just been saved by Jesus, or branded. A yuppie type dragged his girl friend through the congestion, declaring himself a "Buffalo Soldier." A Rasta in a stubby stove-pipe hat exhaled a pungent cloud and widened his gap-toothed grin. The band played, and Ziggy started, "Yeeeaah, this is the official invitation to the Conscious Party."

The nineteen-year-old Marley looked young. Wearing checkered parachute pants, a print sweater and suede vest, Ziggy was well dressed, almost dapper. He stood in front of the microphone and sang while the sweaty audience hollered their approval.

The new messiah of reggae music projected not an attitude but a voice; a rich, mellifluous, caring voice. He delivered his message of peace, love and racial equality with a deliberate and thoughtful simplicity. He played along on his small black triangular guitar on some songs, and on others he closed his eyes and "felt" the music. He seemed aware of the commotion in front of him but unconcerned.

The band, meanwhile, was playing *hard*. Dalol, the Chicago-based Ethiopian back-up band, laid down lilting rhythms with a kick. Fifteen-year-old Stephen Marley added his dense percussion, and sisters Sharon and Cedella, along with singer Erica Mewell, were exciting to watch as background vocalists. Their colorful dresses and animated movements gave life to the production, which was bathed throughout in deep-hued red, green and blue spotlights.

About thirty-five minutes into the set, the band hit a groove with "Tumblin' Down." Later, during a song called "Lee and Molly" about a "white guy in love with black beauty," Ziggy hopped around the stage, clearly carried away by the rhythm. A few times he addressed the audience with a hearty "Yeeeaah," and he was eagerly answered with a "Yeeeeeaaah!" Otherwise, he concentrated on his lyrics.

At about 12:55 A.M. he left the stage and then quickly returned for an encore. "This is the official invitation to the Conscious Party!" he exclaimed again, and the band proceeded to play the new album's title song. Behind the singer, a huge banner with likenesses of former Ethiopian emperor and Rastafari god Haile Selassie was spotlighted. "Get conscious," Ziggy sang in the song's refrain. "Get conscious." Then the music faded, and he walked off the stage.

With the Marley troupe back on the road, reggae music will probably gain a vast new audience this summer. If Ziggy and the Melody Makers have raised consciousness in any way, it has made record buyers more aware of reggae as a powerful pop sound.

After the show, Marley aficionados—black and white—lined up in the lobby to buy *Conscious Party* merchandise. Ziggy Marley and the Melody Makers T-shirts sold well. So did shirts picturing Bob.

Slyght of Hand

CARTER VAN PELT

400 Years
1996

It's a typical evening at Sly Dunbar's Mixing Lab studio in Kingston. The large and comfortably secure chamber of the city's most famous modern recording facility seems a world away from the dark city streets outside. A television monitor on a wall spews out a continuous stream of mindless images as an engineer sits over an array of fader bars at the main mixing board.

At the back of the room, proprietor, entrepreneur and production master Sly Dunbar sits intently behind an Akai 3000 drum machine, wheeling every control, honing every meter, listening for the perfect sound. Dunbar's casual appearance (denim clad with sunglasses and a roundtop baseball cap) belies his significance to reggae music.

Nearby, singer Pam Hall carefully reads over her lyric sheet. Dunbar sets the opening measures of "Choice of Color" by the Heptones in a continuous loop. Over the classic Studio One rhythm, thundering bass and a keyboard lead erupt from the hands of Robbie Lyn. Sly descends with a modern drum loop patterning the original, and Lloyd "Gitsy" Willis sweeps over it all with tougher than tough rhythm guitar.

Although Lowell "Sly" Dunbar is primarily known as the drumming half of the team of Sly and Robbie, he currently spends all of his time as the principal operator of the Mixing Lab and associated Taxi label, co-owned by he and partner/bassist Robbie Shakespeare. Since being launched into international stardom with Black Uhuru in the early 1980s, Dunbar has devoted his time to developing reggae music from the producer's chair. Dunbar is soft-spoken and sincere as he discusses his work and career.

"I look at [dancehall] as part of the lowest form of music," he says, explaining his approach to legitimizing dancehall as a music with longevity. "Rock steady I think is the best form [of music], 'cause we have songs. So we can do the same thing for dancehall [if] we just work on it, 'cause rock steady came to that level. People like Boris [Boris Gardiner, rock steady session bass player] and all those people, they work on it and bring it to that level. So we could take dancehall and bring it to that level too. That is what we are trying to achieve. And I think it can work [if] you get the singers into it."

Sly explains that the work of Chaka Demus and Pliers, who hit in 1993 with "Murder She Wrote," was an important stage in the development he is seeking. Since the track involved a singer as well as a deejay, it broke with the trends of the time and became an international hit. "I think people want to listen to a record that last forever," says Dunbar. "Some dancehall is a one-hit thing and it's over. But I want to take dancehall and [make] it last forever, just like today you pick up and play 'Murder She Wrote' and it's like, yeah!"

The primary obstacle to Sly's goal lies in the nature of the international record market. He feels there are too many different varieties of music to combine to make one cohesive dancehall reggae album. "If you were working [in America] with an artist, you do country and western, rock and roll or R&B, you [don't] mix it. With us in Jamaica you have to make reggae, and there is so many different version of reggae. You have reggae which is one-drop, you have the dancehall sound, you have lovers' rock style. And then you have like Chaka Demus, with a kind of ska feel that you have to do, [and] hip-hop. So you have like five different kind of music on one album for you to go into the international market. If you do a straight-up reggae album, some of the record companies can't sell it, because hip-hop has gotten so big. You have to dilute the reggae with the hip-hop for it to go into the channel. So this is the problem we are faced with now."

Modern production trends have caused Sly to program more rhythms, but he still plays a drum kit from time to time, depending on the needs of a given producer. "What is lacking in Jamaican music now, you're not getting the real soul of Jamaican records as you used to get. You can't tell when every record sound the same way. And the way you would listen to a drummer and say, 'this fill is wicked,' you don't hear that no more. We try not to lose the regular live-session sound."

Sly is also concerned about the effect of programmed production on the ability of young drummers in a live setting. "The thing about reggae live—it haven't got any feel [anymore]. The drummer what they using haven't got a feel to know when to jerk this rhythm some more; they don't know how to push high-hat—jerk it and make it real. Sometime you listen to it and it feel like this [he makes a weary droning sound]. If you're playing a one-drop, you [have to] make it sound solid. When you go into a studio they can get it sound perfect, but when they do a live concert and listen back to a cassette, I don't know. With machine technology I don't think it giving them a chance."

While the electronic revolution has changed the playing field, Sly says reggae is still growing and evolving. He says that comparing reggae to rock and roll or reggae to R&B over a given period shows relatively how much reggae has changed. "If you go back and listen from the first time you heard reggae until now, it's so much changes it has gone through you would believe that it's the only kind of music that keep adding new color to it every time. It just keep on growing."

Dunbar likes to produce every style, from the sparsest, most hardcore dancehall rhythms to mellower, one-drop roots and everything in between, but his primary focus is finding great singers and songwriters to use his rhythm tracks. Among the artists who commonly record for the Taxi label are Ambelique, Anthony Red Rose, Chaka Demus, Ini Kamoze, Red Dragon, Yami Bolo, Bounty Killer, Michael Rose and Pam Hall. In reality, almost any successful singer in Jamaica has voiced at the Mixing Lab at one time or another.

Sly is continually searching for the next direction for reggae. He gives the example of a version of Marcia Griffiths's "Truly," originally recorded for Sonia Pottinger in 1979 and rerecorded by Taxi several years ago. Sly combined a dancehall drum pattern without a bassline (in the same style as the "bogle" rhythm used on "Murder She Wrote") and a sustained chord (like one would find in a soul tune) to complement her vocal. He felt the experiment was ahead of its time musically, even though it didn't run out to be a hit. Sly encourages his engineers to experiment and take chances as well. He elaborates on a number of current production trends, some of which may sound bizarre.

"What's going to happen now is merging the dancehall with R&B and dancehall with like country western—just to make it different. Some of the engineers are trying to do so many mixes, and [they] start merging a dancehall beat with a soul type of keyboard, and it's working. So we gonna take it now and experiment on it and try and get some singers to come and write songs to it. It would be an element of the hip-hop beat and parts of the dancehall beat instead of changing the dancehall beat to hip-hop beat. And we're going into samba, the Brazil kind of rhythm—the salsa. We're going to incorporate the whole of that. You might not sell a million copy or even ten thousand copies, but if people see what you're trying to do, people probably appreciate the musicians trying to do something that sounds good. That's what we are really all about, putting little changes into the music, keep on updating."

Sly Dunbar's achievements as a producer are enough to earn him a permanent place in reggae history, but his contribution to reggae percussion is equally remarkable and influential. His youth in the Waterhouse district of Kingston (where he was born in the early 1950s) and his passion for music were the catalysts for his career. He laughingly remembers taking his lunch breaks from school and spending all his lunch money "punching" Studio One records on a local jukebox. He also fondly conjures up memories of watching *Jamaica Bandstand* and seeing the original Skatalites in all their glory.

"I was really a Studio One fanatic—like everything I owned. Coxsone greatest one I ever known. I used to sit up and listen to all his things. Jackie Mittoo and Lloyd Knibbs were the ones who really inspire me, because when me listen to Studio One records, I listen to the way Jackie play piano or Lloyd Knibbs play drums. When you see them live you could see the soul. I'd say, Man! Wicked! Wicked!

"After that me really get interested, 'cause it was like all my life, wherever you were, like in Waterhouse there was so many sounds, King Tubby's—music every day, every day, twenty-four hours just keep on playing."

Sly started drumming for organist Ansel Collins at age fifteen. His first record was a Collins production with the Upsetters called "Night Doctor." He then played on the Dave and Ansel Collins record "Double Barrel," which became a hit in Jamaica. "[Ansel Collins] was the one who really guide me on the instrument, 'cause he used to play drums. So when he need to do a session, I would be his personal drummer. He [would] do a floor show sometime, and he would teach me how to play for a floor show, 'cause I didn't have the experience." Sly also gained experience playing with Tommy McCook and the Supersonics, and then with Ansel Collins and Lloyd Parks in Skin Flesh and Bones. The latter outfit worked at Dickie Wong's Tit for Tat Club on Red Hills Road in Kingston in the early seventies, becoming known for an early soul-inflected flavor of reggae.

"A lot of people don't know that most of the musicians in Jamaica, we grew up playing more R&B in clubs than reggae. I remember playing a typical dance; we play for an hour, and in the hour you could play like six reggae songs versus the rest had to be soul [or] R&B. So when we start making crossover, it's not that we were trying to cross over, but we just think of recording some funk."

It was during this time that Sly met Jo Jo Hoo Kim of Channel One Studios. Jo Jo gave Sly some work in his session band that became known as the Revolutionaries. It was a good choice on Hoo Kim's part, because it led to Sly's first major rhythmic innovation. Late in 1974 the Diamonds scored a number one with "Right Time," thanks to the revolutionary drumming of Dunbar, who made a rhythmic alteration that subsequently became characteristic of the "rockers" sound.

"That was the turning point for rockers style. It was the first time the drum was being played in that kind of pattern," explains Dunbar, referring to the rhythm played on the rim of the snare drum. "The first time it came out a lot of people didn't think I was playing, they thought it was some effect from the board. Every song we make [at Channel One] we used to cut a dub to see if the drum sound was alright. When you listen to the Channel One sound you can hear the drum was up front in the music."

By 1976 the rockers sound dominated the scene, dub albums were selling by the carload, and Sly Dunbar, firmly established at Channel One, was as well respected in Kingston studios as top sessioniers Santa Davis, Horsemouth Wallace, Mikey "Boo" Richards, and Carlton Barrett. Sly's bass partners in the Revolutionaries were Lloyd Parks, Ranchie MacLean and Aston Barrett's youthful protégé Robbie Shakespeare. At Channel One, Sly also did occasional work for Bunny "Striker" Lee. These sessions were always credited to the Aggrovators and subsequently mixed at King Tubby's Studio—becoming immortalized in the dub tradition.

Sly had in fact become so popular from the mid to late seventies that by some estimates (including his own) he actually played on a majority of the tracks recorded in

Jamaica. Virgin Frontline went so far as to release two Sly Dunbar albums—*Sly Wicked and Slick* and *Simple Sly Man*. By the end of the decade the Revolutionaries were working at Treasure Isle Studio with Sonia Pottinger (see the classic Culture albums of the period), and Sly was also spending some time at Joe Gibbs's studio with the Professionals.

Dunbar made two significant career choices in the mid-seventies. The first was to solidify his rhythmic partnership and close association with Robbie Shakespeare. The other was to focus his production attention on an old Waterhouse friend and singer named Michael Rose. Sly began producing Michael Rose and his brother Joseph; when Joseph Rose died in a car crash around 1976, the younger brother became more intent on a musical career.

In 1977 the original lineup of Black Uhuru (Garth Dennis, Don Carlos and Duckie Simpson) separated and Duckie Simpson joined forces with Rose and Jays' singer Errol Nelson. That incarnation of Black Uhuru was produced by Prince Jammy on the *Love Crisis* album with Santa Davis playing drums (while Sly and Robbie were on tour with Peter Tosh).

In 1978 Puma Jones joined Black Uhuru in place of Errol Nelson; the classic lineup had materialized. With Sly and Robbie producing for their new Taxi label (Michael Rose had actually been its first artist and founder), Black Uhuru recorded "Shine Eye Gal," "Plastic Smile," "Guess Who's Coming to Dinner" and "Abortion"—all of which became big hits in Jamaica in 1979. Those cuts and several others were collected on the Black Rose label as *Showcase*. The album was picked up by Virgin Frontline for European distribution, putting Black Uhuru on an international trajectory.

The Dynamic Duo then produced *Sensimilla*, which was released by Island Records in 1980. The album is often considered among reggae's all-time greatest studio work. Over the next three years, Island would release four Taxi-produced Black Uhuru albums—*Red, Tear It Up, Chill Out, The Dub Factor* and *Anthem*. The group was at the top of the international reggae scene when Michael Rose left to become a farmer in 1985. Though Black Uhuru continued under the leadership of singer Junior Reid and Duckie Simpson, it will always be ultimately considered the principle creative product of Michael Rose, Sly Dunbar and Robbie Shakespeare.

Sly explains that the ultraprogressive sound of vintage Black Uhuru came from translating his observations of the three singers into music. "It was just looking at the artist and playing. If you're around people and you see what they need, you just get out that music. Like sometime you're seeing people moving. We didn't know what it was, we [were] just playing what we felt. We didn't know what was going to happen. We just go for it."

The Sly and Robbie/Black Uhuru sound became known in Jamaica as the cutting edge, but Keith Richards's appearance on "Shine Eye Gal" revealed the group's early rock interests. "If you listen to the drumming in Black Uhuru, and if you go back and listen to some of the reggae [of the period], it's not the same thing—it's different. I'm playing R&B or a heavy-metal pattern kind of drumming. I wasn't playing the one-drop. So what I did to the drum was give it more power . . . really open the snare and really bang on it, so this is where the whole 'cutting edge' come from. . . . That's what helped it to break [internationally] faster, 'cause people could really relate to the beat when they heard it."

The success of Black Uhuru obviously owes a debt to the rhythmic styling and direction of Sly and Robbie, and Sly doesn't hesitate when asked about defining moments of creativity in his playing with the group. "'The World Is Africa.' It was supposed to be like a four bar [bridge]. When you're playing live everybody can look at everybody, and they look at me to give them the roll. So me pick up and continue playing for another four bars and it really swing. Every reggae drummer is like four bars [and] solo. Me like, 'No mon, get creative.' So it would be like a fever kind of groove."

Sly attributes his desire to break new ground to the sheer amount of time he spent working on reggae rhythm tracks. "If you're a drummer, and you come in every day and play kick . . . drop, and you play that for a year, don't tell me the next year you want to play the same thing. You want to improvise and make it better. You always stand a chance to play something creative. [When] you deal with beats you realize early on that the drum is where the whole thing is, cause when the drum is there, everything will lay around it."

Michael Rose, who has worked with Sly for well over twenty years on some of reggae's greatest tracks, unreservedly calls Sly a genius. "Sly come a long long way and up to now he still holds it. Genius, man—genius at work. Him know when fe change the sound, cause when him change the sound, everything change, [and] when the sound change, no matter what, he is always there."

Thanks to Ernie Smith for the trip to the Mixing Lab and the introduction to Sly Dunbar. For more reading on Sly Dunbar look for Ray Hurford's informative article published in *More Axe, Black Star* (1987).

[Originally appeared in interview format.]

Introduction to *Reggae on CD*

LLOYD BRADLEY

1996

Reggae on CD? *Reggae* on CD? Don't be absurd.

When you come out with it like that, it just doesn't seem natural. Almost a cultural contradiction, in fact. Reggae is all about *singles*. Trojan, Bluebeat, Bamboo, Pressure Beat, Pyramid, Pama, Attack, Upsetter, and so on. And when you had more than just Saturday job money to spend, singles meant fresh-from-Jamaica prerelease items, with plain paper covers, no centres and even less information on the label. Singles that came at you first in a sound system dance or in the cramped confines of Musik City in Ridley Road, Dalston, or Paul's in Finsbury Park, or Desmond's Hip City in Brixton. In each case you would have *felt* them as much as heard them. The bass boomed out of speakers so big you could raise a family in them and thumped you firmly in the guts. Reggae in its intended environment would show such a total lack of respect for the sonic range that anything that wasn't driving those eighteen-inch woofers would be forced through high-frequency horn units capable of only the absolute top of the treble. A couple of two-bob bits Sellotaped to the turntable arm's headshell would be the only concession to increased fidelity.

Not exactly intermodulated, twin-processor, 24-bitstream, oversampled digital clarity, is it?

And the only way to measure your reggae collection was by the size of your box. Your box full of seven-inch singles, that is. Singles that always seemed slightly thicker than their mainstream counterparts; with labels fixed somewhere near the centre. A bit of dreadlock pressed into the groove would be held up as a badge of authenticity—hell, even a B-side was an optional extra.

All of which tends not to equate reggae for domestic consumption with the sleek, shiny sophistication of your compact disc. Indeed, it wasn't so long ago that the notion of reggae on an LP was a bit much to deal with. With the exception of *Prince Buster Live On Tour*, that is, which, even as early as 1968, kids far bigger and hipper than you carried about with them in the most ostentatiously casual way possible. But largely, like pre–Isaac Hayes/Norman Whitfield soul music, reggae artists' long-playing offerings stood or fell by how many existing/potential hit singles they had on them. And this meant, as salable propositions, they often shot themselves in the foot, for the people most likely to buy them would already own several tracks. The only reggae albums anyone took at all seriously were compilation sets: the *Tighten Up* series—fourteen shillings and sixpence for a dozen or so of the most recent reggae hits—*Club Ska '67, Club Reggae,* and so on. And they were *collections of singles.*

However—and this would be typical of reggae's "on the downbeat" approach to life—the reasons the music never lent itself to the LP are precisely the reasons why it works so well on CD. Because, quite simply, you can collect a lot more singles on the one CD than you can on twelve inches of vinyl. Check it. The more album-oriented mainstream act feels the need to extend the usual forty-five minutes of an LP to well over an hour to fill the average CD. Which often results in at least twenty minutes of music you could (should?) live without. Reggae-style means you'll finish up with half a dozen more killer tunes. In fact, you could almost say that reggae on CD is so spot on a proposition that, in many cases, it will eclipse rock as The Reason CD Was Invented.

All of this, of course, only applies if your name's not Lee Perry or Augustus Pablo. In their case, something on the "conceptular" side of innovative would be taken as read. The longer player is then the only format that could do their work justice—work that has a centric thread, with themes, moods and musical ideas that need to be stretched out to be fully appreciated. Thus, and this would be another nod in the direction of the digital revolution, the longer it plays the better.

But these two artists, and the legendary dub master King Tubby, are exceptions rather than the rule. Reggae was always instant in its relationship between player and audience. It is a mass-participation event, with the emphasis on the mass, as far removed as anybody could get from the sadly solitary notion of sitting about listening to records over headphones, nodding to oneself and murmuring how "brilliant" it all is. Indeed, progressive rock and its slipstream seemed to bypass Jamaica more or less completely. From day one, back in the late fifties, reggae's direction was dictated by the people it was aimed at. And all those people ever wanted when it came to VFM (Value From Music) was to move their bodies.

Ska, rock steady, reggae—the indigenous Jamaican music industry—grew up out of Kingston ghetto dances. It was the deejays and sound system operators who were the earliest record producers, cutting the sides and initiating musical changes in direct response to their crowds' demands. Being able to road test their musical ideas instantly meant that when they did take the lead it was only ever to where the dancers wanted to go.

Thus it came to make sense to serve reggae up in an easy-access, self-contained, almost self-celebratory fashion, the whole purpose of which being to provide three minutes of excitement and enjoyment on a dance floor: shuffling, stepping, skanking, rocking, holding up a girl, or just plain showing off. And in ram-packed blues dances in north London in the early seventies, it wouldn't have made sense any other way. An aspect that, more than twenty years later, hasn't changed at all. It's still all about that vital three minutes.

The successful performers understood this too. After all, they were often alarmingly youthful and only one step removed from being in the audience themselves. It was this perpetual stream of hopefuls looking for a route out of poverty that kept reggae close to its ghetto roots. A situation perpetuated by the fact that, until very recently, it was nigh on impossible to get rich from reggae, so its practitioners were never able to stray too far from the source. In fact, reggae has remained more or less the exclusive property of the black Jamaican bloodline for thirty-odd years. Take the most expensive American or British session musicians and none of them could ever play reggae that will genuinely move a crowd from the dark sides of Kingston or Harlesden.

But then again, what we're dealing with here is the cultural rather than strictly musical. If you grew up in the "wrong" part of Kingston or its unofficial colonies—Stoke Newington, Hornsey, Willesden, Peckham, Handsworth and the like—reggae was a vital part of life. It was also, quite naturally, a reflection of that life. In much the same way that Trinidad's calypso kept its people, both at home and abroad, informed with local news and views, so Jamaica's musical output quickly earned its nickname of "the ghetto's newspaper." From ska onward, just by buying records and hanging out at sound systems, kids in coldest Dalston could keep informed of such JA occurrences as the sustained ghetto violence and rioting that were the rude boy wars in the early sixties, the Rasta revolution, gun court justice, election shenanigans, economic decline or the rise of the posses. Of course it would never be as fact-checked accurate as, say, the international pages of the *Times,* but it was always going to have a better bassline. Likewise it was always going to be an up-to-the-minute source of the latest yard slang or style affectations. In short, reggae has always been inseparable from its environment. It could never, ever, be anything other than an expression of where it came from. This is a music with genuine soul.

Soul that lives on—literally—thanks to CD and its revisiting of past glories and an accessible cataloguing of all things present. The reggae industry, both in the U.K. and Jamaica, embraced compact disc technology somewhat belatedly. But what was lacking in punctuality has been more than made up for in enthusiasm, and reggae on CD is currently one of the fastest growing areas in the music business. It is an activity that is based more in the past than in the present, as back in the day there was just so much reggae about. During the fifties and sixties the producers ruled the business, there was no such thing as royalties, and the closest most artists got to a recording contract was a few dollar bills for cutting a record. Thus the only way to make ends meet was to cut an awful lot of them. Or, as became almost regulation in the seventies, you set up your own studio, so that you could make as much music as you liked, when you liked.

All these factors led to a situation whereby Jamaica—with a population half the size of London's—boasted more record labels than the entire U.K. Most of these labels were so precariously financed, however, that they didn't last too long, so much of this vast output has long since disappeared. But, happily, it's precisely these hard-to-get-hold-of gems that are now coming out on CD, both as repackaged compilations and as original albums.

The CD drive really began at the start of the nineties, with a few tentative CD collections that were more the compiler's labour of love than a serious commercial proposition. But these early CDs were very well received, and seemed to trigger a tidal wave of nostalgia—which, naturally enough, stimulated supply. With quality rising as rapidly as quantity, today a CD reggae reissue is such a big deal that only the very best need apply. The presentation and track-listing standards set by such revival market leaders as Blood and Fire, Rewind Selecta and Island's Reggae Refreshers would put the most big time labels to shame.

Now add this rapidly escalating back catalogue to a new generation of reggae performers and producers who may be entirely digital-friendly, but have never managed to remove themselves from the high-output-singles format—thoroughly modern reggae that still takes the idea of albums little further than a string of recent, highly desirable, fast turnover collections, with titles like *Romantic Ragga*, *Boglemania* and *Dancehall Killers*. When Keith Stone at specialist London reggae shop Daddy Kool talks about labels' CD catalogues being "current this afternoon, but probably completely different by lunchtime tomorrow," he's only half joking.

As with *Soul on CD* (Kyle Cathie Ltd.), the rules of inclusion for this book are very straightforward. Does the act in question have a worthwhile CD on the shelves at the time of writing? If the answer is yes then they're in. (Except for a very select few, who are there because they *ought* to have a CD on offer.) "Worthwhile" means: Has said disc in some way contributed to reggae as a whole other than just selling by the bucketload?

The yardstick is all to do with *soul*. That certain vibrant something that connects all the best reggae to its roots as a modern-day black folk music. A dark mixture of hope, happiness, love and a sense of community, steeped in four hundred years of sufferation but as capable as any other genre of enjoying a pointless knees-up or looking to, er, capture the gal. It doesn't matter if the folk making it are from Trench Town, Tottenham or Brooklyn either—they're all branches of the same spiritual tree.

Spirit that Bob Marley had on tap. As did Duke Reid, Coxsone and Prince Buster. Likewise the dub masters Lee Perry, King Tubby, Keith Hudson and Augustus Pablo. So, too, do singers such as Burning Spear, Gregory Isaacs, The Mighty Diamonds and Sugar Minott. Or, deejay style, U-Roy, Big Youth, Jazzbo and Prince Far-I. Then as well as these old-timers there's the new blood: Bobby Digital, Garnett Silk, Buju, Tiger, Capleton, Steely and Cleevie, Chaka Demus, Pliers, Spanner Banner, Spragga Benz and Shaggy. Spirit so strong the music has survived and thrived for nearly forty years without deviating too far from its essence. A crossing of chronological and geographical boundaries illustrated with circular efficiency by the tune "Oh

Carolina": a hit for the acoustic Ffolkes Brothers in Jamaica in 1958, and a worldwide smash in 1993 for the New York raggamuffin Shaggy. Although both renditions are utterly different, noticeably they're both exactly the same.

Once more, as with *Soul on CD*, forget all that dreadful old tosh about CDs not being "the real thing"—that bizarre conversational twilight zone in which people try to claim that this new, sparkling computer-controlled presentation of the music is, somehow, not nearly as desirable as seven inches of scratched-up, warping, fuzzy-sounding vinyl. It's almost as if the "realness"—whatever that means—of a piece of music increases in direct relation to the age of your copy and in inverse proportion to its condition. Or that a tune will only have any bearing on anything if it's been commercially unavailable for about twenty years. As if artistic value is in some way linked to fiscal value.

My aim in life, probably the aim of most music fans for that matter, is to have as much music as I can—i.e., as much as my wife and my bank manager will let me—going back as far as I can, and to be able belatedly to catch up, through rereleases, with anything I might have missed. I want it sounding as close as possible to how it was played at the recording session too, not deteriorating with the passing of years or number of plays. And it'll help if it's in a handy-sized format that'll work in my car, in my office, in my living room, on the beach or on the bus. If CD satisfies all the above conditions—which it does—then it's got my vote. Period.

You don't even need to think too hard to realize CD is nothing more than reggae deserves.

Reggae: Better Late Than Never

ELENA OUMANO

Billboard
15 July 1995

Two decades after the release of Bob Marley's *Catch a Fire,* his legend continues to grow, but the wave of reggae artists that was expected to follow him and establish reggae music stateside never materialized . . . until now.

The years 1991 and 1992 saw the door to mainstream success crack open with Shabba Ranks's two consecutive gold albums, *Raw as Ever* and *Xtra Naked.* Others followed him into the charts: Snow, Shaggy, Super Cat, Buju Banton, Inner Circle, Mad Cobra, Patra, Chaka Demus & Pliers, Dawn Penn and Cutty Ranks.

This year is only half over and already a full squadron is scoring on U.S. R&B and pop charts: Ini Kamoze ("Hot Stepper"), Capleton ("Tour"), Terror Fabulous and Nadine Sutherland ("Action"), Vicious ("Nika"), Mega Banton ("Soundboy Killing"), Diana King ("Shy Guy"), Mad Lion ("Weeded") and Shaggy ("Boombastic"). They are the beachhead for a full-scale invasion, an extensive reggae lineup dropping albums in North America this summer and fall. This may be the year reggae delivers on its two-decade promise to create a powerful and consistent presence on stateside pop charts.

What, if anything, has changed? What has been learned from the long history of trying to market reggae in the United States? "The market has changed a lot," says Island Group chairman Chris Blackwell. "In the seventies we were the main company marketing reggae. Now lots of companies are marketing reggae to a wider audience and doing it extremely well. There's a whole interest where there wasn't before."

"THE WAY WE ARE"

Despite reggae's recently increased chart presence, many still view it as the new music. "Generally, the one shortcoming in marketing reggae so far is that a lot of one-off records have broken through, but, with few exceptions, no great follow-up success for the artists themselves," says Priority reggae A&R director Murray Elias. Some fault labels for signing artists without understanding the culture in which they developed, or the fact that reggae has several, often radically different, styles and deliveries. "It may not be just about going in the dance hall and shaking up," says Grove label's Stephen Stewart. "So they take on a message artist, and they can't place him. This is not R&B, this is not hip-hop. Bob Marley said, 'There's a natural mystic running through the air,' and it's in the music. It's how we live, and to project us is to understand the way we are."

Fans of traditional reggae in particular feel left out of dancehall. "Reggae needs to take a full step [toward] involvement instead of just allowing hip-hop, dance-oriented stuff through," says veteran California club spinner Ron Miller. "Over the years we've seen volatile reggae songs that weren't particularly dance or hip-hop oriented get through to popularity. We can't see what reggae as a whole can do until it's given a fair chance."

The reggae community attributes reggae's failure to crack the mainstream to a lack of label commitment. "I don't know that they've gone all out for an artist or done the extra work to make sure they got a record played on radio or in clubs," says WNWK/WBLS radio jock Pat McKay.

Rather than license to a U.S. label, producer Donovan German distributes his Jamaican-produced Penthouse products from his own Miami base. "I'm not going to give up on it," he says. "Sometimes if you stay on it for another week or two, the right doors open."

ARTIST DEVELOPMENT

The pioneering model in reggae-artist development was set recently by former Epic A&R Vivien Scott with Shabba Ranks, Patra and, later, Vicious. Most labels have neglected this crucial component. "There was a time when the majors all came down and everyone was signed," says Clive Hunt of Tuff Gong and Ugly Man Records. "I'm glad some [artists] got money, but in terms of promoting, marketing and the sustainability of the artists, I'm always concerned. Sometimes an artist in Jamaica comes up from the street and he doesn't know much. He has a hit song or two and someone signs him. He still needs basic training. We should work slow on development. If they had signed five or ten acts on a long-term basis during Bob Marley's days and worked until now, when reggae broke out in America, it would be bigger."

Another key aspect of label commitment is pushing for a broader market. Blackwell attributes recent reggae successes to marketing plans that "went in full blast like they've got a big hit act on their hands, rather than creeping up with a minority music. By taking that approach, they've made it happen."

NON-BODACIOUS MARKETING

Elektra senior marketing director Karen Mason handles reggae just as she does R&B. "At the same time, you come up with a plan that fully represents what the artist is about," she says. "If that artist is lovers' rock, you don't make him look like a thug. Or if he's hardcore dancehall, you don't want him all suited down. Your campaign says clearly that you understand how this music is going to develop, with packaging coordinating with a certain image that sends the right message to the consumer.

"Then you put together a marketing plan: when and where you advertise, when you go to the clubs, what radio formats you go to and when do you go to the tape masters first or the sound systems first [with a dub plate]? Do you send different records to radio and the sound systems simultaneously? You don't come out with a bodacious plan, because the core audience will suck their teeth and keep stepping. Your plan has to show you know what you're doing. Before we even rereleased 'Action,' we released 'Gangster Anthem' with a video—which we didn't expect to succeed commercially—for the grass roots and underground, to let folks know that we understood their importance and to build confidence in our ability to market the genre.

"We followed with *Number 2* [the first "pepperseed" riddim release], again to the underground," Mason continues. "Then we rereleased 'Action,' a hit two years ago. But we felt it could have commercial success and open doors for Terror Fabulous and Nadine Sutherland, and it was still embraced by the grass roots."

Loose Cannon president Lisa Cortes's plan for Buju Banton's *'Til Shiloh* also presents the artist as hardcore reggae and as mainstream star. "We're building on a foundation established on the last record," says Cortes. "I never say Buju's reggae–hip-hop, reggae-pop, reggae-R&B. He's a reggae artist. Our imaging is about that. We went to the core base in February with 'Only Man,' using Penthouse's distribution for seven- and twelve-inch vinyls with the Loose Cannon logo. Now we have 'Sensimilla Prosecution,' another vinyl out to our core market, and a West Coast/hip-hop mix on 'Champion.' Remixes are promotional tools to sell an album."

Banton is also touring extensively: a nine-city PA tour last May, the Reggae Sunsplash U.S. Tour in June and part of July, and concerts internationally the remainder of the summer. "This has been a three-year-long artist-development process, and before I got involved he spent years with Penthouse, performing and creating a catalog of singles," says Cortes. "I rereleased *Mr. Mention* in the United States to the independent distribution system through PolyGram. We sold forty thousand. We then released *Voice of Jamaica;* we did a quarter of a million copies here. It's not album-to-album, it's a continuous process of building the artist."

Another key to mainstreaming reggae is industry-wide education. "Aside from signing an artist, the majors have to educate radio and TV personnel about this music in the process of educating them about a particular product," says radio's McKay. "It becomes a dual task. The extent to which it's been done well has meant the success of artists like Shabba Ranks and Super Cat. Those artists were embraced wholeheartedly by the hip-hop community, and that had a lot to do with how large they got."

TO BLEND OR NOT TO BLEND

Some view reggae's recent commercial breakthroughs via hip-hop and R&B flavoring or all-out remixes with a jaundiced eye. They stress the long-term importance of maintaining reggae's stylistic integrity. But blending reggae with American pop styles is nothing new. "The world is ready for reggae, is reggae ready for the world?" asks Super Cat. "Bob Marley never did go out with straight reggae. He [used] the rock guitar in his music, and it became roots, rock, reggae."

Ini Kamoze, whose "Hot Stepper" went to No. 1 on *Billboard*'s pop singles chart, refuses to be limited to the "reggae" label. "When Stevie Wonder or Lionel Richie or Blondie did a reggae song, nobody said they were crossing over," says Kamoze. "We want that same freedom. If you're from Jamaica, they automatically put you in a special section and give you airplay only when they have a reggae program. I want to be played behind Madonna or Guns 'N Roses or whoever."

DEFINED AND UNDILUTED

What is reggae, after all? "If 'Hot Stepper,' 'Shy Guy' and other songs also hit in the Jamaican marketplace, will people say this is not Jamaican music?" asks Columbia A&R person Maxine Stowe, a Jamaican who worked with Studio One and V.P. "You can't really define a 'reggae song.' 'Hot Stepper' made it on a hip-hop remix, but, for me, it's still a reggae song, a Jamaican artist looping stuff into different things, which we've been doing since I know Jamaican music. If you open the door, maybe there'll be more interest in straight-ahead, undiluted reggae. Jamaican ethnic reggae will always be there. The challenge now is to make a connection with that base and get successful artists from there into mainstream.

"But the music will continue to be made in a gritty fashion, or like now, moving to a roots and cultural style," Stowe continues. "All that can happen is a more enriched marketplace. People want to know if a dark dancehall record from the roots of Jamaica will be No. 1 on the *Billboard* chart. But that is not the logic of success for the music form."

At the same time they're wooing the R&B, pop and hip-hop markets, majors are acknowledging also the importance of the ethnic/grassroots market. "The U.S. majors should have people on marketing and promotion staffs from the reggae grassroots/ethnic arena who feel it and know how to sell it," says Yonnie of New York–based Road International sound system. New York–based veteran reggae promoters include Van Gibbs's multiservice Palm Tree Enterprises, Frankie Felicien's Frankie's Wire, Tree Street Promotions and independent publicists Amy Wachtel, Michael Robinson, Sharon Gordon, Christie Barber, Kim Smith and Lisa-Anne Stephenson.

There are at least a thousand [mom-and-pop stores] in the tri-state area," says Felicien—as well as countless more studded throughout Caribbean communities across the United States, all selling vinyl—and innumerable radio programs spinning 45s, both key to starting reggae sales in the street. "[Because they don't have SoundScan hookups], *Billboard* has no way of knowing what that little guy in Flatbush sold, or Top Line in Queens, Unique on Long Island, Pearl and MCM in Brooklyn, S&J in Mount Vernon," says Felicien. Those gateways to reggae's core market should receive the same discounts awarded to volume-buying mega chains, says radio jock/*Dub Missive* editor-in-chief Las.

"The ethnic market is a small percentage of the pie," says Chris Chin of V.P. Records. "But, for the artist's longevity, they have to service it."

"You must always satisfy your core, ethnic audience first," says Germain. "Then you move to the next level, the American audience. If you go to the American audience and it doesn't work and you've negated your Jamaican audience, you have a long way to fall."

Sometimes, though, the reverse occurs. "Hot Stepper" went to the top of the charts in the United States first, then Jamaica; Patra became an international name before she was known at home.

PRINT, CLUBS AND ROOTS

Interfacing with the scattered U.S. grassroots community is a daunting task. Magazines like *The Reggae and African Beat, Reggae Report,* and *Dub Missive* are informal networking devices, as are the local radio shows. The grass roots can be found in New York, for instance, at clubs like Brooklyn's Legend, Act III in the Bronx, the Q Club and Sandals in Queens, and in Manhattan at S.O.B.'s on Tuesday nights or Sunday's at the Lion's Head and Club Downtime for JA Sting, a cutting-edge party that bridges all reggae styles, Coxsone to Capleton.

New York, always an active market, is now in high gear. Long-established recording studios such as Philip Smart's on Long Island and Don One in Brooklyn have been joined by the new midi, twenty-four-, sixteen- and eight-track Kingston Lane studio. Among the city's annual reggae concerts are this August's fifth New York Reggae Music Festival and the many shows clustered around the Labor Day West Indian Parade. Another option is to go online with Reggae Ambassadors, an international network of more than four hundred reggae fans and industry people.

RADIO RESISTANCE

But as labels broaden their perspective, radio, for the most part, refuses to lift restrictions. "Look at Ace of Base and UB40," says Germain. "They're doing the same thing. But they're white and get a level of commitment from radio that we don't." Some dedicated reggae jocks actually pay to play.

Every gain seems to be countered by a loss. Just as New York's Hot 97 changed to an urban format, adding several hip-hop/reggae programs, KISS and WBLS switched in the opposite direction. KISS now plays classic oldies.

"Why can't I hear a 'Redemption Song' on KISS but I can hear an old Teddy Pendergrass?" wonders Felicien.

"It's still a regional thing," says Elias. "Records like 'Action' or 'Tour' were big in certain markets only. Occasionally, an Ini Kamoze goes all the way. Suddenly people stop looking at it only as reggae or rap or alternative. It becomes 'pop' because it's selling everywhere. It's very similar to the early stages of hip-hop, when you were selling in four or five cities on the East Coast. But every record knocks down the door a little more for the next."

"Most [programmers] can't hear reggae and can't understand it," says Gibbs. "But the feedback from the street gives them indicators. I try to make them aware that there's a reggae base along the Eastern seaboard and in all major cities, and things can happen."

"Hot Stepper," remixed by Gibbs's son Salaam Remi, "came at the right time; we had already developed our feed to the street, about sixteen to eighteen promotion people nationally," says Gibbs. "We go wherever we can get it played, starting with the street-consciousness base and letting it come up. The programmers feel it, as opposed to trying to listen and understand."

SUMMER SPECTACLE

Part of Gibbs's plan involves a national dancehall tour this summer, featuring sound systems instead of bands, and DJs Shabba Ranks, Spragga Benz, Mega Banton, Vicious and others added to various dates.

One innovative recent solution to the exposure dilemma is *Irie Jam*, a simulcast program that began September 10, 1994, and is heard on IRIE-FM in Jamaica and WRTN 93.5 FM in the New York area, every Saturday. Featuring disc jockeys on both sides, *Irie Jam* strengthens links between two crucial base audiences.

Meantime, some reggae acts that languish in the U.S. market are booming in Europe, Latin America and Asia. While majors wait for reggae to catch a fire in North America, they might take a cue from the music's universal point of view, broadening their focus from strictly North America to include the entire world.

Get Creative or Pay Up

Rhythm Vibes
November 1996

Did you see the notice on copyright infringements published by Tuff Gong in the Jamaican newspapers earlier this year? It was warning the copycats against "unauthorized usage of any portion of the music and/or lyrics of these songs" and suggests that "all music recordings originating in the Caribbean must be cleared (licensed) by Tuff Gong International Limited prior to its release." Finally, somebody has the courage. But can they back it up?

It does not take a rocket scientist to figure that, especially in this "cultural renaissance," a lot of artists will have a lot to answer for. Maybe it is action like this that will spur artists to strive to be even greater than Bob. Let the true artists begin to emerge.

In these days of production-line reggae, all it requires to turn out a "culture song" is to take an existing rhythm track, a piece from Bob, a little piece from a church hymn, and "yow" you have a hit.

Aside from certain early singles which were rereleased on albums, the Wailers never did two songs on any one rhythm. That required work. This has been the case with many of the older artists. Reason: In the case of the Wailers, they were all musicians; the rest were either musicians themselves or worked with producers who used studio bands.

Basically, all of the "hits" of the eighties and nineties to date have been based on other's people's workmanship. Is it that the music is already made? That can't be for the same reason that the Wailers never did versions. Should the current crop of artists be made to pay for such blatant plagiarism? Depends.

Earlier this year Bunny Wailer was reported as denying an agreement in relation to a proposed release of Wailers music. According to the published report, Bunny promised that legal hostilities would be over only when the Wailers were given the respect, rights and justice due to them by any party, company or organization that has access to any of the group's work. Then there was the action by Bob Andy against Penthouse Records even earlier, which was settled in Bob's favor.

If the Jamaican government cannot begin to set an example, by vigorously enforcing the copyright laws on the books, then it is going to demand that individual labels and artists take the bull by the horn. Such actions can only benefit the music and help bring back food to the tables of the countless musicians in the country who are being denied by the computer-aided productions.

This highlights another existing fact: Only a very few music publishers would be involved in whatever proceeding would be instigated, compared to the vast number of producers and artist/producers, most of whom have been around between ten and fifteen years.

It also shows that during the same period, despite the hype and glamour, since Bob flew away the music has not gone much further; and this is despite the Grammys.

So, a little action to get the creative juices flowing. Bring back the studio bands; improve artist development, leading to more and better tours, more sales, and more impact abroad. That can't be all that bad.

PART FOUR

SKA

From *Reggae, Rastas and Rudies:*
Style and the Subversion of Form

DICK HEBDIGE

Occasional paper of the Centre for Contemporary Cultural Studies,
University of Birmingham, England
1974

Before "ska" (the forerunner of reggae), Jamaica had no distinctive music of its own.
The satirical and articulate calypsos of Trinidad were processed and pruned down
before being played to the tourists. Jamaican calypso or "mento," which developed in
the 1950s, was never more than a mild emasculated form derived from what had
originally been very potent stuff indeed. Beyond this and Harry Belafonte, the North
Coast did the samba to the strains of Willy Lopez and his swish Latin orchestra. But
in West Kingston, R&B, imported from America, began to attract attention. Men like
Duke Reid were quick to recognise the potential for profit and launched themselves
as disc jockeys forming the flamboyant aristocracy of the shantytown slums, and the
era of the sound system began.

Survival in the highly competitive world of the backyard discos, where rival disc
jockeys vied for the title of the "boss-sound," demanded alertness, ingenuity and
enterprise, and, as American R&B began to lose its original impetus in the late fifties,
a new expedient was tried by the more ambitious DJs who branched out into record
production themselves. Usually an instrumental recording was all that was necessary,
and the DJ would improvise the lyrics (usually simple and formulaic: "work-it-out,
work-it-out," etc.) during "live" performances. Certain important precedents were set
by these early recordings.

Firstly, the musicians were generally selected from the vast bank of unemployed
labour; used for one session, paid a pittance and returned to the streets. The ruthless
exploitation of young talent continues unabated in certain sections of the record
industry. Secondly, the music remains, even now, essentially tied to the sound
systems and is designed principally for dancing. Thirdly, the tradition of "scatting"

across a simple repetitive backing with impromptu lyrics continues to produce some of the more interesting and exciting reggae. Lastly, and most important, the "ska" beat made its debut on these early unlabelled discs. Ska is a kind of jerky shuffle played on an electric guitar with the treble turned right up. The emphasis falls on the upbeat rather than on the offbeat as in R&B, and is accentuated by the bass, drums and bass sections (trombones were an indispensable part of early ska). Ska is structurally a back-to-front version of R&B.

Once again, as with language and religion, distortion of the original form appears to be deliberate, as well as inevitable; inversion seems to denote appropriation, signifying that a cultural transaction has taken place. However, the alchemy which turned soul into ska was by no means simple. The imported music interacted with the established subterranean forms of Jamaica. The Kumina, Big Drum, and burra dances had long since resurrected the rhythms of Africa, and the context in which these forms were evolved directly determined their shape and content and left an indelible mark on the semantics of ska.

The burra dance was particularly significant. Played on the bass, funde and repeater drums, the burra constituted an open celebration of criminality. Since the early 1930s it had been the custom for the inhabitants of the West Kingston slums to welcome discharged prisoners back into the communities with the burra. The music consolidated local allegiances and criminal affiliations at the expense of commitments to the larger society beyond the slums.

As the locksmen began to clash regularly with the police in the late forties, a liaison developed between locksmen and hardened criminals. The dreadlocks of the Rastamen were absorbed into the arcane iconography of the outcast, and many Rastas openly embraced the outlaw status which the authorities seemed determined to thrust upon them. Still more made permanent contacts in the Jamaican underworld whilst serving prison terms for ganja offences. This drift toward a consciously antisocial and anarchist position was assisted by the police who attempted to discredit the movement by labeling all locksmen as potentially dangerous criminals who were merely using mysticism as a front for their subversive activities. As has been observed so often elsewhere, predictions such as these have a tendency to find fulfillment, and men like Woppy King, who was later executed for murder and rape, joined the Rastafarian fraternity and affected the extravagant style of the dreadlocks.

In time the locksmen took over the burra dance completely, calling the burra drums "akete drums." Inevitably the criminal ambiance which surrounded the music survived the transference, and the Niyabingi dance which replaced the burra translated the original identification with criminal values into an open commitment to terrorist violence. The crime and music of West Kingston were thus linked in a subtle and enduring symbiosis; and they remained yoked together even after the infiltration of soul. Moreover, the locksmen continued to direct the new music, and to involve themselves creatively in its production.

Meanwhile a survey in 1957 had revealed that 18 percent of the labour force was without work, and, as the Doxey Report was to state twelve years later, it had now become conceivable that "many young persons will pass through the greater part of their lives having never been regularly employed." The embittered youth of West Kingston, abandoned by the society which claimed to serve them, were ready to look to the locksman for explanations, to listen to his music and emulate his posture of withdrawal. Thus it should hardly surprise us to find that behind the swagger and the sex, the violence and the cool of the "rude boy" music of the sixties stands the visionary Rastaman with his commodious rhetoric and his all-embracing metaphors.

And so, ska was resilient, armoured music; "rough and tough" in more ways than one. Its inception guaranteed it against serious interference from above or manipulation at the level of meaning. The stigma which was originally attached to ska by the official arbiters of good taste in Jamaica relates directly to the criminal connotations of the burra dance, and the early attempts on the part of the government at manufacturing a national sound were frankly unsuccessful.

Eddie Seaga, who set up one of the first record companies in Jamaica (West Indies Records), was one of those who tried to promote ska to the world as a representative (and therefore respectable) "native" form. His admission to the Labour Cabinet encouraged him in this project, and he recruited Byron Lee and the Dragonaires, a "class act" which was currently playing the North Coast, and sent them first to West Kingston to study the new music and then to New York to present the finished product. The music suffered somewhat in the translation. Byron Lee was too polished to play ska properly, and raw ska was too "rude."

So, ska was left more or less to its own devices. Before I attempt a critical analysis of the content of the music, I shall briefly summarize the chronology. In the early sixties the record industry developed under the auspices of Seaga at West Indies Records, Ken Khouri at Federal Studios and Chris Blackwell, a white man and son of a plantation owner, at "Island" Records. But Blackwell did not confine himself to the West Indies; he soon went on to exploit the market in England, where more records were being sold to the homesick rudies than to the native Jamaicans. Blackwell bought premises in the Kilburn Road in London and began to challenge the monopoly which the Bluebeat label had managed to acquire over the West Indian record market in Britain.

Blackwell's triumph over Bluebeat was publicly acknowledged in 1964, when he launched the first nationally popular ska record, "My Boy Lollipop," sung with an endearing nasal urgency by the sixteen-year-old Millie Small. Blackwell set up another label, Trojan, which dealt with most of the British releases and left Lee Gopthal to supervise the distribution from South London.[1] Then, sometime in the summer of 1966, the music altered recognisably and ska modulated into rock steady. The horns were given less emphasis or were dropped altogether, and the sound became somewhat slower, more somnambulant and erotic. The bass began to dominate, and as rock steady, in its turn, became heavier, it became known as reggae. Over the years reggae attracted such a huge following that Michael Manley used a reggae song, "Better Must Come," in the 1972 election campaign.[2] His People's National Party won by an overwhelming majority.

But this does not mean that the music had been defused; for simultaneously, during this period, the rude boys were evolving a visual style which did justice to the tessellated structure of ska. The American-soul element was reflected most clearly in the self-assured demeanour, the sharp flashy clothes, the "jive-ass" walk which the street boys affected. The politics of ghetto pimpery found their way into the street-talk of shantytown Jamaica, and every rude boy, fresh from some poor rural outback, soon began to wheel and deal with the best of them in the ubiquitous bars of Ghost Town and Back o' Wall. The rude boy lived for the luminous moment, playing dominoes as though his life depended on the outcome—a big-city hustler with nothing to lose. And, all the time, rock steady, ska and reggae gave him the means with which to move effortlessly—without even thinking. Cool, that distant and indefinable quality, became almost abstract, almost metaphysical, intimating a stylish kind of stoicism—survival and something more.

And, of course, there were the clashes with the police. The ganja, the guns, and the "pressure" produced a steady stream of rude boys desperate to test their strength against the law, and the judges replied with longer and longer sentences. In the words of Michael Thomas, every rudie was "dancing in the dark" with ambitions to be "the coolest Johnny Too Bad on Beeston Street." This was the chaotic period of ska, and Prince Buster lampooned the Bench and sang of Judge Dread, who on side one sentences weeping rude boys ("Order! Order! Rude boys don't cry!") to five hundred years and ten thousand lashes, and on side two grants them a pardon and throws a party to celebrate their release. The dreary mechanics of crime and punishment are reproduced endlessly in tragicomic form on these early records, and the ska classics, like the music of the burra which preceded them, were often simple celebrations of deviant and violent behaviour. Sound system rivalries, street fights,[3] sexual encounters,[4] boxing matches,[5] horse races[6] and experiences in prison[7] were immediately converted into folksong and stamped with the ska beat. The disinherited Dukes and Earls, the Popes and Princes of early ska came across as music hall gangsters, and Prince Buster warned in deadly earnest, with a half-smile, that "Al Capone's guns don't argue."[8]

But in the world of "007,"[9] where the rude boys "loot" and "shoot" and "wail" while "out on probation," "the policemen get taller" and "the soldiers get longer" by the hour; and in the final confrontation the authorities must always triumph. So there is always one more confrontation on the cards, and there is always a higher authority still, and that is where Judgment Day works itself back into reggae as the Rastas sing of an end to "sufferation" on the day when Judge Dread will be consumed by his own fire.

The Rastafarian influence on reggae had been strong since the earliest days—ever since Don Drummond and Rico Rodriguez had played tunes like "Father East," "Addis Ababa," "Tribute to Marcus Garvey" and "Reincarnation" to a receptive audience. And even Prince Buster, the "boss," the Main Man, the individualist par excellence, at the height of the anarchic rude boy period could exhort his followers in "Free Love" to "act true," to "speak true," to "learn to love each other," advising the dissident rudies that "truth is our best weapon" and that "our unity will conquer." In the burlesque "Ten Commandments" Prince Buster is typically ambivalent, prosely-tizing and preaching and poking fun all at the same time; but the internalization of God which marks the Rasta Creed is there nonetheless, behind all the blustering chauvinism:

> *These are the ten commandments of man given to woman*
> *By Me, Prince Buster, through the inspiration of I.*

As the decade wore on, the music shifted away from America toward Ethiopia, and the rude boys moved with the music. Racial and class loyalties were intensified, and, as the music matured, it made certain crucial breaks with R&B, which had provided the original catalyst. It became more "ethnic," less frenzied,[10] more thoughtful, and the political metaphors and dense mythology of the locksmen began to insinuate themselves more obtrusively into the lyrics. Groups like the Wailers, the Upsetters, the Melodians and the Lionaires emerged with new material which was often revo-lutionary, and was always intrinsically Jamaican.

Some rude boys began to grow the dreadlocks, and many took to wearing woolen stocking caps often in the green, gold and red of the Ethiopian flag to proclaim their alienation from the West. This transformation (if such a subtle change of gear deserves such apocalyptic terminology) went beyond style to modify and channel the rude boys' consciousness of class and colour. Without overstressing the point, there was a trend away from the undirected violence and competitive individualism of the early sixties, toward a more articulate and informed anger; and if crime continued to offer the only solution available, then there were now distinctions to be made. A rude boy quoted by Rex Nettleford in *Mirror, Mirror* exhibits a "higher consciousness" in his comments on violence:

> It's not the suffering brother you should really stick up, it is these big merchants that have all these twelve places . . . with the whole heap of different luxurious facilities.

He goes on:

> What we really want is this equal rights and justice. Everyman have a good living condition, good schooling, and then I feels things will be much better.

At the risk of oversimplifying the issue (and overstating my case), I would suggest that, as the Rastas themselves began to turn away from violent solutions to direct the new aesthetic, the rude boys, steeped in ska, soon acquired the locksmen's term of reference, and became the militant arm of the Rasta movement. Thus, as the music evolved and passed into the hands of the locksmen, there was an accompanying expansion of class and colour consciousness throughout the West Indian community.

Of course, I would not isolate the emergence of a "higher consciousness" from larger developments in the ghettoes and on the campuses of the United States. Nor would I dismiss the stimulative effect of the Jamaican Black Power movement, which by the late sixties was being led by the middle-class students and was clustered around the University of the West Indies.[11] But I would stress the unique way in which these external developments were mediated to the rude boy (in South London's Brixton as well as Kingston's Back o' Wall), how they were digested, interpreted and reassembled by the omniscient Rasta Logos situated at the heart of reggae music. In spite of Manley and Seaga, reggae remained intact. It was never dirigible, protected as it was by language, by colour and by a culture which had been forced, in its very inception, to cultivate secrecy and to elaborate defences against the intrusions of the Master Class.

Moreover, the form of reggae itself militated against outside interference and guaranteed a certain amount of autonomy. The dialectical process which lay behind the formation of reggae enabled it to escape the limitations of a Western aesthetic; and, if it imposed its own boundaries, then these were never immutably fixed. So, reggae reversed the established pattern of pop music[12] by dictating a strong repetitive bassline which communicated directly to the body and allowed the singer to "scat" across the undulating surface of the rhythm. The music and the words are synchronised in good reggae and coordinated at a level which transcends meaning and eludes a fixed interpretation. Linguistic patterns become musical patterns; both merge with the metabolism until sound becomes abstract, meaning nonspecific.

Thus, on the "heavy" fringes of reggae, beyond the lucid but literal denunciations of the Wailers, Count Ossie and the Mystic Revelation of Rastafari condemn the ways of Babylon implicitly, taking reggae right back to Africa, and the rudie DJs (like Big Youth, Niney, I-Roy and U-Roy) threaten to undermine language itself with syncopated creole scansion and an eye for the inexpressible. Language (foreign in the first place, if we really want to be retrospective) abdicates to body-talk, belief and intuition; and, by definition, reggae resists definition.[13] The form, then, is inherently subversive, and it was in the area of form that the Jamaican street-boys made their most important innovations.

NOTES

1. In Brixton, for instance, 80 percent of the black population came from Jamaica, and the record shops in the area soon began to specialise in bluebeat and ska.

2. Manley also won support in the rural areas, where a Holy Roller type of religion still lingers on, by appearing in public carrying a stick which he called the Rod of Correction with which he promised to beat out all duppies (ghosts) and drive injustice away.

3. See "Earthquake," in which Prince Buster challenges a rival to do battle on Orange Street.

4. See every other record of this period.

5. See Niney's "Fiery Foreman Meets Smokey Joe Frazier."

6. See the Pioneers' "Long Shot Kick the Bucket," about a horse which dies with everybody's money on it.

7. See "54–46" by the Maytals; this is the number Toots Hibbert was given when imprisoned on a ganja charge.

8. Lyrics from "Al Capone" by Prince Buster.

9. From "Shanty Town" by Desmond Dekker.

10. Cunchyman says that the Americans "don't know how to move slow" (*Rolling Stone,* July 19, 1973).

11. *Abeng,* the official organ of the Black Power movement in Jamaica, translated Rastafarian "metaphorics" straight into Marxian dialectics. Economic analysis jostled uneasily against the intensely personal testimonies of individual "sufferers" in the columns of the paper.

12. Though "heavy rock" also has an emphatic and hypnotic bassline, there is nothing equivalent to the "scat" in rock. Some modern jazz plays with language at this level, but this jazz is produced principally by black musicians (Albert Ayler, Roland Kirk, Pharoah Sanders, John Coltrane, etc.).

13. In a similar way, the syntax of "heavy" soul obviates the need for lexical meaning. James Brown looks at the relationship between "the pronunciation and the realisation" in "Stoned to the Bone" and gives a catalogue of the various words used to denote "mind-power" ("vibes," "E.S.P.," "positive thinking," etc.) but discards them all by discarding language itself: "But I call it, What it is what it is." This tautologous equation is repeated again and again until it synchronizes with the strong, repetitive backing and is eventually absorbed.

The Sounds of Young Jamaica

BRIAN ARNOLD

Ska-tastrophe
December 1995

In April of 1964 the Jamaican government sent a small troupe of ska artists to the New York World's Fair in the hope of promoting tourism. Singers Millie Small, Prince Buster, Jimmy Cliff, the Blues Busters and Eric "Monty" Morris were backed by Byron Lee's Dragonaires. Other popular artists, like the rude boy Wailers and the ganja smoking Skatalites, did not attend because they did not possess the proper image the Tourism Council wanted to project. Accompanying the performers was Jamaica's own Carol Joan Crawford, holder of the 1963 Miss World title, to demonstrate the ska dance for the American audience.

While the effect this envoy had on American culture was minimal, the same cannot be said for its influence on the A&R men of U.S. record companies. Over the next few years every major label tried to imitate the success that bluebeat music (as it was known overseas) was achieving in England. Although most of the attempts were somewhat tame and uninspired, there are a few of these records worth tracking down. In this article I'll discuss U.S. releases of sixties ska.

By far the most well known artist in the World's Fair lineup was Millie Small. At that time she had a worldwide hit with "My Boy Lollipop," released on the Smash label in the States. Recorded in 1963 by Chris Blackwell for his Island label, the song went on to sell an amazing six million copies. Smash released an album with the same title that featured a cover of Derrick Harriot's "Sugar Dandy" as well as some R&B and soul standards. All this material is classic bluebeat. After the release of her second Smash single, "Sweet William," Millie's career sank as quickly as it had risen, although she has a soul single, "My Street," available on the Brit label.

Then billed as Jamaica's No. 1 band, Byron Lee and the Dragonaires started as a calypso tourist act playing in fancy clubs and resorts. They soon graduated to ska music after seeing its popularity rise in the shantytowns. Still, the ska that Byron Lee produced always retained that polished and professional character. The Dragonaires were foremost a show band, and the music as a result is not always the most inspired ska.

In 1964 Byron Lee struck a recording deal with Atlantic Records that resulted in the Dragonaires releasing tracks as the Ska Kings. The most easy-to-find record by the Ska Kings is the "Jamaica Ska" single. On the flip side is Monty Morris with a rerecorded version of "Oil in My Lamp" that includes additional backing vocals not appearing on the Jamaican release. Most used-record shops with a large inventory should have a copy. Atlantic released a second Ska Kings single with two mediocre instrumentals. Also available is the *Jamaica Ska* album that features various artists backed by Lee's band. It's pretty tough to find and not really worth the effort.

Even before the World's Fair, Asnes Records—a doo-wop label from New York— had released a single by the Jiving Juniors in 1961 as an attempt to cash in on the vocal-group craze then sweeping the States. The members of the group were living in New York City and flying back to the island for recording sessions. However, the U.S. single "Moonlight Lover" was recorded in New York and lacks the stripped-down, soulful feeling of their Jamaican recordings.

Occasionally American labels would take songs that had already proven themselves on the Jamaican charts and try to copy that success. Such was the case with two early vocal duos. Joe Higgs and Roy Wilson, who recorded as Higgs & Wilson, had a massive hit in 1959 on the Jamaican WIRL label with "Manny, Oh." The single sold thirty thousand copies on the island. Time Records picked up the song and released it here in 1961. A few years later the Blues Busters (Lloyd Campbell and Phillip James) struck gold when they released "Behold" on Byron Lee's BMN label. Although the single sold a reported one hundred thousand copies in Jamaica, it didn't fare as well when it was released in the States by Capitol Records.

THE BLUE BEAT IS HERE reads the sleeve of Prince Buster's 1967 album on RCA Victor, and the eleven tracks on *Ten Commandments* more than make up for all the previous lackluster U.S. releases. The entire album is pure ska and rock steady. If you locate a copy, it could set you back a bit, but it's well worth it. Available in both mono and stereo, the mono pressing is superior. The song "Ten Commandments (From Man to Woman)" is available as a single on the Phillips label. (The answer record by Princess Buster, on RCA Victor, can be found with some patience; a rarer pressing on the King label also exists, with a Byron Lee instrumental on the flip side.)

The Prince's three singles from 1964 are the ones to really look out for. First we have "Jamaica Ska" on Amy Records. This is not the Ska Kings song but a version of Buster's "Chinaman Ska." Absolutely classic. Next up is "That Lucky Old Sun" (aka "Wash Wash") on Atlantic, credited to the Ska Busters. Recorded in England, not Jamaica, this still has a classic sound. Last is an unknown and extremely rare single on Stellar Records. I have never seen a copy, only the label and a number in some catalog once.

Another record worth finding is *The Real Jamaica Ska* on Epic Records. Coproduced by Curtis Mayfield, this 1964 compilation album has two ska tracks by a young

Jimmy Cliff. An original copy will cost a fortune, so you might want to settle for the budget-line CD reissue released a couple of years ago by Sony Music.

Although it's not ska, collectors of Jamaican music will be interested in the MGM single by Jackie Opel released around 1965. Opel is best known for his incredible ska recordings for Top Deck and Studio One in Jamaica. Featuring two of his most well-known ballads, "Shelter the Storm" and "You Gotta Cry" (aka "Cry Me a River"), this single may exist only as a promotional record.

Also of interest to collectors is the album *Big Bamboo* by the Hiltonaires. This hotel band—who claim to be the originators of "ska-lip-so" music—recorded their first album, *Ska-motion in Ska-lip-so,* at Studio One and released it in Jamaica on WIRL Records. While *Big Bamboo,* on the U.S.-based Hillary Records, is not as good as that first album, when located it should cost you only a few bucks.

While this is certainly not a complete listing, hopefully it will aid collectors and fans in their search for Jamaican ska records.

The Ska Above, the Beat Below

JAY COCKS

Time
7 April 1980

Not *boom, boom, boom, boom.* It is more like *chi-boom, chi-boom, chi-boom.* Come down easy on the offbeat, like a rhythmic shrug of the shoulders. Kind of bluesy. Kind of calypso. Kind of fun.

Ska—a back-pocket onomatopoeia for the distinctive sound of the beat—means no harm, carries no heavy freight, sets out to make you happy and keep you dancing. Ska is the no-account stepfather of reggae, the blues-inflected Jamaican soul popularized Stateside by Jimmy Cliff and Bob Marley and seen to splendid advantage in *The Harder They Come,* one of the best and most popular cult films of the '70s. Reggae shouldered a lot of political burden and social outrage, sometimes sounded almost introverted in its island concerns and religious visions. By contrast, ska is flat-out party music played faster than reggae and meant to be, if not frivolous, then feckless.

Reggae has already been absorbed into the English punk scene. The Clash perform their own blistering versions of reggae tunes. But a group called the Specials, as well as their allied band, Madness, have dusted off ska and made it shine like new. Both bands have had hit singles and albums on their home turf. Now the records have been receiving an encouraging amount of FM airplay here, while Specials and Madness concerts around America have been enthusiastically attended by disenfranchised new wavers and punks without portfolio. Ska may or may not be the latest crest of the new wave, but it is at least clear that the Specials and Madness could safely join in a proud chorus of Stranger Cole's 1963 ska tune, "We Are Rolling."

Stranger's original version, along with fifteen other vintage ska songs, is available on a recently released compilation called *Intensified!* (Mango Records), which offers some interesting source material to set against the carnival modifications of the young English revivalists. Most of the *Intensified!* tunes have a loping energy, even when the recording quality is dense and almost smothering, as if the musicians were trying to play their way out of a bowl of tapioca. Both the Madness and Specials albums (the latter produced by the sullen genie of punk, Elvis Costello) are careful to preserve a spontaneous sound that just skirts being primitive. The groups rock a little harder than their forebears too. "We were the first band which wanted to combine punk and reggae," says Jerry "General Dankey" Dammers of the Specials, "because we liked them both." Bass player Horace "Sir Horace Gentleman" Panter adds, "Both were rebel music." Notes Jerry: "Humble beginnings, what?"

Humble enough for musical comfort. The seven members of Madness are middle-class kids from north London, who range in age from eighteen to twenty-three. The seven Specials all hail from Coventry, in central England, and will remain grounded right there because, according to Panter, "it's a small town and we know all the kids." "People there know we're nothing special," adds Dammers, who is the son of an Anglican minister. "It's important to keep on the same level as the people who buy your records."

Out of a grand total of fourteen members, only two—vocalist Neville Staples and guitarist Lynval Golding, both of the Specials—are black, yet these bands have forged some common musical bond with the island music, doing it honor but making it their own in much the same way that the early Rolling Stones, the Animals and the Beatles excelled in revisions of American rhythm and blues at a similar point in their careers. The Specials flirt with social commentary and take on racial injustice in "Doesn't Make It Alright," whose straightforward lyric and fine-tuned beat steer way wide of solemnity. Specials and Madness members even dress in good-humored approximation of the Kingston "rude boys" of the '60s, from the careless cuffs of their pegged pants up to the porkpie hats that sit on their heads like a street hustler's version of cap and bells. In performance, both bands leap about in transports of benign dementia. The highlight of a Madness show is a ska version of *Swan Lake* that features a couple of roadies conking their noggins together like a couple of billy goats in a brawl.

The effect of all this is much less that of a musical masquerade than of a soulful affiliation of outsiders who share a taste for a strong dance beat and a sense of fun as strong as all that ganja Bob Marley goes on about. Besides roots, both Madness and Specials hold similar suspicions about mainstream rock. "Me mum had a lot of Beatles records," admits Madness organ player Mike Barson. "I reckon they're pretty good, but a bit wimpy." Observes the Specials' Panter: "I think the Rolling Stones have been playing 'Honky Tonk Women' for the past ten years. It must be quite tedious for them." To stave off occupational hazards, the Specials have formed their own label, 2 Tone, which has no offices, no secretaries and no official phone number, but which nevertheless has managed to sign up a diversity of new bands like the Beat and the Body Snatchers. 2 Tone, in fact, released Madness' first record, and will continue to circulate all new efforts by the Specials, who have just gone back into the studio to cut their second album.

Says Madness drummer Dan "Woody Woods" Woodgate: "Our music is spontaneous. If we knew what we were going to do next week, it wouldn't be worth it." For the new Specials effort, Dammers promises a little more experimentation and a wider range of styles, even speculates in a bemused fashion on a possible wedding of ska, reggae and "lift music—the stuff you hear in America in McDonald's and department stores. It's so absurd." Step back, watch the closing doors. Going up.

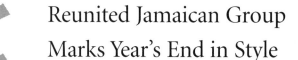

Reunited Jamaican Group
Marks Year's End in Style

FERNANDO GONZALEZ

The Miami Herald
30 December 1994

Before rock steady and reggae there was ska. And much, much before the Police, the Clash, UB40 or Bim Skala Bim there were the Skatalites, a group of studio musicians who backed up Bob Marley, Jimmy Cliff and Desmond Dekker and laid the foundation for much of the music that has come out of Jamaica over the past thirty years.

The Skatalites survived tragedy, breakup and the vagaries of pop music fashion. Now they have a new album, and Saturday night they celebrate in style with a New Year's Eve show at the Marlin Hotel in South Beach.

Saxophonist Tommy McCook, leader and founding member of the Skatalites, recalled in a recent interview how the group was formed.

"We were all session musicians, and people liked what we did and were always asking who did what on the records, so I proposed to form a band," he explained. The name of the band is a blend of *ska* and *satellites,* a passion of the day.

"Satellites was the thing happening at the time," McCook recalls. "It was 1964, America was trying to go to the moon, these satellites were always orbiting the earth—but I thought it shouldn't be Satellites but Skatalites because we were playing ska."

Ska—a bright propulsive style with a sensual bounce—draws from rhythm and blues, jazz and Jamaican folk music and is paced by a choppy guitar and punchy brass accents. It was created in 1959 by a group that included future Skatalites trombonist Rico Rodriguez and saxophonist Roland Alphonso.

The term *ska* was invented "before my time," explains McCook. "It was introduced by [bassist] Cluet Johnson, the leader of the Blues Blasters. His nickname was Skavoovee. That's the way he would greet everyone—'What's happenin', Skavoovee?'—and since he was instrumental in creating the music, that's the way it had to be called."

Some have compared the Skatalites to the MGs, the studio band behind the great Stax/Volt hits, or the Chess or Motown session players. But McCook, Alphonso, the late trombonist Don Drummond and most of the original Skatalites were not R&B or blues aficionados but jazz musicians.

"I started in Big Band music," says McCook. "In 1943 I was playing American orchestrations, Count Basie, Glenn Miller, Duke Ellington, later Stan Kenton, Gene Krupa. The whole thing. But in the dance bands I played, especially in the Bahamas, the tourists didn't want to hear any jazz at all. They wanted to hear island music—rumbas, calypsos, whatever. The minute we started an American standard they would say, 'We don't want no American music, we just left that at home. We don't want that here.' But it was fine with me. By 1963 I was tired of it."

The group reworked Hollywood movie themes—"Guns of Navarone," "Exodus"—into improbable hits, headlined in hotels and worked as a backup band for up-and-comers such as the Wailers, Marcia Griffiths and Toots and the Maytals.

But on New Year's Eve 1965, disaster struck: Drummond murdered his wife in a fit of jealousy and was arrested and confined to a mental institution. He died in 1969. The Skatalites disbanded.

"Don was finished, and he was our featured artist, our most popular artist," says McCook. "People started leaving the group, there were all these things going on, tensions, so I said, 'Let's call it a day.'"

McCook organized his own band; rock steady and then reggae took center stage. The Skatalites did not reunite until the organizers of Sunsplash '83 suggested it, "to show the people where reggae came from," says McCook. It was a hit.

McCook moved to the United States in 1985, riding popularity brought on by neo-ska groups in the States and England, and the group has since toured North America, Japan, Europe. "We did 'Navarone' in Germany and the place almost came down. They knew the words. They were singing as we played. I was in awe."

The re-formed group, which features six original members, also recorded two albums: *Skavoovee* (1993) and *Hi-Bop Ska* (1994), which, coming full circle, features jazz luminaries such as Lester Bowie, David Murray and Steve Turre.

"I knew people would like the music if they got a chance to hear it," he says. "But this kind of response is unbelievable."

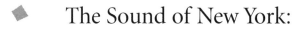

The Sound of New York:
Ska. Ska? Yes, Ska.

NEIL STRAUSS

The New York Times
27 October 1995

The hunt for thriving regional music scenes has become an important one in the record business. Music labels in New York regularly send talent scouts to places like San Diego and Louisville, Kentucky, to make deals with new cadres of bands hoping to replicate the success of the Seattle grunge scene that spawned Nirvana and Soundgarden and the Berkeley, California, punk scene that produced Green Day and Rancid. What most of these record companies do not consider, however, is that for a dozen years a scene has slowly been expanding right on their doorstep, and it is close to exploding. It is perhaps the only underground musical movement that New York can now call its own. T-shirts in record stores and cover artwork on compact discs proudly proclaim it in large letters: NYC SKA.

Ska is an odd-looking word: short, punchy, almost funny. So is the music at times, a light, bouncy, horn-infused grandfather of reggae. (The word itself comes from the sound a guitar makes.) Ska has arrived in three musical waves, beginning in Jamaica in the 1950s and '60s as a homegrown version of rhythm and blues performed by collectives of former jazz musicians like the Skatalites. The music traveled to England along with Jamaican blue-collar laborers, quickening its tempo as it mixed with punk and working-class youth sounds in the 1970s. A second wave of interracial ska bands, including the Specials, the Selecter and the English Beat, first appeared on England's 2 Tone label, registering in America as a quick spark on the pop charts. But that spark slowly ignited an international fire as New Yorkers like Rob "Bucket" Hingley (a veteran of the English movement) and Jeff Baker not only started bands like the Toasters and the Boilers, but also helped to establish a solid underground network, connecting ska groups in New York with ones in Brazil, Japan, Germany, Hawaii and elsewhere through newsletters, fan magazines and record labels.

"It was New York that galvanized the national scene with bands like the Toasters touring," said Mr. Hingley, who runs Moon, the premier ska label in the United States, in addition to playing guitar and singing in the twelve-year-old Toasters. "The music really hooks people once they finally hear it. First you meet a kid at a concert, next they have a band, then they're opening up for you and the next thing you know, you're putting out a record of theirs."

Five years ago, ska concerts in New York City were strictly underground events, where green-haired punks, skinheads and stylish ska fans known as rude boys danced to the holy triumvirate of New York ska bands: the Toasters, the Scofflaws and the N.Y. Citizens. Now there are concerts every weekend at downtown clubs like Wetlands, New Music Cafe, the Cooler and Coney Island High, and the audience is a broad, multiracial mix, where hippies meet skinheads and college jocks dance with rude boys.

"You used to know everybody in the scene in New York, if not personally, at least by face," said Mr. Baker, a former member of the hardcore band Murphy's Law who now plays in the ska bands Skinnerbox and the Stubborn All-Stars. "Now I look around and I see almost no one I know. It's not exclusively a rude boy and skinhead thing now. There are people from fifteen to fifty at the shows. And I know why: It's the only music that makes me dance without thinking about it."

BANDS AND MORE BANDS

Chris Zahn, who books concerts at Wetlands in the TriBeCa neighborhood of New York, said he had noticed not only an expanding audience for ska, but also an increasing number of people playing the music.

"What we have to do is package the ska shows, turn them into multiband nights with five or six groups," Zahn said. "There just seem to be bands coming out of nowhere. I'm getting tapes from all over the coast that even people involved in the ska community have never heard of. I had a ska band from Venezuela here the other night dropping off their tape, and there's an Argentine band interested in playing here."

"But as popular as ska is getting, it's still surprising how many people don't know it," he added. "On a typical Friday we get tons of phone calls about what's playing. When we say it's a ska show, there's always a pause and then we hear: 'Ska? What is ska?' We've gone so far as to say, 'Think of it as Jewish reggae: Imagine "Hava Nagilah" and then put some island rhythms in there.'"

Not every club in New York has such an open attitude toward ska. "I don't book ska shows anymore," said the manager of one club, who spoke only on the condition of anonymity. "If there aren't fights inside, you have nearby restaurants and neighbors complaining about skinheads loitering around with forty-ounce beer bottles in their hands."

But other club bookers and concertgoers say that fighting at ska shows is becoming a rarity. The attitude of ska music has always been one of having fun in the face of oppression, as encapsulated in a warning made famous by the Jamaican legend Prince Buster: "Enjoy yourself. It's later than you think."

At Wetlands this month, when the New York band the Slackers opened for the English 2 Tone band the Selecter, the scene was peaceful and friendly. With fast, shuffling guitar-strumming, infectious drumming on the offbeat and a horn section worthy of a sixties soul revue, the music had even the most awkward of club denizens skanking, or bouncing from leg to leg and swinging their arms.

Where most rock bands get by with three or four members, ska bands may have as many as a dozen. In addition to guitars, bass and drums, they often have an entire horn section. These groups sometimes find older players from the jazz or Latin music worlds; other times they recruit young people who have just graduated from their high school jazz band. Either way, it makes for eclectic music. At eleven members, the Slackers are among the more diverse and unpredictable bands in New York.

There are many different styles of ska being played today, but the main schism is between the bands that try to blend it with punk and hardcore music and the traditionalists who look back to Jamaica for a purer sound.

It is this first style that fans and record executives alike predict will make ska part of the fabric of popular music. The Mighty Mighty Bosstones, from Boston, performed this summer on Lollapalooza, the alternative-rock package tour, exposing new audiences to high-energy ska-core, as the group's hard, fast hybrid is sometimes called. More recently, the California punk band Rancid (which was formed from the ashes of Operation Ivy, a ska-influenced band) put out a ska single called "Time Bomb," which has been played heavily on MTV and pop radio.

But the Slackers have their own dream of a slower, rootsier ska finding success. "The more modern stuff is what they're expecting to break through in the wake of Rancid," said Marcus Geard, who plays bass in the Slackers at night and delivers trees during the day. "But I think the VH1 audience is a perfect traditional ska audience. I think they dig the groove and the vibe more; they're more sophisticated and don't get put off by Latin and jazz influences. The beat's infectious, and then the other influences make it more interesting."

INVESTING IN A GENRE

Profile Records in New York has become one of the biggest American record labels to make an investment in New York ska. Its rock division, Another Planet, recently signed the Stubborn All-Stars, a rotating New York supergroup with an old-time sound featuring members of the Slackers, the Toasters, the Insteps and Skinnerbox, along with the tenor saxophonist from the original Skatalites. The label has also signed the Insteps and is courting one of the New York ska scene's brightest hopes, Mephiskapheles.

"Ska is probably the biggest underground network going right now," said Fred Feldman, the general manager of Another Planet Records. "Moon Records has a 15,000-name direct-marketing list, and the Toasters are selling at least 25,000 to 30,000 records now, most of it through nontraditional retail outlets. I think the bigger labels are still waiting to see what happens with this Rancid song and to see how Green Day does with the ska band it signed to its 510 label, the Dance Hall Crashers. If any of it becomes huge, then you'll see a feeding frenzy."

Many bands, however, remain skeptical. For a long time some musical pundits have written off ska as creatively defunct without ever having listened to the stylistic extremes of the music, which range from the swing- and bebop-influenced instrumentals of the New York Ska-Jazz Ensemble to the industrial electronic ska of World Service. As Mr. Baker said, "One of the strengths of ska is that the foundation is so simple but so effective that it can endure a lot of changes but still maintain a relationship to the original style."

Nonetheless, Mikal Reich of Mephiskapheles added: "Ska is almost the marketing kiss of death. We've been talking to record labels and they're always telling us they don't know how to market ska; they don't know who to sell it to. I used to think people in the record industry were barracudas and would jump on anything. Here you've got Rancid with a ska single in MTV's Buzz Bin and I still have to spell *ska* to people over the phone."

Steve Shafer, who is in charge of promotion at Moon, speculates that one reason for ska's obscurity is that it is stereotyped as a revival. "What happened with ska was that the 2 Tone revival was labeled as a rehash of the Jamaican sound, and critics couldn't see it as a reexamination and reinvention of that kind of music," he said. "There was punk and anger and frustration in it. And now it's still growing and going off in different directions: ska punk, ska-core, rootsy stuff that sounds like it came out of the sixties. We have our *Spawn of Skarmageddon* compilation coming out, and there are forty-three bands on it from all over the U.S., and none of them sound the same."

BEYOND THE CLUBS

Ska is not just a club event in New York anymore. In February, Moon Records opened a store in New York's East Village, selling records, T-shirts and books. It also serves as a general clearinghouse for information on concerts and on ska lore, usually courtesy of a counterman, Noah Wildman, who is working on a book on ska.

And for more than a decade, rude boys up and down the East Coast have been buying their Doc Marten boots and Fred Perry shirts at 99X, also in the East Village. Rude boys were originally unemployed youths-turned-gangsters from Jamaica's shantytowns who dressed in the latest clean-cut fashions to intimidate and impress. Their narrow-brimmed porkpie hats, close-shaven haircuts, wraparound sunglasses, skinny ties and sharkskin suits with tapered legs have survived in ska wear today, as have the checkerboard patterns (symbolizing black and white unity) of England's 2 Tone look.

"Whenever there's a big show in New York, the store gets packed because all these people come into town from all over," said Alex Pietropinto, who works at 99X. "Their style hasn't changed. You can look at pictures of people thirty years ago, and see a rude boy now, and they look the same."

Another factor that has helped ska endure is the word itself. The word *ska* can be combined with almost anything. There have been Skalapalooza tours and Skampilation records; this weekend there's a Skalloween concert in the East Village, and in December, New York is to have its first Skanukkah concert.

"We thought we'd exhausted all the variations we could come up with on the word ska," Mr. Zahn of Wetlands said. "But then last week we booked a Skanksgiving show."

The New Old Ska:
Reverence or Retrowank?

NOAH WILDMAN

One Man's Ska Annual
Summer 1995

All that is old is new again, and all that is new becomes . . . unfashionable. The latest trend in ska music is not only a healthy reverence for the traditional sound of the Skatalites and early Coxsone Dodd, but taking the original hit sound wholesale to produce new music.

Many of today's newer, less-known ska bands play strongly traditional-influenced sounds: New York's Stubborn All-Stars, Slackers, Bluebeats, Ska-Jazz Ensemble and Insteps; Boston's Allstonians; California's Hepcat and Jump With Joey; Germany's Yebo; and more. Why is this?

The most obvious answer is that it is a reaction to where ska has gone since the late 1980s. The British label 2 Tone started the original urge to combine the catchy dance rhythm with rock and pop music, and latter-day ska has followed that musical ethos to a logical conclusion: the fragmented genre-blending of Skankin' Pickle and the heavy-metal ska-slam of the Bosstones.

Both bands reside in a popular idea of ska, but neither band actually plays "ska" in the proper sense—they play fusions of music that involve ska. The bands realize this, and shy away from being pegged as a "ska band," because that would be like writing the ingredients label for Doritos and leaving out the last twenty chemical preservatives.

Today's established American ska bands play a ska blend that resembles the 2 Tone model: the Toasters, Bim Skala Bim, Dance Hall Crashers, Let's Go Bowling and (Canadian) King Apparatus. In a cultural sense, these bands fit snugly into the "ska" label but, like 2 Tone, musically bear only a strong stamp of traditional ska, as a son resembles his father.

Part of the fun of becoming a ska fan is joining the elite club—one of the few in-the-know herberts who can't believe that more people don't dig it. Whether your subculture choices run toward rude, skin or mod, or you're one of those New Age ska types with the checkered sneakers and plaid everything and a tuft of hair poking out of the top of your forehead, ska music has been a calling card of the scene since Rob Hingley decided to start jamming the ska on the Lower East Side in NYC back in '83. Small, hip, cool, underground.

Dig the worms and grubs out from under the ground and place them in the hot sun, they shrivel and die. Ska is picking up momentum in the overground. A semi-major label, Continuum, put out a compilation of the bigger ska bands around today that has since been bouncing around the *Billboard* reggae charts. *Details* magazine has declared ska the next big thing (or should I say the next big thing to be embraced, fucked with and spat back out, à la grunge). Moon Records, the largest indie to concentrate solely on ska, has expanded enough to open the first storefront/office that sells ska and skinhead-related materials exclusively. The sun is shining on ska music today.

Forces like *Details* are good for the music as a whole—national exposure in a magazine broadens the audience and customer base for touring ska bands. On the other hand, the "small hip cool underground" image can only be blunted by expensive clothing lines that embrace retro-glam last week, mod-ska this week, and space-age jockstraps next. These forces have caused a rift in the very core of the national ska scene—the "third wave" ska musical style can now be seen as two distinct flavors, let's call them *modern* and *trad*.

The modern sound is what is represented on Continuum's compilation; it is what *Details* has predicted will be the next trend. Musically it's like 2 Tone—not a far cry from good ol' rock and roll. On the other hand, the trad sound harks back to what the 2 Tone phase irreverently copied and spoofed—the Big Band–derived sound of 1950s Jamaica. It is this new trad wave where a segment of the ska community who greatly value distinctiveness from the mainstream get to keep their "hip cool underground" credentials.

Or is that a bit cynical? The 2 Tone sound was envisioned by Jerry Dammers as a polyglot of styles, starting with rock and ska and working outward from there. As bands like the Bosstones raise the frightening specter of a day when ska does not resemble ska anymore, a refocusing and redefinition is called for. The new trad sound need not be simply a move by a snobby elite, but can represent a genuine curiosity and growing love for what originally inspired the 2 Tone sound to self-start. While England may have had Desmond Dekker and Prince Buster high in the charts back in the sixties and seventies, Americans have no collective conscious that remembers and appreciates these world-class artists. With the advent of the trad sound of the third wave of ska, then, we finally play catch-up to the ever-so-tasteful English!

Is the new push toward a trad sound in modern ska ultimately a pitiful attempt by self-important scenesters to make their music less intelligible to the average herbert, or is it a natural growth in the music, because as ska matures in the United States a natural curiosity for the roots of ska needs to be fed?

It depends on the quality of the new music. Is it derivative and brittle, or is it adding a new and original element that makes the old new again? This early in the trad game, I think that is strictly a matter of personal conjecture. As the bands get more original, put out some more albums, tour the country a bit and make bigger names for themselves, we'll see how the next (and perhaps mainstreamed) wave of ska music works itself out.

PART FIVE

DUB

The Sound of Surprise

RICHARD WILLIAMS

Melody Maker
21 August 1976

How can I persuade you not to laugh when I say that the technique of dub may well be the most interesting new abstract concept to appear in modern music since Ornette Coleman undermined the dictatorship of Western harmony almost two decades ago?

First, I'm assuming that you're aware of dub's existence. For those who unaccountably aren't, the briefest of rundowns: It's what you find on the flip side of most reggae singles, where the producer has taken the A-side and fed it through various equalisation facilities (sound-modification devices) available on his mixing board.

Vocals and instruments appear and disappear with what at first seems a bewildering anarchy, often shrouded in echo or distorted beyond recognition.

It's completely bizarre, and yet among Jamaicans the dub records are usually more popular than the straight versions of the same tunes. It's not abnormal for several dubs of the same basic track to appear, and prerelease dub albums sell at enormous prices in considerable quantities.

What I want to discuss, however, is not necessarily dub in its present application, interesting though that may be.

It strikes me that there are possibilities inherent in this aberrant form which could perhaps resonate through other musics in the years to come; this may seem wild prophesy, but it could change the nature of some areas, and the nature of the ways in which we both play and apprehend music.

THE ROOTS OF DUB

Dub had its beginning in the mid-sixties, when Jamaican disc jockeys first started making funny noises through their microphones in time to the records they played;

this eventually found its way onto the records themselves. A primitive and popular example would be Prince Buster's hit "Al Capone," where a voice provides a curious and persistent quasi-percussive accompaniment.

A few years later, gathering courage, jocks like U-Roy started making up impromptu verse on top of the records, and when this too was reproduced in the studio, the original singer's voice was frequently faded in and out around the overdubbed chanting (or "toasting," as it became known).

The next step was to muck around with the sound of the instruments themselves, and with the whole arrangement of the track.

Producers like Lee Perry (the rawest), King Tubby (the most innovatory), and Jack Ruby (the most sophisticated) vied with each other to create the most eccentrically ear-bending effects.

A couple of years ago dub had become so popular that an album called *King Tubby Meets the Upsetter* (a kind of battle of the boards between Tubby and Perry) bore, on the rear of its sleeve, large pictures of the mixing consoles used by the two protagonists. Not a human in sight.

Currently, and perhaps most interesting of all, certain reggae bands are beginning to duplicate dub in live performance.

As yet they haven't managed to reproduce the full panoply of bass and drum techniques, but the use of heavy sporadic echo on lead instruments like harmonica and guitar is being featured.

THE AESTHETICS OF DUB

One's overriding impression, on initial exposure to dub at the high volume for which it is intended, is that this is the nearest aural equivalent to a drug experience, in the sense that reality (the original material) is being manipulated and distorted.

I have no doubt that this was an important motivation in dub's development, whether consciously or otherwise. That's quite interesting but ultimately insignificant when compared with its other and more sophisticated effects on the listener.

Because it's most often applied to an already-familiar song or rhythm track, dub has a uniquely poignant quality: memories are revived, but rather than being simply duplicated (as when we hear a "golden oldie" from our youth on the radio) they are given subtle twists. Memory is teased rather than dragged up, and is thereby heightened.

It is, above all, the supreme sound of surprise, whether that of an anguished, Echoplexed scream, or a rimshot mechanically flared into a facsimile of thunder, or a steady bass riff suddenly and mysteriously disappearing in the middle of a bar (with an effect like that of stepping into an empty lift shaft).

Ideally, therefore, no dub performance should be heard more than once.

Its evanescence and randomness make it perhaps the most existential of musics, and its most stunning implication comes with the realisation that no dub track is ever "correct" or "finished": it can always be done again a thousand different ways, each one as "correct" as any other.

For the nonaligned (i.e., non–West Indian) listener to cope with this, some values must be adjusted in order to accept and enjoy the constant sense of shock it provides when the hands of a Lee Perry or a Tappa Zukie are at the controls. Once assimilated, though, it can have the invigorating effect of the best so-called Free Music.

Does it, can it, have a wider implication? I think so, and we may already be on the road. Two examples:

1. When Roxy Music was formed, it was Brian Eno's function—him again!—firstly to introduce relevant sound effects (the standard and expected sirens, bleeps, whooshes, and so on), and secondarily to modify the form and content of what the musicians onstage were playing. (In the early days, Eno's synthesizer and tape machines were positioned at the mixing desk.)

A couple of weeks ago Phil Manzanera was quoted in this paper as saying that, then, he was never sure how his guitar would sound once Eno had finished interfering with its output.

As Roxy Music became more conventional, stripping away one by one the original experimental factors in a curious instance of success actually inhibiting exploration, Eno became more of a "player" in his own right and less of a modifier . . . and then he left. A missed opportunity.

2. Late last year one of the young groups currently fashionable on the punk rock scene recorded a song which purposely employed elements of dub: repeat-echo on harmonica, delay and superimposition of rhythm guitars, and the occasional tweak on the lead vocal.

Although it has yet to be released, the track was a complete artistic success: the tension which resulted from these devices was wholly congruous, thoroughly in keeping with the spirit and atmosphere of such music.

Looking elsewhere, one can spot other signs. Ever since "What's Going On," Marvin Gaye has been developing a kind of sound-stratification which allows for a certain randomness within the overall texture.

This is slightly misleading, because Gaye's records (I'm thinking particularly of "Let's Get It On" and "I Want You") must be the result of many hours of forethought and care and patience, all of which would appear to be inimical to the crucial spontaneity of dub.

Miles Davis's last release, the in-concert *Agharta*, displayed an almost dublike nonchalance and disregard of "planning"; but here the difference is that all the musicians are left to their own devices, unhindered.

I have sometimes felt, too, that the loud and apparently arbitrary synthesizer interjections which Joe Zawinul is prone to perpetrate during Weather Report concerts (but not their records) have something of the spirit of King Tubby—although that is perhaps being too lenient.

THE POLITICS OF DUB

In its present "natural" state, dub has no inbuilt politics; were it to be utilised by nonreggae musicians, though, these would arise and create controversy, for one of its major principles is the denial of the right of the musician to control completely his own output.

While advocating its study and wider use, I am not of course suggesting that it would benefit everyone. Only a fool would maintain that the formal purity of a Joni Mitchell or the majestic poise of a John Coltrane could be improved by meddling.

But, in the hands of adventurous groups and composers, it could be a fascinating tool. It seems to me to be a gripping and revolutionary idea that an outside agency—in other words, the man at the mixing desk—could control the actual content of a live performance, choosing exactly what he wanted to be heard, so that while (say) a bassist might be playing throughout a piece, only an unpredetermined proportion of his contribution would be heard. And he'd be as surprised as anybody by what did (and what didn't) come out.

Rather than the performers serving as an interface between composer and audience, therefore, the composer himself would assume that function, standing very relevantly between the players and the listeners. (Another precedent comes to mind: Anyone who's seen Gil Evans conducting an orchestra will know the way he seems to draw out punctuations and colours at will.)

At the lesser end of the scale, dub offers a range of new playing and recording gimmicks which could be plagiarised and thereby enliven all kinds of styles, from Chinn-and-Chapman to Anthony Braxton. At the limit of its potential, it proposes nothing less than a new kind of composing.

SUGGESTED LISTENING: Prince Buster, "Al Capone" (Blue Beat 45); Big Youth, *Screaming Target* (Trojan LP); No artist, *Bag o' Wire* (Klik LP); Tappa Zukie, *M.P.L.A.—Version* (Klik 45); Scratch and the Upsetters, *Super Ape* (Island LP); Brian Eno, "Sky Saw," "Over Fire Island" from *Another Green World* (Island LP); Davis/Evans/Tubby, *Miles Davis and Gil Evans Meet King Tubby at the High Altar of Dread* (Dub LP)

Instrument of Expression

GREG KOT

The Chicago Tribune
13 February 1996

At the Empty Bottle in Wicker Park on Sunday nights, an unlikely cross-cultural exchange has been taking place for months. There, the Deadly Dragon Sound System, a handful of deejays with deep connections to Chicago's underground rock community, spins records by the likes of Lee "Scratch" Perry, King Tubby, Horace Andy and other lesser-known giants of the Caribbean's dance-and-trance musics, reggae and dub.

Like salt, a ubiquitous if somewhat overlooked seasoning, dub reggae seems to go with everything. Name the most significant musical innovations and movements of the 1990s—techno, jungle, ambient, trip-hop, alternative rock—and dub is the spice that flavors them all. Although it has been around for decades, dub is pretty much the province of musical connoisseurs, the shadow kingdom of brilliant eccentrics such as Perry, who is known to consecrate his hundreds of finished recordings by gleefully blowing marijuana smoke on the master tapes before they go to the pressing plant.

When most North Americans think of reggae—the syncopated soul music of Jamaica—they might come up with the name of Bob Marley, or perhaps that of a recent hit maker such as Shaggy or Shabba Ranks. But the deejays in the Deadly Dragon Sound System—which consists of Chicagoans Richard Smith, Casey Rice, John Herndon and Daniel Givens—are well beyond the music's pop surface.

These local rockers are avid fans of producers and mixers such as Perry and Tubby who pioneered the art of dub, in which reggae tunes are stripped of vocals and most accompanying instruments except for the drums and bass, then rebuilt with patches of the original melody or vocals, additional noises and tape manipulations. In this musical sleight of hand, threads of melody and hypnotic riffs disappear and reappear, sometimes only as a faint echo. Like exploring a hidden cavern, or floating lost amid the stars, or sinking to the ocean bottom, dub evokes an alternative world, a suspension of time, a complete reconfiguration of musical space, in which sounds don't so much fade as decay before the listener's ears.

It is this approach to record making, in which the studio itself becomes an instrument and literally hundreds of variations of any given tune are possible, that has begun to pique the interest of the rock underground. A handful of all-instrumental rock bands have begun to emerge that incorporate aspects of dub into their sound, most notably the Chicago-based Tortoise.

"In doing this kind of music, it's just to show that our musical identity is not shaped by one type of thing," says Deadly Dragon's Rice, who is also Tortoise's live sound-mixer. "Chicago is good for that because there are so many different kinds of music here. We aren't anywhere near the level of the people who made dub what it is, but a group like Tortoise isn't just ripping it off. It's way more multifaceted."

Tortoise shared the bill at Metro over the weekend with the Deadly Dragon Sound System, which pumped appropriately spaced-out sounds onto the dance floor between sets, and with headliners Dub Syndicate, essentially a sound laboratory for the dub experiments of the London-based producer and mixer Adrian Sherwood. Although Sherwood does not tour, his spacy rhythmic concoctions are fully elaborated by a five-piece band led by his collaborator, drummer Style Scott, and the sound-board manipulations of mixer David Hamilton.

The Metro performance showcased both the strengths and limitations of dub as a live art form. Essentially, the stars of the dub medium are its producers, and the lack of a vocalist or even an instrumental focus on stage makes the music a bit difficult to watch, in the traditional sense of being entertained at a concert.

This was particularly the case with Dub Syndicate. In many ways this ensemble, which has been recording steadily since the early 1980s, is the starting point for the current underground scene. Sherwood merged his talent for mixing and for creating futuristic soundscapes with the deep bass rhythms of the vast community of Caribbean expatriates in London. The initial Dub Syndicate records were notable for the way they expanded dub reggae's boundaries, incorporating Middle Eastern and industrial grooves, turntable scratching, avant-garde jazz eruptions, and the odd Jim Morrison vocal sample. Sherwood's On-U label, which only recently has acquired distribution in the United States, is where the worlds of dub and rock connect.

At Metro that synergy was made explicit by the massive drum groove of Style Scott, whose command of the reggae rhythm vocabulary is without peer. His left-hand tapping out high-hat Morse code, his right exorcising thunderous eruptions out of the snare, Scott was the foundation upon which the dub was built. The other key component is the bass of Daniel Thompson, who played a six-string "stick" cranked so loud that the tones rattled the sternums of listeners on the dance floor.

Where Dub Syndicate is lacking, however, is in the area of composition. At times its songs are little more than recurring riffs, a groove without a place to go. So while dub remains an essential art form, it is also a narrow one, and must enter the mainstream by combining with other musics.

Arguably the forerunner of the movement, Tortoise began as a side project for members of several prominent Chicago rock bands, including Eleventh Dream Day, Gastr del Sol, Bastro and the Sea and Cake.

Their instruments lined up like a fortress across the foot of the stage, Tortoise performed at Metro as though they were playing for themselves in a studio, hidden in the shadows and oozing sobriety, if not aloofness. The quintet builds songs around the double-bass attack of Doug McCombs and David Pajo, with John Herndon, Dan Bitney and John McEntire alternating among drums, keyboards and vibraphone. At times the music suggested the rhythmic shifts and jazzy flourishes of 1970s fusion bands such as Weather Report and Return to Forever or a spaghetti western soundtrack, but was at its best when it lurked on the fringes of several genres instead of embracing just one. It is in this ill-defined space that Tortoise created something new, not just connecting with the innovations of Jamaica but expanding on them.

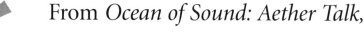

From *Ocean of Sound: Aether Talk, Ambient Sound and Imaginary Worlds*

DAVID TOOP

1995

REPLICANT

Dub music is like a long echo delay looping through time. Regenerating every few years, sometimes so quiet that only a disciple could hear, sometimes shatteringly loud, dub unpicks music in the commercial sphere. Spreading out a song or a groove over a vast landscape of peaks and deep trenches, extending hooks and beats to vanishing point, dub creates new maps of time, intangible sound sculptures, sacred sites, balm and shock for mind, body and spirit.

When you double, or dub, you replicate, reinvent, make one of many versions. There is no such thing as an original mix, since music stored on multitrack tape, floppy or hard disk, is just a collection of bits. The composition has been decomposed, already, by the technology. Dubbing at its very best takes each bit and imbues it with new life, turning a rational order of musical sequences into an ocean of sensation. This musical revolution stemmed originally from Jamaica—in particular, the tiny studio once run by the late Osbourne Ruddock, aka King Tubby, in Kingston. "This is the heart of Kingston 11," Dave Henley wrote, describing the location of Tubby's studio for a reggae fanzine called *Small Axe*. "A maze of zinc fence, potholed roads and suitably dilapidated bungalows. After dark, the streets become remarkably deserted (by Kingston standards, anyway, considering that loafing on the corner is a favourite Jamaican pastime), giving the impression of an eerie tropical ghost town."

Urban, rural, tropic, aquatic, lo-tech, mystical. This was the source mix from which William Gibson drew (sentimentally, some critics think) when adding the humanising element of Rastafari and dub to his *Neuromancer* narrative of tech-Gnosis. When King Tubby first discovered dub, the revelation came, like so many technological discoveries, through an accident. There were other Jamaican recording engineers, of course: Sylvan Morris, Errol T. Thompson and Lloyd "Prince Jammy" James helped to create the sound of albums such as Joe Gibb's *African Dub All-Mighty* series, or Augustus Pablo's *King Tubby's Meets Rockers Uptown* and *Africa Must Be Free by 1983*. But it was Tubby, cutting discs for Duke Reid at Treasure Isle, who first discovered the thrill of stripping a vocal from its backing track and then manipulating the instrumental arrangement with techniques and effects: drop-out, extreme equalisation, long delay, short delay, space echo, reverb, flange, phase, noise gates, echo feedback, shotgun snare drums, rubber bass, zipping highs, cavernous lows. The effects are there for enhancement, but for a dub master they can displace time, shift the beat, heighten a mood, suspend a moment. No coincidence that the nearest approximation to dub is the sonar transmit pulses, reverberations and echoes of underwater echo ranging and bioacoustics. No coincidence, also, that dub originated in a poor section of a city on a Caribbean island.

The first moment of dub has been pursued by reggae historian Steve Barrow through numerous conversations with important reggae record producers such as Bunny Lee. In *Dub Catcher* magazine, Lee conjures some of the excitement of those late 1960s, early 1970s sessions when King Tubby began to experiment with what he termed the "implements of sound": "Tubby's, right," recalls Lee. "With all the bass and drum ting now, dem ting just start by accident, a man sing off key, an' when you a reach a dat you drop out everyting an' leave the drum, an' lick in the bass, an' cause a confusion an' people like it. . . . Sometime me an' 'im talk an' me say, 'Drop out now, Tubby!' An' 'im get confuse an' me jus' draw down the whole a the lever . . . you hear *pluck* an' jus' start play pure distortion. Me say, 'Yes Tubbs, madness, the people dem like it!' an' just push it right back up . . . An' then Lee Perry do fe 'im share a dub too, ca' 'im an' Tubby's do a whole heap a ting . . . 'im an' Niney [producer nine-finger Niney "the Observer"] an' musician jus' play, an' 'im jus' [makes discordant noises and laughs]. 'Im drunk, drunk yunno—the engineer a go stop 'im an' [he] say, 'You no hear a vibes? Mad sound dat man.' An' when 'im come the people dem like it."

Tubby worked with equipment that would be considered impossibly limited by today's standards, yet his dubs were massive, towering exercises in sound sculpting. Legend records that he cut four dub plates—special, one-off mixes—for his hometown hi-fi system at the end of the 1960s. Playing these instrumental versions at a dance, with U-Roy toasting verbal improvisations over the music in real time, he was forced to repeat them all night, dubbing them up live as the crowd went crazy. Tubby worked for some of Jamaica's most creative producers: Lee Perry and Augustus Pablo, in particular, were recording increasingly exotic and distinctive music during the 1970s. On albums such as Perry's *Super Ape* and Pablo's *East of the River Nile* the mixing board becomes a pictoral instrument, establishing the illusion of a vast soundstage and then dropping instruments in and out as if they were characters in a drama. Lee Perry was a master of this technique, applying it to all his records, whether vocal, dub, instrumental version or talkover, all of them rich in his dub signature of rattling hand drums and scrapers, ghostly voices, distant horn sections, unusual snare and hi-hat treatments, groans and reptilian sibilations, odd perspectives and depth illusions, sound effects, unexpected noises and echoes that repeat to infinity.

Dub also anticipated remix culture. In 1974 Rupie Edwards, a producer of celebrated Jamaican artists such as I-Roy, the Ethiopians and Gregory Isaacs, was the first to compile a "version" album—*Yamaha Skank,* twelve different versions of the rhythm of a song called "My Conversation." Although these were not dubs, they grew out of the idea of dubbing a track, shaping and reshaping its "implements of sound" as if music was modelling clay rather than copyright property.

PRINCE FAR I'S VISION

> . . . *city of nine gates, magical moon, circling clouds, marvel of miracles, twilight world, beauty unfold, in living memory . . .*

SUNS OF ARQA, "CITY OF NINE GATES"

WORLD OF ECHO

After the first wave of dub albums during the 1970s from King Tubby, Lee Perry, Augustus Pablo, Yabby U, Keith Hudson and the producer stables of Bunny Lee, Coxsone Dodd, Joe Gibbs and Niney, many of dub's innovations were applied to fresh contexts in America and the U.K. New York dub emerged, almost as an inevitability, from the disco tape editing and remixing of DJs such as Tom Moulton and Walter Gibbons. Moulton, whose hectic career as the pioneer of disco mixing came to a halt after a serious heart attack during a mix, restructured funk tracks with a razor blade, shaping for the ecstasies and libido release of the dance floor; a Walter Gibbons mix, on the other hand, entered the listener into the chaotic heart of King Tubby's "implements of sound." Although many of his mixes, particularly of material from the Salsoul label, were relatively functional, he could also play Lee Perry–style tricks with sound balance, sudden track dropouts or perspectival distortions. His long remix of Bettye LaVette's "Doin' the Best That I Can," released on New York's West End label in 1978, redefined the logical hierarchy of instrumentation.

Walter Gibbons could make a dance floor move to a glockenspiel or a hi-hat. A constant collaborator with the late Arthur Russell—New York singer, cellist, percussionist and minimalist/disco composer—he used sound relationships rather than electronic effects to create wonderfully strange music. These reach their apex on the Arthur Russell 12-inch singles "Let's Go Swimming" and "Treehouse/School Bell"— songs of innocence and experience; convoluted slitherings of sharp sounds, chopped and dislocated; antipathetic to the modular, even-number construction of disco; formed in the eternal shape of the self-devouring Uroborus dragon of alchemy, a flow without beginning or end; contrasting/merging the developmental improvisation of Indian ragas with the hypnotic, human-interlock accretions of Fela Anikulapo-Kuti's Nigerian Afro-funk.

Like Gibbons, Russell played the studio as an instrument, understanding the freedom inherent in present-day recording. For example, sound recorded in a studio live room or direct onto tape is unnaturally dry (unless recorded in special reflective rooms), so extraordinary illusions of distance are possible through contrasting dry, forward sounds with the distancing effects of a huge range of echoes. Another point: the number of "performances" that can be permutated from a multitrack recording is infinite. *World of Echo,* Russell called one of his solo albums.

Russell studied at the Ali Akbar Khan school in San Francisco, where he played cello. "Cello is Ali Akbar Khan's favourite instrument," he told me in 1986. He collaborated on projects with John Cage, Laurie Anderson, Phill Niblock, Philip Glass, François Kervorkian, David Byrne, Steve D'Aquisto, the Ingram brothers, Peter Gordon, Larry Levan, Allen Ginsberg and many others; poets, filmmakers, disco mixers, pop stars, soul musicians, contemporary composers. Forbidden border crossings. When Russell performed his *Instrumentals* piece at the Kitchen in Manhattan, the use of a drum kit caused a stir. "A lot of people turned off," he told me. "They thought that was a sign of some new unsophistication, a sign of increasing commercialisation. Then if you try to do something different in dance music you just get branded as an eccentric. Maybe I am an eccentric, I don't know, but it's basically a very simple idea. I like music with no drums, too. Partly, I guess, from listening to drums so much. When you hear something with no drums it seems very exciting. I always thought that music with no drums is successive to music with drums. New music with no drums is like this future when they don't have drums any more. In outer space, you can't take your drums—you take your mind." DJs told him that nobody would ever play "Let's Go Swimming." "I think eventually that kind of thing will be commonplace," he said. He was right, but neither he nor Walter Gibbons lived to profit from this new era of sound experimentation. Arthur Russell died of AIDS in 1992. Walter Gibbons died in 1994.

MY LIFE IN A HOLE IN THE GROUND

The New Orleans torture scene conjured in hallucinogenic close-up by David Lynch in *Wild at Heart*—a slowed-down Adrian Sherwood production, "Far Away Chant" by African Head Charge—adds further dimensions of hoodoo otherness to Lynch's trademark shadeworld of sexual violence, Prince Far I's warping sandblast vocals rising up from the catacombs . . . in this unholy place a steady throb of Rastafarian repeater and funde drums somehow twisted in the unconscious to draw on archaic fears: fear of voodoo, fear of the primeval occult, the old unhealthy fear of Rastas as "menacing devils with snake nests for hair."

Working with a floating pool of musicians in London, Adrian Sherwood had been pushing reggae deeper into the echo chamber for years, maybe running an entire track backwards, highlighting strange instruments, layering fugitive ambiences from the elemental simplicity of drum, bass and vocals, creating polyrhythmic ricochets, noise bubbles and chimerical voices. His mixing techniques on Creation Rebel's *Starship Africa,* the late Prince Far I's *Cry Tuff Dub Encounter* series of albums, and

African Head Charge's *My Life in a Hole in the Ground* were epic explorations of mood, experiments in bass as an enveloping cloud, premonitions of the marathon dub and ambient mixes of the 1990s.

I played flute and African thumb piano on *Chapter III* of the Prince Far I *Cry Tuff* albums, East London's Berry Street studio boiling hot, air-conditioning broken down, Far I (like King Tubby, soon to become a murder victim of Jamaica's random gun law) solemn and silent, sitting by the mixing desk wrapped in scarf, hat and jacket as if we were working in arctic conditions. The session was a madhouse of post-punk experimentation, indicative of the role dub had assumed as a deconstructing agent, a locus of crosscurrents from reggae, rock, jazz, improvisation and the extra-human conjectures of technological processes. Sherwood has admitted that his initial inspiration for *My Life in a Hole in the Ground* was the David Byrne and Brian Eno collaborative album, *My Life in the Bush of Ghosts:* "I was reading in the paper," Sherwood told *Dub Catcher* magazine, "where he [Brian Eno] said, 'I had a vision of psychedelic Africa,' or something like that. So I had to laugh. The idea was to make a psychedelic, but serious, African dub record."

Shocks of Mighty

MICK SLEEPER

http://www.oanet.com/homepage/sleeper/scratch.htm
July 1996

NAME: Rainford Hugh Perry

AKA: Lee, Little, King, Scratch, The Upsetter, Pipecock Jackson, Super Ape, Ringo, Emmanuel, The Rockstone, Small Axe, and dozens of others

BORN: March 20, 1936, Kendal, Jamaica

HEIGHT: 5'4"

CURRENT
RESIDENCE: Zurich, Switzerland

OCCUPATION: The Man

With a cat as legendary, mysterious, and eccentric as Lee Perry, the story of his life is a mix of fact and fiction, newspaper clippings and ghost stories. An official biography of the man has never been written, and so much of what we know about Perry is open to conjecture, point of view, bad ganja, and grains of salt the size of golf balls. None of this is made up, but I make no apologies for taking artistic license in telling Scratch's story, since I'm sure that the Upsetter would want it that way.

"I came, I saw, and I conquered." Lee Perry's early life mirrors most of Jamaica's musical superstars: he was born poor in a small village, earned an early reputation as a tough guy, came to Kingston in the late 1950s, heard the music, learned the moves, got the groove. His first job was with pioneering record producer Clement "Coxsone" Dodd at his soon to be legendary Studio One: gofer, bouncer, spy, talent scout, uncredited songwriter, and—eventually—performer. His main job was DJ at Coxsone's ska raves, and when he wasn't spinning records, Perry's gig was to help get rid of the sabotaging thugs hired by Duke Reid (a rival of Coxsone's) by karate chopping them in the teeth. He cut his first records in the early 1960s, although nobody knows which was the very first. "Chicken Scratch" was his first bona fide hit in 1965, but it was a drop in the Studio One bucket.

In 1966, after almost seven years with Studio One, Perry left in a flash of lightning, pissed off at Coxsone for not giving him enough money, recognition, or chicks over the years. He crossed the street and joined forces with greenhorn producer Joe Gibbs, cutting his first signature tune, the sinister "I Am the Upsetter," as a warning to Coxsone and anyone else who might try to screw him. Gibbs wasn't really a producer at first, just some guy with sunglasses and a lot of cash, but he realized that Perry had the groove, so in 1967 he hired Perry to run his new Amalgamated label for him. Perry wasted no time and produced a string of hits for Gibbs, including the Pioneers' "Long Shot," which was the first song to use a new rhythm in Jamaican music—it didn't have a name at the time, but a year later someone christened the beat "reggae." "Long Shot" and other Perry works from this time are therefore evidence for those who claim that he actually *invented* reggae.

Perry's productions mashed up the place, but since Gibbs wanted a "silent" partner, he was asking for trouble when he decided to put Perry on the elbow list. Furious once again for being slighted, Perry split from Amalgamated with a mighty roar and retaliated with "People Funny Boy," which was another "screw you" song aimed straight to Gibbs's head. Ironic, since Perry's big hit for Gibbs had been "Upsetter," which was a "screw you" song aimed at Coxsone.

In 1968 Perry decided that since he couldn't work with any of Jamaica's producers without furniture being broken, he would do it himself. He wanted to hire the best guns he could to help him take over the world, and he approached a young band he knew called the Hippy Boys: Aston "Family Man" Barrett on bass, his brother Carlton playing drums, guitarist Alva Lewis, Glen Adams on keyboards, and Max Romeo doing vocals. The Hippy Boys had recorded a few singles without much success, and so knowing about Perry's reputation as a badass, they decided to become his studio band. Perry immediately renamed the band after his current nickname and his new record label—now they were the Upsetters.

The Upsetters used to hang out with Perry all day on the hot streets of Kingston, heading off to the movies in the afternoon to watch as many violent spaghetti westerns as they could before heading back to the studio for an all-night session. Galvanized by the shoot 'em ups, they cut violent, spooky instrumentals like "Kill Them All," "The Vampire," "Dig Your Grave," and what became their signature tune, "Return of Django." "Django" became a Top 10 hit in England in 1969, and Perry took the Upsetters on a six-week British tour on its strength—a first for a reggae band. They were a sensation everywhere they played. Once the Upsetters returned from Britain, they were rather pissed off with Perry, who—ironically, given his past dealings with Coxsone and Gibbs—apparently had taken the lion's share of the cash from the tour.

One day three roughnecks who called themselves the Wailers came to visit the Upsetters on Charles Street and find out more about the British tour. The Wailers had mashed up the place a few years earlier with Coxsone, but at the moment they were struggling. The supremacy of kings like Coxsone and Reid was being challenged by new, independent producers and labels. After years of a two-crown monarchy, Jamaican music was in the midst of a civil war. Success was up for grabs; every man for himself. The Wailers knew this all too well—they needed to jump-start their sound or die trying. Young producers like Perry were creating new sounds that would pull the rug out from under the feet of the "old men" of the Jamaican music scene. The Wailers were amazed that the Upsetters had been so popular overseas; before long, Bob Marley realized that a collaboration between them and the Wailers could be an unstoppable combo. After a few rehearsals and jam sessions together, Marley talked the Upsetters into abandoning Perry's ship and joining the Wailers.

When Perry found out that Marley had stolen his crack musicians from him, he was understandably furious. He actually threatened to kill Bob. The two of them met one day to have it out, and judging from the volume of their voices, everyone around thought that it would end up with someone's head being broken. Instead they emerged from behind closed doors hours later, all smiles and slapping each other on the back. The Upsetters were still joining the Wailers, but their exclusive producer was to be—of course—Lee Perry.

Perry pounded his fist in the studio and turned the two bands into killers. Unlike most other producers at the time, Perry wasn't into horns, preferring Alva Lewis's aggressive guitar riffs and Glen Adams's unstoppable organ to lead the way. He got Bob to tighten up his voice and told Peter and Bunny to stop the sissy backing vocals and sing from the gut. The Barrett brothers laid down rhythms that moved the earth—bass and drums steady as a rock and unstoppable as thunder. Lewis's guitar came in razor-sharp stabs, and Adams's organ flowed like blue and orange water at high tide. "*This* is how reggae should sound!" Perry insisted. Soon they were recording what became a turning point in their careers and in the history of Jamaican music, according to most reggaeologists.

Although it will probably never be known who influenced who, the chemistry between Perry, Marley, the Wailers, and the Upsetters proved to be phenomenal. Together they produced classic songs like "Small Axe," "Duppy Conqueror," "Fussing and Fighting," and many others that changed the course of reggae and laid the foundation for Bob Marley's subsequent success. Many of the songs were rerecorded later on in Marley's career, but the magic of the Perry sessions has never been surpassed.

Success—and a lot of fantastic music—continued through 1969 and 1970. By 1971, however, the Wailers/Upsetters' honeymoon with Perry was over. Dynamic as their personalities were, it was only natural that Perry and Marley would share a love/hate relationship. More arguments (and at times, violence) over chart success and credit where credit was due led to a final bust-up. Soon after, the Wailers took the Barrett brothers and formed a new band, signed to Island Records in 1973, and became reggae superstars. The original Upsetters went their separate ways, but Perry kept the name to refer to the floating band of killer musicians that played for him over the next few years.

In 1972 Perry and his family moved into Washington Gardens, a posh Kingston suburb, and it was here that he took his newfound independence to the limit and began to construct his own recording studio. When it was completed in 1974 he painted the words BLACK ARK above the door, for it was here that Perry reckoned that he would lay down the Ten Commandments of reggae. For any other producer this would be an eccentric boast; in retrospect, Perry was being modest. The music that was recorded at the Black Ark over the next five years was absolute magic from one of reggae's most radical sorcerers.

The magical aura of the Black Ark began to attract Jamaica's greatest performers, from veterans like the Heptones to obscure singers such as Neville Grant and newbies like Susan Cadogan. Such was Perry's passion for producing that he routinely gave unknowns a first try and gave has-beens a shot in the arm. While other studios had performers punching a clock, Perry was only too happy to spend as long as it took to get the right groove. Classic, ganja soaked, dub-drenched albums from Max Romeo (*War in a Babylon*), the Upsetters (*Super Ape*), Junior Murvin (*Police and Thieves*), the Heptones (*Party Time*), and the Congos (*Heart of the Congos*), along with hundreds of singles flowed from the Black Ark between 1976 and 1979.

While things were heating up in Perry's studio, so was the political climate in Jamaica. The island's two political parties had a long tradition of settling arguments out of court on the streets of Kingston. Each party had hired gunmen who routinely went apeshit in the weeks before an election and shot at anything that moved. Antiviolence songs and lyrics that foretold a coming apocalypse became the order of the day, such as Max Romeo's "War in a Babylon," Niney the Observer's "Blood and Fire," and Perry's own fevered plea for sanity, "City Too Hot." Never a stranger to extreme words and imagery, Perry's outer-space productions seemed to mirror the current heat and confusion of Jamaica perfectly. Against this vivid backdrop, Perry's sound was becoming internationally famous. In 1975 he had secured a worldwide distribution deal with Island Records, and his productions had attracted the attention of white rockers such as Paul McCartney, Robert Palmer, and the Clash. With the world beating a path to his door, the Black Ark soon reached the boiling point, and a point of no return for Perry.

One morning in 1979 Perry set fire to the Black Ark and burned it to the ground. The torching was both epic and tragic, as Perry simultaneously acted out his own Charge of the Light Brigade and shot himself in the foot. His wife Pauline had left him and taken the kids, apparently tired of dealing with Perry's second marriage to his music. This separation, combined with the alcohol and ganja-fueled eighteen-hour recording sessions he had been doing for years, had pushed Perry over the edge. His torching of the Ark was an attempt to (literally) burn all of the bridges of the past behind him. He suffered a mental breakdown and began his now famous eccentric behavior, including covering the ruins of the Black Ark with cryptic graffiti and small crosses. Perry's antics would have kept agents Mulder and Scully occupied for months as he became a walking X File: journalists arrived at the Black Ark to find Perry worshipping bananas, eating money, and baptizing visitors with a garden hose.

Perry spent the next few years traveling between Europe and Jamaica, residing in Amsterdam for a time and recording erratic records of little consequence. He made the decision to stop producing other artists and concentrate on his own music, of which there now seemed to be an endless well. In 1980 he temporarily changed his name to Pipecock Jackson and returned to Jamaica in a weird attempt to resurrect the Black Ark. New equipment was installed, but Perry cut all the wires and dug a duck pond in the studio instead. After three weeks with no ducks in sight, Perry abandoned the project after casting a bad spell on the people involved and split.

Nineteen eighty-one saw him on a U.S. tour with a white reggae band from New York called the Terrorists. Most of the people who attended the concerts agreed that they were the worst in reggae history. In 1982 Perry sacked the Terrorists and teamed up with another white reggae band, the Majestics, and recorded his first definite album since the Black Ark torching, the slick but substandard *Mystic Miracle Star*. A similarly duff album, *History, Mystery, and Prophecy*, was released in 1984 on Island, but Perry's already shaky deal with the label crumbled when he swore that Island head Chris Blackwell was a vampire and responsible for Bob Marley's death.

Nineteen eighty-six saw the release of *Battle of Armagideon* on Trojan, recorded while Perry sipped a mix of blackcurrant juice and gasoline and wore an electric heater on his head. The album sounded like the reality of Perry's situation: After years of slumber, the Upsetter was slowly waking up. The following year he teamed up with hipster English producer Adrian Sherwood and made a *real* comeback with the great *Time Boom X De Devil Dead*. Working with Sherwood's house band the Dub Syndicate (in many ways a modern version of the Upsetters), *Time Boom* was a digital throwback to Perry's glory days at the Black Ark. Several tracks from these sessions were deemed "too good to entrust to any record company" by Perry and remain in his private vaults.

In 1989 Perry relocated to Switzerland with his new bride, Mireille Ruegg, a shrewd Zurich businesswoman who became Perry's manager. One of the first actions Mireille took as his manager was to tangle with Coxsone Dodd over the "illegal distribution" of the songs Perry had just recorded with Dodd in New York. Reunited with his mentor/nemesis after many years, Perry recorded an album's worth of new material with his old boss, *The Upsetter and the Beat*, which—due to the legal battle—was not released until 1992 alongside *Lord God Muzick*. He calmly confided to interviewers that it had taken him ten years to build himself back again (1989 being the 10th anniversary of the Black Ark torching), and so he had no need for lawyers since they would perish by natural law. The next year, after vowing never to work with Adrian Sherwood or Island records again, the three were reunited for *From the Secret Laboratory*, his second monumental album of the decade and the finest work Perry has done since the days of the Black Ark. The early part of the 1990s had Perry on very successful European tours, playing concerts that sometimes went over three hours in duration.

Erratic releases of both old and new material have been the norm for the past few years—discoveries of lost treasures such as 1992's *Soundzs from the Hotline*, and lukewarm efforts with Mad Professor. At the time of this writing it's been reported that Perry and his son Omar have been working at what's left of the Black Ark in an attempt to rescue some long lost master tapes. At the same time, in the basement of his Zurich home, Perry began to build a new home studio for himself, calling it the Blue Ark—his "secret laboratory" that "no man has entered before" (well, almost: his wife's washing machine is down there).

At the moment Lee Perry remains the proverbial mad scientist, sitting comfortably in his own moutaintop fortress—a nice family home overlooking Lake Zurich with a BMW in the driveway. He may visit Earth from time to time, but he lives in his own universe, which is every bit as expansive and mysterious as the real thing. Which brings us to the big question that any Lee Perry biography must ask: Is he or isn't he crazy? Some say Perry is as crazy as a bottle of potato chips (which is pretty crazy if you think about it for a moment), others say it's a clever disguise put on by a completely sane genius. My own theory is that the Upsetter is certainly eccentric, but not genuinely insane, at least by strict psychiatric standards. His loony behaviour is part of a persona that helps propagate his legend, and after years of acting out this zany dogma, he has come to truly believe it, like a director trapped inside one of his own films. In this case, Lee Perry is trapped inside one of his songs, a fate which he certainly must face with a big grin. Combined with this DIY legend (and no doubt as a result of it) is no shortage of wild acclaim, and Perry must truly feel like the giant that critics, fans—and the Upsetter himself—have made him out to be. He has created such a monumental niche in modern music that even his most eccentric boasts seem modest in retrospective.

Lee Perry's musical universe is one of vampires and archangels, flying saucers and scatology, hitmen and cartoon characters. Art may imitate life, but for Perry there's no difference between the two. He literally paints, writes on, sculpts, films, records, and sings about everything he encounters. His repertoire makes use of a wide variety of references—personal, Biblical, Rastafarian, sexual, musical, and megalomaniacal. What—if anything—does it all mean?

As compelling as it might be to decipher all of Perry's rantings, it would also spoil the fun. Lee Perry's world is one of a kind, and so when he decides to broadcast messages to Earth via the recording studio, we should just hold tight and enjoy the ride, no instruction manual necessary. "I am a magician. Yes! A magician should do his magic and then disappear!" Perry sings in the autobiographical "African Hitchhiker," and if any one phrase from his work can serve as his raison d'être, that's it. As interesting, entertaining, and fascinating as Lee Perry's life and personality is, it can almost all be forgotten and replaced with one simple idea: His music always has and always will speak for itself.

From "'It Dread Inna Inglan': Linton Kwesi Johnson, Dread, and Dub Identity"

PETER HITCHCOCK

Postmodern Culture
September 1993[1]

> *The trouble with the English is that their history happened overseas, so they don't know what it means.*
>
> THE SATANIC VERSES, SALMAN RUSHDIE

◆   ◆   ◆

Dread is underlined by dub. Dub sharpens the defiance by writing over the OED, by spelling the sounds of actual English usage in the anglophone African/Caribbean community. Dub itself describes the paradox of the poet's voice, for dub means both the presence and the absence of Jamaican speech rhythms. Again, a confrontation with deconstruction's primary reflex might seem in order (the word as the presence of an absent voice), but that only partially explains the paradox at issue.

Dub is instrumental reggae, reggae with the lead vocal track removed and replaced (by a sound engineer) with various sound effects (echoes, reverberation, loops, vocal bites, etc.). Dub reggae's very emphasis on production, on mixing, is itself a challenge to the ideology of the artist as performer or originator (and is sometimes snubbed by reggae artists precisely because it threatens or subverts their copyrights). This feature emerges in many other forms of popular music (for instance, rap, techno, punk, and rave), which all sample one another with wild abandon, but often as much with the voice track as without.

But if dub reggae mixes out the vocals, dub poetry lays down the voice as an instrument within the reggae beat; indeed, the voice is so closely allied with this beat that if you remove the reggae instrumentation you can still hear its sound in the voice of the poem. Dub means simultaneously instruments without voices and voices without instruments. This neat chiasmus is not a tribute to the wily signifier so much as a product of dread identity, subaltern subjectivity as sound, silence, and warning. Dub is underlined by dread.

The paradox of dub as it signifies dread is a function of its multileveled etymology. Obviously the lingo of the sound engineer is paramount, although this was formerly associated with the manipulation of sound and voice tracks in cinematic production or the copying of film onto film. Copying is important, both as a productive capacity and as a logic of repetition. Because of the question of property rights, dubbing is tantamount to repetition as sedition (*dub* has also meant "to forge keys" as well as "to lock up"; and "to invest with a dignity" as well as "to smear with grease," in two other instances of self-deconstruction).

Coincidentally, perhaps, dub has an onomatopoeic function, specifically in "dub" and "dub-a-dub," the sound of a beating drum. As Linton Kwesi Johnson recalls in "Reggae Sounds," the drum is integral to the beat: "Thunda from a bass drum sounding/lightning from a trumpet and a organ/bass and rhythm and trumpet double-up/team-up with drums for a deep doun searching."[2] I will say more about the bass in due course, but the point here is to emphasize dub's undecidability and its technical associations, which are both highly evocative of its cultural politics. The latter, ultimately, is what dread is all about.

Although dub poetry is now associated with a number of poets (Oku Onuora, Mikey Smith, Mutubaruka, Brian Meeks, Breeze, Anita Stewart, etc.), it is almost synonymous with Linton Kwesi Johnson.[3] Indeed, he claims to have coined the term in the early seventies.[4] For LKJ, dub poetry should be distinguished from dub lyricism, the latter being the process by which deejays lay down their own voice track over reggae (he has in mind Big Youth, U-Roy, I-Roy)—we know this more commonly as "talkover" or "toasting."[5]

Dub lyricism is the voice at its most spontaneous, for (with the original voice track removed) the deejay can directly involve his or her audience through call-and-response methods, or by using current events to recontextualize the dread. Toasting, then, is a special skill tuned in to the tenor of the live event, which in the seventies and early eighties was epitomized by the one-thousand-watt-plus sound system discos (either those of the clubs, or the more underground roving systems set up in abandoned houses or warehouses or sometimes just in the street until the police or authorities found a way to pull the plug). Obviously there is some overlap in LKJ's work: "It Dread Inna Inglan" on the album *Dread Beat an' Blood* begins with call and response and features a crowd chanting "Free George Lindo" (the reference is to a wrongful arrest case in Bradford).

Also, the fact that LKJ himself has released dub versions of his dub poetry (most conspicuously, the album *LKJ in Dub*) and thereby allows his music to be "talked over" would seem to make the practical separation of dub poetry from dub lyricism problematic. The main difference, however, is that dub poetry privileges the word over the music, or else incorporates the rhythm of the instruments into its enunciation. For

LKJ in particular, the poetry should outlast its musical accompaniment or affiliation. This is an oddly purist and antipopulist stance, but it has several explanations.

The first is that LKJ considers himself a poet and not a reggae artist. Clearly he has learned much from reggae and the musical traditions on which it is based (like mento, ska, rude boy, and rock steady), but he does not believe that reggae can exhaust the possibilities of poetry in African/Caribbean cultural expression. Indeed, in a scathing review of Bob Marley in 1975, LKJ suggests that it is reggae music's commercialization which underlines the danger in the poet becoming overly dependent on it. He cites the example of Marley being "found" by Island Records' Chris Blackwell (referred to as the "descendant of slave masters") and promoted as a "Rasta rebel" to boost lagging record sales. The irony is obvious:

> The "image" is derived from rastafarianism and rebellion, which are rooted in the historical experience of the oppressed of Jamaica. It then becomes an instrument of capital to sell Marley and his music, thereby negating the power which is the cultural manifestation of this historical experience. So though Marley is singing about "roots" and "natty," his fans know not. Neither do they understand the meaning or the feeling of dread. And there is really no dread in Marley's music. The dread has been replaced by the howling rock guitar and the funky rhythm and what we get is the enigma of "roots" and rock.[6]

One wonders what LKJ would have to say about Shabba Ranks and other notables of ragga (a hybridization of rap and reggae) or dancehall stylee. Dread, here, seems to contain its own fear, in this case connected to the rock industry's economic and race relations: in short, the twin demons of sellout and crossover. For LKJ, commercial dread is either dreck or simply a contradiction in terms: it is reggae shorn of its sense of crisis, of its political edge.

One could argue that Marley contradicts LKJ's case, but LKJ's musical career itself proves that the rock industry is not quite the monolithic capitalist entity that he makes it out to be. Indeed, LKJ's break into pop occurred a couple of years later, in his relationship with Virgin Records. Initially he wrote biographies to accompany Virgin's emerging list of reggae artists, but eventually he got a chance to cut a record of his poems—drawn principally from the *Dread Beat an' Blood* collection—with a reggae backing. (LKJ had been doing this since 1973 with his band Rasta Love, but without a recording contract.)

While it was Mike Oldfield rather than reggae that catapulted Virgin toward multinational Goliath status, LKJ's point about capital remains pertinent: the corporate deployment of reggae directly supports those it putatively opposes. Taking poetry seriously simultaneously distances the white-dominated media conglomerates for which multiculturalism means capital diversity, while it also assures that the poetry itself can only have a local effect.

With the market for printed poetry being so small, the dub poet must rely on live performance as the focus for the message, but for LKJ this means reading principally without the reggae band. Since his "farewell performance" in December 1985 in Camden, LKJ has made less band-backed appearances, although the release of a new music collection, *Tings an' Times,* in 1991 underlines that his concert farewell did not end his desire to produce reggae albums. Yet if economic exigency can be seen to compromise LKJ's poetic principles, the general rule remains that he is suspicious of reggae more because of the industry in which it is entwined than its tendency to demote the voice and the dread it embodies.

◆ ◆ ◆

I have been trying to suggest how the voice of dub poetry instantiates a version of making history: the voice, here, as an active component of community identity. In the main, reggae has provided dub with its dread riddim, but as we have noted, LKJ believes that dub is not reducible to reggae, even if it owes it a rhythmic allegiance.

As with most "sound" protest, dub's doubling provides a subaltern community with a medium for resistance and active intervention in the political arena. While this might seem to confine dub poetry to the margins as subculture, this does not mean cultural subservience. In fact, I believe it is closer to what Deleuze and Guattari have examined as the deterritorializations of "minor literature," but in this case as a textualizing voice.[7]

LKJ's "Bass Culture" is typical of the (sub)cultural (sub)version of dub. Obviously the title puns on bass as being both the instrument of the beat and as being somehow obnoxious or repulsive. Who finds the bass base goes to the heart of the politics of culture that dub foregrounds.

On the face of it, "Bass Culture" exudes all the major features of dub: the thumping beat of bass is its subject matter, here tied to the beating of the heart but also to Kamau Brathwaite's pithy saying that "the hurricane does not roar in pentameters";[8] it is a poem about dread, both as threat and as cultural identity ("dread people"); the violence it registers has everything to do with the tropical storm it imitates and the history of oppression it records and from which it learns; the voice is both musical as it follows the bass line, and noisy as it makes a thunder crack ("scatta-matta-shatta-shack"), a slogan of defiance; the voice is specific about its own musical moment ("an di beat will shiff/as di culture altah/when oppression scatta"), which will pass according to a particular historical situation. In acknowledging the power of the voice (partially indicated in the dedication to Mr. Talk-Over, Big Youth) it makes no claims as to its originality but instead emphasizes a shared sense of "latent powa" as a bloodline of history, a "muzik of blood"; and the dread is a threat because it challenges the norm ("the false fold") in its language, in its riddim, and, of course, in its title.

But there is also an ambivalence of context in "Bass Culture" that allows dread to signify simultaneously in two moments of identity. The first is the colonial condition in which dread is the "latent powa" that eventually comes "burstin outta slave shackle/look ya! boun fi harm di wicked." The second moment, however, is the dread present, where this same latency must be utilized to "scatta" oppression within postcoloniality. Dread keeps the "culture pulsin" with bass riddim as long as it is "bad out dey"—a situation that did not necessarily end with the independence of Jamaica or the migration of some of its population to Britain.

Dread, then, becomes a conceptual as well as experiential link in the story of Afro-Caribbeans. Thus when I suggest that dub identity is about being-in-between, this does not mean that the community voiced by LKJ has not arrived in England (we have already noted that it "stan firm inna Inglan"), but that arrival in itself does not end the legacy of racism that structures England's national selfhood. The dread beat still has that to beat.

NOTES

1. A shorter "version" of this essay was first given at the MLA conference in New York, December 1992. The talk was backed with dub reggae, and the intonation of each sentence picked up on that bass beat. The form of the presentation, therefore, attempted to demonstrate the instrumentation of voice in dub poetry. This, of course, included an example of LKJ's performance—the poem I will discuss later, "Bass Culture." The present "remix" pushes against the impossibility of reproducing that event even as it admits the importance of this form of irreducibility. It is itself a dub version, the voiceless B-side of a reggae record—toned down, of course! A longer version will follow. For more on versions, see Dick Hebdige, *Cut 'n' Mix* (London: Comedia, 1987). Hebdige's book exemplifies the ability to hear and read the riddim crucial to dread.

2. Linton Kwesi Johnson, *Tings an' Times:* 18.

3. LKJ was born in Chapelton, Jamaica, in 1952. When his mother left for England, LKJ soon followed, at the age of eleven. They lived on the outskirts of Brixton, well known for its Afro-Caribbean community, where LKJ experienced not only a taste of home but a new perspective on the metropolitan center. He recalls: "I [saw] a white man sweeping the streets. All the white people I saw in Jamaica drove fish-tail cars and smoked cigars. So when I saw someone, a white person, actually sweeping the streets it was a bit of a revelation." See Mervyn Morris, "Interview with Linton Kwesi Johnson," *Jamaica Journal,* 20:1 (February/April 1987): 17–26.

4. The earliest reference in his work I can find is an essay from 1976. See "Jamaican Rebel Music," *Race and Class,* 17:4 (1976): 397–412. Even so, this still contradicts Stewart Brown's contention that the term was first used by Oku Onuora in 1979. See "Dub Poetry: Selling Out," *Poetry Wales,* 22:2 (1987): 51–54. There are references in the music press as early as 1974, but these are usually tied to "talk-over" rather than LKJ's sense of dub *as* poetry.

5. For more on talk-over and toasting, see Hebdige, especially Chapters 10 and 11. Given LKJ's distinction, it would seem rap is closer to dub lyricism than dub poetry because the latter can function as its own instrumentation.

6. See Linton Kwesi Johnson, "Roots and Rock," *Race Today,* 7:10 (October 1975): 237–238.

7. See Gilles Deleuze and Felix Guattari, *Kafka: Toward a Minor Literature,* trans. Dana Polan (Minneapolis: University of Minnesota Press, 1986). This will be developed in a subsequent "version." For an application of "minor literature" to postcolonial discourse, see Paget Henry and Paul Buhle, "Caliban as Deconstructionist: C. L. R. James and Post-Colonial Discourse," in Paget Henry and Paul Buhle, eds., *C. L. R. James's Caribbean* (Durham, NC: Duke University Press, 1992): 111–142.

8. I refer here to Brathwaite's provocative essay "History of the Voice," first presented at Carifesta '76 in Jamaica and subsequently expanded and revised as a lecture given at Harvard University, August 1979. The full text with bibliography has been published as Edward Kamau Brathwaite, *History of the Voice* (London: New Beacon Books, 1984). My efforts here are strongly influenced by Brathwaite's emphasis on orality in his essay (his talk, like mine, had an audio track).

Dub Diaspora:
Off the Page and Into the Streets

RON SAKOLSKY

from *Sounding Off! Music as Subversion/Resistance/Revolution*
1995

So unheralded are dub poets at Reggae Sunsplash that, according to Adugo Onuora, in 1991 they were actually paid *not* to perform on the originally contracted "Night of Consciousness." Aside from the more internationally known poets Mutabaruka and Oku Onuora, the scheduled appearances of Yasus Afari, Cherry Natural, Nabby Natural and Durm I were canceled at the last minute by Sunsplash organizers and the poets were literally left waiting in the wings backstage. The official rationale of time restrictions belied political silencing of reggae dissidents, as was evidenced by a three-hour wait for the band Third World to begin the next set.

For those dissatisfied with the continued neglect of the dub poetry idiom, Toronto's Dub Poetry Festival International was indeed a revelation. Held May 8–15, 1993, at venues ranging from the streets to high-rises to community centers and art galleries to university settings, the festival showcased the most conscious and rootsy dub poetry from all over the Caribbean, North America and England. Formats for the events included panel discussions (in which the distinction between panel and audience quickly dissolved into an egalitarian sharing), poetry readings and musical performances.

While not all the artists represented would call themselves dub poets in the strict sense of the term, the dub poetry concept and the festival's theme, "Off the Page and Into the Streets," ultimately proved inclusive enough. As Ras Mo (Domenica) put it, "In Domenica we don't find the term 'dub poetry' but rather 'peoples performance poetry.' . . . In the Eastern Caribbean when you say 'dub,' people relate it to Jamaican reggae and dancehall DJs; but I have nothing against the term because 'dub poetry,' 'performance poetry,' 'rhythm poetry' and 'rapso' are all based on the same form from different islands."

Moreover, the influence of dub poetry goes beyond the African presence in the Caribbean. An active participant in the festival was Allen DeLeary, of Anishinabe origins, who flatly stated, "The African diaspora doesn't apply to Indian cultures," but talked of how reggae and dub poetry influenced the music of his band, Seventh Fire. South African dub poet Mzwake Mbuli confided to the audience in a heartfelt aside during his exuberant, hard-as-nails performance at York University's Underground Club, "I *am* because of *you*. I drew my inspiration from the Caribbean."

Of course it makes sense that dub poetry should come full circle in Africa. As Mutabaruka (Jamaica) elaborated, "The commonality is not jazz, reggae or even dub, but the African oral tradition—though they take we outa the country, they never take the country outa we." This placing of the origins of the tradition in Africa offers a refreshing change of pace from the endless discussions about which came first, dub poetry or rap, that can sometimes degenerate into an esoteric debate about how many angels danced on Kool Herc's turntable. Accordingly, the festival brought together griots from all parts of the African diaspora. As Oku Onuora (Jamaica) put it, "This festival is a grounding between brothers and sisters." It was a chance to meet and greet counterparts from around the world, and to reunite with old friends and comrades.

The spirit of sharing was often intense in terms of both agreement and disagreement. As Ras Mo observed, "It was a time to thrash out a number of issues in terms of not only form but content." The two most controversial content issues over the course of the festival related to sexism and homophobia. As for the former, not only dancehall slackness but the Rasta ideal of the "African Queen" were challenged by some of the sisters. Sister Jean Binta Breeze (U.K.) questioned the virgin/whore dichotomy imbedded in the queen concept while still recognizing its difference from the pampered protectiveness of the Eurocentric pedestal. Though she directly confronted her male dub poet counterparts, it was never done with hostility. As she said, "I challenge sexism with such love that men will have to deal with me."

In marked contrast to all the paeans to African queens and princesses, Breeze offered her musical anthem to the strength, independence and unbounded sexuality of "Caribbean Woman" to a very appreciative audience at her Opera House performance. Later, as Cherry Natural (Jamaica) succinctly put it, "I'm Rasta, but I refuse to be the 'weaker vessel.'" One of the men most attuned to the issue of sexism seemed to be Michael Pintard (Bahamas), who in a dramatic appearance after being hospitalized a day earlier read a poem of solidarity with women that extended to the intimate level of their menstrual cycles.

Partly in response to Buju Banton's dancehall record calling for violence against gays, ahdri zhina mandiela (Canada) urged the formation of coalitions with the gay and lesbian community based on a recognition of mutual oppression. As she said, "We must give people the space to exist as who they are." Accordingly, she specifically included gays and lesbians in the lyrics of her poem "african by instinct," which she performed on stage with her little daughter belting out the choruses.

Yet the issue of gay rights was by far the most controversial, with some present considering homosexuality immoral, refusing to accept gays as equals, and others denouncing their appropriation of the tactics of the civil rights movement. As Mutabaruka said, "Not every oppression is the same oppression. I am a black nationalist." In the end, Flo O'Connor (Jamaica) had the last word when she explained that while Caribbean people living in Toronto may have different priorities than those living in Jamaica, "Just because we don't take up a cause doesn't mean we are not concerned. Ultimately, you must deal with it in your own heart."

Aside from such emotional moments at panel discussions, the poetry performances themselves provided their share of emotion. Sister Breeze's spirited reading of four poems by the late Mikey Smith (the martyr of the dub poetry movement, to whom the festival was dedicated) not only surprised those who expected her to do women's poetry (thus expertly turning the tables on her male protagonists), but her deep feeling for these poems and her obvious grief at the loss of a revered fellow poet led to a rousing ovation with many people visibly moved to tears.

Later in the week Breeze performed her new poem, written out of the experience of the festival and titled "Skin Teeth Don't Make It Right," in which she reflected on the differences aired among poets and the male posturing which often accompanies the espousing of deeply held values. She directly challenged Mutabaruka's earlier African essentialist statement that "if you bring a cow into a pigsty, it is still a cow." Finding it lacking in an understanding of the complexity of the situation, she offered her more nuanced interpretation of historical events by playing off Mutabaruka's often stated connection of the struggles of Africans and Native Americans in this hemisphere with these lines: "Cow and pig don't mix/But Arawak and Maroons did." In arguing for a more cosmopolitan interpretation of Africanness she later said, "Yes, we are Africans, but we must be free to be Africans anywhere in the world." As Clifton Joseph (Canada) noted in another context, "Repatriation doesn't necessarily mean going back to Africa—the African diaspora has come home."

Mutabaruka, for his part, gave his concert poetry performance without musical accompaniment. In his extemporaneous remarks in between poems he "marveled" at the way in which racism works in the music industry. "Shabba has never hit with reggae music but only a hip-hop Americanization of Jamaican lyrics over American rhythms, and a white youth like Snow, who has never been to Jamaica, has carried the Jamaican language to number one in America." He further chided Nelson Mandela for "talking too much" to the untrustworthy apartheid regime then in power. In a similar vein, Oku Onuora did an uncompromising rendition of "Bus' Out" which shook the rafters with the sound of revolution. This was in turn echoed by the ringing of Brother Resistance's (Trinidad) bell during his rapso set. Christian "Ranting Chako" Habecost (Germany) provided comic relief with a hilarious satirical take on the stereotypical white Rasta wannabe titled "Blacker than Blackman" that was warmly received with much laughter at his "I-tal Performance" set.

So, in spite of the no-show of British-based dub poetry luminaries Linton Kwesi Johnson and Benjamin Zephaniah, the Dub Poetry Festival International was a rousing success in terms of who did come and what they contributed to the proceedings. Even some publicity problems were pulled out of the fire by (appropriately) a word-of-mouth grapevine campaign that assured the performers of good-sized audiences at all venues except the out-of-the-way York University campus, whose own large Caribbean student population was not in evidence because classes were out of session.

As for the city of Toronto itself, it proved to be an excellent location for an event of this nature. As Lillian Allen (Canada), the organizer who had originally conceived of the festival and a dub poet in her own right, said to me in the St. Christopher House kitchen, where a (down) home-cooked meal was being busily prepared for the evening's poetry performances, "In Toronto we already constitute a diversity of dub poets. We're all from different backgrounds and countries, a microcosm of the international."

The organizers' stated goal for the festival was "to illustrate the social, aesthetic, political and cultural scope of dub poetry, and to develop its potential as a highly creative and culturally responsive art form with the capacity to both articulate social needs and generate energy for social change." Perhaps no one better exemplified these goals than Mikey Smith. As Oku Onuora, in reflecting on the death of his fallen brethren, put it, "Mikey might be dead, but the festival continues his work."

Word soun' still 'ave power!

Tackhead's Heady Tacktics

BART PLANTENGA

The Paris Free Voice (France)
June 1990; revised 1996

Keith LeBlanc, Tackhead's drum mobster, once boasted that Tackhead was to rap music what calculus is to arithmetic. More like a Molotov cocktail compared to a firecracker. A radio exploding under my arm couldn't change the way I listen to music more than Tackhead (and by extension the entire On-U Sound conspiracy from London, and Jamaica, Africa, Japan . . . As a radio DJ I've made On-U an almost weekly habit going on eleven years now).

So what *is* Tackhead? Well, we know what provocation is: the forcing of attention to arguments to establish conditions for discussion, and that they've done. They've never been flashy megafame boys seeking pop deification; instead they prefer to arouse discomfort, destabilize the received signs of the status quo, *détourn*ing their Luddite way up the media towers of power babel.

Putting heavy beats to intelligence is like putting joy inside menace—imagine Dick Gregory and Phil Ochs in King Tubby's studios. Listen to Tackhead's *Mind at the End of a Tether,* Wimbish's bass sounding like strummed high-tension wires, the perfect coagulation of gloom and celebration—samples declare both "Our time is now" and "There ain't no heaven on earth," reprocessed info-overload that speaks directly to our own postmodern malaise.

Tackhead has pushed Bronx ghetto-rap murder casualty Scott T. La Rock's own extrapolations of how Hendrix fused politics and transcendence into aural global politic. (Were Tackhead's covers of Hendrix's "Crosstown Traffic" and "Hey Joe" ever recorded?) Call it outlaw-hardcore-dub-ska-punk-funk-industrial-jazz-rap but call it LOUD. Beeping and a bopping with the sonic boom of a B-52: the MC5 + Fela, so you can dance, dance atop the abandoned bomb shelter, shards of shrapnel jutting from your hemp threads. Survival—and the glory beyond mere survival.

So how did three NY (and NJ) b-boys, responsible for the seminal (circa 1980) Sugar Hill sound of socially conscious "modern rap," e.g., Grandmaster Flash's "The Message" and Melle Mel's "White Lines," end up in London? LeBlanc was recruited by wizard of Oz-mological megamixing, Adrian Sherwood, to come work in the On-U Sound studios. LeBlanc beckoned the rest of the trio, Doug "bass in your face" Wimbish and guitarist Skip McDonald.

The alchemy begins: fat dubby beats for Fats Comet, lots of empty space to—as Tackhead—pour their postmodern cut-up–inspired (via Mark Stewart) sonic political mayhem into. All this spun around Sherwood's know-how (which he learned as a precocious young DJ from the likes of King Tubby, Prince Far I, Lee "Scratch" Perry—check out "African Rubber Dub" on Bim Sherman's Century Records). Prince Far I's (Kingston murder casualty) ghostly gravely voice threads homage roots through most everything Sherwood does: e.g., Singers & Players, Dub Syndicate, African Head Charge. While the rambunctious Perry's influence on Sherwood is enormous, his mixing concoctions of all manner of kinks, loops, snippets, gunshots, mad laughter are duly reconfabulated, as Perry is now produced by Sherwood to make Tackheady, provocative dub meant to "coordinate with verve," as the sampled, disembodied and ominous voice of Andy Fairley explains the On-U strategy.

With Sherwood (Phil Spector as anthropologist) at the knobs, Tackhead has produced some of the deffest "Science Fiction Dancehall," whether it be the mellifluous voice of Bim Sherman (himself a reggae singer veteran of Roots Radics, Prince Far I, Sir Coxsone, and 100s of other projects), or Gary Clail (confrontational street toaster; Billy Bragg in dub?), or soulful Bernard Fowler. Tackhead makes heavenly dissonant dub, which has become one of the most borrowed and reconfigured sounds around. "We're trying to set up a continental landslide," Doug Wimbish once said, referring to their goal of shaking up the industry (a noble failure) and their tendency to sample (organizing sound snatches that, when used properly, create complex and unique aural tapestries) and wend these snatches through other projects and songs, like leitmotifs, to coordinate with verve an even larger matrix of sound. They sample Margaret Thatcher, various military talking heads and apparatchiks, Lenny Bruce, Einstein, Bishop Tutu, Malcolm X, Martin Luther King, Prince Far I, William Burroughs, various televangelists and dominatrixes; throw in the sounds of missiles, soccer fandemonium, and paranoid newscasts, anchored to the bass-ic echo-inflected counterfrictional lassitude of their dub-hop, and you have Funkadelic caught in a Beirut cross fire, a sound at the edge of 1996 way back in 1987.

From today's undulating borders, fickle nationalisms and manufactured styles of rebellion we see emerging new languages—global music(s), musics that borrow, collaborate, hybridize, unite and re-fuse to become mere hard copy or property. The art of the remix elaborates the notion of this perpetual flux, of a zone where the contradictions of spirit (defiance and spiritual acquiescence, anger and joy, well-being and angst) are blended as an unstable yet exhilarating cocktail, all produced in a bedouin encampment of sonic barter somewhere near an Interzone of shifting sound waves: Alhambras filled with J. G. Ballard's "singing statues" along the neuronal trade routes; veins as phone lines "across the vagaboundaries" (as Ron

Sakolsky puts it in *Gone to Croatan*) between temporal and tympanic; a medina of megawatts, P.O. boxes, plain brown wrappers, B. Traven's elusiveness, campfire "bolos," Cedex, websites, white-noise squat punks, ghosts in the wires, "Tunes from the Missing Channel," André Breton's *Nadja*, allusion, absinthe, absence.

TACKHEAD CHRONOLOGY

—1979–83: Doug Wimbish, Skip McDonald and Keith LeBlanc lay down "streetwise" trax in a New Jersey studio, effectively making jazz out of disco. Become Sugarhill Gang band, backbone to Grandmaster Flash, Melle Mel, Funky 4+1, Spoony G . . .

—1984–86: Trio moves to Tommy Boy (rap) label, where LeBlanc produces (arguably) first sampling record, "No Sell Out/Malcolm X." Trio cowrite "Unity" for James Brown and Afrika Bambaataa; cowrite/produce/perform Bambaataa's *Beware (The Funk Is Everywhere)*; work with Force MD's. LeBlanc, at behest of Adrian Sherwood, upon suggestion of Mark Stewart, moves to London. Wimbish and McDonald follow, form Fats Comet. Tackhead "invented" in 1986: the trio plus Sherwood and a round-robin of sampled voices and various singers/toasters such as Gary Clail, Bim Sherman. First disc *War*. LeBlanc does *Major Malfunction* with Wimbish and McDonald; they become the Maffia behind Mark Stewart. Sherwood always close to the controls.

—1987–91: Wimbish with Fats Comet, LeBlanc with Arthur Baker. Wimbish and LeBlanc on Little Steven's *Freedom, No Compromise* and Mick Jagger's *Primitive Cool*. Tackhead produces *The Game* (4th & Broadway) and *Mind at the End of a Tether*. On top of the game of sound. On *Friendly as a Hand Grenade* use soul singer Bernard Fowler (Peech Boys, Rolling Stones). Produce *Sound System, Tackhead Tape Time* and *Mark Stewart*. In various forms they work with Shriekback, Robbie Robertson, B. B. King, Nine Inch Nails, Godfathers—everyone wants the Sherwood treatment. Add to this collaborations with ex-PiL Jah Wobble, Keith Levene, Martin Atkins, Lee Perry, Mikey Dread, Bonjo I, Style Scott, Bim Sherman and Sly and Robbie.

—1992– : Growth, dispersal, commercial disillusionment, cross-pollination: Wimbish becomes bassist in Vernon Reid's Living Colour; Wimbish and McDonald help Annie Anxiety (ex-Crass) on her *Short & Sweet*; McDonald explores blues roots as Little Axe (first ambient dub blues); LeBlanc works with Neneh Cherry, Bomb the Bass, DJ Spike; Gary Clail goes "solo" and on the road with his briefcase of Tackhead backing tapes. Strange Parcels: the hybridizations and sonic dialogues continue. Mark Stewart cuts *Control Data* and appears on Tricky single "Aftermath." Is there a collaboration in works?

SELECTED DISCOGRAPHY

The Wolf That House Built—Little Axe (Okeh)

System Vertigo—Andy Fairley (On-U)

The Strange Parcels—The Strange Parcels (On-U)

Tackhead Tape Time—Gary Clail's Tackhead Sound System (On-U)

Time Boom X De Devil Dead—Lee "Scratch" Perry & Dub Syndicate (On-U)

As the Veneer of Democracy Begins to Fade—Mark Stewart & the Maffia (Mute)

Dub Power: The New Connections

LAURENT DIOUF

Octopus (France)
Winter 1995

After a long inertia, dub is coming back in force, like a phoenix from the flames. Techno and its musical byproducts, including ambient, have incorporated dub's creative strength, thus contributing to its rediscovery and renewal. The rebirth was inevitable. Note that dub—an instrumental music—initiated the remix era, and in fact dub plates are the precursors of the techno DJ's white-labels.

As comedown and break from the BPMs, ambient is definitely—in its ethereal aspects—the successor of the "space out" music of the 1970s. But this open and intelligent music is not restricted to the realm of synthesizers; it is comprised of reliefs and mixes, a whole range of special effects. Its connection to dub is obvious.

Beyond Records confirmed the ambient-dub assimilation with the release of the first "ambient dub" compilation in 1992. Soft, square, fun—all aspects of this music trend are represented by the Insanity Sect, Original Rockers (renamed Rockers Hi Fi), Mimoid and H.I.A. Banco de Gaia, who made their first appearance on Beyond, perform an ambient, trance and tribal dub (*Last Train to Lhassa*, on Planet Dog), as do Horizon 222 (*Through the Round Window* and *The Three of Swans*) and their clone Ingleton Falls (*Absconded*) on Charrm Records, thus following the path opened by the Orb. On the other hand, Subsurfing offers a more subtle symphonia of ambiances and collage: a light and ethnic dub (*Frozen Ants*, Apollo/R&S) close to 23° (*An Endless Searching for Substance* and *Born of Earth's Torments*, Silent Records). Stemming from the industrial trend, Richard H. Kirk, with his Sandoz project (for the Touch label), performs surprisingly kitsch compositions. To the contrary, Transcend are avant-gardiste in their decomposition of the bassline (*2001–2008*, N-Tone). Common ground: a utilization of sound libraries for mixes and extended tracks—the ultimate being the Woob's 30-minute-long "On Earth" (Em:t 1194). From the Infinite Wheel (Brainiak Records) through Sub Dub (when on Instinct Ambient), Astral Engineering (*Chronoglide*, Worm Interface), *Ambient Rituals 2: A Trip into Dub* (D.O.V.e/Hypnotic) and Dub Tractor (Flex Records) to Electronic Dub (Rising High), ambient dub has exercised an increasing number of approaches and seems to never lack for resources—the potential borrowings, influences and *mix*tures are infinite.

It would take too long to make a list, group by group and title by title, of all the sounds copied from the dub masters, which often go unnoticed by an audience lacking in reggae culture. But this is where ambient deserves credit: it gives a second wind to dub without giving up a deep-rooted memory; it reasserts the immense flexibility of the dub structure through the diversity of mixes; it exposes dub to another audience and drags along other types of music in its wake.

Let's go briefly over the associations among dub, house and the kind of commercial productions put out by Guerrilla Records, which carries Liquid and the Groove Corporation. Temple Roy alone (*Deaf and Dumb*, Different Drummer) sticks out of this house-dub club trend, with soulful lyrics and a bass-based sound. After ambient, it is bass that relaxes the sore ears of an audience keen on repetitive beats. Technologically, dub wears the colors of this trend: sharp rhythms and a heavy bassline make the body pulse and vibrate, the mind lost in the complexity of the mixes. This type of collective and musical hypnosis, the true basis of sound systems, has been (re)discovered by the ravers' generation.

As a consequence, the dub has become space- and/or acid-based, with Cosmic Connection (*Zincode*, Double Space Records) and DP-Sol ("Spacecakes," *Live in Oslo*, The Spacefrogs), or even electro-deep with Braindub (*In Your Brain*, Sun), Blue (*Resistance*, Sabres of Paradise Ltd.) and Five-H-T (*Neurotransmitter*, Hypoxia Records). Without any compromise, the rhythm becomes speed: see (hear) Blue Bommer (*Dub*, Nation Records). Zip Doc Records, with Emperor Sly and especially Dubolition, is one of the premier labels of what must now be called techno dub. Here again, a series of compilations assert this association: *Club Meets Dub* and *Triangle Dub Clash*. But some other groups, such as Moody Boyz or Bandulu (*Cornerstone*, Blanco y Negro), refuse to make a choice in their compositions and play both.

Another hybrid form is the ragga/techno breakbeats connection—hardcore even—as a base for jungle. Expert ears can sometimes identify old reggae themes tumbling along this musical electric current. Jungle dub with its hard beats exists: Neon of Rhys Chatham and Martin Wheeler on N-Tone, the compilation *Jungle Dub* on Hardleaders and of course Mad Professor (*Mazurani: The Jungle Dub Experience*, Ariwa). Abstract dub? Try Signs ov Chaos, *FrankenScience* (Earache Records). The wanderings of Strongpoint and DigiDub (*16 Millionths of an Inch*, Incoming!) are quite meaningful on this drift too. And what the drum'n'bass conjunction could take from dub begins to appear when—for instance with Osymyso (*Being Born* and *Peter and the Wolf*, Handsome)—this musical style moves away from the clean and calibrated sounds of FM radio to become baroque. The drum-and-dub symbiosis is even more striking when crossbred with sounds from India (Calcutta Cyber Cafe, *Drum + Space,* Omni) or the Orient (Ebn E Sync on WordSound).

Scene change. At the bridge of jazz, funk, soul and rap, bands that claim to play acid jazz did not hesitate, for one or two tracks, to explore reggaeland dub; *par exemple,* the Humble Souls and Raw Stylus. The Acid Jazz label released two opuses by the Hazardous Dub Company and rereleased Mannaseh's *Dub the Millenium.* A subdivision of the label, Acid Roots, especially deals with roots and instrumental reggae. Still, one would have expected Acid Jazz to produce such jazz-tainted dub as Shake Keen's *Real Keen: Reggae into Jazz* (LKJ Records) or Deadly Headly (*35 Years from Alpha,* On-U Sound). Another synthesis, at the limits of acid jazz and hip-hop, is trip-hop, which acquired its nobility on the Mo' Wax label. On Beechwood, the second volume of the series *110 Bellow/Journey in Dub:* Trip *to the Ship* Chop packs innovative trip-hop dub.

Taking advantage of these musical trends, a new dub wave anchored in the reggae scene has asserted itself. There are two tendencies. On the one hand, a new age is dawning for roots dub without excessive fioritura: deep bass, a round and polished sound. Alpha & Omega are representative of this renewal. This duet knows how to update a mystical and religious dub, down to the images of icons that decorate their record covers (*Daniel's in the Lion Den/King and Queen* and *Watch and Pray/Over-standing,* A&O/Greensleeves). Dub Judah is definitely the main producer/director of this trend. The Rootsman (*In Dub We Trust* and *Into the Light,* Third Eye Music) and the Disciples (*For Those Who Understand,* Roots Records) are two of the bands that have helped revive the roots spirit while taking into account today's resonances (*Res-onations,* Cloak & Dagger). Various sound systems represent this new roots dub on such anthologies as *Dubhead* (Shiver M&D), *Dub Revolution* (ROIR) and *Dub Out West* (Nubian Records).

On the other hand, bands such as Zion Train exude a more "lay" dub—often a faster one (*Natural Wonders of the World in Dub*)—and are tuned in to the English techno/dance scene (with *Siren*). Their label, Universal Egg, provides good examples of this other dubscape. Iration Steppers (*Original Dub D.A.T.,* I.S. Records) has a *warrior* style, with a rhythm sustained by an abrupt and almost metallic sound. Together with Small Axe and Powersteppers (*Bass Enforcement*) they belong to the hardcore dub galaxy—no compromise. In the end, a new school is coming in (Mixman, Armagideon, Bush Chemist, the Dub Specialists, Shotgun Rockers, etc.) that credits those who came before them (see [hear] the remixes of Dub Syndicate's *Research & Development,* On-U Sound).

Left are the "nonaligned" who, through their background, their processes and their music, de-partition dub, muddle up its notions and blow up its rules. One of the first of these bands was Scorn, which made a breach in performing an oppressive, dark and cold dub that revolves around a bass of frightening depths (*Evanescence,* Earache). These bass experiments go on with Bill Laswell (*Bass Terror*), who spread the dub mushrooming with *Automaton, Axiom Dub,* and *Possession.* Kevin Martin's *Macro Dub Infection* (Virgin) compilations present an almost complete scope of the various metastases of dub, thus showing the contagious sprawling that encompasses even Coil.

Future dub? In this game the rules seem to be abolished: Silk Saw (*Come Freely, Go Safely,* Sub Rosa), for instance. The first photos of the "dark side of dub" came to us from Brooklyn via WordSound Recordings and its manifesto-compilation *The Red Shift.* The promised land as no-man's-land: chaotic breakbeats and deafening bass— dub-hop, or a melting pot of elements borrowed from dub and hip-hop. Dub is also a restrained and supressed violence, as with WordSound's *Crooklyn Dub Consortium 1* and *2* and *Equations of Eternity.* No fun, but if this dub is dark, it is above all because it feeds on black music: reggae, ragga, jazz, funk, etc. The Australian label Extreme has started to move in this direction with its subdivision Extreme Dub! As for the combination of dub and ritual/industrial music, the Missing Brazilians (*Warzone,* On-U) and Mark Stewart & the Maffia have been there and done that.

Rebellion and deviousness are the touchstones of DJ Spooky (*Necropolis,* Knitting Factory, and *Songs of a Dead Dreamer,* Asphodel) and the actors of illbient. They dispatch a noisy maelstrom, rough, wild and tormented: music is an organized noise, so is dub. In this way the *Serenity Dub* compilations on Incoming! extend dub's range. Some of its bands are far from reggae, but through their use of bass and their sound technical approach can be associated with dub: Muslimgauze for the roundness of some of its LPs; Rapoon for its use and mixes of loops; Scanner, S.E.T.I. and Nonplace Urban Field, pirates of the electronic avant-garde.

Incoming!, the bass-label precursor of this patchwork, has proposed the term *neodub,* which defines quite well the spread of the sound into various new-music currents. Not many have been spared the dub virus, and incubation continues.

[Translated from the French by Nicole Macintosh; extract adapted from article originally titled "Puissance Dub."]

Dub, American Style

MARC WEIDENBAUM

Pulse!
October 1995

Much has been made of late of the brave new dub-influenced pop tunes wafting across the Atlantic. All manner of this danceable British music, from the ambient-techno encounters of Aphex Twin to the dreamy songs of Tricky and Portishead, is permeated by dub, a meditative studio methodology that originated a quarter century ago in Jamaica, the home of reggae.

More quietly—if anything can be said to be quieter than ambient music—a dub revival is also coalescing in the United States. But aside from the Beastie Boys, whose percussion-and-organ instrumentals betray youths spent under the spell of such Jamaican innovators as Lee "Scratch" Perry and Clement "Coxsone" Dodd, none of the dub-influenced U.S. rock bands have achieved the notoriety of their U.K. brethren. Such groups as the Dub Narcotic Sound System (from Olympia, Washington) and President's Breakfast (from San Francisco) are using dub as a creative launchpad, but their work is too disparate to fit easily under a rubric like "trip-hop," the umbrella term for much of the new British dub-influenced pop.

Dub's rise in America is particularly strong on the West Coast, where beach culture would make for a nice climatic correlation with Jamaica if dub—a studio art—weren't by nature an indoor activity. (Well, there's always the hemp connection.)

A little history. In dub, a song's backing tracks are treated with simple studio effects to create new versions. These dub compositions focus the listener's attention not on the familiar strengths of pop music—melody, lyrics, instrumental leads—but on the simple pleasure of a heavily echoed drum reverberating into seeming eternity; or on the repetition of a horn blurt, severed from the original full horn section by liberal use of the mute button. Dub's emphasis on reverberation carves out imaginary spaces for contemplation—and casual partying. The result is an odd form of spiritual music: one that is indebted to technology, however primitive.

The founders of this movement were such prolific producers as Augustus Pablo and King Tubby; in their heyday their sound systems, or studios, produced more music than the average-size record company. Today's dub-influenced pop echoes these pioneers in several ways: by using such dub standards as unnaturally exaggerated reverb and the recycling of riffs and rhythms; by often adopting dub's languorous pace; and, most importantly, by conveying the implicit message that technology is not the enemy of humanity, but a tool of artistic expression and personal reflection. (Island Records, for one, has recognized the new dub explosion with a series of historical reissues, off to a great start with a Pablo overview, *Classic Rockers,* and an updated edition of the *Raiders of the Lost Dub* compilation, now titled *Time Warp Dub Clash.*)

In drawing from dub for inspiration, Aphex Twin, Tricky and their U.K. cohorts are simply the latest in a British line of reverse assimilation that includes the Clash, the Specials, Eric Clapton and the Rolling Stones; U.K. pop's creative debt stretches back almost half a century, to the first wave of Jamaican emigration.

Lacking a prominent Jamaican community on the order of England's, America has allowed for more diffused absorption of dub's musical lessons, in settings that include everything from Meters-style pop instrumentals to highly experimental jazz.

Dub Narcotic Sound System leader Calvin Johnson had a modest purpose when he formed the group. "A lot of people in town here are in bands, but when they have a party they're not listening to the same kind of music they make," he says on the phone from his Olympia, Washington, studio for which he named the band.

Johnson should know Olympia's scene better than most; he founded K Records in the early 1980s to document, and eventually fuel, the city's musical community. "I thought it would be neat to make a record that someone in Olympia might actually play at a dance party—not that I know if that's happened yet."

In the spirit of his prodigious Jamaican role models, Johnson's Dub Narcotic has during its year-and-a-half existence released a full album of instrumentals, an EP of songs and a handful of 7-inch singles and cassette-only recordings. The band's lineup is as informal as a party, as is its attitude toward recording. *Ridin' Shotgun,* an EP the band recorded with Memphis producer William Brown (Stax's first black recording engineer) while touring the States this past summer, is due out at the end of October. Also in the dub tradition, Dub Narcotic accepted a commission from the Jon Spencer Blues Explosion to rework one of the band's songs, the result of which is featured on the Blues Explosion's *Experimental Remixes* EP (Beastie Boy Mike D contributed to a remix, too).

"One of the ideas that I draw from Jamaican music is that there are these rhythms that get used and reused in different contexts—with singers, DJs, instrumentalists," says Johnson. "That's incredibly exciting to me." Some of the tracks on the *Industrial Breakdown* EP add lyrics to material worked out on the band's exceptional vocal-less album, *Rhythm Record Volume One,* a catchy smattering of simple grooves atop which Johnson's melodica playing suggests Ennio Morricone as much as it does Augustus Pablo. On the title track Johnson intones Marxist axioms over the band's spare arrangement. Dub, the narcotic of the indie-rock masses?

"In terms of using samples," says Johnson, "in Jamaica there's no shame in taking someone else's song and making your own song out of it. And I never saw dub as a type of music, but as a process," he adds, extrapolating from his sense of a free exchange of intellectual property. "The fact that it originated in reggae is inconsequential."

A key ingredient in the Beastie Boys' fine mess is Money Mark, or Mark Ramos-Nishita. His keyboards were essential in the Beastie Boys' transformation from a studio concoction to a true live act over the course of their last two albums, *Check Your Head* (1992) and *Ill Communication* (1994). And recently Nishita's been moonlighting with his own music, as well as recording with George Clinton, Beck and the Blues Explosion.

A homespun 10-inch of his organ-noodling appeared in record stores last year. It's since been collected with additional material for the lengthy, nineteen-track *Mark's Keyboard Repair* on Mo' Wax, the influential London-based label. The record is thick with the porn-flick funk that pervades the Beasties' recent work. Freed from the sermonizing and antic rapping, Nishita's favor for pretty melodies and scratchy, off-kilter keyboard sounds is allowed full fruition. ("It's kind of an act of defiance from the stuff I do with the Beastie Boys," he says from his Gardena, California, home, just back from London.) Nishita does sing a bit on *Keyboard Repair,* sounding on "Cry" like Mose Allison guesting on *Sanford and Son,* but it's the attenuated vamps like "Insects Are All Around Us" that invite repeated listening.

Nishita says he's excited to be included in an article that mentions the Dub Narcotic Sound System. Turns out that he played along with the band's *Rhythm Record Volume One* for an in-store performance at London's Rough Trade the day before he returned to the States. "I'm gonna do some records where you can add your own part," he jokes. "That was my idea when I played live to that record—like, There's enough room here; let me be in the Dub Narcotic band."

Though Nishita doesn't aim for the sort of authenticity with which Johnson's band toys, his album is rich with dub overtones, with its sturdy basslines, deep acoustic resonance and occasional melodica, horn and flute solos. And like the Dub Narcotic Sound System, Nishita understands his studio smarts to be an inherent part of his music making. "The first keyboard I bought was a Fender Rhodes," he says. "I played that all night long and the next day I had to go out and buy a four-track—so I've never really separated my musicianship from my recording hobby."

Bill Langton, like Dub Narcotic's Johnson, champions dub as process, or metaphor—more means than end. "I guess our dub sounds pretty different from normal dub, stripped away stuff," says the leader of President's Breakfast from his home in San Francisco. Among the band's members are guitarist Will Bernard (T. J. Kirk) and keyboardist Dred Scot (Alphabet Soup); widely recorded saxophonist Glenn Spearman guests. President's Breakfast's recent sophomore album, *Doo Process* (Disclexia), is a wildly experimental mix of studio invention and live performance. "We certainly try to revere the form," says Langton, who goes by the name Click Dark, "and put other stuff on it that might also give you some idea of a relationship between dub and jazz, dub and funk."

Doo Process is thick with dub resonances, but what truly places the band in the tradition of Jamaica's studio innovators is its ability to combine Langton's studio technology with live improvisation. "Odpharb" is virtual reggae, with a spongy beat and ska horns, but check out "Yahh!" on which a sample of breaking glass fills in for a climaxing horn section, or the band's take on Wayne Shorter's "Nefertiti," here rendered as low rider anthem.

The album's finest track, "Sounds Spectacular," makes a deep impression with its thin array of samples and riffs, which the band works into an incredibly rarefied brand of funk. "It's very much an excursion into sculpting," he says. "I filled up what must have been forty or fifty tracks, full of horns and synthesizers, and gradually came to strip away so much that literally 15 percent of the total sound is all that I had left anymore. I was just shaving more and more rock and was eventually left with this Brancusi form sticking out in the middle."

And despite the heavy emphasis on prerecorded material, Langton insists that the band thrives on live performance. The most exciting material on *Doo Process* is when the musicians are clearly interacting with Langton's sampling, and where Langton is responding to their ideas with his array of effects. In February Langton's Disclexia label will release *Wood Squares* by Bar-B-Que Dali, a live collaboration between key members of President's Breakfast and clarinetist Don Byron (like Langton, a New England Conservatory of Music alum).

Bob Green is getting somewhat used to the dub label, though he denies any particularly deep involvement in the music. When he calls from San Francisco he reports that he just got off the phone with a Canadian writer who claimed that *Grassy Knoll*, his band's self-titled debut on Nettwerk/Verve, is steeped in dub. (*Grassy Knoll* was first released by Nettwerk in late 1994; the new Verve edition adds a pair of studio demos.)

"For me that's kind of weird," says Green, who recently returned to S.F. after a stint in Austin, "because I don't hear the dub. Well, the basslines, because of my fondness for Jah Wobble, show that influence. But dub always seemed to me to be an afterthought, where you have established tracks and go from there. Though in my music I do make a lot of having adverse ideas coming together. In a way it's kind of a dub idea, to take fragments and combine them."

Green's statement exemplifies how dub's influence has been disseminated over the years. Englishmen such as Wobble, the former PiL bassist, and Adrian Sherwood of On-U Sound System have enlarged dub's listenership and its definition. Green's music also bears the mark of Bill Laswell's best work: impenitent jazz-rock fusion unabashedly transformed with postproduction techniques, music riddled with flavorful samples and draped under film-score textures. *Grassy Knoll* is a tremendous album, thick with hard grooves and powerful playing by clarinetist Beth Custer, trumpeter Chris Grady and other San Francisco musicians, including a tabla player and a DJ. Notably absent is the guitar, which Green, who plays bass and other instruments on the album, said he eschewed in order to keep his album from being labeled "industrial."

As with President's Breakfast, it's the self-consciousness of Green's studio techniques that make the strongest musical impression—the layering of melodies, the haloing of fragments, the shifting postproduction arrangements, the additions of telling samples. A 1995 Emigre Records sampler (*Dreaming Out Loud*) featured a Grassy Knoll track titled "Noe Valley," much of which consisted of meditative music fused together from the manipulated scratches of vinyl records; the effect was more Satie than Public Enemy.

"Those sampled tracks of LP records' pops"—or scratches—"are samples unto themselves," says Green. "They're not with anything else [musical]. So if you get a bunch of them going, you can control where the pops land, and synch them up so you can create rhythms with that as well."

Grassy Knoll shows Green to be comfortable with cacophony and contemplation. Expect a harder album this spring (with guitar, he promises), after the label has had the opportunity to (re)introduce Green's music to a listening public so enamored of the acid jazz and studio-generated pop of his British contemporaries.

What's apparent on both sides of the Atlantic is that dub has become the reigning metaphor for reconciling the tradition of live musical performance, as old as mankind, with the abstract art of using the studio as a recording instrument. It's as though the reverb echoes of Augustus Pablo and his kin have failed to dissipate over the years. Instead, the reverberating waves of their sound systems have grown wider and more far-reaching, only to encompass the most creative pop music of our day.

PART SIX

DANCEHALL

When Rap Meets Reggae

JOHN LELAND

Newsweek
7 September 1992

Clive Campbell was twelve when he moved from Kingston, Jamaica, to the Bronx in 1967. Tall and athletic, he ran track and attended Alfred E. Smith High School, a vocational school for auto mechanics. And he gave parties. Following the model of the Jamaican reggae acts back home, he assembled a sound system—a powerful mobile PA setup and a crew of emcees, or "toastmasters," who would chat up the crowd and protect the gear if things turned heavy. He called his featured dancers the Nigger Twins and his sound system the Herculords; he was Kool DJ Herc. In a Bronx club called the Hevalo, Herc and the Herculords made musical history. From these parties—from this casual synthesis of Jamaican toasting and American funk—came the most significant popular innovation of the last twenty years: rap.

Almost two decades later, the paths of rap and reggae have come together again, merging in a dynamic hybrid that is as far from the soothing reggae of Bob Marley as it is from Elvis Presley. Like American rock and soul, Jamaican music has been racked by a generation gap since the age of Marley, a rift widened by the hard politics of the eighties. With the turbulent change from Michael Manley's socialist government to the capitalist system of Edward Seaga in 1980, says Maxine Stowe, a reggae-industry veteran who now scouts talent for Sony, "the Rastafarian culture and Afrocentric talk started dispersing. Kids became less Afrocentric and more New York–centric." This new Jamaican music, like rap, has become harder, simpler, more urban and more conspicuously market wise. Dancehall style—the vernacular, often sexually nasty sound of Jamaican dance clubs—has all but eclipsed the more spiritual "cool reggae" of Marley and Jimmy Cliff. In Jamaica, says Super Cat, one of the stars of the new dancehall style, "it's all about the hard core: survival, facts of life."

Super Cat, born William Maragh, is emblematic of the new music. Wearing his hair cut short—a style the Rastafarians, who favor long dreadlocks, dismiss as "bald-head"—he calls himself "The Don" and appears on his album cover dressed as an American gangster. Living in Kingston as well as New York, Super Cat is fluent in the idioms of both cities; his music is a spare, brutal intersection of reggae and rap. "They're both ghetto music," he says. "We express ourselves the same way. Everything is in this music: girls, guns, fast living, roots and culture."

The music is finding an audience here and adding flavor to American acts like Kris Kross, the top-selling Atlanta rap duo who affect Jamaican speech patterns. Shabba Ranks, whose "slackness," or risqué rhyming, has made him the current dancehall ruler, recently scored a No. 1 single, a feat Marley never accomplished. And where Marley's American audience was white baby boomers, says Stowe, "this new sound sells to a young black audience. It's more dynamic now." For many Americans, dance-hall represents the raw, outlaw wildness once symbolized by rap. At Jamaican shows, says Ranks, audiences often show their approval by firing gunshots into the air. "That's a salute of honor," he says.

Having absorbed funk, rhythm and blues and elements of jazz and rock, rap is now advancing by consuming its roots. The result is an international street music, an expanded turf for both rabid machismo and pointed social commentary. Dynamic, multicultural and often cruel, it's a music for the nineties.

Introduction to
The Official Dancehall Dictionary

CHESTER FRANCIS-JACKSON

1995

Dancehall music in its purest form, bubbling with all the intensity, colour, and high drama of Kingston's urban ghettoes, is at its best in its home environment. Attempts such as this to seek to shed light on this burgeoning music, for all the research, etc., will always be superficial because of the inability to communicate the electricity, the atmosphere, in short the vibes of the dance hall, the home environment; whether this be in London, New York, Germany, Sweden, or in Jamaica.

The dance hall and the music it gave birth to is an experience which spawned its own food, drink, fashion, and, case in point, language. The original music itself draws heavily on the colourful Jamaican experience, using a vocabulary that is totally visually descriptive.

Figuring prominently in the music's vocabulary are the more notorious of Jamaican ghettoes; references to the island's two major political parties and their strongholds; and the choicest of cusswords. The harmonious combining of these and other experiences has evolved into the sheer theatrical drama of dancehall music. It is intended that this compendium will more than offer a summary interest to the reader, but will create an experience akin to the reality.

And while the language paints and illustrates the music, and graphically so, earning itself the label *slackness*—much to the dismay of reggae purists, notably columnists—interest in the music, its relatively obscure lyrical content notwithstanding, has not been diminishing as has been predicted. In fact, we can say that in spite of the relatively foreign language in which dancehall is sung, recorded, etc., interest in the music has skyrocketed internationally.

Trend? I think not. Phase? Nope!

Labels such as these are, at best, superficial attempts to explain away the dancehall phenomenon in pretty much the same way that attempts were made to curtail the phenomenon of reggae before Bob Marley accorded it respectability. These labels ignore the development and history of what is now the phenomena booming from sets, nigga boxes, and being worked on dance floors in Jamaica, the U.S.A., Britain, Germany, Italy, France, Poland, and/or Ibizia.

In an interesting and informed programme on the subject of dancehall carried by the BBC in May of 1991, the question was posed: Was Jamaica now turning its back on *roots reggae* (my emphasis) a la Bob Marley? The interviewee, Neville Garrick, friend of the late Bob Marley who now directs the Bob Marley Museum in Kingston, Jamaica, replied, "No." And indeed, no it is. Dancehall music may have gained international prominence within the last two years or so, but it was there right from the very birth of reggae, in a class titled then and now as ragamuffin. While reggae went on to earn respectability and its place on international playlists, the dancehall ragamuffin sound took hold in the ghettoes of Jamaica.

The music is admittedly still largely identifiable only with ghetto circumstances, albeit on an international scale. And those who radically label it a trend—and a passing one too—rush to point out (as a means of bolstering their position) that the music is yet to storm into international charts and yet to be of significance by way of longevity. But this is in reality an expression of the ignorance of the music itself.

The current popularity of the music was not achieved through the slick and professional promotion accorded mainstream music. Dancehall made its way from the ghettoes of Kingston via the undergound—chanting slackness, debasing our womenfolk, and appealing to our baser instincts all the way. Its pathway consisted largely of specialist record shops and the creative machinations of a few individuals, with little or practically no airplay—the surest way of crossing over and the surest conventional method of attracting attention—outside of specialist stations or programmes. The exception here was John Peal of BBC Radio 1—a local, that is to say a British-based, radio station that consistently plays both reggae and dancehall.

Mainstream radio largely ignores dancehall reggae; a number of reasons being advanced include programme directors not "liking" the sound or slackness content; the violence; etc. and etc. But the music itself is no longer that of the underground crowd. (Who wants to keep a good thing to themselves?) It has now established itself as a floor-filler on the mainstream scene. This has led to some mainsteam dance acts seeking to engender a new style incorporating dancehall into . . . you name it, it's being attempted. And herein lies the greatest fad potential.

Of slackness: In the mid-1980s, at about the time when the musical world was caught up in Bob Marley nostalgia following his death, Winston Foster, a teenage orphan who had spent his growing years at Eventide Home, a home primarily for the aged, infirm, and indigent situated smack in the middle of many of Kingston's ghettoes, rose to DJ prominence and very soon after was hailed as DJ King. Bob Marley, the King of Reggae, was dead; a new king was crowned, albeit not of reggae but of reggae's underside.

Foster, truly a physically unattractive young man, took the stage name Yellowman (an acknowledgement of his being an albino, a physical state which automatically stigmatized him and shunted him to the edge of society as an abnormal freak) and became, paradoxically, the darling of the new generation of reggae lovers, using lyrics that tore everything apart.

He spared nothing. Himself, homosexuality, the various ethnic groups of Jamaica, the prevailing social order, and the social practices and habits of his audience then— the underprivileged underclass—were all taken to task in the *raw-chaw* language of the environment. As his popularity increased and his lyrics (not fit for airplay) began being recited by four- and five-year-olds, the Jamaican media took an active interest in his lyrics, branded as indecently offensive and degrading to women.

Yellowman achieved cultlike status, and curiously enough his popularity soared, particularly among women.

And what is slackness? As performed by Yellowman and as is being performed today by practitioners of the art, it is the ability to unabashedly call a spade a spade— the word *sex* may be more pleasant to the ear, but *fuck* is what, by and large, is meant, so this is the word used, or the current substitute common to the vocabulary and experience of dancehall *massives*.

Of culture: Of the other style of DJing practised by dancehall DJs, "culture" is the name given to this vein. The "cultural" DJ deals with *livity* and *up-fullness*—he avoids the usage of slackness lyrics and basically sees himself as part of the musical process promoting social consciousness, awareness, and change.

Basically the slackness DJ sees himself as a social commentator. On the other hand, the cultural DJ operates as a social activist—a vehicle for change. Of the two it is the latter—the cultural DJ—who artistically identifies with the lyrical legacy of Bob Marley (that is, within the dancehall vein).

Since Yellowman first unleashed slackness (to a receptive public), several dance-hall DJs have emerged from out of the musical woodwork riding the slackness rhythm all the way to the bank. With this new and growing trend have come the new styles of DJing. Not all the new crop of DJs "check fi de slackness," but the awareness that "a slackness time now" has led to an inventiveness, both among those who DJ in praise of slackness and those inclined to promote "culcha," which has only enriched the dancehall "stylee." The tendency by the commentator to label all dancehall style as "ragga" is off mark.

Ragga, or ragamuffin—the actual parent of ragga, which these same commenta-tors wrongly claim to be a sort of black sheep, if you like, offspring of reggae—is just one of the prevailing styles. And as the word *ragamufffin* indicates, this "style" is hard-core dancehall stuff, lyrically. The heavy dub—instrumental, characterized by a heavy bass—will be found in all styles. And here I point out that style is used to indicate

(a) personal delivery
(b) general vein, as in: dubwise, ragamuffin, rub-a-dub, lovers' rock, or slackness.

Within the dancehall DJ fraternity it is those with a distinctive individual style—a consistent wheeze; a bansheelike wail; a gravelly sound; stuttering; chanting; or the ability to rhyme, all backed with theatricality—who author and enjoy *don*like status.

And, whichever vein a performance DJ makes his own, the lyrical content of dancehall music has been and remains largely anecdotal. Where it is alleged that DJs advocate violence, this is arguable, as what is usually alluded to is defensive violence. The exception is violence as an act of aggression against male and female homosexuals. And this prejudice, while not excusable, could be said to be a Jamaican trait, amplified by the ghetto circumstances, which provides the inspiration for the lyrics to the music.

As stated earlier, reggae music is largely available from specialist shops. This is especially true of Europe, but in North America this is not the prevailing mode—a situation which tends to contribute to the marginalization of the music. However, where there is a recognition of the sales potential, reggae charts are used to quantify sales. Interestingly, where these charts obtain (they do on both sides of the Atlantic) it is the dancehall strain of reggae, which is in the ascendancy, particularly the slackness style. That Shabba Ranks was signed to CBS—the biggest reggae signing in recent history—is an acknowledgement of the status of dancehall reggae—long an established part of the Jamaican dance scene. The recent inroads it has been making on the international scene says it's more than the flavour of the month.

But more on the music. Reggae has been described thus: a type of popular music from the West Indies with a strong, continually repeated beat; the music from the Caribbean island of Jamaica made popular by Bob Marley, characterized by its heavy, often repeated bass. The Collins Dictionary gives this definition: Reggae—a type of West Indian popular music having four beats to the bar, the upbeat being strongly accentuated.

All the definitions of the word *reggae* taken from these different sources stress the "repeated" bassline. *Dancehall* has not yet earned a place in world dictionaries, but it would be interesting to see what definition it would be accorded. Unlike reggae, dancehall style is not necessarily identified by its heavy repeated bassline. In fact, quite often the bassline does not exist at all, and the accent is away from the bass and on the artiste. It is the style the artistes perfect which largely accounts for dancehall's popularity. Lyrics and bass follow.

And, when it comes to the rhythm (bass), the tendency has been to move away from the "accented" standard reggae bassline to a more up-tempo type rhythm, a sort of electro-exploration—with liberal samplings from soul and/or disco material. The end result is that while reggae's bassline is its identity card, dancehall, while it incorporates the bassline, has moved away from within the structures of the established rhythm to embrace a wider expression. In short, the bassline is no longer king.

This up-tempo style rhythm, with its electro-exploration and sampling, it should be noted, often follows a pace that is dictated by the particular DJ's style.

The DJ Tiger, with his hoarse throaty roar; Ninja Man with his stammering (stuttering) style; the wailing Sweetie Irie are a few examples of the main characteristics of dancehall: the music (rhythm) is usually composed after the lyrics, to accommodate the DJ's style. The most common method, however, of putting together dancehall music, at least by the majority of newcomers and a few "ranking" DJs, is to adapt an existing rhythm to facilitate the DJ's style. Often, adapted versions of established rhythms show no real or noticeable rearrangement. And when a rhythm or a whole record achieves dancehall prominence, whether its origins are in soul, disco, dancehall, etc., the adapted versions will number in their tens of tens.

Rhythms and/or records are not the only areas of dancehall where large-scale adaptation occurs or is attempted. For every successful DJ with his own "inimitable" style, there are several aspirants to be found imitating him. This trend is not only confined to Jamaica but is also to be found in cities such as Toronto, Miami, New York, and London.

But of particular relevance to this compilation is the growing awareness of, and the effect dancehall is having on, the wider music and new-music world. Not only has there been a growing interest internationally in dancehall reggae, but there has been a corresponding awareness of and active interest in its subculture and language. As the streets and corners of most musical cities, particularly those with large ghettoes, underground culture, faddish population, continue to blast dancehall music from motor vehicles and sets, the language of these specific populations has been changing: "the new talk" comes straight out of the dance hall. To be sure, many using the language do so without fully grasping the essence of the spoken word—as one German acquaintance of mine, after attending a reggae dancehall "shakedown" in Berlin went about for days reciting a line he'd picked up from one of the many performing DJs. The line "She jus a kin out her saul," which in as approximate a translation as is attainable means "she's exposing her vagina," was not at all understood by my German acquaintance, but because it "sounded cool" and was used by a currently *stinging* DJ he thought it very hip to be using it. He had the accent and emphasis down to a tee. Needless to say, I was and still am amused whenever I think of my acquaintance happily humming "She jus a kin out."

I resisted earlier attempts by associates to have me compile this book and have it published, as I had feared that by doing so I would only further assist in the sterilization of dancehall music. Like calypso, which originated in the Caribbean isles of Trinidad and Tobago, the lyrical component cannot be separated from the sound any more than in the case of dancehall. The tendency to classify dancehall as "slackness" is ill informed. Slackness is but one of many dancehall styles.

So, why this dictionary? With the language of the dance hall becoming more widely spoken by dancehall enthusiasts, it is experiences such as those with my German acquaintance referred to earlier, plus by having viewed an interview given by a group of young musicians (a pop group) in which they laid claim to being originators of a number of dancehall words, which spurred me to compile this book.

I fervently hope that in picking it up you will find it illuminating and entertaining and will have a much deeper insight into the music and culture it sprang from.

SELECTED ENTRIES

BATTY RIDER   a skirt or pair of shorts which exposes more of the buttocks than it conceals

BIG-UP YUHSELF   enjoy your status, you've earned it

BOW-CAT   a man who indulges in fellatio

CRABBIT   (*Ja.*) 1. good: *u.* a crabbit piece of music 2. coarse individual: *u.* Yuh too crabbit.

CRISS   anything new or attractive: *u.* De outfit criss; de gal criss.

CUT EYE   to stare malevolently then turn away with eyes closed: *u.* Nuh cut yuh eye after me.

DIBBY-DIBBY   (*Ja. derog.*) lowlife: *u.* dibby-dibby bwoy

DIGITAL   state-of-the-art; modern

DON   title of respect, not necessarily of a criminal

FLEX   hot dancehall buzzword (due mainly to a hit by Jamaican DJ Cobra, titled "Flex [Time to Have Sex]," meaning ready for sex)

GAL A TEK LIFE   a woman who is a head-turner; a very attractive or well-dressed woman

GORGAN   a toughie; roughneck: *u.* De man is a gorgan.

JACKET   a man who unknowingly accepts the social responsibility of fatherhood for a child not thought to be his genetic offspring: *u.* A fi 'im jacket that.

MASSIVE   a large crowd; a group of friends (amount)

MR. MENTION   someone who is very popular

RAW-CHAW   1. the naked truth 2. vulgar, unadulterated

RUB-A-DUB   heavy instrumental music; also type of dance

STING   the flavour of the moment; breathtaking: *u.* A dat a sting.

WASSY   wild; very good: *u.* De music well wassy.

WINE   sexual gyration; to dance in a sexually suggestive and provocative manner

YUSH   hush; be cool: *u.* Yush an tek in de music./*Hush and listen to the music.*

Jamaica's Rhythm Twins Still Reign Supreme

BALFORD HENRY

The Jamaican Weekly Gleaner
21 August 1992

They certainly are Jamaica's rhythm find of the 1980s.

Now, in the 1990s, even with a renewed challenge from the veterans Sly and Robbie, Steely (Wycliffe Johnson) and Clevie (Cleveland Browne) have remained tops among producers of reggae rhythms.

Who are they? Well, if you are not into modern dancehall vernacular, they are the musicians who create the rhythms on which dancehall music's rapid success is being built.

No doubt that Sly Dunbar created a rude shock, reminding all and sundry that he is far from a spent force when he went to India, experimented with bhangara music and emerged with the "bangara" rhythm (sometimes called the "Bam Bam" rhythm).

But, Steely (keyboards) and Clevie (drums) still reign supreme as far as Jamaican dancehall rhythms are concerned.

MANY HITS

Their rhythms have spawned a number of hits, including "Ting-a-Ling" and "Trailer Load" by Shabba Ranks; "Stamina Daddy," "Love Me Browning" and "The Grudge" by Buju Banton; "Wife" by Joseph Stepper; "Coca Cola Shape" by Simpleton; "Fire Burning" by Marcia Griffiths; "Tempted to Touch" by Beres Hammond; "Fresh Vegetable" and "Sweet Jamaica" by Tony Rebel; "When" by Tiger; "Mama" by Baby Wayne; and "Ghetto Red Hot" by Super Cat.

Steely and Clevie are the masters of the "Bogle" beat, which has spawned the current dance of the halls. In fact, says Steely, "Most musicians have been copying us for the past ten years, because we create all the new styles." They also have their own label, the Steely and Clevie label, operating since 1988 and distributed by Dynamic Sounds.

Both musicians regard themselves as fine examples of what producers really are. "The public needs to know the difference between a producer and an executive producer," said Steely. As Clevie explained, "The executive producer finances the project, while the producer deals with the whole technical aspect of the recording." They are both producers and executive producers. In fact, they have become fine examples of what can be achieved through mastery of local music.

Both men drive shiny new Mercedes Benzes, and apart from owning their own label and producing hit songs for themselves as well as creating new rhythms for other producers, they are also composers and are soon to open their own studios.

"Prior to now we were just producing but not being paid the royalties we deserved as producers and originators of the rhythms," Clevie explained. "We had to cut back working for other people in the business. In Jamaica most 'producers' don't acknowledge the input of the musicians into the creative aspects of the music by granting them publishing credits. Gussie [Clarke] started doing that, recently.

"But, since we were responsible for the change in the music, we refused to work without being accorded publishing rights. Normally we ask for 50 percent of the publishing for both of us."

WATERSHED?

However, Billy Ocean was here in April and they were able to work out a deal with him in which they shared 33⅓ percent each, which could be a watershed in local music publishing.

They had done a remix for Jive, a U.S. label, which impressed the head of the company so much he decided to have them work with a new rap group signed by the company fusing reggae and hip-hop. They also did a remix for Yo Yo Honey from England.

All this led to the contract to work with Ocean, a big rhythm-and-blues star of the eighties, whose hits include "Caribbean Queen" and "Suddenly." They produced two rhythms for Ocean—one a house-music rhythm and the other a reggae fusion.

Prior to that they produced rhythms for Carron Wheeler, "Jamaica" and "Proud." Wheeler led Soul II Soul's "Keep on Moving" and "Back to Life." They also worked for Jazzy B's Funky Dread label, a Motown subsidiary. Recently they were in the studios with Daddy Nuttea, a French dreadlocks deejay whose label, Labelle Nyr, is distributed by Virgin. On Shabba Ranks's summer album for Epic they produced "Ting-a-Ling," "Goody Goody" and "Bedroom Bully."

PLAN STUDIO

For Lt. Stitchie's album for Atlantic, Steely and Clevie produced "Jamaican Addiction" and "Ton Load a Fat" as well as a third, unnamed tune. They also produced six songs for Tiger's album and one for Cobra's.

Now this talented duo are working on setting up their own studio.

"It will be ready in another three months on Worthington Terrace," says Steely, "and it will be known as Studio 2000."

"We are futuristic: we're looking ahead," said Clevie. "We are pacesetters and we don't follow; all the styles we have created come from our natural heritage.

"When we started playing computerised instruments, people were afraid that the computers would push musicians out of jobs, but we welcomed it and we tried to stay ahead of the game."

They honour the late Jackie Mittoo as a mentor of theirs. "We both love him," said Clevie. "He was a genius." Said Steely, "Jackie was great, man." And they admire guitarist Ernie Ranglin, who they refer to as the "maestro," as well as other late greats from Studio One, including Aubrey Adams, Jackie Jackson, Lloyd Brevett, Lloyd Knibbs, Jah Jerry Ricobaca Frater, Leroy Sibbles, as well as Boris Gardner and Dwight Pinkney.

They also have an immense amount of respect for Studio One's founder, Clement "Sir Coxsone" Dodd. In fact, in tribute to Studio One's contribution to local music they recorded an entire album of hits from that era, *Steely and Clevie Plays Studio One Vintage*, currently available on CD through the U.S.-based Heartbeat Records.

COLLECTOR'S ITEM

"This is going to be a collector's item," Clevie suggested. "They are our favourites, but on modern, multitrack recording. It is music that we love and we think should be preserved."

They still hold high respect for their competitors, Sly Dunbar and Robbie Shakespeare, the original rhythm twins.

Whenever they tour they have a band, the Don Band, which appears with them. The band is comprised of Steely and Clevie as well as Danny Browne and Robbie Lyn.

They are against both drugs and "slack" tunes: "We keep away from drugs," said Steely. "Not even cigarette smoke we tolerate." Clevie pointed out that Shabba Ranks's current hit "Ting-a-Ling" was loaded with slack lyrics; they refused to produce the hit until the lyrics were rewritten.

They also own one of the island's leading sound systems, Silver Hawk, whose musical repertoire includes two "specials" done by Billy Ocean. Steely is so ambitious, he wants to ask Michael Jackson to do a "special" for Silver Hawk, through their relationship with Sony.

In addition they are looking for what they call "culture singers" for their label. "Dancehall will be big, but there will always be a demand for the singers of cultured lyrics," said Clevie.

They have a lot of confidence in the future of Jamaican music. "This music will be here well into the next century," says Steely. "There will always be the raggamuffin/dancehall sound," said Clevie, "but I expect that we will see more conscious and cultured lyrics towards the middle of the nineties."

Reggae Sound Systems

ANDREW C. CAMPBELL (AKA TUFFIE)

Black Majesty International Reggae Web Site
http://members.aol.com/baseodyssy
1996

This essay is an attempt to capture and relay the essence of reggae sound systems through the eyes of one who grew up around his father's sound and now owns his own. It's offered as a primer for those who seek knowledge and understanding of this continuously evolving subculture.

The phenomenon of reggae sound systems (also known as "sounds" or "sets") has intrigued observers in Jamaica and across the world. Started as an underground movement in the reggae industry, sound systems have risen to become an integral part of reggae culture. In fact, the roots of dancehall reggae can be traced to the formation of local and nationally popular sound systems more than twenty years ago. (Kilamanjaro, a sound based in Jamaica, was formed more than twenty-five years ago.)

What makes up a sound system? People are often surprised by the number of components involved. Sounds vary in size, from locally popular sound systems to those of international fame. Although there is no set composition to a sound, an ideal sound is made up of the following: the selector, mike chatter, owner/promoter, technician, moving staff, sound followers, equipment, and last but definitely not least, the records and dub plates. It is important to note that while not every sound has all of these components, some of them are indispensable; for example, a sound without a selector or records is like a refrigerator without electricity: "It jus naw go work!" It is also important to note that some roles may overlap. For instance, the selector might also be the mike chatter and owner of the sound.

THE SELECTOR

Probably one of the most important roles on a sound is that of the selector. The selector is responsible for managing the turntables—selecting and playing the records. The skill required for this role (at least if you want to be considered any good) and the difficulty involved is often underestimated. A good selector has to know hundreds of records, including the artists and location in the record box, off the top of his head. Playing the records in an order and manner that is pleasing to the crowd, or selecting, requires a high level of diligence. Also, a selector must be able to make a smooth transition from one record to the next (mixing). These skills can take years to develop, but are done with such style and ease by the good selectors that they often go unnoticed. A bad selector, on the other hand, can easily be pointed out, and the displeased crowd will usually not hesitate to make their disapproval known.

Rory from Stone Love Movement, who originated the popular "radio personality voice," is said to be the best sound system selector in the world, but with the rise of so many young selectors—such as Squingy, Glamma G, and Lenny from Bass Odyssey Sound—this can be disputed.

THE MIKE CHATTER

The mike chatter is the selector's right-hand man, and vice versa. He is responsible for introducing the records being played ("intro"), hyping up the crowd ("building vibes"), encouraging crowd participation in singing the popular tunes ("conducting chorus"), and requesting that a record be played again immediately (this is called a "forward" or a "rewind"). The mike chatter is much like the emcee of a live show, and he forwards the records upon indication by the crowd—usually by screams, shouts, chants, whistles, holding up of lit lighters, pounding on the walls, and waving handkerchiefs (or "wipers"). The mike chatter may tell jokes, announce upcoming events, and in some cases even make political commentaries. In a sound clash the mike chatter's role becomes even more crucial. In this setting he is responsible for verbally ridiculing his opponent—the other sound—by taunting them ("toasting") and telling embarrassing jokes that may or may not be true (referred to as "drawing cards").

Ricky Trooper, who selects for Kilamanjaro Sound, is said to be the best mike chatter in the world, while Tony Matterhorn from King Addies comes in at a close second.

OTHER STAFF MEMBERS

In addition to the selector and mike chatter there is the owner/promoter, who owns the equipment and is in charge of hiring the other members of the sound. This person is also responsible for negotiating contracts and booking dates for the sound to perform ("play out"). The technician is in charge of assembling ("stringing up") the hardware components of the sound system (including the speakers, turntables, and amplifiers) and making sure that everything sounds crystal clear. If a problem arises with any hardware before, during, or after an event, it is the technician's duty to fix it or arrange to have it fixed. The moving staff (or "box boys" as they are called because they lift a lot of speaker boxes) are in charge of transporting and positioning the equipment. Some sounds go as far as purchasing a truck and hiring a permanent truck driver to haul their equipment.

SOUND FOLLOWERS

The sound followers are what make or break a sound. These are the people who follow and support the sound, in much the same way a congregation supports a particular church. Sound followers attend the dances (or "bashments") that the sound system plays; they collect and trade the sound system's cassettes ("cassette freaks"); and they support the sound system in a sound clash. Although most dancehall fans are casual sound followers (they simply acknowledge a certain sound as their favorite), there are others who take this more seriously. These "crews" or "massives" support the sound in such a way that their name sometimes becomes synonymous with the sound itself. These serious sound followers will often accompany the sound when it plays internationally.

So what's in it for the sound followers? Getting bigged-up at the events that your sound plays; free passes; a proud feeling when your sound wins a clash; or simply a feeling of identity with something. Providing support for something one enjoys can be a very rewarding experience.

Afrique sound (dubbed the girls' number one sound) from Brooklyn, New York, is said to have the largest following of devoted female fans in the world—from hairdressers to lawyers. So extensive is this following that once a year Afrique holds an awards ceremony where various trophies are given out in a show of appreciation. I even saw a granny at an Afrique dance once, and I have the videotape to prove it.

THE EQUIPMENT

The equipment of a sound system is all the electrical hardware that makes up the sound. Collectively, these components are also called the "set." A set can easily consist of thousands of dollars worth of hardware, including turntables, mixers, tape decks, CD mixers, echo chambers, amplifiers, speakers, power supplies, wires and cords, storage and travel parcels, and backup equipment.

Although size is not necessarily the ultimate factor in distinguishing a good sound, it does play a huge role, and a fast way to increase the popularity of a sound system is to increase its physical appearance. Some sound systems (such as King Jammy's from Jamaica) are so huge that stacked side by side the speakers may surpass the length of an average city block and can be heard across some parishes (Jamaica has fourteen parishes, similar to boroughs). Of course, the speakers are stacked vertically and are usually divided into two matching towers, both displaying decals showcasing the name of the sound.

RECORDS

Last but not least are the records and dub plates. A sound system may own thousands of records and CDs. A good sound system may also own valuable out-of-print vinyl records, such as classics on the Studio One and Coxsone labels. While the amount of records a sound has is not necessarily a reliable indication of how good it is, variety helps when you are playing for a very diverse crowd in terms of age and background, and in the event of a sound clash quantity becomes especially meaningful. David Rodigan, selector and sound owner from England, boasts one of the most comprehensive collections of reggae records.

WHAT ARE DUB PLATES?

Dub plates—also called dubs, specials, or samples, although there are differences among these—are another unique thing about sound systems. A dub plate is basically a record on which a recording artist mentions the name of the sound (in effect identifying it as a top sound and backing it). Dub plates are unique because of the fact that they are usually renditions of hit songs the artists have made. My friend Scrappy D gives this fine example: "Buju [Banton] may do a [dub plate] for Stone Love saying, 'Stone Love sound like a champion, play like a champion, what a piece a sound, Rory [Stone Love's selector] tell mi where you get it from.'" This dub plate is a rendition of Buju's hit song "Walk Like a Champion." The effect is similar to Lou Rawls singing in a Coke commercial.

Sound systems have been successful in getting popular artists outside of reggae music to do dub plates. Some honorable mentions include the classic vocal group the Temptations (recruited by Bodyguard from Jamaica) and the rap artist Mad Lion (recruited by King Addies from New York City).

SPECIALS AND SAMPLES

On a technical note, laymen usually confuse dub plates, specials, and samples. Although these terms are often used interchangeably, they actually refer to very different things. A dub plate is a song that any sound can get from an artist, if they can afford it. A special is a song that the artist agrees to make only for one particular sound, thus the saying "no other sound can play this." A sample is similar to a special, except that it is usually something that sounds like nothing any other artist, or the artist himself, has done. When Beenie Man did his hit song "Maestro" in "opera style" for Kilamanjaro Sound long before the song was released, it was considered a sample because no one had yet heard the opera style done in dancehall reggae.

THE ROLE AND COST OF DUB PLATES

Many artists got their start by doing dub plates for local sounds. Popular recording artist Beenie Man was performing on sound systems in his locality, such as Black Scorpio Sound, for more than ten years before he got his big break. For established artists, besides providing an additional source of income, dub plates are a means of returning to their roots (especially after going off to sign contracts with international record labels).

The cost of a dub plate varies, and although I am not permitted to quote the prices that artists charge, let's just say that if the dub plate you are seeking is the rendition of a current hit song, "If you have to ask, then you can't afford it!" Although the price of dub plates at times seems outrageous, dub plates are an important way for a sound to remain in the top ratings. Furthermore, as you will later read, in a sound clash dub plates are of the essence.

DETERMINING A SUPERIOR SOUND SYSTEM

So what then determines a superior sound system? No one factor, but rather many things make a sound top-notch (or "Number one," as we say). For starters, the sound system must be technically sound, with CD-quality voice and tweeters and solid round bass. The selectors and mike chatters must be competent in their respective roles. Furthermore, it doesn't hurt to have a strong following of stylish ("hotty hotty") females and men. Even the price and frequency of the events a sound holds in a particular vicinity will affect its popularity; after all, a sound system must remain accessible—especially to the locality from which it originated.

If the sound attracts a lot of celebrities that brandish a lot of new styles (clothes) and new dances, this can be an asset. The quality of dub plates a sound produces is another determining factor; the more popular the artist and the songs, the better. Although all of the above are very important, probably the single most important factor used to determine if a sound is in fact a number one sound is its performance in a sound clash.

WHAT IS A SOUND CLASH?

A sound clash is a musical competition where selectors and mike chatters from opposing sounds—two or more, but usually two—match wits in selecting, hyping up the crowd, and toasting (ridiculing the other sound's members). It usually takes place in a large building or on a lawn with the sounds set up at opposite sides.

THE EARLY WARM-UP

At the very beginning of the clash, called the "early warm-up," the opposing sounds take turns (usually an hour each) to play music for the people. Each turn is called a segment, and a pair of segments (one from each competing sound) is called a round. During these early rounds, little if any reference is made to the clash that awaits, and the sounds usually big up each other as well as the crews and massives at the dance. At this point in the dance the guys are usually checking out the ladies, and vice versa.

LATER ROUNDS

In the wee hours of the morning the clash begins to develop, and the sounds use their dub plates to toast and musically chastise—as the reggae artist Lt. Stitchie puts it— each other. The segments now become shorter; usually each sound gets to play two half-hour rounds each, then two rounds of fifteen minutes each followed by two or three rounds of five minutes each. In each segment the selector tries to discredit (or "counteract") the songs played by the opposing sound in the previous segment by playing more-popular songs or dub plates. In the meantime the mike chatter is hyping up the crowd by singing the songs, making jokes, and toasting in order to foster discontent and disapproval for the opposing sound.

While the selector is dropping tunes on the turntable, the crowd, usually led by the avid followers of that sound, are cheering, hollering, showing lighters, pounding on the walls, and waving wipers in support of or against the songs and dub plates that are being played. Interestingly enough, this is usually one part of the dance where you rarely find males and females interacting, because they are all caught up in the competition. If the song or dub plate was an extremely good choice, the people will shout for a forward (to have the record played again). Good dub plates usually get forwarded three or four times (although I've seen a Bounty Killer dub plate forwarded more than eight times). Sometimes the selector plays only a couple of seconds of a dub plate and that's enough to drive the entire crowd into a frenzy.

THE CLIMAX—DUB FI DUB

After a couple of rounds back and forth, the clash finally simmers down to the moment of truth: the dub fi dub round (also called one fi one). In this final round the sounds are allowed to play only one record or dub plate per segment, then the other sound immediately attempts to counteract it with a better dub plate (called the answer). This round is very important, because if the selector makes a bad choice it is usually hard to recover, since the opposing selector is going to play a counteraction immediately (as opposed to the longer segments of earlier rounds, where a bad choice can skillfully be covered up by subsequent better selections).

In dub fi dub the motto is "Do or die and take no prisoners!" The selector and mike chatter now play the very best and original of the dub plates they possess. If you slip ya slide, and sooner or later the superior selector causes the weaker to play all of his good records and dub plates, leaving him with no more records worth playing; this is called running a selector out of tunes. The superior sound must now ask the people if the other sound has lost: "Him dead?!" If the crowd says no, then the clash continues to a second round of dub fi dub. But if the crowd screams yes!, then the selector of the winning sound plays a final tune (or burial) to officially do away with (kill) the losing sound and discredit the selector— "flop him career like John Crow wings"—thus ending the clash. At this point the victorious sound asks the loser to "lock off" his sound, which he must or face further embarrassment.

OTHER POSSIBLE OUTCOMES TO A CLASH

The "death" of a sound is the climax of the dance—and what everyone has paid their money to see. However, in a sound clash this is not always the outcome. Sometimes a sound loses in the early rounds (usually the case with an inexperienced sound, for example, or one experiencing technical difficulties). Sometimes a sound quits the clash for various reasons (a "walkout") and the opposing sound wins by default. At other times an act of God (or man) causes the clash to end prematurely—for example, rain in an outdoor clash, or the eruption of violence. In addition, a sound might win a sound clash but by such a small margin that the victory is considered a "lucky chance"—in this case the other sound merely lost as opposed to being "killed."

But probably the most interesting ending to a clash is a draw. This is where both sounds have played so excellent that the crowd is split 50/50 as to who is the winner.

In these cases, somewhat rare, the sounds usually agree to a rematch at the same location at some point in the near future. Both sounds get credit for the dance, although the underdog coming in usually gets more "ratings" (widely accepted approval).

A popular clash still talked about was King Addies versus Black Kat (from Jamaica) in 1993 at the Biltmore Ballroom in Brooklyn, where the entire world was split 50/50 after the match. If I was to choose which clash was the biggest clash ever, it would have to be one of two: The first is Kilamanjaro Sound (from Jamaica) versus King Addies (Brooklyn's number one sound killa) at Portmore (for sure!) in Jamaica in 1995. (These two sounds had clashed several times before, but this time Kilamanjaro put an end to the confusion, by a slight margin—or was it King Addies?) The second is Saxon Sound (England's undisputed number one) versus Third World (New York City's ruler back in the early 1980s from the 90s area in Brooklyn). This dance is still being talked about today. In fact, a stranger offered me a good sum of money recently for a copy of the Saxon versus Third World clash, now dubbed a highly valuable cassette among collectors. (I gave it to him for free.)

The important thing to note here is that after the clash the members of the two sounds are friends again and everything is back to normal ("Everything criss!"); after all, it's only a musical competition.

CONCLUSION

Sound systems are more than just sources of music or proving grounds for the latest dances; they can be viewed as a sport, or even an art form. As for what makes a sound number one, it's ultimately a personal choice I guess. An abundance of whatever particulars a listener feels is important. Whatever it is, we can all agree that reggae sound systems are an invaluable part of reggae music and culture, and will be around for many years to come.

As one of the selectors on Black Majesty International, I can appreciate what goes on behind the scenes to make a sound, and what goes into making a sound number one. It can be a full-time job filled with headaches and burdens. But I'll tell you this, there is no other feeling in the world like the feeling you get when you stand behind your turntables in a clash and the crowd cheers you on and anoints you with the ultimate final command that you have sorted records all day to hear, played dub plates all night to hear: "Murder di tin pan sound!" It is at that moment, when your sound is crowned victor, that you realize why you play a dance for twelve hours straight at a time, spend thousands of dollars on records and equipment, and come out in the cold to play a dance: It's for the people!

Nuff respect.

APPENDIX

Big-up to all selectors and sound systems worldwide, past, present, and future. It's all about one love and the promotion of reggae music straight back to infinity. Honor goes out to all avid sound system fans, including Father Teddy and 949 Fam, Princess, Paul & 90s, Accurate and BMI Crew, 3 Di, 6 Di, Essence, X-Amount, Donnettes,

Technites, UB, Fordham, Sterling, all JA and NYC crews, and the Stewart Town Crew. There are literally hundreds of sound systems worldwide, and to each I say, *Continue to keep the music alive!* Here are just a few:

Action Pack	Jah Love
African Love	Jamrock
African Star	Juggler
Afrique	K.C. Soundstation
Baby Wayne Movements	Kilamanjaro
Bass Odyssey	King Addies
Black Kat	King Barka
Black Knight	King Fila
Black Magic	King Jammy's
Black Majesty International	King Mellow Sound
Black Scorpio	King Slata
Black Star	King Turbo
Bodyguard	Krystal
Bullet Proof	L.A. Benz
Changez	Lee's Unlimited
City Rock	Legacy
Classique Climax	Liberation
Class One	Libra Love
Conquering Lion	Lone Star
Creation HiFi	L.P. International
Dogheart International	Massive B
Downbeat	Mellowtone
Dub Plate International	Metromedia
Dud Star	MP International
Earthquake	Outlaw
Earth Ruler	Pieces
Electroforce	David Rodigan
Exodus 4x4	Renaissance
Exodus Nuclear	Rhythm Track
Mikey Faith	Road Block
Fatal Attraction	Road International
Firgo Digital	Rocket Force
Galaxy	Saxxon
Gemini	Silver Hawk
Ghetto Super Power	Snow White
Golden Axe	Soldier One
Heatwave	Soul Supreme
Impressions	Soundquake
Inner City	Sound Wave

Spectrum
Star Tone
Stereo One
Stereo Sonic
Sting International
Stone Love
Stone Wall International
Stur Grav
Stur Mars
Super Dee
Super Saint
Super T
Suzy Q

Sweetness Sound
Techniques
Teddy's Hi Fi
Third World
Too Tuff
Travellers
Turbo Crown
Twin Tower
V Rocket
Waggy T
Yaried Crew
Young Hawk

Stone Love Live!

SHARON GORDON

Dub Missive
December 1994

Twenty-two years ago, when Stone Love sound system was founded by Winston Powell, aka Wee Pow, dancehall was still a Jamaican "thing." Then, on any given Thursday night Stone Love could be heard flinging down selections at the trendy Tropics Night Club in the heart of New Kingston. Roadblock was the norm, as devoted patrons formed lines and jammed the open-air club.

Since those early days, Wee Pow has always stood apart from other selectors. The manner in which Rory and Cancer (Stone Love's official selectors) work the turntables demonstrates exceptional talent as well. Selecting only the wickedest tunes, they are forever making a statement with that certain style of selecting—the Stone Love style. No one leaves a Stone Love dance un- or under-entertained, righttt!

During the mid-eighties, sound systems started traveling to New York, London and other major cities, where weekly dances were promoted in the form of sound clashes—foreign set versus set from yard. It wasn't long before Wee Pow, the entrepreneur, realized that he needed to bring his set to foreign. Stone Love began to make movements; hence the name Stone Love Movement.

By the late eighties, Wee Pow, Rory and Cancer had become household names, due to the influx of Stone Love tapes and their visits to places as far north as Toronto and as far east as Japan. It was about then that Barney Dudley, Wee Pow's longtime friend, became Stone Love's booking agent and road manager. Since then Stone Love have become globe-trotters—taking the sound of Jamaican music to virgin territory and ears.

As the saying goes, good things come to those who wait, and Stone Love Movement is now reaping due rewards. Recently Mike Cacia, longtime reggae collector, producer and collaborator (he produced the original Gemini live dancehall album recorded at Skateland, Jamaica, back in the late seventies), along with Jaime Stewart, introduced Wee Pow and Barney to Rob Holt of November Records. This meeting proved successful, as November Records proposed that Stone Love record a live album for their label. Needless to say, all parties involved are excited about this venture. November Records is prepared to extensively promote and market this album. According to Rob, "We plan to put a lot of effort into marketing the album on an international level. We are positive this is a great venture for all those involved." There are plans to record and release at least two or three of these albums.

The debut album is being recorded at a series of live Stone Love dances to be held in New York. The first session was on November 6 at S.O.B.'s in Manhattan. It was incredible; spirited live performances from Brigadier Jerry, Junior Cat, Screechy Dan, Bajja Jedd, Mad Lion, Dougie Fresh, Lady Apachie and Junie Ranks were captured. On November 19 Stone Love did another live recording session at the Biltmore Ballroom in Brooklyn, alongside Spectrum Disco, L.P. International and Stereo Sonic. The third and final recording session will take place on November 26 at the Q Club, when Stone Love will be appearing alongside London's number one disc jockey, David Rodigan.

Considering the journey Wee Pow has made with Stone Love, it is destiny that such great opportunities should come his way. Much continued success to Wee Pow, Rory, Cancer and their crew. And, massive and crew, stay tuned for updates on *Stone Love Live! The Album.*

Buju Banton:
Dancehall's Cultural Griot

TRAINER

Dub Missive
August 1995

His name is often mentioned delightfully throughout Jamaica, England, Canada, Japan, the United States and reggae communities worldwide. His first album, *Mr. Mention*, broke all previous album-sales records in Jamaica, including those of Bob Marley, John Holt, and the Blues Busters. He has had more number one singles on the Jamaican charts than previous record-holders John Holt, Bob Marley or Yellowman. He has thrilled audiences with his electrifying performances.

With these credentials on his resume, the brilliant and prolific young DJ Buju Banton journeyed to New York in the summer of 1993 for the official listening party for *Voice of Jamaica*, his debut album for Mercury Records. His dreams were transformed into reality: a handsome contract with a major record label, his tunes bubbling on the Top 100, the limousine, the star treatment, the life. This was what he had worked so hard for. But, somehow his triumphant entrance was being overshadowed by a controversy that had the potential to derail his career.

Mark Anthony Myrie was born on July 15, 1973, into a classic Jamaican satellite family of fifteen—thirteen sisters and one brother. His mother, Miss Dottie, named her chubby "wash belly" (youngest) Buju. The young Mark Anthony grew up in Barbican, a Kingston suburban community with an eclectic mix of the affluent, the ambitious, and the impoverished. Barbican is a study in contrasts: manicured gardens and mansionlike houses overlooking tenement yards and dilapidated houses. But Barbican was a relatively safe neighborhood, one where Miss Dottie could raise her brood away from the crime-infested environment that shattered strength and spirit, scattering them like broken glass.

A descendant of the mighty Maroons, Miss Dottie raised her children to be strong, caring, respectful and God-fearing, providing them with a sense of duty, perseverance and the knowledge that hard work builds character. At an early age Buju knew he wanted to be an entertainer. "From birth. From I come outta my madda belly," he replied when asked about his realization of blessedness.

As long as music has been played in Jamaica, its home has been the dance hall. From the late fifties, when the tube-amplifier rigs of Coxsone Dodd, Tom "the Great" Sebastian, and V-Rocket ruled, to the eighties, when the tube monstrosities gave way to transistorized megawatt control towers, music has been an elixir to the people. As Bob astutely observed, "One good thing about music, when it hits you you feel no pain." It has provided relief from the oppressive systems under which people have struggled.

To an impressionable youth, the entertainment business fueled visions of grandeur, the glamorous life, and money. Buju was just twelve when he began working in earnest to make his dreams a reality. His apprenticeship commenced in earnest on Whitehall Avenue with entertainers like Flourgan, Daddy Lizard, Red Dragon, Sanchez, Clement Irie and Wayne Wonder on a sound called Rambo International. In deference to his favorite DJ, Burru Banton, Buju took the name "Banton." Daily after school he would find his way to Whitehall Avenue for "extra lessons." Soon he was considered good enough to voice "specials."

By 1985 dancehall had caught fire and was the talk of the town. DJs had supplanted the singers. Yellowman was king. From Charlie Chaplin—the Principal—and Josey Wales—the Colonel—lyrics flowed like Heineken at a "cork" session. A struggling DJ then, Buju dreamt of the time he could imprint his voice on vinyl. His break came in 1986 when fellow DJ Clement Irie took him into the studio to record his first song, "The Ruler." This was followed by a second single, "I Got to Leave You," for the young producer and singer Robert Ffrench.

Encouraged by his initial success, he continued commuting from studio to studio, producer to producer, standing in line with dozens of other youths, begging for a chance—a chance to stand behind the mike and surrender the rights to his tunes, a common practice in Jamaica and a necessity for any artist wishing to make it in the Jamaican music industry. By the time he was fifteen, Buju had recorded tracks for several producers, including Patrick Roberts of Shocking Vibes and Bobby Digital of Digital B fame. Simultaneously, he was doing the dancehall circuit, sparring with the aforementioned entertainers.

In 1988 Buju linked up with Clifton "Specialist" Dillion, then an aspiring producer, and recorded for his Shang label the now-infamous "Boom Bye Bye." In 1989 he hooked up with Stumpy, an engineer at Penthouse Studio. Stumpy would eventually bring Buju to the attention of Dave Kelly, then Penthouse's creative force, its riddim maestro. Buju's first two singles for Penthouse were "Man Fi Dead" and "Jackie & Joyce."

With his stock rising, Buju voiced "Stamina Daddy," "Big Up" (a duet with Don T.), and "Bring You Body Come to Me" (with singer Frankie Paul) for producer Winston "Technique" Riley. Of the lot, "Stamina Daddy," released in late 1990, enjoyed reasonable success, even making it into the Canadian Top 10 reggae chart.

. . .

In late 1991 Buju recorded for Penthouse his first major hit, "Love Mi Browning." Like a rocket, the song zoomed to the top of reggae charts in the Caribbean, U.S.A., Canada, Europe and Japan. While a certifiable hit, its lyrics—"Me love me car/Me love me bike/Me love me money and ting/But most of all me love my browning"— generated plenty controversy. Controversy which only served to sell more copies.

In a country like Jamaica, to openly praise women of lighter complexion at the expense of their darker-skinned sisters was regarded as an affront to their African heritage, a resurrection of Jamaica's colonial legacy. But Buju was smart, and in an effort to placate the uproar caused by the bluntness of his lyrics, he offered "Love Black Woman" as an affirmation of his own personal feelings toward dark-skinned women. His quick and timely response to the ensuing debate assured him a preeminent place in the hearts of all women. "It [the song] was never intended as an insult to my sisters. It was just a reflection of the reality I saw around me. Browning [brown-skinned girls] was a carry de swing." The controversy turned out to be the boost his career needed.

From late 1991 through 1992 Buju sparked with a series of hits, primarily for the Penthouse label. With Tony Rebel, Marcia Griffiths, Buju, and Wayne Wonder on his label, Donovan Germain became a force in the biz, and 56 Slipe Road became a hit factory.

Buju's profile remained high as he fulfilled the expectations of his fans and answered the critics—especially those who had written him off as a flash-in-the-pan DJ—with an incredible string of hits: "Woman No Fret," "Love How the Gal Flex," "Batty Rider," "How the World A Run," "Who Say" (a duet with Beres Hammond) and "Bogle," the dancehall anthem for the summer of 1992. His efforts were not confined solely to Penthouse; he also recorded tracks for Techniques ("Gold Spoon"), Xterminator ("Yardie") and Digital B ("Good Looking Gal"). When Penthouse released his debut album in Jamaica, *Mr. Mention,* it immediately broke all album-sales records.

Sunsplash '92 was Buju's coming-out party. His thirty-five-minute performance served notice that Miss Dottie's son was dancehall's newest sensation. Buju had become a knight commander of lyrical distinction. At Sting '92 his polished presentation and energetic execution drove the crowd wild. Witnessing his spellbinding performance was Lisa Cortes, then A&R rep for Mercury Records, who immediately signed the Banton. Buju-mania continued into 1993 as he garnered more awards than any other DJ: Best New Artist at the Tamika Awards, the Caribbean Music Awards, the Canadian Music Awards . . . and the list goes on and on. With all the awards sitting on the dresser, Buju retired to the studio to work on his debut album for Mercury.

The controversy over "Boom Bye Bye" [the lyrics of which suggest that homosexuals be shot—Ed.] is more than just homophobic behavior on Buju's part. It represents a clash of Jamaican conservativeness and American liberalism. Dancehall is littered with a litany of antigay songs, many of which never make it out of the dance halls. What made the difference in the "Boom Bye" case was that the song was released on the same rhythm as Mad Cobra's gold single "Flex." American disc jockeys found the beat irresistible and the song exploded. Incensed by what they viewed as "the promotion of gay-bashing," GLAAD (Gay and Lesbian Alliance Against Defamation) and GMAD (Gay Men of African Descent) retaliated. Buju's smiling face was plastered all over the front of the *New York Post* with headlines that screamed "Hate Music."

Damage repair started immediately. Buju issued a carefully crafted response: "I do not advocate violence against anyone and it was never my intention to incite violent acts with 'Boom Bye.' However, I must state unequivocally that I do not condone homosexuality, as this lifestyle runs contrary to my religious beliefs." But the controversy represented only a part of a rather complex picture that involves free speech, censorship, power, hypocrisy and ignorance. The reality is that in America, gay power is real. Gays hold decision-making positions, not only in the entertainment industry but in all media. And they can inflict plenty damage.

In Jamaica there is no such notion. In a land where homosexuality is condemned from the pulpit, "batty-man" better remain in the closet. For Buju to offer an apology to the gay community would be tantamount to committing professional suicide. Shabba "bow" and look what happened.

Despite his troubles in America, Buju's popularity worldwide remained high throughout 1993 and well into 1994. He toured extensively in France, Germany, Japan and the U.K. to appease and please his fans. He also added five international music awards to his collection.

But the meaningless murders of fellow DJs Panhead and Dirtsman in 1994 seem to have triggered a spiritual awakening within the dancehall community. For Buju the tragedy was personal. These were not just two other guys, but colleagues, individuals with whom he shared time—on the fence, in the studio, and on the stage. Deeply saddened by their deaths, Buju expressed his abhorrence with "Murderer." Its antigun message confirmed his personal rejection of violence while eloquently illuminating society's disgust with the constant killing: "Murderer, yuh inside mus' be hollow . . ."

In the last decade popular Jamaican music has undergone an evolution: from the "blood and fire" cry of the sufferah seeking deliverance, to the cravings of a very cosmopolitan and materialistic generation weaned on televised images of sex and violence. But as the situation worsened, it became clear that man cannot live by bread alone. The success of "roots and culture" artists—notably Tony Rebel and Garnett Silk—in the dance hall ignited a cultural revival that was slowly influencing the dancehall fraternity. For Buju the controversy over "Boom Bye Bye" had made him more aware of his responsibility as an artist and a role model. But more important was the realization that the members of his generation had refused to honor the cultural legacy inherent in the music. For Buju that wisdom came with the acceptance of Jah. *What was hidden from the wise and prudent is now revealed to the babe and suckling.* It was the realization that reggae should not only cuss and preach, it should teach positive values.

Naturally, Buju's newfound consciousness was questioned. And rightly so, especially when so much band-wagonists were hopping on board the cultural train. Was he a wolf in sheep's clothing?

"Browning" was the first demonstration of Buju's ability to articulate the Jamaican social environment, of which he had become an astute observer. His proficient use of dialect, idioms and popular expressions, and his uncanny knack for discussing relevant social issues, revealed him as one of dancehall's most intelligent lyricists. Although risqué and suggestive at times, he has refused to resort to the obscene lyrics prevalent among his peers. By showering his female fans with praises and compliments, he became the number one girls' DJ and changed the direction of dancehall DJ lyrics. Buju a nuh follower, 'im a leader.

Throughout his career Buju has often chronicled the hardships, the joys and the irony of the disenfranchised. Like his spiritual mentor, Bob Marley, he has provided them with the hope and inspiration to sustain their defiantly determined struggles. His catalog is replete with such offerings: "How the World A Run," "Deportees," "Good God of My Salvation," "Murderer." From "How the World A Run": "True, the poor can't afford the knowledge, dem nuh get none/The rich man 'ave the dollars and no wan' give we some/. . . Dem no wan see ghetto yout' elevate outta the slum."

It is always prudent to judge a person by their works, their action, and not their utterances. On Monday, June 27, 1994, Buju and the Penthouse crew launched one of the most ambitious projects of the 1990s, the Operation Willy campaign in Jamaica, in aid of children who are affected by the HIV virus or AIDS. Enlisting the help of many in the medical profession, the foundation's efforts are focused on prevention through education. Proceeds totaling over J$50,000, all from sales of the single "Willy Don't Be Silly," have been donated to the foundation.

Asked why, Buju replied, "Nuff people willing fi go ah dance, but them nuh want do nuthin' positive. If we don't do it, then who ah go do it? We haffi tek care of the youths." And while he is the only artist who has committed to the project, Buju is hopeful that others "will realize how important this type of t'ing is and get involved."

In 1994 Buju also completed work on his own studio, Cellblock 3-2-1. With so many studios in Jamaica, why one more? "To help all sufferah youth who don't have it fe go ah studio. Some of the t'ings I had experienced in my time. Me come yah fi help dem." For Buju, helping his fellow man is only natural; it is his way of giving thanks for the blessings he has received.

Garnett Silk's untimely death in December 1994 was not only a shocker, but a reminder that time waits for no one. For Buju Banton the time is now. As a soldier he can't afford to "lay-lay." He has to get the message across now. He is about to release his third album, *'Til Shiloh,* on Loose Cannon. Without a doubt the fifteen tracks represent Buju's most philosophical and poignant effort ever. Filled with socially conscious lyrics delivered in an eclectic blend of rhythms and innovative stylistic approaches, *'Til Shiloh* will undoubtedly redefine dancehall music. The album delivers on its promise to entertain and educate while showcasing Buju's growth. "I want to be an instrument of peace in this time of war," he declares. "Too much slack lyrics did ah run, ya know. We haffi teach the youths. I want to be a Marley for my generation."

Like a griot, Banton is telling his stories through his music, continuing the tradition of his African ancestors. And despite the glitter and the glamor, he strives to remain humble. "I remember where I come from, down ah Salt Lane bottom. My music universal, it reflect the suffering of poor people not only ah Yard [Jamaica], but all over the world. I just wan' people to listen to this record with open hearts and open minds." If Buju continues to embody the hopes and aspirations of his generation, then we will be listening, forever.

Postnationalist Geographies:
Rasta, Ragga, and Reinventing Africa

LOUIS CHUDE-SOKEI

African Arts
Autumn 1994[1]

The whole world is Africa . . .

BLACK UHURU

Hear me now raggamuffin: we run all sounds, and we run the nation. So mek we just control the borderline.

ANONYMOUS PIRATE DJ

Ring the alarm, another sound is dying . . .

TENOR SAW

Because "Africa" has been called upon to justify so many movements of liberation and exploitation, and because it has functioned not only as a physical reality in the making of Western culture but also as a central concept in the canons of institutional (and revolutionary) knowledge, it is hard to mark a clear space between the layers of discourse and desire and any Africa which may lie beyond. It is in many ways very difficult to extricate what is said of Africa from what Africa says of itself. Perhaps it is impossible. But if indeed "Africa" spoke, how would it speak and what would it say? What "itself" would it express, and could the sound of that voice be understood by ears still ringing with myth?

After all, a native sound connotes a system of native knowledge, and as Paul Gilroy has so well argued, national and cultural belonging—especially within the various populations of the black diaspora—cannot be fully understood in the realm of literacy and print media. Native knowledge cannot be accurately traced or located in the writings of the literate few. Instead it is articulated in and disseminated by what I call the sound/culture nexus: that discursive space where Africa ceaselessly extends and invents itself in an epistemological matrix coded not in words but in sound. Why sound? Because the discourse in sound is separate from those of the literary, of the logos; it is a space independent of the centered semantic structures of science, freed from the objective bias of literacy. It is necessarily the space of oral knowledge, the space of both magic and postmodern technology. Indeed, for this generation within a black diaspora, sound is closer to culture than "race" ever was.

For me, Africa speaks in those shadowy historical moments which go unrecorded, those moments of the reflection when diaspora asks the question asked by Harlem poet Countee Cullen in 1925: "What is Africa to me?" But in these moments, the language is opaque, as with all oracular dispensations, and the events which mark them often very threatening. Take for example the stoning of Bunny Wailer at Sting '91. On the level of popular knowledge—as opposed to the towers of "critique"—the stoning of this semilegendary Rastafarian singer, the last living member of the original Wailers (Bob Marley and Peter Tosh both dying in the 1980s), signifies a crucial moment in diaspora. For you see, Wailer was more than just a singer: he was perhaps the last living symbol of black revolutionary desire from his generation. And his was a generation that helped thrust a mythic "Africa" to the forefront of black popular culture in the West Indies and, via reggae music and Rastafarianism, the world.

His being stoned in Jamaica by this new generation, the raggamuffin generation, signifies that something has radically changed in certain suburbs of the city I call diaspora. Certainly Africa constantly changes, but the meanings of Africa change too; they change and are adapted to fit the local notions of black identity and cultural survival. In this case the "Africa" central to a Rastafarian Pan-Africanism has been symbolically dislodged. The generation which celebrated Marcus Garvey as a prophet and Africa as "Zion" has been assaulted by the children birthed by it. This is because new economic and cultural conditions require new gods and symbols; old ones stagnate or become malevolent and repressive. In short, what we have in the raggamuffin/dancehall[2] (sub)cultural movement is a very harsh popular critique of what Africa means to us at this moment in a post-/neo-/omni-colonial world.

Emerging out of the Seaga-Thatcher-Reagan triumvirate in the 1980s and fueled by a booming international cocaine trade, ragga stepped boldly onto the diasporan stage as first an overturning of that Rastafarian mythos which celebrated a universalized notion of black racial and cultural identity; an essentialized vision of diaspora which exercised a sort of oppressive control over Jamaican cultural production. In its most sincere moments, Rasta fetishized black cultural origins, rooting them in a fixed source of "anciency" called, according to the Old Testament, "Ethiopia." And as the Rastafarian influence in reggae music grew and came to dominate in the 1970s, this obsession became crucially linked to the driving bass and drums of reggae "riddim." The music and its ideology, then, became so fastened to "roots" and ethnic/cultural authenticity that many felt challenged to speak to the raw present of Jamaican ghetto life—that which reggae had once directly addressed. Specificity was lost because of the obsession with global "Pan-African" discourses, racial metaphors, and religio-political allegories. And the ideology of "roots" did not offer a framework within which to contend with the changing environment of music, multinational capitalism, and global communications technology.

The raggamuffin generation then positioned itself as a serious challenge to any attempt to narrate diaspora based on similarities of oppression or pigment. Certainly Pan-Africanism has been criticized in the past for some of its racial essentialism, but to criticize the logic of essentialism is not in any way to halt its currency on the street. With the stoning of Bunny Wailer, the much maligned raggamuffin sound/subculture has announced itself as the latest in a long line of exiles to ask Cullen's question and to violently reassess their position within the vagaries of black cultural history. For this generation, the slippages made between race and culture by their forbears have become the space in which new notions of belonging and becoming are being asserted.

Where the Rastafarian "Africa" was a cultural commodity available to all those with black skin, one that could be traded across and beyond the Atlantic by Garvey's "Black Star Line" of ships, or could be invented in sound by the open metonymic spaces of heavy dub echoes, the signifiers of ragga/dancehall ground themselves firmly in a "blackness" produced out of a specific cultural history. For the Rastafari brethren, "Zion," the promised land of Ethiopia, was both precolonial utopia and the imminent future of black people who were destined to survive the time span of Babylonian hegemony. With ragga, however, the abstraction of Ethiopia/Africa in what I have elsewhere called the "Discourse of Dread" gives way to Rema, Tivoli Gardens, and Jungle, particular "Yard" (Jamaican) realities which do not function as global signifiers of black exile because they are so rooted in the urban myths of Jamaica's postcolonial history. And these signifiers and symbols quite clearly belong to "Yardies" who spend much time carefully "controlling the borderline" which separates one blackness, one idiosyncratic cultural experience, from another.

Rasta-reggae too had moments of specificity in its narratives—for example, "Trench Town" as mythic space, or "Dungle"—but they were always linked directly to some global narrative of black oppression. With raggamuffin sound, which currently dominates the ideologies of Afro-Caribbean youth and black Third World pop/ghetto culture, one is challenged to find references to the mythic signifier of black identity that is Africa. And most important, there is no longing for it. As a matter of fact, the few references in dancehall music to that distant memory of a continent are usually halfhearted attempts to criticize and condemn the present by evoking the moral authority of some always fictitious golden age. The sentiments of raggamuffin music and culture are very different from the nostalgia and longing for "elsewhere" that characterizes much of the kind of reggae and cultural production that comes out of Bob Marley's generation. The "Waiting in Vain," "Back to Africa," "Rasta Waan Go Home" exile narratives have given way to cultural expressions from those who see the new battles as immediate and local—through gun sights and across dirty inner-city streets. From an aesthetics of exile and absence to an aesthetics of raw, materialistic presence.

Instead of dwelling psychically "elsewhere," the narratives of dancehall feature an exploration and celebration of the microrealities, the obsessive minutiae of Jamaican urban life which holds little meaning for all outsiders. They also investigate the noirish street-level intricacies of a postcolonial underclass navigating a global network of immigrant communities. Outsiders to the culture of ragga, Jamaican and non-Jamaican, tend to find these narratives rude, crude, scatological, and "slack." This, however, is what DJs (read MCs, or rappers) describe as "strictly reality." Everything from local politics and crime to ghetto morality, from graphic depictions of murder to very explicit and pornographic details of the bedroom, gets put to rapid-fire boom-beats and is broadcast throughout the global community of Yardies. Lyrics, which in most cases are community property, belonging only to the moment of expression, range from the sublimely terrifying to the incredibly stupid.

Take for example the latest masterpiece in the "gun talk" genre, that subcategory of ragga chats which are devoted exclusively to the celebration of guns and the street credibility and power derived from them: "Shine and Criss" by the massive Shabba Ranks. Some gun-talk tunes are explicitly metaphorical, celebrating the fierce competitions within sound culture; but these metaphors get strained due to that proximity between life and art, that closeness between a metaphorical "sound-boy killing" and, in the words of Terror Fabulous, "Literally Killing." I quote from "Shine and Criss" not because it is definitive but because it is the latest and the most self-conscious of the genre. It is also a major hit:

> *Oil up all a the gun dem, keep them shine and criss*
> *A copper shot, you fe carry inna you gun,*
> *mek a bwoy turn purple any time him get it, Lawd . . .*

The opening sampled phrase "original gangster" (the voice of Ice-T) in this song is of course the ultimate statement of ghetto-political authenticity in Afro-American "gangsta rap." And this is where the potential in a hip-hop/ragga cross-cultural discourse was first articulated on the street level. But what Shabba does in "Shine and Criss" is offer a view into the mind of a Yardie whose world is one of extreme violence, a world that has no time for what Barbadian writer George Lamming called *The Pleasures of Exile*. Guns are a sign of entirely different assumptions about cultural positioning; or as Mad Cobra has said in his massive "Shot No Talk": "Fe me gunshot/don't hold no argument." Some of these tracks are so vivid and violent that they are merely long, wrenching descriptions of slow torture and boasts about the most brutal ways to kill—not only one's enemy, but his family and friends (and one ridiculous line which pops up every now and then involves the murder of the family cat!). Indeed, some tunes are merely lists of the dead ("Roll Call" by Tenor Saw, or Super Cat's "Nu Man A Dead") and celebrations of one's own homicidal history. As for the incredible stupidity—especially as it relates to sexual "slackness"—more on this later.

For those within this floating cultural context, Africa is less important—in fact it often gets in the way of—contemporary Third World ghetto life. As a British rudie once said to me, "Africa nah go mek me bullet-proof."[3] More important, though, raggamuffin and dancehall narratives map out a sprawling Third World urban geography which stretches from the gun-loud poverty of Kingston to the bass-heavy housing estates of South London and over to that place that Raymond Williams located as the center of modernist exile—New York City. This is a discourse that is obsessively local but well aware of the global network of Afro-Caribbean migration and the discontinuous histories of black diaspora. Inside the dense sound-sculpting of ragga mixology, the references begin at and return to Yard, but in between the signifiers travel through the Jamaican communities in England (London massive, Brixton crew), New York (Brooklyn massive, Flatbush posse), and Canada (nuff respect, Toronto massive!). This is the matrix of dancehall music and culture: creating a new sense of national belonging beyond the boundaries constructed by politics and geography. Community is narrated there in that very tense space between the local and the global: the space they call "the borderline."

Although Seaga's Jamaica, Thatcher's England, and Reagan's America gave ragga the kind of painful birth necessary for their mythic function, they really were always there. They were overshadowed by the spectacle of Rasta and its pious moralisms, but they were there nonetheless, stalking Jamaica's neocolonial streets and consuming American cowboy and gangster films as well as the Old Testament and Pentecostalism. They existed within Rasta from the moment it defined itself as an urban phenomenon and as a place for those suppressed by the hierarchical and color-stratified social structure of Jamaica. During the sixties, before the hegemony of Rasta in the consciousness of ghetto sound, the earliest manifestation of the ragga can be located in the rude-boy phenomenon which swept the tiny island. The rudies, like today's "gangbangers" in America, were young males who had little access to education and were victims of the incredible unemployment endemic to Third World urban centers. Their political consciousness was as developed as the Rastafari, but where the Rasta solution was one which often refused to engage directly with the harsh realities of ghetto and Third World life and frequently got lost in cloudy moments of rhetoric and myth ("roots and culture"), the rudies clung fiercely to "reality"—that trope central to today's ragga/dancehall culture. They terrorized the island, modeling themselves after their heroes from American films and glorying in their outlaw status. They killed, robbed, and looted, celebrating their very stylish nihilism. And ska and reggae—especially DJ-reggae,[4] the beginning of rap/hip hop— were their musics.

Today the dreadlocks vision has been superseded—at least in the realm of sound and culture—by the rudie vision. The crucial differences between them can be seen quite vividly in their relationship to Babylon. Where in Rasta and other forms of popular Negritude there has always been some degree of nostalgia for a precolonial/preindustrial/precapitalist Africa, raggamuffin culture is very forward looking and capitalist oriented—as are most black people, despite the fantasies of many self-appointed nationalist leaders. These rudies focus their gaze instead on America absorbing commodity culture from the fringes of the global marketplace, responding to it positively.

This means that in the context of a Third World ghetto where there are more guns per capita than anywhere else in the world, where legitimate employment is often a fantasy, where the drug trade and music provide the only available options for success, these young men find affirmation in the various messages that radiate out from America, an America that is not the center but rather an imagined source of transmission. Messages like *The Godfather* get picked up and translated into island style. For example, one of the titles of utmost dancehall respect is "don."

The raggamuffin pantheon is full of DJs with names like Clint Eastwood, Johnny Ringo, Al Capone, Josey Wales, and Dillinger; and today's dons boast names like Bounty Killer, Shabba Ranks (named after a famous Jamaican gunman), and John Wayne. Also, the Jamaican underworld has always been full of characters who inscribed themselves into ghetto myth by renaming themselves in much the same way. Male identity in this context is a necessary pastiche, and the allegorical representations of America's dreams of itself become rewritten with a pen soaked in the blood of colonialism, slavery, and black ghetto style. The gunfighter/outlaw image has always been there in reggae; it is now, however, without overt references to the Western world as the "sheriff," as in Bob Marley and the Wailers' classic "I Shot the Sheriff." For the ragga, this metaphor is no longer apt, for now they shoot each other in a lawless postcolonial terrain. Indeed, Ninjaman has described Jamaica as a "Cowboy Town."

These names—and the notion of crime as political/cultural resistance that they signify—were there during Rasta's moment; but where the more Afrocentric embraced the Marley vision, the ghetto youth, the "bad bwoys," were smuggling in specialized weaponry like M16s, Glocks, and Bushmasters, killing each other and following their favorite sound systems[5] around the island. And, of course, the cocaine and marijuana trade was booming. In fact, it was booming in such a way that in the 1980s a few of the more enterprising Yardies invested some of this money which came to the ghetto in—believe it or not—state-of-the-art digital computer technology. Thus began what Jah Fish (Murray Elias), an avid follower of Jamaican music, has called "the modem era"[6] of Afro-Caribbean sound and culture.

This, then, should help describe the raggamuffin sound, what Dick Hebdige has called "an ultra-modern maisonette where all the surfaces are clean and shiny":[7] a highly produced digital and floppy-disk-driven sound from a country which, ironically, has no significant computer technology to speak of. The ragga youth are immersed in this technology, fascinated with it in much the same way that early reggae mixers and producers were with multitrack technology. For them, this technology and the highly experimental rhythms that they produce in it—as much akin to German and Eastern European avant-garde synthesizer music as to West African percussion and calypso—allow them to play with the signifiers and symbols of cultural history in the ontological space of sound. It also plugs them into an information network spread across the Atlantic, one focused on the potential for cultural and economic exchange in the New World instead of a fixation with their roots in the Old. This is all summed up, I think, in the words of the truly large Cutty Ranks:

> *London, Paris and even California,*
> *down a Japan or me gone down a Africa*
> *down a New Zealand or even inna Canada,*
> *yes, Cutty Rankin' a go kill you with the lingua . . .*

Let me provide a practical example of how this specific network within diaspora operates. The legendary team of Steely and Cleevie in Jamaica, or maybe Bobby Digital in Kingston, may send a floppy disk with the basic rhythm track to Daddy Freddy, who is in London with the up-and-coming production team of Mafia or Fluxy (or maybe Fashion, today's dominant U.K. sound). This track may feature the latest craze in dancehall rhythms—sampled Indian tablas mixed with Jamaican mento[8] patterns from the 1950s. After a brief vocal session, that same information could go to Massive B in the Bronx for hip-hop beats or to Sting International in Brooklyn where R&B touches are added. Again, all of this is by modem or by floppy disk. Within a few days this mix is booming down the fences at the weekly "sound clash" between Metromedia Hi-Fi and the mighty Stone Love Sound System somewhere in a crowded field in West Kingston. Or in a community center in Brixton. An "authentic" Jamaican product! And this trade goes both ways, circulating through diaspora. (Even in Lagos, Nigeria, I have sat listening to Igbo rude boys and Yoruba dreads rap in Jamaican patwah about the virtues of Eddy Murphy!)

Here we can witness an attempt to connect the various points of black/Afro-Caribbean disembarkation into one transnational, commodity-based space. One postnationalist city of blackness—but with many, many suburbs. Maybe this is the only Zion possible: a place where the subversion and redefinition of First World technology and the loosening bands of racial/nationalist ideologies allow dancehall to create a new "Africa" within the postmodern networks of multinational capital; a virtual "black" community informed by the very arbitrariness of the racial signifier itself. And, like the Rastafari before them, they use sound to invent this space of black belonging. Sound which conveys cultural and historical meanings encoded in beats, grooves, and samples: digitalized culture production.

Tragically, violence and the drug trade follow this same route—these young men and women die in diaspora as quickly and as often as they enter into it. The bullets and gunshot sounds central to dancehall music, and the lyrical gun-fetishizations of the DJs, are not simply rhetorical figures; they reflect a certain reality. And the obsession with space, with controlling borders, is such that on the micropolitical level it leads to some of the fiercest territorial and aesthetic disputes in the world. Not only has reggae and dancehall been known for their deep intimacy with crime, but the very rituals of sound-system culture celebrate a certain ruthless parochiality. Sound clashes often end in violence, with DJs and posses killing each other over lyrics, money, and volume disputes. And the lyrics of many ragga-chats are about the celebration of one's belonging to and willingness to kill and die for one's sound. Also, one of the most heartfelt ways of showing appreciation for the selector (he who controls the psycho-acoustic space of the dancehall and spins the records) is by firing real guns into the floor or off into the Jamaican night sky. These days applause has been replaced in sound sessions by the verbal chants of "Bo! Bo! Bo!" or "Booyaka!"— imitation gunfire. Here, borders are patrolled because there is ever the fear of having some other sound encroach upon yours.

But it is in language that the cultural barriers between blacknesses are more clearly visible. There have always been fast-talkers in various West Indian musics, and the vernacular has been long accepted as the medium of truly popular discourses throughout the Caribbean. Rasta also featured its own language, one subtly independent of the Jamaican vernacular. Some called it "lyaric" and thought of it as the first step to complete semantic freedom from the "politricks" of neocolonial structures of power. The ragga strategy, however, is not to escape the language, but to use it to stress their specific "Yardness." They so stress their Jamaican patwah, by exaggerating, stretching, and speeding it up (almost to and sometimes beyond the point of parody), that it is incomprehensible and intimidating to those on the outside. This language is consciously as fast as the ragga beats, as garish as their style, replete with in-jokes, neologisms, specific island/cultural references, and full of more assertions concerning class and gender than racial authenticity.

Indeed, where Rasta and various Black Nationalisms and Negritudes tended to segregate women into a phallocentric ghetto—voices, identities, and bodies covered in some kind of revolutionary propriety—the ragga moment is one which is dominated by explicit representations of the sexuality of black women. In addition to urban tales of survival, machismo, and violent retributions, the body of the black woman is at the center of ragga cultural discourse.[9] Not as metaphoric "Mama Africa," to quote Peter Tosh (or any of the poets of French Negritude), but as a threatening physical and economic presence. An aggressive and predatory figure to be guarded against in some cases and catered to in others. This is important because in Rasta, women were a conspicuous absence in the rhetoric and in the rituals of culture. And except for women like the I-Threes, who sang back-up for Bob Marley and the Wailers, they were absent in the iconography. But not only do women function in the symbolic order of raggamuffin sound, they are very present in the culture itself. They consume more records than the men do, and they control the dance floor. Most DJs today—acknowledging the market—orient their lyrics toward these women. From a Western liberal-feminist perspective these lyrics, because they are boldly heterosexual and disdainful of bourgeois sentimentality, seem very sexist and objectifying of women. However, down there in the mire of postcolonial reality, where power is a rare but prized commodity, these women find both affirmation and power in the fear that their sexuality creates in the men. It allows them the freedom and security to navigate in and around a world of brutality, violence, and economic privation.

And because this aesthetic is one of raw materialistic presence, where the pressures of history succumb to the intensity of the moment, the obsession with the body of woman—admiring it, celebrating it, possessing it, controlling it or fearing its power—

seems to pick up where the obsession with "Africa" left off. But here it is without the gendered romance of Negritude or Rasta-nationalism. Here racial romance has given way to something much less pastoral and much more vicious. With titles ranging from "Want a Virgin" and "Love Punaany[10] Bad" ("Punaany it is so nice/Punaany it so slick/Come put your lips on a twelve-inch d**k), and with lyrics ranging from horrific celebrations of male sexual aggression ("Me ram it and a jam it 'till the gal start to vomit") to lyrics mapping out the rituals and morality of ghetto relationships, this music articulates a world completely devoid of sentimentality and intimacy—a world where one is, in the words of Don Gorgon Ninjaman, "Married to Mi Gun." And many of the women who pick up the mike today and attempt to "ram up session" demand not equality, but that their dons "ride and provide."

It is also important to note that the particular uses of language in raggamuffin sound culture tend, as was my point earlier, to consciously separate them from blacks met in New York, Miami, or London. They use language, as many Afro-Caribbean immigrants have, to signify and create cultural difference within the nationalist monolith of "blackness." Despite the fact that Pan-Africanism is in many ways an invention of the West Indies, the specific racial dynamics of the ideology require that culture often be elided for the sake of "race," that the specifics of one African experience be lost in the Atlantic for the sake of an historical, transcendental "ness." This has created certain hostilities which conveniently escape the annals of black historiography—nationalist or otherwise—because they would strip "racial" affiliations of their often merely rhetorical power. The long-standing tensions between Jamaicans and black Americans in Harlem—between Garvey and the Harlem "Niggerati," for example—attest to this crisis of affiliation. This use of language and culture, this particular intraracial silence, functions as a reaction to the shock of seeing each other; to be ambivalently placed between an assumption of racial affinity and the differential truths of black history. Once again, the "borderline" that figures so prominently in raggamuffin sound.

None of this, however, is to suggest that there is no ground of commonality—as with history, racism, slavery, exploitation. Not even the most nihilistic "dogheart" DJs would assert such a thing. By now it is clear to me that diaspora is a memory bank of signifiers and symbols of black authenticity constructed over the last century or so and is moored by an assumed racial/cultural commonality. Without this assumption there really is nothing to talk about; there really is no "we" or, in some cases, "them." But due to it, the assumption, there is now more exchange between and among blacknesses than there has been since the slave trade! The ragga response, however, is not to accept themselves as passive victims in an overwhelming Babylonian structure; not to represent themselves as "wailers," as victims of history belonging to a helplessly innocent race. This can be seen in the incredible boasting and self-assertions that are typical of dancehall and the "fearless" rude boys who "ride the riddim." Instead, they see themselves in many ways as being free within Babylon to destroy history and rebuild community—to, in T. S. Eliot's words, "murder and create."

Unfortunately this equation tilts too often to the "murder" side—as in two recent ragga hits, "Murder She Wrote" and "Murder Dem!"—due to the intense competition, violence, and wanton bloodshed central to the crack/cocaine trade, the Jamaican record industry, and the vagaries of ghetto living and grassroots capitalism. Nevertheless, the ragga are here, there, everywhere, stalking the ever-extending streets of diaspora with a lethal and dangerous style. Imagining freedom within the virtual networks of dissemination and consumption, they circulate, never achieving a fixed moment of landfall. They follow their sound and their sound follows them, defiantly asserting noisy difference in the center of that dream space called diaspora.

> *Now big up all massive, London massive, New York bad bwoy, Toronto massive—all crew! Rude bwoys a foreign and rudie's a Yard big up cause you know say all a we a Jamaicans. And we know that no dibby-dibby sound bwoy can cross the border, cause if him test it, him a go dead—pure gun-shot inna him head! So come now, my selector, come with a next riddim cause we no skin teeth and fret fe the sound bwoy dem. Come, raggamuffin, enter inside this ya sound. . . .*

SKYJUICE, SELECTOR FROM METROMEDIA SOUND SYSTEM

LISTENING GUIDE

Considering that the ragga/dancehall industry is a singles industry releasing over two hundred new singles a week, and considering that its infrastructure is still very close to the West Indian grassroots and sound-system subculture, it is at this point very difficult to obtain those specific tracks which characterize the form at any given moment. Most fresh singles reach certain American record stores in a limited quantity and are snatched up by selectors, DJs, and those "in the know." And the albums which are widely available tend to feature a DJ's two or three hits and acres of bad material. However, acknowledging this scenario, many independent and major labels have made available dozens of compilations featuring the major hits of the last few months. (These, of course, are notoriously late, since there is such a high turnover rate of hits and artists and since things get laughably old in a matter of days.)

I would suggest any of the following compilations because they all fairly well give an idea of what I have been trying to describe:

Bam Bam It's Murder. Features the major hits "Murder She Wrote" by Chaka Demus and Pliers and "Them a Bleach" by Nardo Ranks. This is very available and highly recommended.

Booyaka: The Ultimate Dancehall Collection. Available on Big Beat Records and featuring many of 1993's best, like Terry Ganzie's "Welcome the Outlaw," Baby Wayne's "Can't Live So," Cutty Ranks's "Open Up," and a reissue of Sister Nancy's haunting "Bam Bam."

Dancehall Stylee: The Best of Reggae Dancehall Music, Volumes 1–4. Especially *Volume 2*, which features Shabba Ranks's "Wicked in Bed," Ninjaman's "Murder Dem," Little Lenny's "Gun in a Baggy," and the very important "Ring the Alarm" by the late great Tenor Saw.

Just Ragga, Volumes 1–6. On Charm Records, London. Very hardcore and "authentic."

Strictly the Best, Volumes 1–13. These tend to balance well the more pop-oriented sounds with the vicious, hardcore slam-jams. *Volume 3* features Pinchers's huge hit "Bandelero" and Ninjaman's "Test the High Power," which is the most well-articulated description of being at a sound session that I have ever heard.

Also, Roof International/Cosmic Force Records have put out a series of dancehall compilations that are well respected in the DJ community. Still, any compilations that you find—especially those that feature bhangra/bangara rhythms or very experimental rhythms that sound nothing like reggae—should serve to make my points clearer. As for major-label albums, I will suggest only a few:

As Raw as Ever and *X-tra Naked* by Shabba Ranks. These two American albums have won Ranks two Grammy Awards and an Afro-American audience that even Bob Marley couldn't get. The latter features the Yard hit "Ting-a-Ling" and a number of American R&B crossover smashes.

From Mi Heart by Cutty Ranks. Includes a handful of very good tunes. But the classic is *The Stopper,* featuring the hit title track.

Don Dadda by SuperCat. This album is highly recommended. Features the hit single "Ghetto Red Hot" as well as the classic "'Nuff Man A Dead." If you can find the Massive B. hip-hop remix of "Ghetto Red Hot" you will have found the most successful ragga/hip-hop fusion single to date.

Raggamuffin Soldier by Daddy Freddy. Despite an incredibly bad debut solo album, this second full album by Daddy Freddy is very highly recommended. In my humble opinion, it ranks as the best and most diverse full ragga album available. Daddy Freddy chats on hard Yard riddims as well as gansta–hip-hop beats and jazz-funk tracks. It's on Chrysalis Records so it is widely available. Definitely check this one out.

Anything you can find from Ninjaman "the Don Gorgon," "the People's DJ," will blow your mind—if you can get through his dense patwah and virtuoso lyrical style. He has ruled in Jamaica for years, and his early albums (pre-1993) feature some incredible verbal, rhythmic, and narrative adventures. His latest is *Nobody's Business But My Own,* featuring "Married to Mi Gun," "Mi Belly Move," and "(The World) Between Her Legs."

Patra has recently been signed as the first major female DJ, and her album on epic, *Queen of the Pack,* features tracks that are definitely "the boom."

And no recommended-listening list would be complete without mentioning 1993's DJ kid sensation, Buju Banton. Nineteen years old, gruff, and truly wicked, his American debut is the aptly titled *Voice of Jamaica.*

This list, of course, is not definitive and is based on my own collection and my experience as a selector/DJ with the sound system Ebony Tower International.

NOTES

1. A slightly different version of this paper was presented at a conference titled "Art, Aesthetics and Politics in Africa and the Caribbean," which was held at the University of California, San Diego, in 1994. It is being published [in *African Arts*] with the proceeds of that conference.

2. *Dancehall* and *raggamuffin* are terms used often interchangeably to describe the new computer-driven music coming primarily out of Jamaica in the wake of traditional reggae music and culture. Although some of it sounds merely like hi-tech reggae, most of it sounds nothing like its predecessor at all. These terms also describe the music's attendant cultural superculture—attitudes, styles, language, and sociopolitical orientation. Originally the dance-hall was (and still is) the physical space—an open field, a rented auditorium—in which sound systems strung up and held public dances. It is in this context that the discourses of Jamaica's urban, working-class culture worked themselves out in sound and expressive culture.

But I prefer to think of a difference between ragga and dancehall music in much the way many see the distinction between hip-hop and rap: the latter is more commercial, dealing with the music that has gotten mass attention and become streamlined for popular tastes; whereas the former also connotes a culture and is more disdainful of popular acceptance.

3. Heartical respect to Welton Irie and all Ladbroke Grove massive.

4. DJ reggae is the form of reggae that dancehall and hip-hop descend from almost exclusively. It features the use of prerecorded instrumental tracks ("versions") or strategic breaks in a tune as spaces for the DJ to improvise new, spoken lyrics. This form of reggae has only recently gotten the international attention it deserves, but has ruled in Jamaica even from when Bob Marley was the global "Reggae Ambassador."

5. Sound systems are one of the black diaspora's most enduring and frequently unacknowledged cultural institutions. Although variations can be found throughout diaspora history, the form they have today can be traced back to those mobile discotheques in Jamaica during the late fifties/early sixties which would set up in empty fields around the more economically depressed areas in Kingston. Cane cutters who were taken to Miami for brief stints of migrant labor would return to Jamaica with the latest R&B records and play them on homemade stereos customized to produce a level of volume that was nothing less than insane. Especially the bass frequencies. These rapidly became the only social and cultural space that catered to the ghetto dwellers. Shunning the popular media—neocolonial radio and television which expressed the views of a culturally insecure elite—these systems became the primary space of cultural discourse in the vernacular. Indeed, it is this sort of discourse that reinvents Africa and celebrates Garvey where the national media evaded such issues; it is here that the fissures in the official narrative of race and nation were opened up for popular scrutiny, culminating in the development of ska, rock steady, and then reggae and ragga.

With the migration of Jamaicans to London in the late fifties, sound systems became a space of exile where, for a loud bass-thick moment, "home" could be invented there in the midst of Babylon. With the success of West Indian music and style in England, the sound-system structure was picked up by various youth subcultures who reaccentuated it, eventually creating the digital sound cultures we see throughout Europe today. And the technical and musical innovations developed in ghetto studios because of the need to circumvent the limitations of poor equipment have become standard in state-of-the-art dance-music production in the West.

In New York, this alternate-media structure was central to the formation of hip-hop music and the foundation of its attendant subculture.

6. S. H. Fernando Jr., "Hip-Hop Meets Reggae Inna Soundclash," *Dub Catcher: The Soul Voice of Jamaican Roots,* Winter 1993.

7. Dick Hebdige, *Cut 'n' Mix: Culture, Identity and Caribbean Music* (Routledge, 1990), p. 151.

8. Mento was the earliest music fully acknowledged as indigenously Jamaican. In the late 1950s its mixture of African and Latin percussion was the foundation upon which subsequent

musical forms were built. Oddly enough, after years of bass-dominated harmonies, mento has returned in Jamaican music via sampling technology; mento has returned to inspire artists to dig into the past and reshuffle (remix) their roots.

9. A much better and more specific discussion of the sexual politics of dancehall can be found in Carolyn Cooper's "Erotic Play in the Dancehall," *Jamaica Journal* 22, p. 14.

10. *Punaany:* crude slang term for the female genitalia. Usage very popular in ragga.

Dancehall DJs in the House

JORDAN LEVIN

The Miami Herald
26 April 1996

It's dancehall night at Cafe Casablanca in Hallandale, and Richie D and crew are at the turntables, spinning out a relentless groove that has the packed floor rocking and jamming like a wildly pulsing heart. A circle of boys in baggy jeans is in an impromptu dance competition, rising up on sneakered toes, knees and hips in liquid flow like Gumby figures come to funky life. A girl in a jumper open over black bikini and sneakers is off in her own private ecstasy, swaying and bouncing to her knees.

"Watch me now!" Richie D calls into the mike, flipping records on and off in thirty-second bites as he works up to Beenie Man's "Ole Dog Like We," the latest dance anthem. When he hits it people jump, scream, blow whistles and point in the air; Richie flips the volume down and the crowd chants the lyrics, never missing a beat. "Oh yeah, everybody wants to do this s***," says Belinda Black, twenty-two, who's at Casablanca for dancehall night every Sunday. "This s*** is hype."

Jamaican dancehall is a fast-moving form of reggae with a hard percussive beat, a bass that echoes like a seismic tremor in your gut, a music with an irresistibly deep groove. Here's how it works: A vocalist/DJ raps ("toasting" or "chanting") over a track that usually consists of just a rhythmic bassline, drums, maybe guitar. It's some of the most energetic black music to come out since hip-hop emerged from the Bronx, and it has spawned a subculture with stars, slang, dances and style. And in South Florida, with its proximity to Jamaica and its large West Indian communities, dancehall is booming.

"Dancehall is really happening," says Clint O'Neil, godfather of Miami's reggae scene, host of a late-night reggae show on WLRN (91.3 FM) since 1979. His seven-year-old Thursday night dancehall set is his most popular show. "And we're getting everybody hooked up in it right now. It's not even underground like it used to be."

Yet for all the buzz, dancehall is one of the oldest forms of popular music. "This is where Jamaican music originated, in the dance hall," says Winston Barnes, news director for Caribbean station WAVS (1170 AM). Barnes, who started working in Jamaican radio in the sixties, says that in the fifties DJs at local dances began rerecording, manipulating and rapping live over their American R&B records, beginning the evolution of Jamaican styles like ska, rock steady, reggae and lovers' rock into contemporary dancehall.

The genre remains club-driven dance music, largely shaped by the DJs, also called selectors. Top selectors and "sound systems"—mobile music conglomerates with selectors, rappers and technicians—can be stars on a par with recording artists and even remix and produce their own records. Jamaica's twenty-four-year-old Stone Love sound system has twenty-one members and tours the world, a traveling music machine.

A dancehall DJ is musician, producer and showman all in one. Jamaican-born Waggy Tee, thirty-two, started playing parties when he was thirteen, graduating to clubs and radio in the 1980s. Now he plays the Caribbean, New York, England and South Beach, drawing up to a thousand to his Saturday nights at the Cameo Theater. Onstage, Waggy is a tranced-out blur in a sea of records, whipping between turntables and boxes, scratching discs, flipping switches, mixing dancehall, house, hip-hop, classic reggae, soca—even disco—into an ever-ascending wave of rhythm.

"It's all in the mix," Waggy says of his high-octane style. "The young generation— they're so hype they get bored if you play the entire song throughout." It takes keen musical instincts and a less definable "feel" for the crowd. "It's a high, like a singer getting into a certain spirit," says Richie D.

Out to party, women often wear elaborate outfits—"either party dress or as close to naked as possible," says "Nuffy" (as in 'nuff, slang for enough), a self-described "No. 1 fan" famous on the local dancehall scene. Some get pretty close to naked—like a gold mesh mini over a skimpy gold bathing suit, or a transparent sheath over a G-string. Custom outfits can cost hundreds, and spectacularly sculpted hair has to be redone every week. "A lot of these people live for the weekend," said a clubgoer at Casablanca.

New dances pop up every few weeks, with names like Butterfly, Sketel, Motley Dread. Ardent dancehall-goers can identify a song almost instantly. "It's a never-ending thing, beats, catering to how they dance," says Waggy. A hit will inspire a train of others incorporating the same rhythm, often plucked from an older song. Rhythms are endlessly manipulated and recycled. "Most of the rhythms you're hearing now are from the sixties and seventies," says Ron Burke, a WAVS host who comanages the reggae/Caribbean club Stinger Lounge in Miramar. "Producers take those rhythms, change them and bring them back."

Dancehall has become the dominant style in Jamaica, still its definitive home. South Florida is the biggest market and scene after the island and New York. Top artists and sound systems play here regularly, and major concerts, like the recent Sting Festival in Miami, draw thousands.

"Miami is very important," says Luther McKenzie, president of Shang Records, label for top artists Shabba Ranks, Patra and Mad Cobra (Shang recently moved to South Beach from New York). "There's a lot happening behind the scenes, and there's more to come, believe me."

South Florida's confluence of cultures makes it fertile ground for a music built on recycling and incorporation. "We exchange a lot," says Eddie Edwards, who manages Stinger's and produces the August Reggae Festival for Jamaican Independence Day. "Here dancehall is not a strange music, it's my friend's music from Jamaica." South Florida DJs tend to mix in other sounds, creating a sort of universal Afro–New World beat.

"When you have a wider range of understanding you get a better vibe in what you're playing," says Waggy Tee. "Now reggae is not just a Jamaican thing. Latin kids, whites, blacks—everyone is listening to reggae now."

Where dancehall and American tastes most readily merge is in hip-hop. "Hip-hop and dancehall have the same beats," says Rory, lead DJ for Stone Love. "You can mix the records, and they will groove." Often American labels will try to widen a dancehall artist's audience by employing a hip-hop artist or producer: Patra has recorded with Salt-n-Pepa and Shabba Ranks with KRS-1; Beenie Man's "Slam" was remixed by Special Ed.

Dancehall has been controversial, largely because of violent, sexual—even misogynistic—lyrics (called "slackness") that dominated until recently. Much like in gansta rap, some said slackness encouraged violence, and dancehall shows got a bad rep. But in the last two years the slackness has gone slack. "You used to have a lot of gun talk and degrading women," says My-Stro, who runs an underground Caribbean/reggae radio station. "Now people speak of God and the problems of daily life." Gospel-oriented artists like Luciano, Capleton and the late Garnett Silk have become popular, and even the hardcore Buju Banton has got religion. Most attribute the change to concerns that slackness and fear of violence were alienating audiences— and boredom. "Everyone just rebelled against it," says Edwards. "It's hard to say why. These things go in cycles." While slackness certainly hasn't disappeared, it no longer overwhelms.

The spiritual resurgence might be part of dancehall's reconnection with roots reggae. At times, the two have seemed generationally incompatible ("You cannot push what you had ten to fifteen years ago on the younger folks," says My-Stro).

But in a broader sense, they are connected. And while Bob Marley's reggae might have opened the world's ears to Jamaica, dancehall might turn out to be the island's most universal music.

"Dancehall is just another manifestation of the music," says Barnes. "The music comes in cycles. I think dancehall is the way it is now because the music is no longer Jamaican music. It is an international music."

PART SEVEN

WORLD

Jamaican Music:
The Foreign Press Again?

WINSTON BARNES

The Jamaican Weekly Gleaner
11 December 1992

While in college in New York in the mid-1970s, I developed this theory about Jamaican language—the language some of us are convinced is unique to us as a people. The same one we call patois. Even at that stage it was obvious our culture was going to impact heavily on that of the world and decidedly on the culture of the U.S. of A.

I took the decision that we should not teach Americans to speak and understand Jamaican dialect. We should, I reasoned, keep back something for ourselves. Maintain our language, which would allow us to communicate without outside understanding. Oh how things have changed since then.

Not only has reggae music and its attendant cultural attachments entered the American music industry, but it is moving into and affecting mainstream American culture. From fake dreadlocks in a variation of stylings, to a profusion of articles (from shoes to belts and headgear) in the red, green and gold colours, to claims about Jamaican ganja, things Jamaican have moved into the United States on a number of levels. Sadly, the Jamaican phenomenon has also included Jamaican posses with their penchant for major violent outburst, if we are to go by the foreign press.

The recent ruckus about that Buju Banton song which promised death and punishment to homosexuals has obviously attracted the attention of what especially in the 1970s came to be known as the foreign press. How are they going to view the song and others of a similar bent?

MYSTERY
Especially to journalists of the American variety, reggae music has provided a certain amount of mystery and fascination. Many have convinced themselves that they have

uncovered this grand mystery, too. Considering that so much of this mystery was of their creation, it would follow that they should be able to explain it fairly easily.

But the travesty dealt reggae music by these journalists has to do with the American proclivity to explain away everything and place everything in some neat cubbyhole and under some easily recognized label. Hence one gets a question which goes something like, Such and such a recording speaks about a certain political reality; what are your thoughts on the politics of this song? Maybe the song has no political connotations whatsoever!

It is conceivably a result of their training, either directly or through learning from other practitioners, but the practice of making certain conclusions and then seeking or sometimes demanding evidence to support their thesis is as commonplace as it is forced and artificial and sometimes plain inaccurate. Even when indications are to the contrary, these journalists have to find evidence—sometimes trumped up or brought out of someone who is hardly knowledgeable or articulate about the music but who happens to be Jamaican.

While there are obviously some foreign journalists who are extremely perceptive and have made some observations about our music which have benefited us and the music, it is even more obvious that so many others have simply jumped on a bandwagon they never recognized or worse, understood.

A classic example: A couple of years ago I interviewed the publisher of an international reggae publication. It was at about the time when a number of very current performers were making recordings with a decidedly gospel-influenced feel and lyrical content. Under the circumstances, I enquired about the influences of gospel music on reggae music. What I got from this publisher of an international magazine was a short response about the minimal influence, or words to the effect that there was none.

Even if the response was about American gospel, it would still have been inaccurate. Gospel music from both the United States and Jamaica has influenced Jamaican popular music since its very birth, from the earliest "movements of Jah music." Toots and the Maytals sang gospel at first. Max Romeo's biggest hit, "Let the Power Fall," was really a gospel song; it has been recorded by local gospel groups since Romeo's version hit in 1971. We are aware that some of Lovindeer's and Admiral Bailey's stuff of a few years ago was gospel influenced; so too is one of Pinchers's songs, "This Life I Owe," hardly recognized for what it really is, a thanksgiving for life to "the man who went to Calvary!"

So let the foreigners come and take another look at Jamaican culture and reggae music, in wake of the stink over Buju Banton's song. But those who talk with them should demand more accuracy in their retelling of what they are told. And we should tell it like it really is and not how these journalists want it told.

Children, You Don't Know Your Own Name

PAN JUMBIE

The Sunday Express (Trinidad and Tobago)
9 October 1988

Pan Jumbie was driving through Petit Valley on Monday night on his way home when he hear pan. The road was pitch black . . . so dark people were holding hands to walk, but Valley Harps were practising.

I wanted to stop and listen because I was sure they were preparing for the inaugural World Steelband Festival, scheduled to get under way here on October 20. But the children in the backseat of the car wanted to hurry home to watch *Alf*, so I had no choice. They don't care about culture. You think I could tell them about pan? They turned me off and start up a conversation about this "hard Maxi" with these "cork dubs" and the bass so loud it could be heard for nearly a quarter mile: "BOOM BU DOOM . . . BOOM BU DOOM . . . BOOM BU DOOM."

"That is cork music boy," said my eighteen-year-old son. "We fed up hearing about those longtime days. We know that the only time Despers ever won a steelband festival was last year . . . and that when they started "Stranger in Paradise" tears of emotion came to your eyes. We have heard that already.

"We know they were considered the Government band because they always won the Prime Minister's Trophy, which, like the music festival, was held biennially, and when it came to the festival . . . after the quarter-finals Despers gone, even in 1966 when they played "Brazil." We know all that already."

Well, the Jumbie get vex, and since I was the "man of the house" I asked his mother to deal with him.

I instructed her to inform him of the importance of this festival, and the input it could make to the nation as a whole.

She was to tell him it was thinking like his which was retarding the progress of the steelband movement, and that he should be proud of people like Len "Boogsie"

Sharpe, who could play a pan turned upside down, or Ray Holman, Robbie Greenidge, Ken "Professor" Philmore, Earl Brooks and Selwyn "Mini Eyes" Springer, who were all fantastic musicians.

She was to add that *Boogsie and the Rebels* was a record of which every Trinidadian should be proud, but he chose to listen to a set of third rated (I cannot even call it) music, loaded with wrong chords.

But even while she was raging, talking about "your father's beliefs," he slipped "Don't Worry, Be Happy" by Bobby McFerrin into the cassette player.

He joking about a serious thing. Friends turn enemies over this music festival thing, the blue ribbon event for pan.

Look, when Dixieland played "Agnus Dei" to beat Invaders with "In a Monastery Garden" in 1960, Myfan (currently in Starlift) lost a good friend because he would not honour a bet he had lost. "I don't care what the judges say, "Agnes Dei" ain't beat that," Fan said, and that was the end of the friendship.

You see me, this week I leaving the kids home, because even Starlift back in the festival—the last time Starlift was in a festival was in 1966 when they played Handel's "For Unto Us a Child Is Born." You think these children want to know about that?

And, for the first time, too, all those foreign bands! Antiguans like to tell people they make pan—but Brute Force coming?

Stay with the Jumbie as he makes the rounds of the festival panyards. I tell you history in the making here.

Beating World Music Into Submission

JOE BOYD

Musician
August 1995

There is no such thing as "pure" ethnic music. The greatest forms in popular music are miscegnated in nature. Jazz was born from the rich cultural melting pot of New Orleans. Tango and samba are products of cultural collisions between Africa and European cultures. Even that most *un*fused of musical forms, the English Morris Dance, derives from sailors' *Moorish* dance in imitation of what they had seen in Africa.

So I have no doctrinaire objection to the world music fusions that have proliferated in recent years. But when I hear Youssou N'Dour or Salif Keita's latest hi-tech effort using top American or European session players, my heart sinks. Likewise when I hear the sampling of exotic melodies over a relentless dance beat that comes straight from Euro-American drum machines.

Musicians from all cultures, particularly those from the Third World trying to crack the Western market, revere Bob Marley, the first and still the greatest World Beat musician. What puzzles me is that this reverence seems to ignore the fundamental lessons of Marley's approach to his music.

His melodies and lyrics are not particularly typical of reggae. Some call to mind Dylan and Lennon, some American gospel or folk, some hark back to early Jamaican mento or calypso. But beneath them is an undiluted rhythmic foundation of powerful, pure reggae. The key to his music was the marriage of his lyrical and melodic genius with a rhythm section which could not have come from anywhere but the heart of Jamaica.

Compare this with N'Dour. He superimposes the Wolof melodies and lyrics of his culture on a kind of mid-Atlantic "modern" rhythm section. At one point in his Virgin Records days, I was approached by an A&R man about producing him. I was sent rehearsal tapes of the new material and much of it was backing tracks without the vocal. I could play that to any number of experts and no one would identify it as even African, much less Senegalese. It was mid-Atlantic World Beat rhythm with plenty of electronic effects diluting the energy of the Mbalax rhythms which propelled Youssou to his place in the galaxy of African stars. Needless to say, my views did not endear me to Youssou and I did not get the gig.

When the great artists (and their A&R men) from both the First and the Third Worlds start to listen to their Bob Marley records more closely and learn the lessons to be found there, we may find some true stars of World Music.

So far, the only concrete result is a trail of unrecouped royalty advances from the immensely costly efforts of the likes of N'Dour, Keita and Kidjo to make hi-tech records which deny their rhythmic roots.

I have more respect for what Paul Simon has done with African and Brazilian music than I do for the depressing fusions of Peter Gabriel, Angelique Kidjo or Deep Forest. Simon starts with the rhythm and from that, everything else grows. The same usually applies to David Byrne. Our Ali Farka Touré/Ry Cooder record has outsold all the Youssou N'Dour or Salif Keita records in the U.S. market by the proverbial mile. It was made in a few days, and Cooder never imposes an American rhythmic sense on Ali's pure Malian music. The result is a gem and it has had the success such an effort deserves. Maybe now the lesson will begin to sink in.

Intereggae

DON SNOWDEN

New America News Service/New York Times Syndicate
8 July 1996

Question of the week: How come the United States is still one of the few countries in the world where reggae's influence is acknowledged grudgingly, at best?

Maybe it's because reggae missed out on its next-big-thing-in-pop-music chance twenty years ago, or that Jamaican artists were measured against the impossible-to-match standard of Bob Marley for years. Maybe it boils down to discomfort with the Rasta religion associated with reggae or the postdisco mindset that any rhythm-based music was inferior to guitar-dominated rock.

In any case, it hasn't prevented many artists in the rest of the world from adopting and adapting the music that has spawned a genuinely universal, alternative (in the original sense of the word) culture in twenty-five years. But it does mean that U.S. listeners who want to sample international reggae sounds usually have to head for the import bins.

Los Pericos: *Pampas Reggae* (EMI Latin H2 7243 8 30872 2 8). There's a broad range of sounds and impeccably solid performances on this 1994 CD by a popular Argentinian band. "Párate y Mira" throws everything from parade rhythms inspired by the Brazilian Afro-bloco drum ensembles Olodum and Timbalada to a salsa Big Band bit into the mix and makes it work. "Cabeza de Policía" goes for mood-setting with an almost sitarish guitar line over a catchy roots bass and those big-sounding horns again. And the economical musical and lyrical hooks to "Más Cera del Cielo" and "Runaway" fit so perfectly they're irresistible.

Skank: *Calango* (Chaos/Sony Brazil 750.214/476429; Brazilian import). ROCK FROM BRAZIL says the sticker on the front of the CD case, but it's really a case of either rock-rooted reggae or reggae done by a pop-oriented rock quartet flavored by horns. The sound boasts an edgy, punchy rock drive with lean, clean tunes mixing straight roots reggae with pushy rub-a-dub and the popular dancehall/1950s R&B hybrid sound on "Proibido Fumar." Brazilian add-ons like the Chico Science–style hard-rock guitar on "A Cerca" and those parade drums again on "Amolacao" and "Pacato Cidadao" simply add more flavors to a natural, unforced musical mix. There's another popular Brazilian band, Cidade Negra, that is apparently working in a similar vein.

El General: *Clubb 555* (BMG/U.S. Latin 74321-31522-2). Moving up to Panama, dancehall en español deejay El General moves in a keyboard-dominated, techno-oriented direction here. He doesn't exactly deal with profound themes—dancing and girls predominate—but he's an engagingly goofy character, knows how to put tracks together and his rapid-fire Spanish fits the rhythms like a glove. "Dámelo" melds (somehow) dancehall with 1950s R&B and rockabilly guitar, "Jingle Belele" goofs on Christmas carol sentiments and the deadly keyboard hook that anchors the brilliant Latin house of rub-a-dub arrangement of "Perezosa" makes it a standout in any dance hall.

Tappa Zukie: *From the Archives* (RAS CD 3135)

Tappa Zukie: *In Dub* (Blood & Fire UK BAFCD 008; British import). A brief pit stop at the Jamaican root source with the veteran toaster (i.e., early reggae rapper) who was first championed by Patti Smith. This is absolutely fundamental roots reggae recorded twenty years ago, and there's still something utterly magical about the simplicity of such tracks as "M.P.L.A.," "Marcus" and "Tappa Roots"—every rhythm, wash of echo, strategic insertion of guitar or horns behind his lazy toasting hits home with maximum impact. The Blood & Fire CD treats tracks from the same mid-1970s era with splendid sound, but the music never takes wing.

Audio Active: *Happy Happer* (On-U Sound UK, ON-U CD 77; British import)

2BadCard: *Hustling Ability* (On-U Sound UK, ON-U CD 78; British import). The second CD by the Japanese group Audio Active is a coproduction with On-U Sound's Adrian Sherwood, and the boundary between where Audio Active leaves off and the On-U crew comes on is often murky. Tackhead members Doug Wimbish and Keith LeBlanc show up frequently, but the prime impetus is Audio Active's arsenal of Space Bloop 2000 keyboard effects and fuzz-bass overload to complement rhythms in the heavy industrial dub reggae vein of recent On-U releases. It's generally powerful stuff, and the force of "Happy Shopper," "Electric Bombardment" and "Wah Wah Zoo Mars" is impossible to deny.

In company with coproducer Carlton "Bubbler" Ogilvie, Sherwood takes a break from the forbidding techno-dub soundscape on "Hustling Ability." The music boasts a lighter sound and more directly Jamaican sensibility—Henry Lowther's trumpet meanders lazily through "Leaving Rome," melodica pops up on "Badder Card" and "Mentally Sk'd (Guns I Will . . .)" takes a ska-cruise by the guns of Navarone. It sounds like a vacation for Sherwood—he should take 'em more often if they come out like this.

Zion Train: *Homegrown Fantasy* (Mesa/Bluemoon 2-92643). The first half of *Homegrown Fantasy* flies by in a blur because this new Anglo dub group apparently suffers from an old musical malady—show-your-chops syndrome. It isn't until "Get Ready" that the Jamaican influences rise to the surface and that most essential of dub qualities—space—enters the arrangements. Too late—the high-energy opening tracks have bludgeoned the brain to the point where the dubwise tracks don't really lock in.

Alpha Blondy's Message Is Dead Serious

CHRIS POTASH

The Miami News
11 February 1988

"I think that a solution is in the hands of the American government, you know? They have enough influence in South Africa to make Mr. [Pieter] Botha change his apartheid policy.

"That's the only problem in South Africa, really. The problem is apartheid. If Mr. Botha would abolish apartheid, I know that the white and black South African can build one nation."

These are the studied but sincere words of eloquent African reggaeman Alpha Blondy. They reflect his current concern: the disparity of power and the absence of justice in the strife-ridden country of South Africa.

"Apartheid is so simple. For me, apartheid is Nazism. So how can, in this twentieth century, we accept this kind of situation?"

Apartheid Is Nazism is the name of Alpha Blondy's third album. He is touring the United States with his thirteen-piece band, the Solar System, for the first time, hoping to draw attention to the social problems in South Africa.

Though not entirely comfortable lecturing about politics, Blondy spoke from Atlanta, where his tour started on Tuesday, about his beliefs and his music, and about the importance of America's sympathy to his antiapartheid message.

"Talking politics, I'm not an expert, but I know that America is so strong politically that it can make an ally like Mr. Botha change his ways."

Apartheid is the government-endorsed policy of separate development of races, official in South Africa since 1948 when the Nationalist Party took control there. Blacks, who constitute 68 percent of the population, have been forced by ruling white Afrikaners (descendants of Dutch settlers) into segregated schools, residential areas and occupations.

In 1984 Botha was sworn in as President under a new constitution that allowed for an authoritarian form of government. Twice since then Botha has declared a state of emergency to mobilize military forces against the country's blacks protesting his apartheid policies. The result: murder and suffering.

"You don't have the right to shoot Jah children I say/'Cause black and white we are all the same," sings Blondy in the title track to the new album. "We got to wipe away hatred I say."

"For me, America has been the teacher of human rights; it cannot allow that [apartheid]," says Blondy, a native of Africa's Ivory Coast and a former student at Columbia University in New York.

"I'm kind of hooked on New York," chuckles Blondy, who frequented Harlem nightclubs during his college days and occasionally jumped onstage to sing. He says that when he returns to Manhattan during this tour, "I'll take a walk uptown, I'll stop in the Village . . . and find some friends that I had before."

"Before" means before his first record, *Jah Glory,* was cut in Africa; before he moved to Paris and cut his second album, *Cocody Rock;* before he dared to sing his song "Jerusalem" in Hebrew at the Festival of Marrakesh in Morocco.

Blondy has experienced much in life but has found strength in a single doctrine. "Hope," he says, "is permitted. We should not close the door to hope and just jump on the battlefield."

Hope, and a healthy conscience, guide Blondy's music and his life.

"I was invited to South Africa by some friends but I refused to go. For me it's hard to go play when you know in the backyard there are people being killed," he said thoughtfully.

"You know, the difference between Alpha Blondy and some reggae singers is that I would never advise people to go mash it up. I would not encourage violence. I think my music can kind of create the consciousness of a peaceful solution, because I don't believe in a mash-it-up solution; I like to have people analyze the problem and try to find another way of solving the problem than a civil war."

He says his approach to his music is more spiritual than political.

"I first try to vehicle the African dialects," he says, "and I also try to bring people together around a spiritual energy." Seven of the nine songs on *Apartheid Is Nazism* are sung in a mixture of French and African languages. Only two are in English. But the happy-time feeling of reggae music infuses the album with good vibes that can be understood by all listeners.

"Sweet love, we need you!/And unity, that's what the wise man say," sings Blondy in "Come Back Jesus." He says he gets his inspiration from both the Koran and the Bible, and that allows him to have faith in world leaders to do the right thing regarding apartheid.

"There are political things that we don't know, that we don't understand. I don't know what they [politicians] are waiting for, but I know that they are aware of the situation and we're just waiting for them to do something."

The Fire This Time

PATRICK ANDRADE

http://www.xtr.com/extreme/firethi.htm
1996

Founded in 1988, The Fire This Time was established as a production and collaborative entity that would lend itself to a wide range of musical collaborations. The
genesis of The Fire This Time arose out of the life experience of Patrick Andrade,
who was born and raised in Jamaica of Jamaican and Haitian parents with black
and Native lineage. In the late seventies his family immigrated to Canada and he
began working with First Nations people. A reggae and Native radio show with Chinese–Cree Indian poet Greg Young-Ing, and diverse artistic collaborations with Native
people that involved traveling among Native communities throughout North America, brought Andrade to a deeper understanding of the cultural links between black
and Native American people.

The focus of the group is to continue a historical tradition that is thousands of
years old—a tradition of cooperation and cultural exchange between Africans and
First Nations people around the world. Joint musical projects have been achieved
among indigenous peoples of Greenland, Peru, India, Costa Rica, South Africa,
Mexico, Chile and various North American Native nations. The Fire This Time
refuses to be limited by artificial borders.

The Fire This Time also traveled to South Central America to work with indigenous people, and as a result of this experience the group was joined by Chilean-born
poet and artist of Inca Native heritage Marcela A. Toro, who also serves as art director
for the group. The Fire This Time enjoys the cooperation of media and network
strategist Errol Nazareth, born in Kuwait and of Indian heritage.

On occasion The Fire This Time describes its sound as "Blakk Indian Music," in
reference to the manner in which it fuses different elements of black music like
reggae, hip-hop and dub with Native American musical forms like traditional singing

and drumming. The group's first recording was the antirape rap "Aboriginal Hitch Hike Rap," an innovative mix of rap, traditional Native singing and industrial beats. Other politically charged musical hybrids followed, including their single "Geronimo Pratt," written about the jailed Black Panther member and American Indian Movement activist Leonard Peltier.

The Fire This Time was the driving force behind the 1991 album *Till the Bars Break* (Cargo Records), which featured the moving poetry of Okanagan Indian writer and artist Jeannette Armstrong. The album received wide international acclaim and a Juno nomination (Canada's equivalent to a Grammy) for best World Beat recording. Armstrong's book of Native philosophy, *The Native Creative Process,* written in conjunction with Douglas Cardinal, has been a lyrical inspiration for the group's current recordings.

Since then The Fire This Time has been busy working with a number of acclaimed producers, rappers and poets who are attracted to and support the group's vision. Their albums feature an all-star cast that includes Augustus Pablo, Mikey Dread, King Jammy, Mad Professor, John Trudell, Chuck D, Harry Allen, Ole Christianson, Santa Davis, Oku Onuora and Don Patrick Martin.

Basslines and Ballistics and *Dancing on John Wayne's Head* (both on the Extreme label) are the first installments of recordings from this creative period. They were recorded in both northern and southern hemispheres—from the northernmost recording studio in the world (in Greenland) to locations in Chile situated at the bottom of South America.

The following narratives by Pat Andrade give insight into the making of these recordings.

NAVAHO NATION

I'm approaching Window Rock, deep in the heart of Navajo territory. I know I'm close to my final destination—the Navajo Nation Fair. I approach a group of Navajo youth and ask for a ride. People are incredibly warm and friendly and a number of them are wearing reggae paraphernalia. I ask one youth skanking away to sounds in his Walkman what he's listening to. He replies, "Augustus Pablo and Israel Vibrations." Serious roots music. People know their music here. A couple of trucks are heading to the fair and everyone wants to ride with them, so I jump in the back of the nearest pickup truck. Soon we are flying along the nearest desert; a couple of cars with Navajo youth follow, blinking their lights and waving at me.

We arrive at the fairground and the sight of thousands of Navajo greet us. Inside the auditorium, different performers are taking the stage. I am introduced to the emcee, an African-American who used to work in Houston. He's now manager of the Navajo radio station, which happens to be one of the most powerful AM stations in the United States. We have a great chat; he describes how he loves working with the Navajo people.

While waiting for my friends, John Williams's all-Native reggae band, to come on, I walk outside. Parked outside is a white van covered with vivid paintings of Bob Marley, Peter Tosh and Marcus Garvey. In large lettering, STOP POLICE BRUTALITY and HOW CAN YOU CALL THE COPS ON THE COPS is painted beside it. There is a stand in front of the van and someone is handing out pamphlets. Soon I'm talking with Cimi Boone, a Navajo artist and activist responsible for the paintings on the van. She explained how Bob Marley had inspired her activism and how, despite the harassment she received from police, she traveled around in her van visiting different Native communities and distributing pamphlets on Marcus Garvey and other Black activists. She is overjoyed to hear about the work I'm doing. I give her copies of our recordings and she gives me a beautiful T-shirt she has made that has a picture of Bob Marley on it with the caption STOP POLICE BRUTALITY.

LA PAZ, BOLIVIA

The capital of Bolivia, La Paz, is a wonderful city to be in, even though the altitude takes a while to get accustomed to. One step up the stairs can leave one panting for breath.

It's summertime and the period preceding a national strike. Telltale signs are everywhere. Soldiers guard the banks and telecommunication sites. On my way to an appointment to meet an indigenous people's representative, Marcela Toro and I stop in the market. We sit under the covered stalls amidst an amazing variety of fruits and cooked dishes. In the distance we can hear the sound of demonstrators marching through the capital.

After a couple of minutes I notice that one of the vendors has started burning a wad of newspapers in the passageway. Suddenly two Indian men in black appear out of nowhere and sit beside us; food miraculously appears in front of them, and to anyone not in the know it would seem that they had been there eating all the time. Someone whispers to us that the woman is burning the newspaper to have the flames ease the tear gas that soldiers are throwing at the demonstrators. We all stay in the marketplace till darkness falls and it is safe to leave.

Reality: indigenous people are on the front line of struggles everywhere.

ZIMBABWE

An inevitable aspect of doing work on an international basis is the crossing of borders and subsequent dealings with immigration and custom officials. Sometimes these encounters can involve a bit of tension.

During a necessary crossing into South Africa from Zimbabwe on my way to meet poet Sandille Dikeni, I'm traveling in a semilegal van packed with people. We approach the South African border, complete with electric barbed wire fences. Entering the immigration office, one is surrounded with large posters with life-size depictions of grenades, land mines and other "terrorist" weapons to look out for. It's 1991; the apartheid regime is still in power but has begun public negotiations with the ANC. An ANC member is returning to South Africa and his credentials have to be verified; in the meantime we are told that everyone in the van has to wait in the courtyard, crammed with about a hundred, mainly white, South African soldiers. For two hours we wait in this courtyard as soldiers return. The heavily armed soldiers are very young white kids; maturity and independent thinking don't appear to be their strong points. On the side I catch the soldiers collecting bribes from passengers who

246

are carrying goods to sell in South Africa. The official political climate in the country is that of a "new beginning," and these soldiers, in an extremely clumsy manner, are attempting to follow official orders.

Another dread is traveling in the van. A bunch of white soldiers approach him and in an "attempt" to be friendly tell him to sing some reggae songs and start touching his dreadlocks. Suddenly one of the young white soldiers in this group turns and sees me in the van. From the look in his eyes it's apparent that I'm immediately another potential candidate to sing and dance for their benefit. That wasn't about to happen. My hair is sacred to me and there wasn't any way that I was about to let some Afrikaner soldier play with it. For about ten minutes we stared down each other as he decided what move he was going to make. The people nearby became very quiet as they realized the potential showdown in the making. Finally, the young soldier, after accurately assessing my resoluteness, slung his machine gun over his shoulder and walked off.

Bob Marley's lyrics come to mind: "Jah would never give the power to a baldhead to come crucify the dread."

KINGSTON, JAMAICA

It's August in Jamaica and I'm in Kingston, in the Waterhouse area. This is the politically troubled area where legendary dub pioneer King Tubby had his studio and also where he was murdered. I'm here working with King Tubby's protégé, King Jammy. Jammy is renowned for his dub plates, and the studio yard is packed with singers.

It's the end of the day and the mixing has taken a bit longer than expected. I realize that I'm dangerously close to missing the last bus to Montego Bay, which is where I'm staying. Quickly I pack my equipment into a bag and call a taxi. I'm fortunate to get one fairly quickly because cabs are often too scared to venture into the area. I explain to the driver that I really need his help to get to the bus depot as quickly as possible or I will be stranded in Kingston. Hearing this, the driver reaches under his dashboard and pulls out his car alarm. He activates it and places it on the roof of his car. To the other cars on the road it appears that we are an unmarked police car with its siren going off.

Sure enough, this ingenious tactic pays off. As we hurtle along, cars pull to the side to make way for us. My anxiety about missing the last bus has eased considerably. However, I glance in the rearview mirror and discover that hot on our heels is an army Jeep and they are signaling for us to pull over. I say to the driver to let me do the talking. We pull over immediately. Four soldiers jump out and train their automatic rifles on us, commanding us to get out of the vehicle with our hands up.

It seems at this point we appear more like potential bank robbers than musicians trying to get somewhere. They demand to know where we are coming from; I explain that I am coming from King Jammy's, that I am trying to catch a bus and if they look in the suitcase on the backseat they will find my recording equipment. Luckily for me, King Jammy's is well known, and after the soldiers check my bags they let us go. What could have been a difficult situation passed without further incident.

P.S. I did catch the bus, but barely.

Reggae or Not: Jazz Goes Dread?

NORMAN WEINSTEIN

Down Beat
March 1987

Caribbean music has a long and not often recognized place of honor in terms of its impact on jazz. Think of Dizzy Gillespie's romance with Cuban rhythms, or Sonny Rollins' playful permutations of calypso. In recent years there has been a steady increase in utilizing Jamaican reggae sounds, a synthesis bringing together a far-ranging assortment of talents: Oliver Lake, Leo Smith, Miles Davis, Arthur Blythe, Kuzumi Watanabe, John Abercrombie, Jack DeJohnette, Don Cherry, Lester Bowie, and the Art Ensemble of Chicago. One can note this reggae influence and leave the matter at that—or one can use the occasion of this new synthesis as an opportunity to ask: can a language be developed to help us better comprehend the manner in which these musicians are absorbing, modifying, and transforming established reggae forms? And can these examples from a reggae/jazz merger also illuminate the manner in which other musical styles are synthesized with jazz?

These questions were inspired by repeated listenings to recordings by Oliver Lake's Jump Up reggae-funk-jazz dance band. Lake grew dreadlocks and donned Caribbean costumes for his shift from avant-garde jazz to reggae. The albums both delight and disturb, revealing how much more than an image shift is required to move into reggae. Jump Up's rhythm section established an authentic-sounding reggae groove—yet a vital spark was missing. Lake's sax solos were unadventurous, brief, desultory, particularly when compared to solos by Jamaican pop-jazz saxophonists like Tommy McCook and Roland Alphonso. The point here is not simply to discredit the dimensionality of Lake's understanding of Jamaican pop music. It is to identify what occurs when an American jazz player of distinction steps into a tradition outside of his immediate experience and borrows surface elements (the conservative regularity of reggae's rhythmic groove) without delving into more subtle deep structures of style. There is no question that the tales drums and bass overwhelmingly tell are a cornerstone of reggae. But what lies beyond this force in the musical style, and how much more reggae can contribute to jazz, is best discovered by listening to the recent music of trumpeter Leo Smith.

Smith wears the superficial trappings of the American jazzman gone dread: natty hair and Ethiopian colors. But Smith's art readily transcends these visually chic cliches. He is an active believer in the faith of Rastafarianism, that visionary brew of Pan-African millennialism that has been the living faith of so many stirring reggae composers, including Bob Marley and Peter Tosh. Smith brings this spiritual perspective directly into the heart of his recent compositions. *Rastafari* (Sackville 3030), *Jah Music* (Kabell 5), and *Human Rights* (Kabell/Gramm 24) are outstanding recordings of Smith's work in this mode.

Rastafari's title cut demonstrates a musical approach radically different from Lake's. The drums and bass which are so crucial traditionally in both reggae and Rastafarian worship music are entirely eliminated. The composition opens with Smith chanting the word "Rastafari" with the piece then segueing into a series of long flowing lyrical lines executed by Smith's trumpet and David Prentice's violin, their crosstalk a passionate dialog about despair and faith—a metaphysical reverie evoking an American Transcendentalist composer like Carl Ruggles just as surely as Marley. Smith's uncanny feel for reggae's essence—even without a rhythm section in his ensemble—is actualized through an exacting arrangement of various intermeshing instrumental timbres, which creates a sense of spaciousness and rhythmic syncopation.

Smith's *Jah Music*, a seven-song cycle by an eight-piece band, does utilize bass and drums marking time. Once you overcome any uneasiness about Smith's meager singing skills (a fault he shares with Lake), you are treated to an astonishing amalgam of jazz, reggae, and rock (enhanced by James Emery's bold guitar solos) in which these musical styles seem to fuse seamlessly. This musical triumph seems to have emerged as the result of Smith's total immersion into both reggae's musical vocabulary *and* the spiritual system which inspired the birth of reggae.

Between Lake's borrowing on a superficial level of reggae's obvious surface traits and Smith's total involvement with the music's deep structures are a spectrum of musicians who move on a continuum from a rare experiment with a single jazz/reggae composition (John Abercrombie's *Night* and Jack DeJohnette's *Inflation Blues*) to an ongoing infatuation with reggae/jazz intersection points (Kuzumi Watanabe's *Mobo* series, Bowie's work with AEC and Brass Fantasy, Blythe's as yet unavailable live sessions with the Skatalites at the Village Gate). Guitarist Watanabe, like Lake, chooses a most obvious feature—the steady rhythmic groove—but chooses to record with the most sophisticated reggae rhythm section in the world: Sly Dunbar and Robbie Shakespeare. Trumpeter Lester Bowie has brought Jamaican song to the Art Ensemble of Chicago with *Jah* on the *Nice Guys* album and *Coming Back Jamaica* to the record made by his own brass band, Brass Fantasy. The humor and ease in these pieces might stem from his time in Jamaica jamming with many of the island's finest reggae and jazz musicians.

Let's shift now from this brief survey of reggae/jazz mergers to my original point of inquiry: can a language be created to precisely talk about how jazz players interact with an influence like reggae? The jokester in me will suggest (with tongue planted firmly in cheek) that Lake is "less than dread," Smith "dreader than dread," and the rest various "dreadful" variations between these poles, "dread" being a multipurpose word in the Jamaican vocabulary somewhat similar to the positive use of "bad" in American black English. A less impressionistic language for analysis might surface if we begin considering whether musicians are content to borrow merely surface elements of a musical style or are seeking to utilize deep structures. Another pertinent question to ask: are musicians borrowing from a style simply to introduce exotic tone colors or rhythmic configurations on a one-shot basis, or is there an ongoing commitment to keep mining a style for new directions? Smith's music even raises the thorny question of whether a musician can or should practice the spiritual faith underpinning a particular style, a question only the Divine Bopper can answer, whether they're reggae or not. Improvisations triggered by these questions will hopefully lead toward creating a new tongue to describe what sparks fly at the intersection points between jazz and other styles.

Bassline in the Yard

ANDY TAITT

Caribbean Week (Barbados)
26 October–8 November 1996

Island Records has launched a new label—Island Jamaica Jazz—in a most remarkable way, with a CD each by Ernest Ranglin and Monty Alexander. It would have been extremely difficult to launch a label with more class than this. And as I sit at my keyboard with the CD drive going, my fingers bounce merrily along and it's hard to concentrate on the writing for the sweet music.

Ernest Ranglin's *Below the Bassline* is the more appealing of the two. It's indisputably jazz, if you want to talk genres, but the reggae in this whole work is so close to the surface that genres no longer make sense.

Unmistakably this is Jamaican music. Anybody can play a reggae rhythm but nobody does it like Jamaicans do. Always, somewhere, whether it is guitar, or drums, or bass or anything else, someone is holding down a reggae rhythm. And they are doing so sweetly. *Sweet* is the word that keeps on cropping up to describe this music, particularly to refer to the chicken-scratch guitar with the tinny scratch blunted just enough.

The first tracks, "Congo Man Chant" and "Surfin," have the swing and bounce of late sixties and early seventies reggae at its most thoughtful. "King Tubby Meets the Rockers" sounds slightly later-era with even more bounce. A classic of nostalgia, the Abyssinians' hit "Satta Amassa Gana" turns up here significantly reworked as "Satta Massagana." It is as haunting and lyrical as the original, but now with some sparkling guitar work and a melodica reminiscent of Augustus Pablo. Toots Hibbert's "54-46 (Was My Number)" comes next, followed by "Ball of Fire," a number in which the performers sometimes seem to forget this is a jazz album and relapse into a classical piece of ska.

A striking feature of this collection is the way in which its tremendous complexity is so smoothly disguised. The occasional flash of pure brilliance, as in the high-speed guitar playing in "Bourbon Street Skank," serves to remind the listener that all the performances here are technically of very high quality, although no one strikes out above the others. What we hear is a very tight, very together band playing a highly textured sound, as each musician spreads a layer, exceedingly scant or rich, over highly efficient bass and rhythm.

The next-to-last last track is the most purely jazz of the eleven titles on this CD, even with a name like "Nana's Chalk Pipe." For the first time there is an almost complete absence of the various Jamaican influences, of whatever era, that have played below the surface. And as if to make up, the final and title track sinks almost to the elemental level of a "version." It is as if the music so far has been created for enjoyment but this last track is down to the real business of music, down to the heavy bassline that keeps all else in order.

The album notes relate how Ranglin came up through the postwar years and was there when most of the trends in Jamaican popular music surfaced and even helped to create some of them. It is evident here.

Monty Alexander's *Yard Movement* starts with a twelve-minute, two-part work, "Exodus," incorporating the theme from the movie and reference to Bob Marley's "movement of Jah people." This opening is far more classically jazz and more ambitious than anything on Ranglin's CD. But even though the Jamaican heritage seeps through repeatedly, somehow the excitement so prominent in *Below the Bassline* is felt less. The second track, "Regulator," makes an attempt to infuse some excitement. The third, "Crying," goes back to a more precise (if jazz can be precise) classical style. These first three tracks were recorded at the Montreux Jazz Festival in 1995, and perhaps the audience is influencing the style. None of this is meant to imply that the music is anything less than top-notch.

The remaining five tracks, all studio tracks and all written by Alexander, sometimes with help, creep more and more deeply into reggae. These include a tiny twenty-second piece, "Momento"—a melodica version of a folk tune and easily mistaken for an intro to the following track.

In both these CDs the mixture of jazz and reggae crops up each time in a different mix of instruments, or from a different era. No two of them sound alike; nothing here is predictable. Most of the music is bouncy and infectious. Since each plays on the other's CD there is a unity, though not a sameness, about the two works.

Altogether, Island Jamaica Jazz has been launched in the very best way. I wonder if there are enough quality jazz musicians in Jamaica to maintain this level of quality over an extended period. I wonder if the name implies the label will release only Jamaican jazz, or will there be performers from other islands or even outside the region. It is going to be very interesting, whatever the answers turn out to be, to see this catalogue grow.

Children of the Ras

JAMES D. DAVIS
(RELIGION EDITOR)

Fort Lauderdale Sun-Sentinel
23 May 1994

At six each morning, the drums begin in Desta Tonge's Margate home as she leads her seven children in praises to Jah.

At about the same time in Boynton Beach, John Moodie kneels on the sand and prays to the Ethiopian king he and other Rastafarians worship.

To most people, the Rastafari faith is reggae music, ganja—Jamaican marijuana— and dreadlocks with an undercurrent of African exotica. What most don't know is that it also is a faith with tenets of self-reliance, return to Africa—and worship of a black God.

"We still seem mysterious to the average mind," says Ras Sam Brown, one of thirteen elders in the Nyahbinghi order, one of the better-known of the half-dozen Rastafarian sects. "Many have said it's a movement of fantasy, a cult of madness. But now we have people in the professions and in many countries. Are they all mad?"

Right now, Rastafarians are providing outsiders with a rare look into their religion. More than two hundred delegates from several countries have converged on Miami for the International Nyahbinghi gathering, which began last Thursday and ends this Thursday. So secretive is the movement that even estimates of its numbers vary wildly—from thirty thousand, to one million, to one million in the United States alone, with perhaps two thousand in South Florida.

That vagueness translates to lack of numbers to some observers. "If the movement was any size, they'd be much more visible," says J. Gordon Melton, one of three editors of the *Encyclopedia of African-American Religions*, published last summer. "It's still a very small community."

Small, perhaps, but undeniably widespread since its evolution early this century in Jamaica. Attending the gathering this week are not only islanders and African-Americans but Asians and Europeans, all easily identifiable by the long thick locks of hair they call "Covenants."

Reggae music, of course, is the port of entry for many who become followers. Among the enduring images of pop music: the late Bob Marley and the Wailers, their locks flying as they churned out bouncy rhythms and tricky guitar work, singing of poverty and liberation.

It partly was the music that drew Terri Larsen of Miami, a blue-eyed Norwegian whose honey-brown hair is "Covenanted." Larsen was attracted to the faith while living in the Virgin Islands during the 1970s. She admired the Rastas who lived off the land and cooked and sang together. And she liked the reggae: "It makes people mellow and happy. There's something about it that touches everyone."

Ironically, reggae isn't authentic Rasta music—Nyahbinghi drumming is. "The rhythms [of reggae] are based on Nyahbinghi, and the lyrics are social commentary," says Tonge, who makes her living as a musicians' agent.

If it's real Rasta music you want, step into the Tonge residence. From the time you enter the upper-middle-class Margate house, drums and chanting will greet you from a stereo. "This is the akete, the drum battery," Tonge says. "We use it in our I-ses, or praises, every morning."

On the wall hangs a poster of the Mother Continent in green, gold and red, plus a giant eye, a rebus for Rasta jargon.

◆ ◆ ◆

Home worship begins at the start of the day. In Tonge's home, that's at 6 A.M., before her seven children go to school. Some members also gather in home worship on Sunday afternoon or evening, singing chants and "Rastasized hymns," as Tonge calls them—such as "Jah's Got the Whole World in His Hands."

The most controversial ritual, of course, would be the use of ganja. During worship, the shredded leaves are blessed, placed in a clay chalice and passed around the circle for everyone to inhale. Rastas consider ganja a natural herb, a gift from God. "'Drug' is a loaded word," says Ras Abraham Peddie, head of the Rasta community in Washington, D.C., during a separate phone conversation. "Even the medical profession is now seeing the value of ganja for things like nausea after AIDS treatments."

One ritual the Rastafari don't do is funerals—to the point of turning over their dead to nonbelievers to bury. "We believe in eternal life; it's just the flesh that dies," Tonge explains. That denial of death extends to their god. Haile Selassie was deposed by a Marxist coup in 1974 and kept under house arrest in his palace. He reportedly died a year later, amid gossip that he was murdered. Only in 1991 was the Marxist regime itself replaced.

Rastas insist that the king is still alive, saying no one has ever found his remains. "He conquered death; he cannot die," Moodie says. Many believers even flocked to Ethiopia in 1992 to celebrate Selassie's centenary.

If he's alive, where is he? The Rastas confess they don't know. But, "I commune with him every day, though he is thousands of miles away," Peddie says.

From "On Reggae and Rastafarianism—and a Garvey Prophecy"

PAMELA O'GORMAN

Jamaica Journal
August–October 1987

The time was October 1986; the place, Brisbane, Queensland—an Australian state whose political conservatism and backwardness are a source of despair and incomprehension to most other states of a country that works hard, if at times a little naively, at being one of the Commonwealth's more liberal and tolerant nations.

I was walking over the bridge that connects the new multimillion-dollar cultural centre to the city of Brisbane proper and was feeling depressed, having just left the art gallery after searching in vain for even one Aboriginal painting. Three-quarters of the way across, my eye was suddenly caught by a lone graffitto, a proclamation in black despoiling the pristine whiteness of the bridge: BOB MARLEY. I stopped dead in my tracks—and all of a sudden found that I was smiling, my depression momentarily gone. What price JA! (Marcus Garvey would have approved too.)

There is, in Australia, an Aboriginal reggae group called No Fixed Address. The name of the group is a clever dual reference to the Aboriginal practice of periodically disappearing "on walkabout" and to the customary status of the Aborigine in Australian society. The group's performance style is African-American. Only the addition of a didgeridoo for special effects in the bass and a certain nasal quality identify it as belonging "Down Under." The song lyrics, composed by a member of the group, are directly descended from the tradition of reggae protest.

> *You can't change the rhythm of my soul,*
> *You can't tell me what to do,*
> *You can't break my bones by putting me down*
> *or by taking the things that belong to me.*
>
> "WE HAVE SURVIVED," LYRICS BY BART WILLOUGHBY

The author of an article on reggae published in the *UNESCO Courier* (1982) was accurate enough in making the following statement:

> The music is obviously an important force within the lives of the black community, whether in Jamaica, the Americas or Europe. In the latter situation it has given strength and resolve to those experiencing the harshness of European racism and prejudice and has forced them to resist these experiences.

The influence of reggae spreads far wider than America or Europe. It has become a political weapon of racial isolates such as the Aborigine and of countless others of the world's dispossessed.

Michael Manley in his introduction to *Reggae International* draws attention to the revolutionary nature of the Jamaican art form as compared to calypso and blues and its acceptance as part of international culture despite the competition of "the bromides and anodynes" of synthetic escape music which exist at the other end of the popular-music spectrum. He hazards the guess that its success owes much to the originality of Bob Marley, whose gifts helped it to gain international acceptance; but, he says, "it must also be true that the protest of reggae, *the positive assertion of moral categories* (my emphasis) goes beyond parochial boundaries. Among other things, reggae is the spontaneous sound of a local revolutionary impulse. But revolution itself is a universal category. It is this, possibly, which sets reggae apart, even to the international ear."

◆ ◆ ◆

It took some three centuries and a lot of bloodshed and exploitation for European culture to attain the position of global preeminence which reached its culmination in the early part of this century, overlapping the genesis of African-American popular music. It has taken the latter a mere thirty years to sweep the world. This can be attributed directly to the invention and development of radio and the long-playing record (the latter of which came on the market in 1948, around the same time that rhythm and blues developed). In countries which have tried to ban the music, it has inevitably gone underground and because of consumer demand has become a black market commodity (its availability no doubt aided by recording machines and the Voice of America).

Anyone who is alert to musical developments worldwide must realize that African-American music is about to take the preeminent position which European music once held. It can be observed on a macrocosmic level (the number of countries—even Communist ones—where African-American music has not penetrated are the exception rather than the rule) and on a microcosmic level: in most societies where African-American music is present, it soon becomes the music most listened to by the greatest number of people.

Is there a reason for this?

I feel that there is. From the time when Western beliefs presided over the dissolution of the ancient unity of music, song and dance—a destruction that was initiated by the early Christian church—and when the Western scientific worldview adopted the Cartesian separation of body, mind and spirit, there has nevertheless developed a concomitant and growing need for a return to human wholeness, unity and communality, especially in urban societies.

This is a need that the purest black culture has always satisfied. In religion, education, healing and the arts, the unity has always remained. But of all black culture, especially that in the New World, black music is the artistic manifestation that has remained most intact. Throughout the diaspora it has preserved its essential unity, even when it has mixed with white culture, its syncopations and rhythmic drive continuously urging the body to assert itself and move, its compositional patterns and social mores continuously urging a communal sharing that has been lost in Western urban civilization. Its inherent approach to time as a circular rather than a linear element denies the Western search for goals which is termed "progress" and subconsciously asserts the importance of time in action over action in time. The message has already been picked up and understood, either consciously or subconsciously, by those who have suffered most from the dehumanizing effects of goal-oriented societies hell-bent on "progress."

No changes occur suddenly. They are always preceded by a long period of preparation and gestation. For years black music has been preparing—and continues to prepare—the way for the acceptance of black culture, black attitudes, a different worldview.

One cannot help feeling that if Marcus Garvey were alive today he would look on this amazing modern phenomenon and recognize it as the manifestation of a prophecy reaching fulfillment.

Surely that great new civilization of which he spoke will come from this hemisphere, where the African slave was brought forcibly centuries ago and where he has become a cultural catalyst and a cultural leader with all the potential of changing the face of the world.

BIBLIOGRAPHY

Allen, Richard. *Skinhead Girls.* London: New English Library, 1972, p. 37.

Andrade, Patrick. Extreme Records website (http://www.xtr.com/extreme), 1996.

Arnold, Brian. "The Sounds of Young Jamaica." *Ska-tastrophe* (December 1995), p. 8.

Bacchus, Clive. "Dub Damage Becomes Permanent." *Guyana Review* (February 1993), pp. 36–37.

Bailey, Khris. "Word Sound Is Power: Reggae's Dub Poets." *The Reggae and African Beat* (April 1985), pp. 12+.

Bangs, Lester. "Bob Marley Aims High, Misses Big." *Rolling Stone* (1 June 1978), pp. 56+.

———. "How to Learn to Love Reggae." *Stereo Review* (April 1977), pp. 64–70.

Barnes, Winston. "Jamaican Music: The Foreign Press Again?" *The Jamaican Weekly Gleaner* (11 December 1992), p. 27.

Bilby, Kenneth. "The Impact of Reggae in the United States." *Popular Music in Society* 5, no. 1 (1977); pp. 17–22.

———. "Jamaica." In *Caribbean Currents: Caribbean Music from Rumba to Reggae* by Peter Manuel with Bilby and Michael Largey. Philadelphia: Temple University Press, 1995, pp. 143–182.

"Bono on Bob." *Rolling Stone* (10 March 1994), p. 29.

Boot, Adrian, and Chris Salewicz. *Bob Marley: Songs of Freedom.* London: Bloomsbury Publishing, 1995.

Booth, Patricia. "Lui Lepki and Yellowman as Reggae 'Folk' Singers." *Everybody's Magazine* (August 1982), pp. 20–22.

Boxill, Ian. "The Two Faces of Caribbean Music." *Social and Economic Studies* (June 1994), pp. 33+.

Boyd, Joe. "Beating World Music Into Submission." *Musician* (August 1995), pp. 12–13.

Bradley, Lloyd. *Reggae on CD.* London: Kyle Cathie Ltd., 1996.

Brother Resistance. *Rapso Explosion.* London: Karia Press, 1986.

Brown, Lloyd W. "*The Harder They Come*: Beyond the Reel Thing." *Freedomways* (third quarter 1981), pp. 180–185.

Campbell, Andrew (aka Tuffie). "Reggae Sound Systems." Black Majesty International Website (http://members.aol.com/baseodyssy), 1995.

Campbell, Horace. *Rasta and Resistance: From Marcus Garvey to Walter Rodney.* Trenton, NJ: Africa World Press, 1987.

Campbell, Howard. "Steven Marley: Ghetto Youths Unite!" *Reggae Report* 14, no. 6 (1996), pp. 20–21.

Cardwell, Diane. "Dancehall Reggae." *Vogue* (July 1992), pp. 72–73.

Chude-Sokei, Louis. "Postnationalist Geographies: Rasta, Ragga and Reinventing Africa." *African Arts* 27, no. 4 (Autumn 1994), pp. 80–84+.

Clarke, Sebastian. *Jah Music: The Evolution of the Popular Jamaican Song.* London: Heinemann, 1980.

Clerk, Astley. *The Music and Musical Instruments of Jamaica.* Kingston: Astley Clerk/Cowen Music Rooms, 1916, p. 16.

Cocks, Jay. "The Ska Above, the Beat Below." *Time* (7 April 1980), p. 75.

Cooper, Carol. "Tuff Gong: Bob Marley's Unsung Story." *Village Voice* (10 September 1980), pp. 33+.

Cutler, Chris. "Progressive Music in the U.K." In *File Under Popular: Theoretical and Critical Writings on Music.* Brooklyn: Autonomedia, 1985, p. 128*n*.

Davis, James D. "Children of the Ras." *Fort Lauderdale Sun-Sentinel* (23 May 1994), pp. 1D+.

Davis, Stephen. *Bob Marley.* Garden City, NY: Doubleday, 1985.

de Leon, Rafael. *Calypso from France to Trinidad: 800 Years of History.* Self-published, 1978.

De Stefano, George. "Remember Reggae?" *The Nation* (26 January 1985), pp. 90–92.

Diouf, Laurent. "Puissance Dub." *Octopus,* no. 3 (Winter 1995), pp. 1–4D.

di Perna, Alan. "Ziggy Marley: His Own Man." *Musician* (July 1989), p. 78+.

Ehrlich, Luke. "The Volatile History of Dub." In *Reggae International* by Stephen Davis and Peter Simon. Munich: Rogner & Bernhard, 1982, pp. 105–109.

Eliezer, Christie. "Aborigines Get Popular Forum Through Reggae." *Billboard* (8 July 1995), pp. 1+.

Fergusson, Isaac. "Blunt Posse." *Village Voice* (22 June 1993), pp. 34–36.

———. "'So Much Things to Say': The Journey of Bob Marley." *Village Voice* (18 May 1982), pp. 39+.

Fricke, David. "Bob Marley and the Wailers: The Roxy, Los Angeles, May 26th, 1976." *Rolling Stone* (4 June 1987), pp. 93–94.

"Get Creative or Pay Up." *Rhythm Vibes* (November 1996), pp. 6–7.

Goldman, Vivien. "Uptown Ghetto Living: Bob Marley in His Own Backyard." *Melody Maker* (11 August 1979), pp. 24–25.

———. "The International Dub." *Melody Maker* (24 March 1979), pp. 39–41.

Gonzalez, Fernando. "Reunited Jamaican Group Marks Year's End in Style." *Miami Herald* (30 December 1994), p. 22G.

Goodwin, Michael. "Marley, the Maytals and the Reggae Armageddon." *Rolling Stone* (11 September 1975), pp. 9–11.

Gordon, C. *The Reggae Files.* London: Hansib Publishing Limited, 1988, pp. 80–85.

Gordon, Sharon. "Stone Love Live!" *Dub Missive* 7, no. 4 (1994), p. 20.

———. "Jungle Music." *Dub Missive* 7, no. 3 (1994), p. 20.

Gore, Joe. "Dr. Know: Slammin' in the Name of Jah." *Guitar Player* (July 1990), pp. 60–65.

Grass, Randall. "The Stone That the Builder Refused . . ." *The Reggae and African Beat* 6, no. 6 (1987), p. 9.

Gutterman, Scott. "Undertone: Rhythm and Rage." *Artforum* (November 1989), pp. 24–25.

Hebdige, Dick. *Out of Many, One Person: Bob Marley and the Worldification of Reggae!* Unpublished manuscript, 1995.

———. *Reggae, Rastas and Rudies: Style and the Subversion of Form.* Occasional paper of the Centre for Contemporary Cultural Studies, Birmingham: University of Birmingham, 1974.

Helander, Brock. *The Rock Who's Who*, 2nd ed. New York: Schirmer Books, 1996.

Henry, Balford. "Screaming Africans Greet Chaka Demus and Pliers." *The Sunday Gleaner* (11 August 1996), p. 6E.

———. "Jamaica's Rhythm Twins Still Reign Supreme." *The Jamaican Weekly Gleaner* (21 August 1992), p. 24.

Hewitt, Christine. "Reggae Legalistics!" *Dub Missive* (April 1996), p. 44.

Hitchcock, Peter. "'It Dread Inna Inglan': Linton Kwesi Johnson, Dread, and Dub Identity." *Postmodern Culture* (http://nimrod.mit.edu/ejournals/b/n-z/PMC), September 1993.

Horovitz, Michael. "Wi Noh Reach Mount Zion Yet." *New Statesman & Society* (17 May 1991), p. 34.

Huey, John. "The Hypnotic Sound of Reggae Floats Far from Jamaica Slums." *The Wall Street Journal* (10 August 1981), pp. 1+.

Irving, Katrina. "'I Want Your Hands On Me': Building Equivalences Through Rap Music." *Popular Music* (May 1993), pp. 105–121.

"Island Hopping." *The New Yorker* (8 March 1958), p. 118.

Jacob, Debbie. "Deejaying Is Here to Stay Says Stitchie." *Trinidad Weekend Sun* (14–16 October 1988), p. 11.

Jacobson, Mark. "Bob Marley Live." *Natural History* (November 1995), pp. 48–53.

Jammin Reggae Archives (http://www.arrowweb.com/jammin). Mike Pawka, ed.

Jennings, Nicholas. "The Hypnotic Pull of the Reggae Beat." *MacLean's* (27 October 1986), p. 69.

"Jimmy Cliff: Paving the Way for Reggae." *Rolling Stone* (6 August 1981), p. 42.

Johnson, Brian D. "Rita Marley: Reluctant Queen of Reggae." *Rolling Stone* (27 May 1982), pp. 49–51.

Johnson, Linton Kwesi. "Jamaican Rebel Music." *Race and Class* (Spring 1976), pp. 397–412.

Jones, K. Maurice. "A Session with Super Cat." *Scholastic Update* (9 October 1992), p. 14.

Kostakis, Peter. "In Concert with the Dub Band: *Linton Kwesi Johnson* (review)." *Down Beat* (May 1986), pp. 30–32.

Kot, Greg. "Instrument of Expression." *Chicago Tribune* (13 February 1996), p. E5:1.

Lee, Peter. "Glory to Jah: Remembering Bob Marley." *Guitar Player* (May 1991), pp. 82–89.

Leiby, Richard. "Dread Reckoning: The Marley Mess." *The Washington Post* (25 August 1991), p. 1G.

Leland, John. "When Rap Meets Reggae." *Newsweek* (7 September 1992), p. 59.

Levine, Jordan. "Dancehall DJs in the House." *The Miami Herald* (26 April 1996), p. 24G.

Lieb, Kristin. "Hunt for 'Next Big Thing' Unearths Ska Underground." *Billboard* (15 January 1994), pp. 1+.

Llosa, Mario Vargas. "My Son the Rastafarian." *The New York Times Magazine* (16 February 1986), pp. 20+.

Luntta, Karl. *Jamaica Handbook*. Chico, CA: Moon Publications, 1996.

McClure, Steve. "Reggae Makes a Lucrative Splash in Japan." *Billboard* (8 July 1995), pp. 1+.

McDonald, Paulette, and Carolyn Cooper. "Dancehall Revisted/Kingston." *Review: Latin American Literature and Arts, Americas Society* (Spring 1995), p. 29–31.

McGlashan, Colin. "The Sound System." London *Sunday Times* (4 February 1973).

Mack, Bob. "Return of the Super Ape." *Grand Royal*, no. 2 (1995), pp. 60–66.

mandiela, ahdri zhina. *dark diaspora . . . in* dub. Toronto: Sister Vision, 1991.

Martin, Jana. "What Is Illbient: A New Sound and Vision Emerge from New York's Underground Clubs." *Village Voice* (23 July 1996), pp. 36+.

Martin, Tony. *Literary Garveyism: Garvey, Black Arts and the Harlem Renaissance*. Dover, MA: The Majority Press, 1983.

Medrano, Rebecca Read. "Reggae, Roots and Razzmatazz." *Americas* (January/February 1984), pp. 35–39.

Mento an' T'ing. Published for Mento Yard '90 by the Jamaica Cultural Development Commission.

Morris, Mervyn. "Mikey Smith, Dub Poet." *Jamaica Journal* (May–July 1985), pp. 39–45.

Nagashima, Yoshiko S. *Rastafarian Music in Contemporary Jamaica: A Study of Socioreligious Music of the Rastafarian Movement in Jamaica*. Tokyo: Institute for the Study of Languages and Cultures of Asia and Africa, 1984.

Nettleford, Rex M. *Mirror Mirror: Identity, Race and Protest in Jamaica*. Kingston: William Collins and Sangster Ltd., 1970.

O'Gorman, Pamela. "On Reggae and Rastafarianism—and a Garvey Prophecy." *Jamaica Journal* (August–October 1987), pp. 85–88.

One Drop Books catalog: Steven Stempel, DH Station, Box 20392, New York, NY 10017

Orth, Maureen. "Jamaican Rock." *Newsweek* (12 February 1973), pp. 94–95.

Oumano, Elena. "Better Late Than Never." *Billboard* (15 July 1995), pp. 48+.

Owens, Joseph. *Dread: The Rastafarians of Jamaica*. Kingston: Sangster's Book Stores Ltd., 1976, pp. 7–8, 55, 90, 154.

Palmer, Robert. "One Love." *Rolling Stone* (24 February 1994), pp. 38+.

Pan Jumbie. "Children, You Don't Know Your Own Name." Trinidad *Sunday Express* (9 October 1988), p. 35.

Pareles, Jon. "Still Tormented, but Less Withdrawn." *The New York Times* (14 January 1997), p. C9.

———. "Dancehall, the New Sound of the In Crowd from Jamaica." *The New York Times* (4 August 1991), p. 68.

Plantenga, Bart. "Tackhead's Heady Tacktics." *Paris Free Voice* (June 1990; revised 1996).

Potash, Chris. "Cliff Promises to Bring the Sun." *The Miami News* (2 June 1988), pp. 1C+

———. "Bob's Son Ziggy Proves To Be a Reggae Biggie." *The Miami News* (28 April 1988), pp. 1C+.

———. "Alpha Blondy's Message Is Dead Serious." *The Miami News* (11 February 1988), pp. 1–2C.

Preston, Rohan B. "Music and Fighting Words." *Chicago Tribune* (26 October 1992), p. 5:3.

Pulis, John W. "'Up-Full Sounds': Language, Identity, and the Worldview of Rastafari." *Ethnic Groups* (1993), pp. 285–300.

Reckord, Verena. "Reggae, Rastafarianism and Cultural Identity." *Jamaica Journal* (special anniversary issue, 1982), pp. 70–79.

"Reggae Power." *Time* (30 April 1973), p. 79.

Robinson, Leroy. "Wailers Wooing U.S. Fans." *Billboard* (24 November 1973), p. 25.

Rodigan, David. "The U.K. Reggae Scene." *Yush* (http://www.yush.com), 1996.

Rohlehr, Gordon. "Jamaican Music: A Select Bibliography." *Carib* (December 1980), pp. 11–12.

Sakolsky, Ron. "Dub Diaspora: Off the Page and Into the Streets." In *Sounding Off! Music as Resistance, Subversion, Revolution*. Brooklyn: Autonomedia, 1995.

Sandman, John. "Feeling the Soul Vibes in North America." *The* (U.S.) *Guardian* (3 July 1991), p. 19.

Santoro, Gene. "Stir It Up." *The Nation* (12 October 1992), pp. 407–410.

Saunders, Alphea. "Dancehall Music: Its Contribution to the Reggae Industry." *Reggae Times* 1, no. 9 (1996), pp. 32–33.

Shaw, Greg. "Will Reggae Make It? Jamaica Says It Will." *Crawdaddy* (June 1973), pp. 64–68.

Sheridan, Maureen. "Third World Vision." *Down Beat* (January 1986), pp. 24+.

Simunek, Chris. "Rastafari Now!" *High Times* (January 1997), pp. 55–70.

"Singing Them a Message." *Time* (22 March 1976), pp. 83–84.

Sleeper, Mick. "Shocks of Mighty" (http://www.oanet.com/homepage/sleeper/scratch.htm).

Snowden, Don. "Intereggae." New America News Service/New York Times Syndicate (8 July 1996).

———. "When Dub Flies—From Jamaica to U.K." *Los Angeles Times* (October 6, 1991), p. 21C.

Soaries, Rafika. "The Television Castration of Buju Banton." *Everybody's Magazine* (February/March 1994), 36–39.

Speech. "Marley Parley." *Interview* (January 1995), pp. 88–93.

Spencer, Marjorie. "Marley's Last: The Song, Not the Singer." *Village Voice* (18 October 1983), pp. 99–102.

Strauss, Neil. "The Sound of New York: Ska. Ska? Yes, Ska." *The New York Times* (27 October 1995), pp. 1C+.

Taitt, Andy. "Bassline in the Yard." *Caribbean Week* (26 October–8 November 1996), p. 61.

Thelwell, Michael. "*The Harder They Come*: From Film to Novel." *Grand Street* 10, no. 1 (1991), pp. 135–165.

Thomas, Michael. "The Wild Side of Paradise." *Rolling Stone* (11 June 1992), pp. 69–70.

Toop, David. *Ocean of Sound: Aether Talk, Ambient Sound and Imaginary Worlds*. London: Serpent's Tail, 1995.

Trainer. "Buju Banton: Dancehall's Cultural Griot." *Dub Missive* (August 1995), pp. 28–33.

Van Pelt, Carter. "Slyght of Hand." Adapted from "Sly Dunbar: Him a Hit You from a Far." *400 Years*, no. 3 (1996), pp. 16–27.

———. "Natural Mystic: The Mystic Revealers." *The Beat* 15, no. 2 (1996), pp. 40+.

Walker, Alice. "Redemption Day." *Mother Jones* (December 1986), 43–45.

Waters, Anita M. *Race, Class, and Political Symbols: Rastafari and Reggae in Jamaican Politics*. New Brunswick, NJ: Transaction Books, 1985.

Weber, Tom. *Reggae Island: Jamaican Music in the Digital Age*. Kingston: Kingston Publishers Limited, 1992.

Weidenbaum, Marc. "Dub American Style." *Pulse!* (September 1995).

Weinstein, Norman. "Reggae or Not: Jazz Goes Dread?" *Down Beat* (March 1987), p. 63.

"West Indian Population Sparks New U.K. Music Trend." *Billboard* (13 November 1971), p. 28L.

Wexler, Paul. "Jamaica's Dancehall Style Takes Hold." *Rolling Stone* (8 March 1990), p. 60.

White, Garth. "Reggae: A Musical Weapon." *Carib* (Decemeber 1980), pp. 6–10.

———. "Rudie, Oh Rudie!" *Caribbean Quarterly* (September 1967), 39–44.

White, Timothy. "Jump Up!" *Rolling Stone* (16 April 1981), pp. 83–87.

———. "Roots, Rastas and Reggae: Bob Marley's Jamaica." *Crawdaddy* (January 1976), pp. 35–41.

Wildman, Noah. "The New Old Ska: Reverence or Retrowank?" *One Man's Ska Annual* 1, no. 2 (Summer 1995), pp. 1–2.

Williams, Richard. "The Sound of Surprise."*Melody Maker* (21 August 1976), p. 21.

———. "The Facts About Reggae." *Melody Maker* (19 February 1972), p. 25.

Wilson, Dr. Basil. "The Dialectics of Reggae Music." *Everybody's Magazine* (August 1982), pp. 17–19.

Winders, James A. "Reggae, Rastafarians and Revolution: Rock Music in the Third World." *Journal of Popular Culture* (1983), pp. 61–73.

PERMISSIONS

INDEX

Entries in **boldface** indicate writers with articles in this book, and the pages on which their pieces begin.